D0862769

OPERATION FLASHPOINT
DRAGON RISING

Welcome to the official guide to Operation Flashpoint: Dragon Rising. In producing this guide, our goal was to create a book that would act as a reference to the game, and ensure that everything a player could want to know was covered in detail. In essence, this is a guide to the game, rather than a basic strategy guide. We have provided as much information about the game as possible, with tremendous support from the Operation Flashpoint: Dragon Rising development team, and presented it in a way that allows players of all skill levels to get the most out of the game.

Of course, there are plenty of strategies in the guide for each of the game's missions, and even separate strategies and routes to help take advantage of co-operative play. There are many possible routes through most missions, and we've focused on the ones the game's designers have recommended as being optimal. These routes are the ones marked in the game by RV Markers, and will get new players through the game with the minimum of trouble. We've also provided alternate routes in many places to highlight different approaches, which may be tactically safer, or just much quicker than following the RV points.

This approach also allows us to point out things in the game that players could easily miss, and give a better picture of some key engagements by showing some of the different ways they can play out. Showing how the game really works, and helping players to understand it better is the aim in all chapters of this book. We hope that you'll find everything you're looking for in these pages.

BASIC TRAINING
CHAPTER 01

In this chapter we will explain everything you need to know in order to get started in Operation Flashpoint: Dragon Rising. The game aims to offer a realistic experience and, as such, players are given a wealth of options on how to tackle and respond to situations. Although the game provides plenty of assistance on the Normal setting to make it as accessible as possible, there is still a lot to take in and get to grips with. Gaining an understanding of the basics is essential, due to Dragon Rising's unique approach to FPS warfare.

BASIC TRAINING
CHAPTER 01

NORMAL CONTROLS (CONTROLLER)

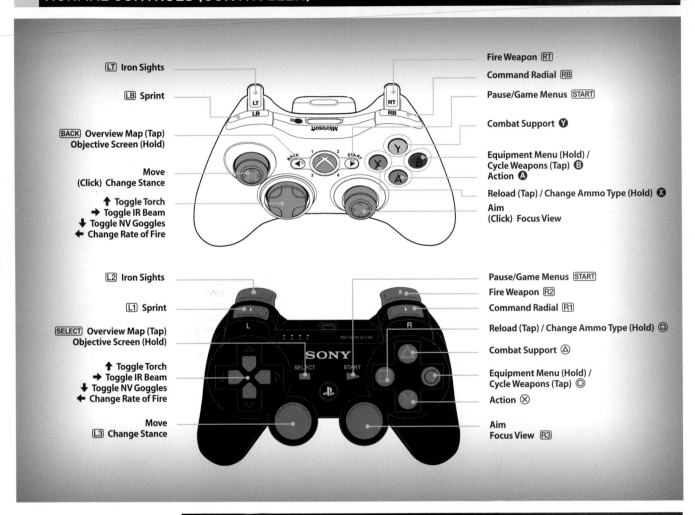

LT Iron Sights

LB Sprint

BACK Overview Map (Tap)
Objective Screen (Hold)

Move
(Click) Change Stance

↑ Toggle Torch
→ Toggle IR Beam
↓ Toggle NV Goggles
← Change Rate of Fire

Fire Weapon RT

Command Radial RB

Pause/Game Menus START

Combat Support Y

Equipment Menu (Hold) /
Cycle Weapons (Tap) B
Action A

Reload (Tap) / Change Ammo Type (Hold) X

Aim
(Click) Focus View

L2 Iron Sights

L1 Sprint

SELECT Overview Map (Tap)
Objective Screen (Hold)

↑ Toggle Torch
→ Toggle IR Beam
↓ Toggle NV Goggles
← Change Rate of Fire

Move
L3 Change Stance

Pause/Game Menus START

Fire Weapon R2

Command Radial R1

Reload (Tap) / Change Ammo Type (Hold) ◎

Combat Support △

Equipment Menu (Hold) /
Cycle Weapons (Tap) ◎

Action ✕

Aim
Focus View R3

First we'll take a look at the default control setup, as displayed on the controller diagrams here. To make reading easier, when referring to specific controls or buttons within this guide, we will use the primary action of the button, rather than using each button's name across all platforms. For example, when you want to chain commands on the Map screen, we will say: To hold down the Shoot button, which you can see in the Controls tables, here is the RT button on Xbox 360, the R1 button on PS3 and the Left Mouse Button on PC.

NORMAL CONTROLS (PC)

Control	Action	Control	Action
W A S D	Move	Right ⇧	Combat Support
Move Mouse	Look / Turn	Function Keys	Equipment Menu
Right Mouse Button	Secondary Fire / Aim Mode	End	Focus View
Left Mouse Button	Fire Weapon	R	Reload
G	Toggle Torch	Hold Left ⇧	Sprint
B	Toggle IR Beam	M	Overview Map
V	Toggle NV Goggles	Q	Quick Command Radial
F	Change Rate of Fire	Z	Prone
Esc	Pause / Game Menus	Left Ctrl	Crouch
E	Action / Interact	Space Bar	Stand

DRIVING CONTROLS

Control	Action	Control	Action
Left Stick / Ⓐ Ⓓ	Steer	⊘ / Ⓨ / Right ⇧	Call in Combat Support
Right Stick	N/A	◎ / Ⓑ / Right Ctrl	Toggle Smoke
Click Right Stick / ↵Return	1st/3rd Person View	Ⓓ / Ⓧ / Space Bar	Handbrake
↑ / Ⓖ	Lights On/Off	L1 / LB / Left ⇧	Switch Seat (Hold)
→ / Ⓑ	Engine On/Off	L2 / LT / Ⓢ	Brake/Reverse
↓ / Ⓥ	Vision Mode	R1 / RB / Ⓠ	Command Radial (Hold)
← / Ⓕ	Turn in or out	R2 / RT / Ⓦ	Accelerate/Drive Forward

COMMANDER CONTROLS

Control	Action	Control	Action
Left Stick	N/A	⊘ / Ⓨ / Right ⇧	Combat Support
Right Stick / Move Mouse	Aim	Ⓧ / Ⓐ / Ⓔ	Exit Vehicle
R3 / Click Right Stick	1st/3rd Person View	Ⓓ / Ⓧ	N/A
L2 / LT / Right Mouse Button	Issue Movement Order	L1 / LB / Left ⇧	Switch Seat (Hold)
↓ / Ⓥ	Vision Mode	R1 / RB / Ⓠ	Command Radial (Hold)
← / Ⓕ	Turn In or Out	R2 / RT / Left Mouse Button	Fire Weapon

PILOTING CONTROLS

Control	Action	Control	Action
Left Stick / Ⓦ Ⓐ Ⓢ Ⓓ	Pitch/Roll	⊘ / Ⓨ / Right ⇧	Call in Combat Support
Click Left Stick	N/A	◎ / Ⓑ / Number Keys	Weapon Select
Right Stick / ← → ↓ ↑	Power/Rudder	Ⓧ / Ⓐ / Ⓔ	Exit Vehicle
Click Right Stick / ↵Return	1st/3rd Person View	Ⓓ / Ⓧ / Space Bar	Toggle Autopilot/Hover
↑ / Ⓖ	Lights On/Off	L1 / LB / Left ⇧	Switch Seat (Hold)
→ / Ⓑ	Engine On/Off	L2 / LT / Right Mouse Button	Order Gunner to Fire
↓ / Ⓥ	Vision Mode	R1 / RB / Ⓠ	Command Radial (Hold)
← / Ⓕ	Decoys	R2 / RT / Left Mouse Button	Fire Weapon

Control Options (gamepads)

The Control Setup screen can be reached from the Main Menu, or at any point when the game is paused. Fully customizing your control configuration isn't possible on the Xbox 360 or PS3, but there are a number of tweaks you can make, subject to personal taste. For console players, the most important of these is the 'Legacy' setting, which switches the Strafe and Turn controls between the Left and Right Sticks. This makes the control more familiar to those players who have stayed with old-style console FPS controls over the years, and it also has an impact on the vehicle controls. **[Screen 01]**

There is also a 'Southpaw' setting, designed to make control easier for left-handed players. This essentially reverses the functions of the Left and Right Sticks, moving all aiming controls to the Left Stick. You can also turn the Vibration function on or off here on Xbox 360 if you are using a gamepad that supports force feedback.

Advanced Controls

Pressing the Reload button on the Control Setup screen will bring you to the Advanced Controls screen. Here you can make further tweaks to the aiming controls. The vertical aiming controls can be inverted to feel more like flight controls. This is another setting that some players will already be more comfortable with, which is really a matter of personal preference rather than something that might improve your aim. There is a separate setting that allows you to invert flight controls only. By default the flight controls are already 'inverted', so only change this if you want your helicopter controls to act in exactly the same way as standard aiming.**[Screen 02]**

You will also find the options to change the Look Sensitivity here, a setting that will have a much more noticeable effect on your ability to aim your weapon. The default setting is 75 for both horizontal and vertical aiming speed. It is recommended that you keep this setting, unless you find the aiming too fast and overshoot your targets when having to adjust your aim quickly. To offset this, you can bring the sensitivity down to 50 or below, although your ability to make fast adjustments, or turn around quickly when taken by surprise, will be noticeably reduced.

Press the Start or Action buttons on the title screen to take you to the game's Main Menu screen. You can then choose from the following menu options, each of which we will take a look at now:

Campaign Game

The Campaign Setup screen allows you to start a fresh campaign by selecting New Campaign from the menu. You can also load an existing campaign from here, or delete your campaign save file. Selecting Continue Campaign will start you from your last saved checkpoint in the most recently played campaign. You can also select Load Campaign to load up a different save file, which can prove useful if you are not the only person playing through the game on your console.

Once New Campaign is selected, you'll need to make a new save file, or choose to overwrite a previous one. You will then be shown the intro movie, detailing how the current conflict on the island of Skira has come about, after which you'll be presented with the Mission Briefing screen for Mission 01. In Campaign mode you will have to play through all 11 missions in order. **[Screen 01]**

Single Mission

This brings you to the Single Mission menu, where you can select any previously completed mission in a campaign to play through. First, you must choose the campaign in which the mission you want to play takes place. By default, the only campaign available will be Dragon Rising, but there may be Fire Team Engagements or other campaigns available if you have pre-order codes or have DLC installed (this includes user-created missions and campaigns for the PC version of the game). You can then select the difficulty setting to play on, and finally select the mission you wish to play from the list shown. **[Screen 02]**

Multiplayer

Here you'll find the Multiplayer menu, from which you can access the co-op campaign and dedicated multiplayer modes, Annihilation and Infiltration. First you must choose between Online play or System Link/LAN play. For the console versions of the game, Online play requires an Xbox Live or PlayStation Network account (and a paid subscription in the case of Xbox Live). System Link play requires you to link up two consoles with an Ethernet cable, and will allow for two-player Co-op play or 1 vs 1 in the Multiplayer modes. For full details on the multiplayer modes, see the 'Online Engagements' chapter later in the guide.

Options

The Options menu provides access to four sub-menus, which are: Audio, Graphics, Game Settings and Control Setup. The Audio settings let you adjust the volume of each element of the game's audio separately. The Graphics menu allows you to adjust the Gamma setting, which is useful if the game appears too dark or washed out on your television or monitor.

The Game Settings let you decide whether to turn the subtitles and tutorial texts on or off. These are both on by default, and it is recommended that you leave them on until you are much more familiar with the game, otherwise you risk missing an important message that could help to point you in the right direction. You can also turn the RV Markers off here, so that even on the Normal setting they won't be displayed on the HUD. Again, this is best left on the default setting until after your first play through the game. **[Screen 03]**

Extras

The Extras page makes it easy for you to keep track of your stats and achievements. The game tracks almost everything you do while playing and presents the resulting statistics while missions are loading. The full list of tracked stats can be found in the Extras menu, and can be filtered by a Global setting or just for multiplayer modes.

You will also find the Achievements option here on Xbox 360, which will bring up the Xbox 360 guide. You can then check which of the game's achievements you have, and which you still need to unlock. PS3 users should use PS3's XMB to check their progress with the game's Trophies. **[Screen 04]**The last two options here are the Credits, which simply allow you to view the game's entire end-credits sequence at any time and also the Bonus Codes menu. Bonus Codes can be entered here to unlock extra content or grant access to hidden features.

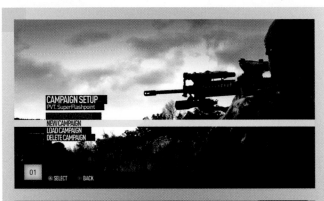

DIFFICULTY

Difficulty in Operation Flashpoint: Dragon Rising is not based on the damage you take or on the number of enemies you'll be up against. The action in the game doesn't actually vary at all between the difficulty settings. What does change, however, is the amount of assistance the player receives through on-screen indicators and checkpoints. The changes between the game's three difficulty settings are listed here in full in the 'Difficulty Changes' table.

DIFFICULTY CHANGES

Feature	Difficulty			Description of feature
	Normal	Experienced	Hardcore	
Aim assist (Stick aiming)	✔	✔	✘	As the player moves their crosshair over an enemy the aiming becomes more sluggish in order to help shots where more precision is required.
Compass	✔	✔	✘	This is the main compass at the top of the screen
Compass when Quick Command Radial is held	–	–	✔	This is the main compass at the top of the screen; only visible when using the quick command radial
Objective Markers (World)	✔	✘	✘	Objective markers that float within the world (can be seen through the scenery)
Objective Markers (Compass)	✔	✔	✘	Objective markers that appear on the compass
Objective Markers (Map)	✔	✔	✔	Objective markers that appear on the Overview Map
Enemy Markers (Compass)	✔	✔	✘	Enemy markers that appear on the compass
RV Markers available	✔	✔	✘	RV markers that appear in the world to help direct the player to areas of cover
RV Markers (On by default)	✔	✘	✘	This is a change to the default setting by having RV Markers appear in the world
Crosshair	✔	✔	✘	The crosshair is the aiming reticule the player can use when un-aimed.
Crosshair Color Change: Enemy	✔	✔	✘	This makes the crosshair change color to red when the player looks at an enemy
Friendly indicator: blue cross	✔	✘	✘	This blue cross will appear when the player looks at a friendly unit (aimed or un-aimed) and is used for reducing friendly fire incidents
Hit indicator: Hit on an enemy	✔	✘	✘	This indicator indicates when the player gets a hit on an enemy unit
Hit indicator: Direction of fire indicator	✔	✔	✘	This indicator shows the player that they have been hit and from what direction
Player injury indicator (where hit and severity)	✔	✔	✘	This indicator shows a silhouette of a human body and shows the player which body location is damaged and the degree of severity
Third-person view in vehicles	✔	✔	✘	This option allows the player to go into third-person view when on board vehicles
Full health regained at checkpoints	✔	✘	✘	When this is on, injured fire-team members are fully healed at checkpoints
Focus View (soldier names)	–	✔	✘	When focus view is used, fire-team members' names appear above their heads (when in view)
Team Mates' names permanently on	✔	✘	✘	Fire team members' names are permanently above their heads
Squad Selector	✔	✔	✘	The squad selector is visible at all times
Equipment Menu	✔	✔	✘	The equipment menu is visible at all times
Stance Indicator	✔	✔	✘	The stance indicator is visible when stance changes
Bleed out meter	✔	✔	✘	The bleed meter is visible if the player is currently bleeding

01

HEADS-UP DISPLAY

As you can see in the 'Difficulty Changes' table, the on-screen elements that you'll see when playing will vary greatly, depending on the difficulty setting selected. Normal mode gives you every assistance you need to make you feel sure about your surroundings and the current situation. This includes HUD elements such as RV Markers, which will lead you towards your next objective. Experienced mode removes some key HUD elements, such as the Hit Indicator. This forces players to receive most of the feedback from their actions from observing the game world, rather than from the HUD. **[Screen 05]**

Although the game itself doesn't change on the higher settings, the nature of the challenge it provides does. On Normal, for example, once you've spotted an enemy soldier, you can line up a shot and watch for the Hit Indicator to flash red, and then quickly look for other enemies who might be in the area. On Experienced or Hardcore, however, you can't be certain that the enemy you shoot is incapacitated, especially from longer distances. This

05

means you have to choose between making sure he's finished off or looking for other enemies who may have been alerted.

THIS IS HARDCORE

The almost total lack of any HUD elements on the Hardcore setting can make for a much more absorbing experience. This, combined with a lack of checkpoint assistance, shifts the focus much more on to spotting enemies well in advance of engagements. Effective use of your fire-team is essential here, as they will still call out enemies they've spotted for you. [Screen 01]

Compass

The top of the HUD is dominated by the compass on the Experienced setting and below. This takes the form of a linear strip showing compass directions and degrees between them. Enemy units (both soldiers and vehicles) appear as red dots along this strip, and will be dead center when you're looking perfectly in their direction. Checkpoints and mission objectives also appear on the compass, but as white dots. Enemies spotted by you or your fire-team will appear on the compass, but they will disappear again if they are out of the line of sight of friendly forces for too long. [Screen 02]

Targeting Crosshair

The crosshair you'll see when aiming a weapon is one of the most important aspects of the HUD. This crosshair is only visible when playing on the Experienced setting or below. The crosshair will turn red when you are aiming directly at an enemy soldier or vehicle. On the Normal setting an additional blue cross appears when you are aiming at allies to further reduce the chance of friendly fire incidents. The crosshair disappears when the aim button is used for aiming through the iron sights or scope of your weapon.

The lack of crosshair on the Hardcore setting means that normal aiming requires much more skill and judgment. This puts more emphasis on the aim mode and on using the iron sights on your weapon, which in turn makes you a more stationary target. [Screen 03]

Current Weapon Info

The Current Weapon Info box appears at the bottom right of the HUD and is on all the time on the Normal setting. This will show a small picture of the weapon you have currently equipped with its name beneath it. It also shows your current ammunition count, both in rounds and clips/magazines remaining. Lastly, there is a dashed bar below your ammo count that represents the rate of fire. Think of each dash as a bullet. The current rate of fire is shown by how many of the bullets are bright yellow. A single bullet means that you are in single-shot mode, while three bullets indicates semi-automatic mode, allowing for short, three-round bursts of fire. If the full five bullets are lit up, the weapon is currently fully automatic, so holding down the Shoot button will result in a continuous stream of fire.

Hit Indicator

Whenever you successfully hit an enemy soldier on the Normal setting you will see a dotted cross appear briefly on screen where you are aiming. This dotted cross can be white or red. If it's white, your shot hit the enemy but did not incapacitate or kill them. Red signifies that the enemy was killed or incapacitated. Incapacitated enemies should no longer be considered a threat, as they will quickly bleed to death unless healed by an ally. The Hit Indicator is an invaluable tool when you are learning how to judge your aim over distances, and it will allow you to finish off weakened enemies easily before moving on to fresh targets. [Screen 04]

Squad Selector

The top left of the screen is where you'll see the squad selector, which gives you a small visual of each squad member and indicates their current condition. Each squad member's icon will change color to show if they are injured or incapacitated. By default, these icons are white, but will turn yellow if the member is injured. If the injury is severe the icon will turn orange and then finally red when the squad member is killed or incapacitated.

To the left of each member's icon you'll see their assigned number and their current Rules of Engagement. A small red icon is visible when they are in a no-fire state, but no icon will appear when they are able to fire at will.

With the Command button held down, you can use the Left Stick (or the number keys on the PC version, for direct unit selection) to move between these icons and then press the Action button to select one or more of your fire-team members. This is very useful for selecting only one or two members and issuing orders that you don't want non-selected members to follow. You can also press Right on the Left Stick/movement keys to view each member's exact Formation, Spread and Rules of Engagement setting. **[Screen 05]**

Overview Map

At any point during an active mission you can hit the Map button to view the Overview Map. While viewing it you can press the Map button again to return to the game. Using the Right Stick (or the Mouse on the PC version), you can move the map so that you can view the whole of Skira and Skirinka, regardless of which mission you are currently playing. The Left Stick allows you to zoom in and out for a closer view.

This is the Overview Map as it appears in the game. The various elements that you'll come across are all shown and explained in this numbered example:

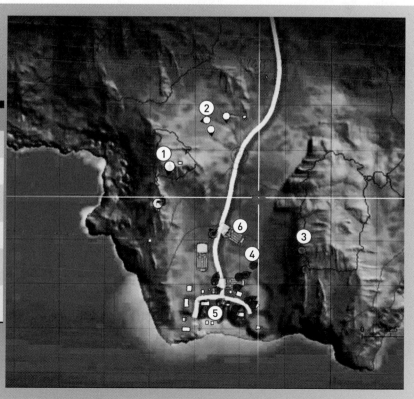

MAP LEGEND

(1)	**Fire Team Leader**	This is your character.
(2)	**Fire Team Members**	These are the squad members under your control
(3)	**Friendly Soldiers**	These are friendly solders that are not part of your fire team, and will not respond to your orders.
(4)	**Enemy Soldier**	This is an enemy soldier in your line of sight
(5)	**Enemy Soldier (Faded)**	This is an enemy soldier that was recently spotted, but only the last known location is displayed
(6)	**Inactive Vehicle**	This is an inactive vehicle, which can be boarded even if it is an enemy vehicle

MAP LEGEND

7	Enemy Vehicle	This is a currently active enemy vehicle
8	Enemy helicopter	This is a currently active enemy helicopter
9	Building	This is a building that can be entered
10	Destroyed Vehicle	This is a vehicle that has been destroyed beyond repair
11	Objective Marker	The marker for your current Primary Objective

MAP LEGEND

12	Friendly Vehicle	This is a friendly vehicle, such as an APC
13	RV Marker	This is your next RV Marker position

MAP LEGEND

14	Friendly Helicopter	This is an active friendly helicopter
15	Inactive helicopter	This is a currently inactive helicopter within visual range of friendly forces
16	Checkpoint	A checkpoint marker before it has been activated

You'll find a Map Control legend at the bottom right of the screen detailing some of the more useful Map functions. This control legend is context-sensitive and reveals a great deal of control over your fire team from the Map. For more on this, see the Advanced Map Use section in the 'Specialized Training' chapter.

FIRE TEAMS

Operation Flashpoint: Dragon Rising gives the player control of a Fire Team Leader, who can give orders to the other member of his fire team. A fire team is a military term for a small group of four soldiers which functions as an independent unit. Squads are usually made of three or more separate fire teams, depending on the size of the operation.

There are different types of fire team, each of which is geared towards a specific task. You'll find full details on these types in the Specialized Training chapter, but for now we'll show an example of a typical USMC fire team that you'll be in control of in Dragon Rising. The weapons shown here are used as examples; the initial weapons for each soldier will vary from mission to mission.

FIRE TEAM LEADER

Primary Weapon: M4A1 Assault Rifle (CQB)	Secondary Weapon: SMAW

This is the character under your control. Other fire team members take orders from the Fire Team Leader, and he generally takes point when advancing. He is also trained to use all types of infantry weapon.

MEDIC

Primary Weapon: M16A4 Assault Rifle (Marksman)	Secondary Weapon: N/A

The medic can heal you when you are injured. He can also be ordered to heal other fire team members. He will use an Assault Rifle in combat.

RIFLEMAN

Primary Weapon: M16A4 Assault Rifle (Marksman)	Secondary Weapon: N/A

In most cases, the team's rifleman is a long-range spotter who should be used in flanking maneuvers and general mid-distance combat. He will usually be acting as your main backup.

MACHINEGUNNER

Primary Weapon: M249 SAW	Secondary Weapon: N/A

Your fire team's machinegunner is very useful for laying down suppressive fire on your order. You should use him to keep enemies pinned down in their position.

MISSION FLOW

Next we'll take a look at the various elements and events you need to be aware of when playing a mission in Dragon Rising. The checkpoint system and the way the game handles taking damage and healing are very different to those in typical FPS games, and it's essential to fully understand them in order to succeed within each mission.

Mission Briefing

This screen will appear before each new mission. Here, you'll find everything you need to know about the mission ahead and you can obtain some useful information about the Primary and Secondary Objectives. You'll also see some estimates of the number and type of enemy forces you'll be up against and the key friendly support that will be taking part in the mission. Press the Reload button here to bring up a detailed description of where the mission fits into the current assault, and where the important staging areas are.

Soldier Loadouts

Before you start each mission you'll get a chance to inspect your fire team's weapons and equipment on the Soldier Loadout screen. To do this, press the Combat Support button on the Mission Briefing screen (you'll see 'View Force' indicated at the bottom of the screen). This will take you to the Force Summary screen, detailing all of the fire teams and support teams involved in the current operation. From here you can press the Combat Support button again to go to the Combat Support screen, or press the Command button to go to the detailed Soldier Loadout screen for the currently selected squad.

You can't actually change the loadout you start with, but it is still worth checking what equipment your fire team has access to. Knowing which squad members are carrying silenced or suppressed weapons on, for example, a stealth mission can make a huge difference to your tactics. Similarly, your fire team is often composed of different specialized combat types, such as snipers or grenadiers, you can plan your strategies around. For more on these types, see the Specialized Training chapter. **[Screen 01]**

Saving and Loading

The game uses an auto save feature to save your progress throughout the campaign and within missions. Progress is saved after each mission is completed, allowing you to continue from the start of the next mission, either in Campaign mode or in a Co-op Campaign. Your current position is saved whenever a checkpoint is reached during a mission (though this doesn't ap-

ply in Co-op). This means that, if you die after reaching a checkpoint, you can restart from that point, with your weapons and ammunition counts exactly as they were when the checkpoint was reached. **[Screen 02]**

Objectives

Each mission has Primary and Secondary Objectives to complete. These are outlined on the Mission Briefing screen before each mission. It should be noted, however, that not all objectives are always shown here, as the nature of the mission can change once you enter combat. During a mission you can see the current objectives by holding down the Map button for a short time.

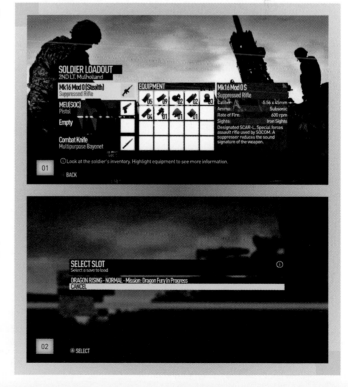

Primary Objectives must be completed in order for you to finish the mission, which means that they are essential if you are to progress within each mission. These objectives will be marked on the map by numbers, and will appear as on-screen markers when playing on the Normal difficulty setting. When a Primary Objective is completed it will usually trigger the next objective to appear.

Secondary Objectives are not required for progress to be made within a mission, but will very often be tasks that can be completed along the route to the Primary Objective. These objectives will usually involve eliminating enemy defenses, or keeping all friendly support units intact. Completed Secondary Objectives will generally make things easier for you when tackling the Primary Objectives, so completing them is a good idea in principle. **[Screen 01]**

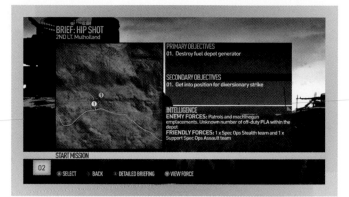

BONUS OBJECTIVES ⓘ

You may notice that the game also tracks Bonus Objectives. These are not pointed out on the Mission Briefing screen but are hinted at in the Achievements or Trophies list. Naturally, each of these will unlock an Achievement or Trophy when completed, ranging from successfully piloting a helicopter to keeping all of the hostages you are escorting alive. The Mission Briefing chapter explains exactly when and how to complete the objectives in each mission. [Screen 02]

RV Markers

Once a mission begins on the Normal difficulty setting, you will see a yellow marker icon on the HUD with a flag and a small arrow. This is your first RV Marker, which is short for Rendezvous Marker. Heading towards it will put you on the right track for completing your current objective (even though it may not actually be leading you in the exact direction of the objective). The RV Markers are placed at regular intervals, often near identifiable geographic markers, which real-world fire-teams would use to plot routes across enemy territory.

When you reach the RV Marker's position, a new RV Marker will appear in the distance. By continuing to follow these you will ensure that you are on course to complete the current objective. Note, however, that they don't always lead you through every checkpoint on a mission, so keep an eye on the Map to ensure you don't miss any. **[Screen 03]**

Checkpoints

Checkpoints are the points in the mission where your progress is saved. The Normal setting has the most checkpoints. On this setting your fire team will respawn with full health whenever you reach a checkpoint. On Experienced there are fewer checkpoints in each mission, usually leaving only one or two, while on Hardcore there are none at all. This means that you'll have to play through the entire mission again from the very start if you die (although, even on Hardcore, the mission's opening checkpoint remains in place to avoid your having to hear the full mission briefing each time you restart). **[Screen 04]**

To activate a checkpoint you need to be within its active radius. Checkpoints are sometimes not positioned on the mission's main path, as indicated by the RV Markers. Check the Map to see where the checkpoints are within each mission and plan your route so that you will pass through them.

Taking Damage

Unless you've taken a direct shot to the head, or have been caught in an explosive blast, getting shot will almost certainly cause you to start bleeding. You will notice that there is now a red circle in the bottom left of the HUD. This is a gauge that slowly depletes itself, representing your current loss of blood. Once the circle has been fully diminished, you will have lost too much blood and will subsequently die. You can avoid this by using a field dressing on yourself, which you can select from your inventory and apply by holding down the Shoot button. **[Screen 05]**

Healing and Dying

The more serious the wound, the faster you'll bleed and you'll notice that your view will slowly lose color saturation and get darker to emphasize this. On Experienced and below you'll also see your current body condition represented in the bottom left corner of the HUD. This will show which areas of your body are currently wounded and provide a color indication ranging from yellow, for minor flesh wounds, to red, for lethal wounds that cause incapacitation.

Light wounds are indicated by yellow patches and occur when a body location has taken damage but still has more than 50% of its hit points. Serious wounds are indicated by orange and occur when a body location has fewer than 50% of its hit points remaining, but still has positive hit points. Incapacitating wounds are indicated by red and occur when a single body location has 0 or fewer hit points. Death is indicated by all body locations coloured red and occurs when a single body location reaches -3 hit points. Typical hit point values for a character in the game are illustrated here (it should be noted that modifiers such as armor values are applied to these for different troops in the game, so they cannot be considered as absolute (i.e. hitting the head with a weapon rated at 4 will not guarantee a kill in all instances). **[Screen 06]**

Yellow wounds don't actually make you bleed, but orange wounds do. Each body location that receives an orange wound has an increased bleeding rate. Light arm wounds cause a minor loss of aim, serious arm wounds a major loss. Light leg wounds cause your possible sprinting time to be noticeably shortened. A serious leg wound will nullify your ability to sprint entirely. Serious wounds to arms or legs will therefore reduce your combat effectiveness considerably and should be treated as quickly as possible. For quick reference, and to emphasize the importance of this, these conditions are shown in the following chart.

HP VALUES

	Hit Points	Body Area
Head	4	Face, Skull
Chest	8	Neck, Rib Cage, Thorax
Abdomen	8	Hips, Groin
Arms	8	Shoulder to Hand
Legs	8	Hip to Foot

WOUND EFFECTS

	Light Arm Wound (Yellow)	Serious Arm Wound (Orange)	Light Leg Wound (Yellow)	Serious Leg Wound (Orange)	Lethal Wound (Red)
Aim Loss	Minor	Major	None	None	No
Sprint Loss	None	None	Minor	Major	No
Incapacitation	N/A	N/A	N/A	N/A	Yes

MEDIC! ⓘ

Applying a field dressing to yourself will only stop the bleeding, regardless of how serious the wound is. To heal the wound, however, and get back to peak condition, you'll need to get a medic to give you the proper treatment. You can order your squad's medic to heal another squad member using the 'Treat Wounded' command or to heal you by using the 'Medic' command. For more on this see the 'Commanding Your Fire Team' section in the Specialized Training chapter. [Screen 07]

THE ENVIRONMENT

Operation Flashpoint: Dragon Rising is set within an enormous and completely open-world environment. In missions without time-sensitive objectives players are free to roam the environment at their leisure. Skira is a vast island, but very sparsely populated, and the majority of its terrain is made up of untouched grasslands and mountainous rocky areas. Exploring the island takes a very long time and will often not reveal anything useful to the player, due to the sheer size of the area involved. However, it is still worth investigating areas that look interesting; a drive around the island will reveal no shortage of these.

Day/Night Cycle

Each mission within the campaign starts at a specific time of day. You can see the mission start times on the timeline that is visible between missions in Campaign mode. This also applies to multiplayer modes, but the exact time of day is not given. Time will pass normally during play, although at a slightly accelerated rate. This means that missions starting just before dawn will usually still be in progress when daylight emerges and have an obvious effect on your visibility.

Buildings

There are many small villages, settlements, depots and buildings on Skira, although the vast areas between them will make each of them seem very remote. Most of the buildings you come across can be entered by use of the Action button, which opens doors. It is worth checking every building in the area, as there may be valuable equipment boxes within them. You'll also find bunkers that can be entered, although they usually won't have doors to open. These can be useful for quick cover, or as defensive positions.

Equipment Boxes

The weapons you start a particular mission with will almost certainly not be the only ones available to you throughout the mission. You'll often find equipment boxes near enemy camps or fortified positions. These may contain some extremely useful weapons and ammunition that will often have a huge impact on how you tackle the subsequent engagements. Equipment boxes will be very important in longer missions, as the ammunition you start with may not be enough to see you through to the end, so it's essential that you search them out. **[Screen 01]**

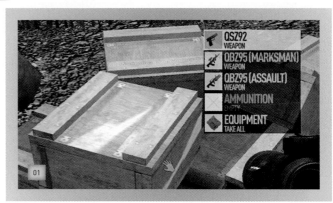

01

BODY SEARCHING

Remember that the bodies of enemy soldiers you have killed can also be searched for ammunition. However, they will generally not have ammunition compatible with your weapons, so you'll have to take their weapons together with the ammunition that goes with them, if you are dangerously low on ammo of your own.

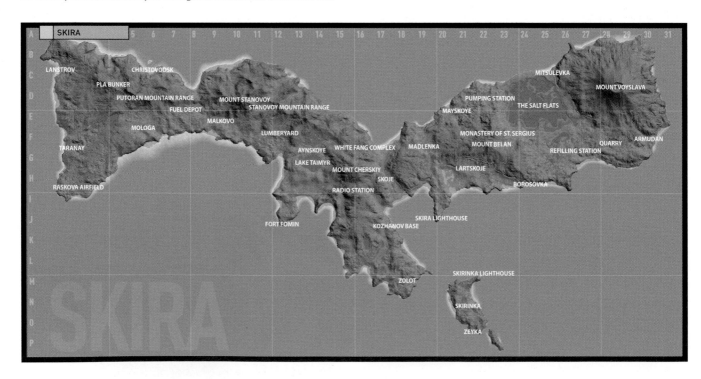

BASIC CONTROLS

Here we'll take a brief look at the most important elements of control-ling your character in the game. Players well versed in modern FPS games will find the basics of control in Dragon Rising familiar, but there are still some subtleties that are very well worth pointing out.

Movement

By default, you will move through the environment using the Left Stick, which has become the standard for other console FPS games in recent years. You do have a degree of control over your movement speed, allowing you, for example, to walk very slowly by pushing forward lightly on the Left Stick. (this doesn't apply when using the movement keys on the PC version). This is important to know during stealth-based missions, as the slower you are moving, the less noise you will make and, subsequently, the less likely you are to alert the enemy soldiers to your presence. **[Screen 02]**

This degree of control also applies to strafing, which is also controlled with the Left Stick (or the defined left and right movement keys on PC). You have three separate speeds at which you can strafe, depending on how far you push the Left Stick to the left or right. The slowest of these speeds is perfect for helping to line up your shots, while the faster speeds are better for dodging fire and moving behind cover.

Stances

You have three stances available to you when moving around the game world: Standing, Crouching and Prone. On Normal and Experi-enced settings your current stance is shown on the HUD at the bottom left of the screen (although this indicator fades away if you remain standing for a while). The icons for each of these stances are shown here:

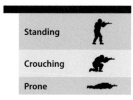

Standing	
Crouching	
Prone	

You can switch between the three stances at any point in general play by clicking the Left Stick (or using the defined Stance key on the PC). Your AI controlled fire-team will automatically adopt the same stance you take. From a standing position you can instantly drop into prone stance by clicking and holding the Left Stick. Crouching will make you move more slowly, although your strafing speed isn't dramatically affected. In prone stance you will have a very limited degree of movement and you will also lose the ability to fire your weapon while moving.

Crouching or going prone will make you a smaller target and will also increase your accuracy, so these stances are a very important element of the game. Try to change your stance as much as possible, depending on the cur-rent situation. For example, crouch when moving towards spotted enemies to get into position for a shot, and then drop into prone if an enemy takes you by surprise from an unexpected direction so that you can assess the situation while avoiding being an open target. **[Screen 03]**

Sprinting

Holding down the Sprint button (see 'The Controls' section at the start of this chapter for specific controls on each platform) while moving forward will cause you to move much more rapidly. This applies to standing and crouching, although you obviously won't be able to sprint at full speed when crouching. While sprinting, you lose the ability to fire or reload your weapon, so it is not a good idea to sprint towards known enemy positions.

You will also begin to suffer from fatigue if you sprint too much. Sprinting will lessen your combat effectiveness should an engagement break out. You'll notice this happening after prolonged sprinting from the sound of your heartbeat getting progressively stronger and faster (and you'll feel it, too, if you are using a gamepad with force feedback and the Vibration setting is on). You will also notice heavy breathing sounds, which are an ad-ditional warning that you are getting fatigued.

Vaulting

When you come into contact with certain obstacles in the environment, such as low walls, sandbags or destroyed buildings, you'll see a prompt on screen to press the Action button. This will cause you to vault over the obstacle in question, which you would otherwise have had to find a way around. This is useful when you need to take a very direct route but will leave you prone to attack briefly if there are enemies in the area. **[Screen 04]**

Also remember that your fire-team will not vault over obstacles but must find a way around them. This can result in their being left behind if you don't take care and make sure there's a route they can take that will allow them to catch up with you.

Equipment Selection

Hold down the Equipment button to bring up the Equipment menu. You can then use Up and Down to navigate through your available weapons and equipment. Stopping on a weapon will automatically select it, if you then release the Equipment button. Give the Equipment button a quick tap to cycle through your available weapons and the currently selected grenade type. This will not work with rocket launchers, such as the SMAW. The latter eliminates the chances of accidentally tapping the button and then finding yourself stuck in the lengthy and highly vulnerable setup process these weapons have to go through.

Binoculars

Your binoculars are an essential tool for scouting out the terrain ahead or calling in air strikes on a specific area. They are always available to you from the equipment menu in both Campaign mode and Multiplayer modes. Once equipped, use the Aim button to bring them up to get much better view of the distant surrounding area. You can also use the Shoot button to fire the binoculars' rangefinder feature. This uses a beam of light to gauge the distance between you and the targeted area or object, which makes it very useful at extremely long range to help you judge your shots correctly and compensate for the ballistics effects. **[Screen 01]**

GIVING ORDERS

Holding Down the Command button (again, see 'The Controls' section for the specific button) will bring the Command Radial on screen. At this point you'll have a huge selection of possible orders you can issue to your fire-team, split initially into two main categories: Tactical and Orders. You also have instant access to the Move command and the Follow Me command by pressing Up or Down respectively from the top level of the Command Radial. [Screen 02]

Sub-categories

Orders are shown in the Command Radial in white text, while grey text represents another sub-level of the Radial, leading to another set of commands. Simply pressing the desired direction when a command is shown in white is enough to issue the command. Within the Orders and Tactical categories there another eight sub-categories, four for each type. Exactly how these main categories are broken down is shown in the Order Categories table here.

ORDER CATEGORIES

Orders	Offense	Defense
	Fire	Movement
Tactical	Rules of Engagement	Medic
	Formations	Spread

The Target Zone

When the Command button is held down, a yellow circle will appear where you are currently aiming. This is your target zone indicator, and it will change size to give a visual clue about how far away it currently is. When giving an order, such as Move or Assault, this target zone is where your fire-team will move to, as soon as the order is given. When you aim at an enemy soldier with the Command button held down, the target zone circle will turn red and the Move and Follow Me commands will be replaced with Assault and Engage commands. You will then benefit from much quicker access to these two key commands in situations where there is no time to spare.

Aiming at a member of your fire-team and holding down the Command button will cause the target zone marker to turn blue. It will also again change the orders that are instantly available, with Follow Target now being assigned to a single press of Up. The Treat Wounded command can be issued by pressing Down, if the fire-team member you are aiming at is a Medic or happens to be currently wounded. This makes for a very quick way of issuing a heal order when engaged in battle or pinned down behind cover. **[Screen 03]**

Note that you can't bring the Command Radial on screen while moving. If you are moving or sprinting when you press the Command button, you will be brought instantly to a dead stop. This makes it very important to plan ahead and make adjustments to your formation and Rules of Engagement before you begin to move. For a detailed run-down of every specific order and command available, see the Commanding Your Fire Team section in the Specialized Training chapter.

Solid copy. Relocating to set up OP. Will advise when we are in position

BASIC COMBAT

Next, let's go over some of the most important things to remember when engaging enemy soldiers or vehicles. The basics of combat are similar to those in other FPS games but, in Dragon Rising, you'll need to place a lot more emphasis than usual on spotting enemies early and using the natural terrain as your cover.

Spotting Enemies

We'll start with spotting enemies, since who-spots-who first is the single most important factor in determining the outcome of most engagements. It is very unlikely that you'll be able to recover from being taken completely by surprise, so your first priority is to make sure this doesn't happen. Always use the scope on your weapon to check the terrain ahead for enemy soldiers or vehicles. If your weapon doesn't have a scope with any kind of zoom then you can use your Binoculars to spot ahead. Otherwise, try to pick up a Marksman-type rifle from an enemy's body. **[Screen 04]**

You can also use your fire-team to spot enemies. Keeping them spread out wide in front of you is perfect for this. If one member of your fire-team has a

Sniper rifle then they will be ideal as the point man, a little ahead of the others. Once you've spotted enemy movement, you can call back your fire-team and plan your approach to give you the best possible advantage in terms of ground level and available cover.

Shooting

Once the enemy force has been spotted you'll need to get into a good position to shoot them from. Ideally, you'll want cover nearby from an elevated position, but this isn't always possible. Try to see how far away you can get while still being able to take an accurate shot. If the enemy hasn't spotted you yet, shooting from as far away as possible will give you at big advantage, although you'll need to maximize your accuracy.

If you can find a clear patch of ground you should go prone and take advantage of the large accuracy boost it offers. The accuracy boost becomes even more accentuated over longer ranges. You should also ensure that you are not fatigued before taking your first shot. At long range you will need to aim above the enemy's head to make allowances for ballistics. Most scoped weapons have height markers for every few hundred meters; these will show you how high you need to adjust your aim. **[Screen 05]**

Reloading

Reloading in Dragon Rising is a more realistic affair than you find in most FPS games. Once the Reload button is pressed you will be totally vulnerable for the entire time it takes to reload your current weapon. If your weapon happens to be a Javelin or SMAW, then that could be up to 10 full seconds, so planning for your reloads and staying in cover for their duration is essential. With a regular Assault rifle it is possible to reload on the move, but this should only be attempted when you are certain the area ahead is clear.

Using Cover

Cover can come in many forms in Operation Flashpoint: Dragon Rising. There are the usual low walls and sandbags that you can make use of, but you'll frequently find the enemy already dug-in behind cover like this. This is because you'll be approaching their fortified positions, usually from open ground, as required by the current mission. **[Screen 06]**

This means that you must look for other forms of cover in order to avoid becoming too vulnerable during your approaches. The answer to this problem is usually in the lie of the land itself. Use hills and undulations in the terrain to give your fire-team cover during your approach and ensure that the enemy don't know where you will be coming from. By staying close to small hills, but avoiding approaching the hilltop, you will be able to control your visibility to the enemy forces more effectively. **[Screen 07]**

Aim Mode

Holding down the Aim button will take you into aim mode. This brings your weapon up to head height for a level aim, using either the iron sights of the weapon or a scope, if the weapon features one. There is a noticeable gain in accuracy when firing in aim mode, but your movement speed and options are greatly reduced. However, you can still change stances while in aim mode.

Grenades

To use Hand Grenades you must equip them from the Equipment menu. Once equipped, you can hold down the Reload button to toggle between the various types of grenades available to you, such as Smoke Grenades and IR Strobes. You can throw a grenade with the Shoot button, holding it down to 'ready' the grenade a little before throwing (note that this doesn't actually pull the pin, so you are not 'cooking' the grenade). You can also use the Zoom button to give a short underarm throw instead of the arcing, long-distance throw. This is useful when engaging targets within buildings, or for rolling grenades underneath vehicles to reach targets just the other side. **[Screen 08]**

Combat Support

Combat Support comes in the form of various types of Air Strikes and Mortars. These are launched from friendly aircraft or naval vessels and must be called in by the player after targeting a specific area. To do this you should equip either your binoculars or a weapon with a zoom-capable scope and then press the Combat Support button once to bring up the available strike option in the command radial. Aim the red circle at the area you want to target and then choose the type of strike you want to call in (generally there will only one type available on each mission) and how concentrated you want the blast radius to be.

CO-OPERATIVE PLAY

Operation Flashpoint: Dragon Rising is designed to be played with up to four players co-operatively throughout its entire Campaign mode. Players can play in Co-op mode over System Link, which means directly linking two or more of the same consoles (or PCs) using ethernet cables (this also requires multiple copies of the game).

Starting a Game

You can start a co-op game from the multiplayer menu, after choosing to play over System Link/LAN or Online. Once you've selected the Co-operative mode, you can either start a new campaign, load up an existing campaign or choose to play a single mission. When loading up an existing campaign or single mission, players can join even if they have not reached that point in the Campaign, but they will not be awarded the "Complete the Campaign" achievement or Trophy for finishing the game from that point.

The Tether Zone

You'll notice a circle to the right of the screen on the HUD in co-operative mode, which has at least two dots inside it. This is the tether zone, and the dots represent you and your fellow human-controlled squad mates. When playing in Co-op mode the squad members who are controlled by you and the other player(s) are limited in how far away they can be from each other. This limit is indicated by the tether zone circle, which is visible on both the HUD and the overview map. **[Screen 01]**

Each player is always positioned at the centre of the tether zone on their own HUD. The tether zone has a radius of 225 meters. If you get this far away from your nearest squad mate you'll be given a warning that you are reaching the edge of the permitted zone. Once you are 275 meters from the nearest other player you'll have reached the cut-off point and will be killed, so you must watch the tether zone indicator carefully when playing and plan around it accordingly.

ACHIEVEMENTS AND TROPHIES

The console versions of Operation Flashpoint: Dragon Rising feature the usual set of Achievements and Trophies that can be collected during play. The majority of these are based on regular progress through the Campaign mode, including completing Primary and Secondary Objectives. Some are bonus objectives that remain hidden; each of these will be explained in full detail in the Mission Briefing chapter. The last few can only be achieved in co-operative play and are based on successful teamwork.

ACHIEVEMENTS AND TROPHIES

Name	Condition	Explanation	Points (Xbox 360)	Type (PS3)
Campaign Objectives				
Tide's Out	Successfully hold the beachhead	Your Fire Team successfully held the beachhead in United We Stand	20	Bronze
Runway Relief	Capture the airfield	Your Fire Team captured the airfield in Eagle Offense	20	Bronze
Sandman's Saviors	Extract the downed air crew	Your Fire Team extracted the downed air crew in Powder Trail	20	Bronze
Resource Management	Secure the fuel depot	Your Fire Team secured the fuel depot in Bleeding Edge	20	Bronze
Uphill Struggle	Eliminate the PLA mortar site	Your Fire Team eliminated the PLA mortar site in Trumpet's Sound	20	Bronze
Ship It	Assault the Naval Base	Your Fire Team assaulted the Naval Base in Dragon Fury	20	Bronze
Without Warning	Destroy Radar emplacement	Your Fire Team destroyed the Radar emplacement in Dragon Rising	20	Bronze
Saber Beats SAM	Disable the SAM sites	Your Fire Team disabled the SAM sites in Blinding The Dragon	20	Bronze
Fly Away Peter, Fly Away Paul	Get to the extraction chopper	Your Fire Team got to the extraction chopper in Hip Shot	20	Bronze
Heroic Rescue	Rescue the hostages	Your Fire Team rescued the hostages in Looking for Lois	20	Bronze
Bug Out	Reach the extraction point	Your Fire Team reached the extraction point in Decapitation	20	Bronze
Bonus Objectives				
Get Creative	Destroy the PLA APC at the top of the beach in United We Stand	Your Fire Team destroyed the PLA APC at the top of the beach	30	Silver
Hip Shooter	Destroy the fleeing PLA transport helicopter in Eagle Offense	Your Fire Team destroyed the fleeing PLA transport helicopter	30	Silver
Hitchhiker	Destroy the PLA armored units around the ghost village in Powder Trail	Your Fire Team destroyed the PLA armored units around the ghost village	30	Silver
Ruthless Efficiency	Eliminate the remaining troops on the second line with one mortar barrage in Bleeding Edge	Your Fire Team eliminated the remaining troops on the second line with one mortar barrage	30	Silver
Keep 'em Rolling	Ensure all of the Abrams reach the supporting fire position in Trumpet's Sound	Your Fire Team ensured all of the Abrams reached the supporting fire position	30	Silver
Vertical Envelopment	Pilot a MH-60S safely to the designated landing zone in Dragon Fury	Your Fire Team flew an MH-60S safely to the designated landing zone	30	Silver
Skirinka Island Tour	Find the PLA helicopter and fly it around Skirinka Island in Dragon Rising	Your Fire Team found the PLA helicopter and flew it around Skirinka Island	30	Silver
Ghost Ops	Eliminate the PLA Commander in Blinding The Dragon	Your Fire Team eliminated the PLA Commander	30	Silver
Fuel the fire	Destroy all of the PLA fuel trucks in Hip Shot	Your Fire Team destroyed all of the PLA fuel trucks	30	Silver
Perfect Rescue	All hostages must survive in Looking for Lois	All of the hostages survived	30	Silver
Two Birds, One Stone	Eliminate Han and the radio station with one JDAM in Decapitation	Your Fire Team eliminated Han and the radio station with one JDAM	30	Silver
Miscellaneous				
Dragon Rising	Complete the campaign on any difficulty	You completed the campaign on any difficulty	70	Gold
Dragon Rising: Hardcore	Complete the campaign on Hardcore difficulty	You completed the campaign on Hardcore difficulty	100	Gold
Shock and Awe	Call in your first air strike	You called in your first air strike	20	Bronze
Hard Rain	Call in your first artillery barrage	You called in your first artillery barrage	20	Bronze
Low Blow	Kill an enemy vehicle with an AT mine	You killed an enemy vehicle with an AT mine	20	Silver
Scrap Metal	Kill an enemy vehicle with an AT weapon	You killed an enemy vehicle with an AT weapon	20	Silver
Clear Skies	Kill an enemy vehicle with an AA weapon	You killed an enemy vehicle with an AA weapon	20	Silver
The Sky is Falling	Kill an enemy with a helicopter without using its weapons	You killed an enemy with a helicopter without using its weapons	20	Silver
Squad Slayer	Kill or incapacitate 25 enemies	You killed or incapacitated 25 enemies	20	Bronze
Platoon Pounder	Kill or incapacitate 50 enemies	You killed or incapacitated 50 enemies	30	Silver
Company Killer	Kill or incapacitate 100 enemies	You killed or incapacitated 100 enemies	50	Gold
Unbloodied Hands	Complete a mission without directly killing anyone yourself	You completed a mission without directly killing anyone yourself	20	Silver
All Patched Up	Apply a field dressing to an injured friend in co-op	You saved the life of a friend	20	Silver
Florence Nightingale Award	Apply the field dressing to other wounded soldiers 20 times	You applied the field dressing to other soldiers 20 times	20	Silver
All Trophies collected	N/A	N/A	N/A	Platinum
	Points total		**1000**	

SPECIALIZED TRAINING
CHAPTER 02

This chapter will give you the full details on commanding your fire team, and will reveal all of the tricks you'll need to know to stay alive through the toughest engagements. Taking full advantage of your fire team requires you to know everything they are capable of. All commands are detailed here, along with insight into the extensive map controls and the game's AI systems.

COMMANDING YOUR FIRE TEAM
CHAPTER 02

In this first section we'll cover everything you need to know in order to lead your fire team to victory. We'll start with the basics, and cover the roles that each squad member is best suited for, and then go into detail on every single order you can issue to your team. Finally, we'll cover the various spreads and formations available to help keep your team in order.

THE BASICS

First we'll take a look at the basic elements of effectively commanding your fire team. This includes how to select individual squad members, and what each of the defined roles means

Squad Selecting

As explained in the Basic Training chapter, you can use the Squad Selector to select one or more of your fire team members to give an order to. You can give orders to your entire fire team either by selecting all of them or by leaving them all unselected. Whether you select all fire team members or none of them makes no real difference; they will all carry out the order given.

Selecting all units and issuing an order (as opposed to having no units selecting and issuing the order to the fireteam as a whole) has the effect of issuing the order to each solider individually. As they are each following this order individually rather than as a group they will not demonstrate any group behaviour whilst carrying out the order, such as formations or bounding. Another advantage to this is that they will all show up on the map as bright yellow circles, instead of muted grey. This also applies to the lines used in plotting movement, and makes finding your team quickly on the overview map a little easier. **[Screen 01]**

Quick View Icons

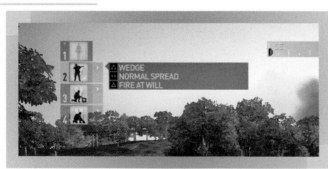

When one or more fire team members are selected in the Squad Selector you can press right on the Right Stick to bring up the quick view icons. These icons show the current Formation, Spread and Rules of Engagement settings for each squad member. These icons are shown here:

Squad Roles

There are small icons next to each fire team member's icon in the Squad Selector. They represent each fire team member's combat type, which is essentially the role they are filling within the team. These can help you assign tasks to the right person quickly, once you know what each of the icons means. For example, once you're familiar with the medic's icon, you can quickly select your medic only and order him to stay back and hold fire. Similarly, you can select only your grenadier and quickly have him engage an incoming enemy vehicle.

There are many more different types of roles than any single fire team can accommodate. Highly specialized fire teams can be made up of snipers, marksmen and combat engineers, for example. **[Screen 02]**

A balanced fire team, however, is far more often the best approach, though there are quite a few ways to reach that balance. A look at the most often used combat types will help to understand what each one's role is within a team. Note that there are other, much less common, roles that aren't included here.

Fire Team Leader

The Fire Team Leader is usually the most experienced member of the squad, and will take on a multi-purpose role while commanding the team. They are trained in all types of weapons, and will usually be equipped with the best one for the mission ahead.

Medic

The medic is an extremely valuable member of any fire team. Trained combat medics are highly qualified to treat wounds, and are also expert marksmen. They come equipped with medical kits with morphine syringes, capable of fully healing fire team members.

Sniper

Having a dedicated sniper on a fire team will add a lethal long-range threat, due to their Sniper rifle. Their presence will allow the team to take slower approaches, as they scout for targets in the far distance.

Engineer

A combat engineer is a versatile squad member, usually proficient with Marksman-type assault rifles. Engineers will usually come equipped with an assortment of explosive gear, from the usual C4 Demo Charges, to AP and AT Mines. Spec Ops Engineers come equipped with a Rocket Launcher as an anti-tank weapon.

Rifleman

Most fire teams should have at least one rifleman among their number, and in fact they are the most commonly used class in Dragon Rising. Dedicated and proficient assault rifle users, riflemen are the ideal general combat soldiers. They usually come equipped with a scoped Marksman-type rifle.

Machinegunner

The Machinegunner specializes in the use of Light Machine Guns, such as the Mk48 Mod 0. Due to the size of these weapons, and the difficulty of aiming them proficiently, they usually do not come equipped with other weapons.

Grenadier

The Grenadier can be considered a hybrid class, albeit one with a strong specialty in Grenade Launcher use. They will use their assault rifles for general combat, but will make good use of the underslung Grenade Launcher attachment when the need arises.

Fire Team Types

The fire team you are commanding (or are simply a member of in multiplayer) will be composed according to the mission or combat requirements at hand. In Operation Flashpoint: Dragon Rising you'll either play as a USMC Infantry fire team, or a Spec Ops fire team, depending on which mission you are playing. Both types of team can and will be made up from the various combat types listed on the previous page, although the marines will have a preference for machinegunners and grenadiers, while the Spec Ops teams will generally include riflemen and snipers.

The two types of fire team are from different branches of the US armed forces and, as such, will each have their own preferences and approaches. You'll notice that the Spec Ops, for example, are much more strict in their use of language than the USMC infantry teams are. There many types of fire teams within these two branches, set up to perform specific tasks or to deal with certain types of threat. Here we'll have a look at the major differences between USMC Infantry and Spec Ops teams.

Infantry

The USMC Infantry fire teams are often deployed as part of a much larger invading or peacekeeping force. With multiple fire teams participating in the operation, some will usually be sent on routes that allow them to cover a wide area, while staying just close enough to provide backup to other fire teams. Infantry are basically an assault force; large numbers of disciplined soldiers designed to take and hold key objectives. As an infantryman you'll generally be advancing alongside friendly forces, and the enemy will typically be in a direction ahead of the force. **[Screen 03]** Infantry fire teams are usually set up to specialize in Assault, Rifle, Security and Support. USMC fire teams in Dragon Rising will have the codename Dagger.

Spec Ops

Spec Ops teams are usually sent into missions as a solo outfit, and must rely on evading enemy contact unless it's absolutely necessary to engage. These teams will generally have weapons with silencers and the most effective Night Ops equipment. Spec Ops are self-sufficient, precision forces designed to take or eliminate high value targets. They'll generally face 360 degree threats as they'll typically be deployed or inserted behind enemy lines. **[Screens 04-05]** There will usually be at least one rifleman on a Spec Ops fire team. Spec Ops teams can be geared towards Recon, Rescue, Stealth Ops, Command and Demolition. Spec Ops fire teams in Dragon Rising will have the codename Saber. Note that the dagger and eagle wings insignia is for Special Forces teams only.

GIVING ORDERS

Here we'll go into a little more detail on the command radial and how to best make use of it. You'll also find a detailed description of each order's basic function and the best uses for them.

Command Radial

The command radial is used to give orders to your fire team from the field (rather than from the overview map). It separates orders into categories, so that similar ones are grouped together to make them easier to find.

Once you know the exact commands needed to give a particular order from the command radial, you can input the commands extremely quickly to issue the order immediately. Since you can't give orders while on the move, issuing them from the command radial as quickly as possible is a valuable skill to learn. **[Screen 01]** In the next section we'll detail exactly what each order is used for and we'll also give the exact series of commands needed to issue the order in question quickly. First, however, we'll describe exactly how the various orders are grouped into the categories seen in the command radial.

Order Categories

Commands are separated between the two sides of the command radial, with Orders on the right and Tactical commands on the left. Each of these categories is then split into further branches. Orders are split between the following categories: Offensive, Defensive, Fire and Movement, each of these categories having three or four commands within them. On the Tactical side, the three categories are: ROE, Formation and Spread. Again, in each of these there are three or four commands that can be given.

Basic				
	Move			
	Follow Me			
Tactical	**ROE**	**Formations**	**Speads**	
	Fire at Will	Vee	Normal	
	Fire on my Lead	Wedge	Combat	
	Return Fire	Line	Tight	
	Hold Fire	Column	--	
Orders	**Offense**	**Defense**	**Fire**	**Movement**
	Assault	Follow Me	Engage	Move Fast
	Flank Left	Fall Back	Suppress	Follow Me
	Flank Right	Halt	Hold Fire	Move
	Halt	Defend	--	Exit

BASIC COMMANDS

MOVE

Quick Command:
→, → → (or ↑ when no context sensitive commands are available)

The selected fire team member(s) will Move to the specified point, as defined by the target zone. They are free to Engage enemy units they encounter while moving, unless prevented from doing so by the Rules of Engagement. Generally you will use the Follow Me or Assault commands instead of a basic Move command, but this can be useful for precise positioning of your fire team members when waiting an enemy on a stealth mission, or planning to ambush enemy units. It can also be used to get your fire team safely behind cover or away from potential danger, such as when an air strike is about to be called in. Note that once this command is given, you'll need to issue the Follow Me command again once they stop moving if you want your fire team to follow you.

FOLLOW ME

Quick Command:
→, →, ← or ↑, ↓, ↑ (or ↓ when no context sensitive commands are available)

The selected fire team member(s) will Move to the player's position and then follow your movements until they are told otherwise. While following you they will be free to Engage enemy units they encounter, unless the rules of engagement prevent them from doing so. This is the most useful command for moving across open areas or between engagements. It will ensure that the fire team's formation and spread remains intact, and leaves you free to focus on the terrain ahead, rather than on your team's positions. Note that your fire team members will follow you into vehicles when this command is in effect.

MEDIC

Quick Command:
←, ↓ (or ↑ or ↓ when incapacitated)

This is a basic command, accessed very quickly from the top level of the command menu when the player needs their wounds treated. If a unit able to heal the player is within range, they will attempt to Move to the player (combat conditions permitting) and heal them. If there is no Medic available when you are bleeding, the nearest fire team member will attempt to apply a field dressing to you. When incapacitated, this is the only command you will be able to give, and you'll be relying on a team member using a field dressing before you bleed to death.

CONTEXT-SENSITIVE COMMANDS

ASSAULT BUILDING

Quick Command:
↑ (When aiming at the interior or exterior of a building)

The fire team will Assault the building you are aiming at. They will Move to the building, Engage units they encounter on the way, then enter the building and Engage any units they find inside. Fire team members will enter the building one at a time and clear rooms before the next member enters. This order can only be issued to the entire team at once. This is not a quick command to execute, as the fire team members must form up and enter one at a time, so it should only be used when you are not under duress. It is perfect for buildings where interior visibility is low and you don't want to risk entering blind. Simply send your team in to clear it out first.

REPAIR

Quick Command:
↓ (When aiming at a damaged vehicle)

A fire team member will Move to, and attempt to repair, the targeted vehicle, combat conditions permitting. This command will only be available when aiming at a damaged vehicle. They will be completely vulnerable while repairing, so this command shouldn't be given while combat is in progress. Repairing can take some time, so using this command to have a member of your fire team do the work is a good idea, as it leaves you free to check the surroundings for enemy threats, or to give covering fire.

OPERATE GUN

Quick Command:
↑ (when aiming at an emplaced weapon)

A fire team member will Move to the targeted emplacement weapon and proceed to use it. If all members are currently engaged in combat, they may not be able to reach the emplaced weapon. This command should ideally be used when setting up to defend an area, before the enemy troops arrive. Make sure you don't have a team member use an emplaced weapon that leaves them vulnerable to an assault from the rear, as they will be unable to defend themselves

FLY AND HOVER

Quick Command:
↑ (when aiming at (or commanding) a friendly controlled helicopter)

The helicopter will Move to the specified point and hover above it. The pilot will hover over the point defined by the target zone until another order is given, and the gunner will engage any visible targets within range of the helicopter's weapons. This command should be issued either from the commander's seat of the helicopter or from the overview map with the helicopter selected. Be careful not to use this command at times when the enemy has anti-air units in the area, as the helicopter will be stationary and defenseless.

FLY AND LAND

Quick Command:
↓ (when aiming at (or commanding) a friendly controlled helicopter)

The helicopter will Move to the specified point defined by the target zone and proceed to land. You can give this order while aboard a helicopter in the commander's seat (or from the overview map) to get the pilot to land instead of performing the landing yourself. In this case, you should switch to the external view to ensure you are above a clear landing zone on flat and even ground.

ENTER (VEHICLE)

Quick Command:
↑ (when aiming at a vehicle)

The fire team member(s) will Enter the target vehicle as defined by the target zone. If you are already inside a vehicle then the fire team members will board your current vehicle when this order is given. You can give this command from a great distance away from a vehicle (or by selecting the vehicle on the overview map), which means you don't have to order your fire team to Move to the vehicle first.

TREAT WOUNDED

Quick Command:
↑ (when aiming at a wounded fire team member)

The selected fire team member will Move to the target (combat conditions permitting) and attempt to heal them. Medics will treat wounds fully, while other squad members will simply apply a field dressing to stop the bleeding. Use this command when one of your fire team members is wounded (as indicated by their color changing in the Squad Selector). If the medic is wounded, he will treat himself without you issuing the order, as long as he can avoid combat for long enough to do so.

FIRE COMMANDS

ENGAGE

Quick Command:
→, ←, ↑ (or ↓ when aiming at an enemy soldier or vehicle)

The selected fire team member(s) will engage the selected target, as defined by the target zone. In combat they may reprioritize their target based on visibility and local threat. They will open fire from their current position, if they are within range and have a clear shot, otherwise they will move closer before engaging. Use this command when you want your fire team members to focus on a single enemy target that you deem to be a high priority. This may free you up to take on a different target, or can be useful when there is a single target that must be taken out quickly, such as an AT gunner posing a threat to your vehicles.

SUPPRESS

Quick Command:
→, ←, ←

The fire team member(s) will lay down suppressive fire towards the target area, as defined by the target zone. They will provide continuous suppressive fire on the area until given another order, even if all enemies are neutralized. This command is great for pinning down enemies while other units flank their position. Even if you can't effectively flank them, keeping enemy units pinned down in one position is a good idea, if only to keep them occupied until other threats in the area have been dealt with. Suppressive fire from a vehicle-mounted weapon can be extremely effective for this.

HOLD FIRE

Quick Command:
→, ←, →

The selected fire team member(s) will cease firing and will not fire again until told otherwise. This is effectively a quick way to change the rules of engagement for the selected unit(s). Use this command to make your fire team cease firing quickly, after taking out their targets in a stealth mission, in order to reduce the risk of alerting other enemies. It is also very useful for preventing your fire team from causing unacceptable collateral damage during an engagement, such as blowing up fuel tanks with stray shots.

OFFENSIVE COMMANDS

ASSAULT

Quick Command:
→, ↑, ↑ (or ↑ when aiming at an enemy soldier or vehicle)

The selected fire team member(s) will attack the target area (not unit), the centre of which is defined by the target zone. They will Move towards the area and Engage any units they find within it. They are also free to Engage enemy units they encounter directly en route. This is the simplest way to send your fire team into a combat zone, and is perfect for tackling areas where enemy presence is assured, even though no enemies have been spotted yet.

FLANK LEFT

Quick Command:
→, ↑, ←

The fire team will use a bounding movement (if there are enemy units in proximity) or move in a formation to advance to the left of the target area. They will Engage any units they encounter as they move. They will first move to a point to the far left of the target area and then advance directly towards it. Use this to have your fire team take the enemy by surprise from their left while you or another fire team member distract them from the front.

FLANK RIGHT

Quick Command:
→, ↑, →

Fire team members will use a bounding movement to advance to the right of the target area. They are free to Engage any enemies they encounter as they move. They will first move to a point to the far right of the target area and then advance directly towards it. This command is used to attack an enemy position from the right, ideally while other fire team members are engaging or suppressing them from the front. Your choice between Flank Left and Flank Right should be made while taking into account the amount of cover and potential obstacles on either side.

MOVEMENT COMMANDS

FOLLOW TARGET

Quick Command:
→, →, ← (or ↑ when aiming at a fire team member)

The fire team member(s) will Move to and then follow the selected target. They will be free to Engage enemy units they encounter along the way. For best results, this command should be given from the overview map. Select the map marker for the target you want your team member(s) to follow and then give the command. The target should be a friendly unit or vehicle, preferably already on the move. This can save you some time plotting out a route for your fire team whenever you want to separate from them. It will also keep them near allied forces and allow them to assist in the engagements friendly fire teams enter into.

MOVE FAST

Quick Command:
→, →, ↑

Units given this command will move individually, and rapidly, to the target location. They can fire at enemies while on the move, but will not go off-path to Engage enemies and will not remain in formation , since getting to the target location quickly is their only priority. This makes it a risky command to use, if you aren't certain that the area is clear of enemy activity or if your fire team are out of your visual range. It is best used for rendezvousing with your fire team after engagements, or when waiting for them to catch up at the times when you've gone ahead to scout for (or snipe) distant enemies.

EXIT

Quick Command:
→, →, ↓ (or ↓ when aiming at a vehicle with fire team members on aboard)

The selected elements will dismount whatever vehicle they are in. This command can be given either by aiming at a vehicle, or any point on it, when you are on board. This includes times when the vehicle is still moving, so you should be careful to not give this command at the wrong moment. You can use it to make the fire team disembark a vehicle when you need to proceed on foot, but they will automatically exit when you do, if you have used the Follow Me command. The most important use for this command, however, is to get your fire team out of a vehicle quickly before it is destroyed by an enemy AT or AA unit, as this would otherwise kill the fire team outright.

02

DEFENSIVE COMMANDS

FALL BACK

Quick Command:
→, ↓, ←

The selected units will move towards the location they've been given, and will lay down smoke between themselves and any enemy forces if they can. They'll use bounding movement to reach this location, so they'll fall back gradually and fire back as they go, though they will not stop to engage enemies. You can use smoke grenades to cover your retreat if your fire team members are wounded and the nearest cover is some distance away. Issuing this command will allow for a tactical retreat, useful when you've gone too far into enemy territory, or when an enemy helicopter is en route to your position.

DEFEND

Quick Command:
→, ↓, ↓

The selected fire team members will defend the target location. The target zone will define the centre of the area to be defended and the fire team members will remain within about 50 meters of that point. They may, however, engage enemy units that move to within 200 meters of the defend position. In this case they will do so from their current location, rather than advancing towards the enemy position. Use this command to ensure that your fire team members stay together when attempting to hold a position. This is very useful in Multiplayer modes which involve defending a target, especially if you have placed mines in the surrounding area and don't want your men to trigger them.

HALT

Quick Command:
→, ↓, → or →, ↑, ↓

Squad members will stop carrying out all previously issued orders. They will then hold their position and await further orders before moving or engaging any targets. This changes their Rules of Engagement to Hold Fire. This is a useful command for canceling other commands, such as Move or Assault, or simply to ensure that your selected fire team member(s) wait where they currently are. Use the Halt command when your fire team is hiding in a building to avoid detection by an enemy patrol helicopter, as this will ensure they don't decide to leave the building for some reason.

MOUNT MY VEHICLE

Quick Command:
↓ (when inside a vehicle)

The selected fire team member(s) will move to the vehicle you are currently in and attempt to board it. This command is only available when you are already on board a vehicle. The fire team member(s) will be far more likely to board the vehicle successfully if it is not moving, although they can board vehicles which are moving very slowly.

[ET]Hunter: Weapons free

RULES OF ENGAGEMENT

FIRE AT WILL

Quick Command:
←, ↑, ↑

Also known as 'weapons free', this is the default condition of your fire team member(s) when a mission begins. While this condition is active, they will engage enemy units as soon as they spot them without waiting for your order. Use this rule before sending your team on an assault to ensure they are free to engage enemies at their own discretion.

RETURN FIRE

Quick Command:
←, ↑, ←

When this rule is active the fire team members will only engage enemy units after they have been fired upon. Issuing this command will cancel any assaults in progress, unless a fire team member is already in close combat with an enemy soldier. This rule is perfect for advancing between engagements, as it makes full use of your squad's spotting abilities.

FIRE ON MY LEAD

Quick Command:
←, ↑, →

The Fire on my Lead rule will make all currently selected fire team members cease firing. They will then not open fire again until you've initiated combat by firing your weapon. They may, however, engage a target that gets within 20-30 meters of them, as not doing so would risk the lives of the fire team.

With your fire team set to Fire on my Lead, you can select each member individually and then tell him to engage an individual target. They will not actually engage the target until you fire first. This allows you to pick another target to fire at, which will then trigger your squad to open fire on their selected targets. You can use this to set up some very effective stealth assaults on enemy positions.

HOLD FIRE

Quick Command:
←, ↑, ↓

As the name suggests, this order will make all currently selected fire team members cease firing immediately. It will not cancel other orders, such as formations or the Follow Me order, unlike using the Halt command. This is simply a quick way to change the selected team member's Rules of Engagement to Hold Fire. With this rule in effect, the affected fire team members will not fire on any targets, even if you fire first.

FORMATIONS AND SPREADS

Formations and spreads may not seem very important, since all they do is change how your fire team moves around. But understanding how they work can help your fire team to survive engagements or avoid being spotted.

WEDGE FORMATION

Quick Command:
←, ←, ↑

The Wedge formation is the default formation that USMC and Spec Ops fire teams use while moving around. This will most likely be the formation that the player's fire team starts with on all of Dragon Rising's Campaign missions. The Fire Team Leader takes point at the front of the wedge, which is an arrowhead shape. One fire team member forms the left flank of the arrowhead and the other two remaining fire team members the right flank.

This formation offers a very large firing arc over the fire team's forward and side flanks and gives the Fire Team Leader great spotting coverage ahead. This makes it perfect for stealth-based missions, particularly those featuring the Spec Ops fire team. Combine this formation with a tight spread to make your fire team harder to spot when on the move.

VEE FORMATION

Quick Command:
←, ←, ↓

The Vee formation is like a reflection of the Wedge formation. The Fire team leader is at the back of the formation, with one fire team member to his left and two more to his right, one ahead of the other, forming an inverse arrowhead. This formation allows the Fire Team Leader to keep an eye on all of his fire team members. It is particularly effective when performing a tactical fall-back order.

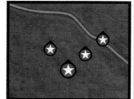

This is a great formation to use in Dragon Rising's Single Player Campaign, especially in the USMC missions. The Vee formation takes full advantage of your fire team's spotting capabilities, and can be great for advancing between engagements, especially when combined with the combat spread.

LINE FORMATION

Quick Command:
←, ←, →

The Line formation sets the fire team up to advance in a straight line, with one fire team member to one side of the Fire Team Leader and two on the other side. This formation means that the fire team is completely exposed to attacks from the sides, but they can focus completely on firing forward. Whilst this gives them the largest firing arc towards the enemy, it leaves the fire team open to ambushes on the flanks.

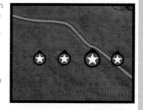

COLUMN FORMATION

Quick Command:
←, ←, ←

The Column formation sets the fire team up in a column, with all fire team members behind the Fire Team Leader. This is a useful formation for hiding your numbers when preparing to engage the enemy head-on. It does present a problem, however, for other fire team members firing forward, so it should be used in tandem with the Line formation or the Wedge formation when an assault or suppression begins.

The Column formation is also useful when moving through hostile territory, where the chances of an ambush are higher, as it offers a lot of protection to the fire team's flanks. It does, however, restrict the view of the squad members at the rear. The Column formation can also be very effective in an offensive capacity, if used with the flanking commands.

TIGHT SPREAD

Quick Command:
←, →, ←

Spacing of fire team members is approximately 2m. This spread is good when you are trying to remain undetected. The downside is that, if spotted, the whole fire team has a greater chance of being hit by explosive damage and spray from bullets. Additionally, in narrow environments and when clearing rooms, this formation can be particularly useful.

NORMAL SPREAD

Quick Command:
←, →, →

Spacing of fire team members is approximately 4m. This is the default spread. It is a nice cross between Tight and Combat spread. An important thing to remember in Normal spread is that the fire team members are usually spaced so that only one or two of them can be taken out by a fragmentation grenade explosion.

COMBAT SPREAD

Quick Command:
←, →, ↑

Spacing of fire team members is approximately 8m. This spread is best used when attacking areas. You are more likely to be spotted, but even if the enemy gets a very accurate fragmentation grenade through, only one member of the fire team will get injured.

COMBAT SUPPORT OVERVIEW
CHAPTER 02

There will be times when something stands between you and an objective that just can't be taken out without some help. This is when Combat Support comes into play. When you have the option to request a Combat Support strike you'll be required to decide on the amount of explosive power needed, and the type of strike that's best suited to the situation. Here we'll go over the available options, so that you'll know which ones to use in every case.

Combat Support Radial

Pressing the Combat Support button brings up a radial menu, similar to the command radial, from which you can select between the various types of strikes and munitions available. Generally, there will only be a limited selection available, depending on the type of off-board support in the area and the enemy's anti-air or anti-naval presence.

Artillery and Munitions

When calling in a naval artillery strike, your first choice will be the type of artillery that delivers the payload. These include Mortars and Howitzers, and have varying degrees of range and explosive power. Once you've selected the artillery type you'll need to select the type of munitions the Mortar or Howitzer will be delivering: explosive or smoke. One is for a destructive strike, the other for a tactical one.

ARTILLERY

Artillery basically means large guns, which come in many forms and deliver highly explosive results. Most artillery is launched from land- or sea-based guns that can be an incredible distance away from the intended target. Artillery will be your most reliable form of combat support, and doesn't rely on the absence of enemy anti-air weaponry in the area.

Mortar

Mortars are perfect against infantry units and soft targets, but are unlikely to do much to heavily armored targets and buildings. Wiping out infantry from key areas will be the most frequent use for Mortar strikes. Use where the enemy troops are most concentrated to get the best results. Recommended patterns are Tight and Barrage. **[Screen 01]**

Heavy Mortar

Great against buildings and soft vehicles, heavy mortar decimates infantry units and can be used against armored targets, but it may only do secondary damage initially. It should be used in the same way as regular Mortars, but you can expect some heavier damage when it's used against buildings. Recommended patterns are Scattered and Harassing. **[Screen 02]**

Howitzer

The Howitzer is capable of destroying almost any target, regardless of the pattern used to deploy it. It has a kill zone radius of around 50 meters, so it's very likely that multiple targets will be taken out in a single strike. Recommended patterns are Barrage, Scattered and Harassing.

MUNITIONS

This choice is often available to you when you are using artillery. You'll need to decide if you want to destroy everything in an area or if it will be more beneficial to use the tactical advantage of extended smoke cover.

HE

High Explosive rounds are perfect against soft and armored targets, including armored tanks and APCs. It is also effective against infantry, and can level entire buildings with a direct hit. Building strikes require large sizes of artillery, such as the Howitzer, in order to be really effective. **[Screen 03]**

Smoke

The Smoke rounds for artillery cause massive clouds that can obscure entire battlefields. These are excellent for preventing the enemy from seeing what maneuvers your fire team are performing. They can be used to mask full-on assaults or even tactical retreats.

PATTERNS

The patterns you can choose from when launching artillery will dictate both the radius targeted in the attack, and the duration between each rounds being fired. Choosing the right pattern for the current enemy positions will help to maximize the effectiveness of the strike.

Tight

This pattern is four waves of four shells over an area of 20 meters. It is an intense, focused attack on a small area, designed to take out armor and buildings. Use this pattern when targets are grouped together in a small area, or when a specific, high priority building needs to be targeted. **[Screen 04]**

Scattered

This pattern is four waves of four shells over an area of 50 meters. It is used more speculatively when there are multiple targets in a large area. It can also be the best choice when a single, high priority target is on the move, as the target is unlikely to escape the blast area before the strike arrives.

Barrage

This pattern is 20 separate shells over an area of 20 meters. A sustained attack on a small area, it is perfect for convoys as they're passing through a narrow valley. This is a great choice whenever you need to keep an area off limits to the enemy for a while. **[Screen 05]**

Harassing

This pattern is 20 separate shells fired over an area of 50 meters. As the name suggests, it is used to harass an enemy that may be dug in. As it involves prolonged sustained fire, it is perfect for keeping the enemy suppressed. It can also be the best option in cases where the enemy's movement is highly unpredictable.

AIR STRIKES

These are strikes delivered by aircraft in the form of guided air-to-ground missiles. Usually you will not have more than one type available, but all types are lethal if called in at the right time.

Small

The small air strike is an infrared, guided AGM 65 Maverick missile. It is particularly good at destroying soft and armored vehicles. It will take somewhere between 15-20 seconds after being called in to arrive at its target, so it is best called in against stationary targets. Although you can target buildings with this strike, it's primarily used against tactical targets such as fuel transports and anti-air defenses. **[Screen 06]**

Large

The large air strike is a SLAM (Standoff Land Attack Missile). This cruise missile is delivered by aircraft and is capable of striking from incredible ranges with pinpoint accuracy. It is very effective at taking out sections of buildings (or sometimes entire buildings). It will also have a lethal effect on vehicles, including heavily armored tanks, and can even target them while they are on the move.

JDAM

The JDAM (Joint Direct Attack Munition) is the largest of the air strikes available in Operation Flashpoint: Dragon Rising. This system allows a 2000lb bomb to be launched as a guided missile. With its gigantic 100m kill radius, it leaves nothing standing in its immediate blast zone and is useful for destroying both vehicles and buildings in a single strike. **[Screen 07]**

COMBAT ANALYSIS
CHAPTER 02

BASIC COMBAT TIPS

Here we will provide some tips and strategies that will apply to general combat, in both the Single Player Campaign and the Multiplayer modes. There are things that should be remembered at all times, and can easily mean the difference between success and failure in some engagements.

Cover

We've already touched on the use of terrain as cover in the Basic Training chapter, but when a single bullet can kill you instantly the importance of cover can't be overstated. The enemy is just as capable of using the terrain for cover as you are. Whenever you approach a hillside that obscures your view on one side, there is the possibility of concealed enemy forces lying in wait, and you may not be able to see them until you either reach the top of the hill or navigate your way around it. Also remember that smoke grenades can be used to generate instant cover, useful for covering assaults, closing open ground and providing defensive cover when healing teammates. **[Screen 01]**

Heading directly over the hill will therefore be a bad move in most cases, as it means you are effectively proceeding blindly. Working your way around the hill, checking the far side as it becomes visible, is a better solution. You should basically think of this situation as being like passing a building with enemies on the other side. When you come to the corner of the building, you'll be exposed to any enemies who may be waiting in ambush.

Finding cover in the environment is usually easy to do, and planning your approaches around cover locations is something that you should quickly learn to adopt. There are often plenty of rocks outside developed areas which are perfect for use as cover. The larger ones can be seen from a good distance away, allowing you to use them for entire approaches. **[Screen 02]**

Accuracy

When aiming normally (outside of Aim mode), you'll have a targeting reticule on screen on Normal mode. This is made up of a central dot with an L-shaped line on either side of it. The closer these two lines are to the central dot, the higher your current accuracy. **[Screen 03]** There are quite a few factors that will affect your accuracy noticeably.

The most important factor is movement. Fast movement will drastically reduce your ability to aim your weapon accurately. Your stance also has an effect on this, as will being fatigued. The weapon you are using is the next most important factor. Some weapons will keep their accuracy on the move far better than others. Some are also a lot more accurate at close range, such as Light Machine Guns. Other weapons are designed for longer-range, single-shot fire, and the recoil will greatly reduce their accuracy when multiple shots are fired in succession.

FATIGUE AND STAMINA ⓘ

As mentioned in the Basic Training chapter, sprinting for too long will lead to fatigue. You can sprint for up to 55 seconds before fatigues sets in, after which you will lose the ability to sprint. Entering combat while fatigued should always be avoided. You will regain your stamina after being fatigued either by standing still, walking or jogging. Stamina will regained at 50% of the standard rate whilst jogging and at 100% while walking or stationary. You can also regain stamina faster by crouching or going prone. By far the fastest way of regaining stamina is by going prone or remaining stationary.

Aiming on the Move

Most assault rifles are best used in Aim mode, especially if the rifle has a scope attached. They can also be very effective when firing from the hip, however, and there will often be situations where this is essential. If you are forced to take on multiple enemy contacts alone, you'll have the luxury of using your scope for the first one, but after that the others will be unlikely to let you stand there and pick them off. Your best course of action is to crouch and then move whilst firing. If you move slowly enough you'll be able to use your movement to line up your shots, while making yourself harder to hit.

This is also great for lining up shots through your scope in stealth missions, where you need to stay crouched to minimize the chances of detection. The long grass may make aiming hard, but moving slowly sideways will bring you above the level of the grass without reducing your accuracy too much. This can give you a good view of your target without your being too exposed. **[Screen 04]**

Torch

All assault rifles come equipped with a powerful torch, which you can toggle on and off at any point. This is a valuable tool on night-time missions, though using it will make you a more visible target in Multiplayer modes. It is also useful for clearing out buildings, since their interiors are often unlit. Another use is to make it easier to find the bodies of enemies you have killed, since they can be very hard to find among the grass, even when it's not pitch dark. **[Screen 05]**

Frag Grenades and Mines

To use Frag Grenades effectively you will need a very good grasp of how to arc them to reach very specific points. It is worth using up some grenades to practice hitting target areas until you are comfortable with them. If you hold down the Shoot button when throwing a grenade, you will delay the throw. This will not 'cook' the grenade, since the fuse is not active. It simply readies the throw, allowing you to 'charge' the throw from behind cover and then pop out and release it very quickly.

You can make good use of Frag Grenades to clear areas ahead when you're advancing into places where your visibility is low. This includes moving over hills, where there is a very good chance that enemies will be occupying dug-in positions beyond your vision just over the crest of the hill. You can throw grenades over the hilltop to either take out their sandbags or force them to reveal their positions. **[Screen 06]** Grenades are hard to see, so it's worth remembering to inform team-mates before throwing them when playing in Co-op.

Mines can be very useful, especially in Multiplayer modes. As with grenades, however, you must inform other team-mates whenever you plant a mine, or you will be risking a friendly fire incident. Mines are best placed in grass, to make them impossible to see, although open roads are usually far more likely places to catch passing enemy targets. **[Screen 07]**

Assaulting Buildings

There is a lot more to assaulting buildings than simply giving the order to your fire team. Doing it effectively requires you to take some precautions, especially if there are likely to be enemies inside. Unlit interiors will usually make it impossible to tell if there are enemies inside. In these cases it might be more advisable to break the windows and throw Frag grenades inside to clear the building than to enter blind. You can also open doors and roll grenades in underarm for a similar effect.

Spec Ops team can use their Thermal scopes to spot enemies inside buildings. If you're taking point when clearing out a building, you should turn your torch on and check everywhere as quickly as possible so as to catch enemies hiding in dark corners. It's works best if you have another team member sweeping the building from the opposite side at the same time whenever possible.

02

FOCUS VIEW ⓘ

Clicking the Right Stick in will take you into Focus View. This will zoom your view in a little bit, but has no effect on your accuracy. Use this to gain an improved view without entering Aim mode (or having to get your binoculars out), and thereby reducing your movement options. For weapons without scopes attached this is especially useful.

Gun Jamming

All weapons in Dragon Rising have a very small (0.01%) chance of jamming each time a round is fired. This means there's a 2% chance of at least one jam when firing a 200-round belt, or 9.5% when over 1000 rounds. This is something you can't be prepared for, as the risk is so low that it will happen only very rarely.

When a gun does jam, you'll need to press the Reload button to remedy the situation. This of course means that you'll have to reload your weapon, even if the current clip is fresh, thus wasting valuable ammunition. Note that missiles and vehicle-mounted weapons are not susceptible to jamming, so you won't have to worry about this when using them.

Tracer fire

Tracer fire is used to identify, and differentiate between, friendly fire and enemy fire in the heat of battle. You will notice that your fire team's tracer fire is always red, while the PLA use green tracer fire. You can easily use this to see, not only if the fire originates from an enemy soldier, but also which direction it comes from, and thereby pinpoint the enemy's location. While it might seem odd for the enemy to give their position away like this, it is an essential tool in avoiding friendly fire incidents, which would otherwise have a devastating effect on the soldiers' morale.

If an enemy has taken you by surprise, then watching for their tracer fire isn't going to do you much good. If, however, you are watching the tracer fire as your allies are fired upon, you'll be able to quickly work out the direction the fire is coming from. **[Screen 01]**

Reloading

As explained in the Basic Training chapter, reloading takes time and leaves you vulnerable until it is completed. With many weapons, however, the delay until you can fire again after reloading is actually much longer than it may seem, and extends beyond the actual reloading process animation. This is especially noticeable when trying to use Aim mode straight after reloading, so take this extra time into account when engaged in a close battle. With most assault rifles the reloading process will also obscure most of your view, so you are strongly advised to stay safely behind cover when reloading. **[Screen 02]**

WEAPON SLOTS ⓘ

You won't be able to carry everything you might want to at once. Weapons can only be picked up according to the slots you have for carrying them. You have room for two assault rifles, for example, but if you want to pick up a rocket launcher then you'll have to leave one of the assault rifles behind. You are also restricted to carrying only one heavy weapon at once, which means you can't carry a rocket launcher at the same time as a Sniper rifle.

ADVANCED COMBAT

Next we'll cover some of the more in-depth aspects of Dragon Rising. Anyone wanting to really understand how the game works, or looking for an extra edge, will find some very useful information in the following section.

Weapon Ranges

In the Ordnance and Equipment chapter you will see that the effective range for each weapon is listed in the tables provided. The maximum effective range of a weapon is very hard to quantify, however, as the distances you'll be firing from will almost never be beyond a weapon's physical range limit in terms of reaching the target. Just because your bullets can travel far enough doesn't mean that they are likely to hit their target, however.

Lining up a shot perfectly, and still having the bullet miss its target, can often happen at extreme ranges. This is because the gradually increasing dispersal of shots at longer ranges makes it increasingly difficult to hit effectively. You will also find that even the most minute adjustments to your aim will have dramatic effects at long ranges, so you'll need to line up your shot again after every round is fired. Therefore, when dealing with maximum effective ranges, it should always be assumed that the shot is perfectly lined up from a prone position and is fired at an angle relatively parallel to the target. **[Screen 03]**

Assaulting an Area

The Assault command is important to use in situations where there are multiple enemy contacts in an area that you need to either get through or take control of. Simply having your fire team Engage each target one at a time is not likely to be successful, since you are limiting your fire team's actions. Letting them make their own choices about which target to engage within an area will usually be a better option.

The diagram here shows the areas that your fire team members take into account when an Assault command has be issued. First, they will move towards the target area, staying within a 20 meter 'tunnel' and will then engage anything within a 30 meter radius of the targeted location. This puts them in combat-ready state, even if there are no enemies visible at the location to be assaulted.

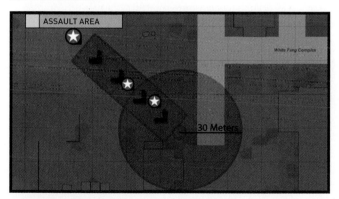

Suppressive Fire

Suppressive fire is a simple tool that can be extremely effective if used in the right way. First you need to remember to use the right type of weapon for the job. Fire team members with machineguns should always be your first choice when giving the Suppress order. The machinegun can lay down continuous fire far better than any assault rifle could, and will have greater stopping power when within the weapon's ideal range.

To take this a step further, you can plan to use an emplaced weapon or a vehicle mounted weapon for suppressive fire. This has the benefit of much higher ammunition capacity for prolonged fire. Vehicle-mounted Heavy Machine Guns also have much greater stopping power than even the best infantry machineguns. Weapons are rated within the game on how effective they are at suppressive fire, and these ratings are shown here. As you can see, the Heavy Machine Guns are the best tool for the job. The Sniper rifles

are surprisingly effective, too, since the likelihood of a one-hit kill can keep enemies pinned down, but they won't have the ammunition to use them for prolonged suppression. **[Screen 04]**

SUPPRESSION RATINGS

Weapon Type	Weapon Examples	Rating
Pistols	QSZ92, MEU (SOC)	0
SMGs	MP5A4, QCW05	4
Assault Rifles	M16A4, Mk16 Mod 0	3
LMGs	M249, QBB95	4
MMG	M240, Mk48 Mod 0	5
HMG	M2 50 Cal, M134	6
Sniper Rifles	M21, M82A1	4
Grenade Launchers	M32	0

Firing Rates

The ability to change a weapon's firing rate can make a huge difference to its effectiveness in differing combat situations. When aiming at a target over long distances you should always use single-shot mode if the weapon allows it. This greatly increases the potential accuracy of the shot, and saves wasting extra bullets that would very likely have missed their target.

3 Round Burst, on rifles that feature it, can prove invaluable in ensuring a kill on single targets. This is because the game's damage system tracks damage to each part of the body, and inflicting enough damage to any one part will mean a certain kill. Generally, if you can land three shots on a single body part, the enemy will be killed outright, but even with 3 Round Burst the level of accuracy required to make all three bullets hit one location makes it unlikely to happen. However, using the prone stance, coupled with a highly

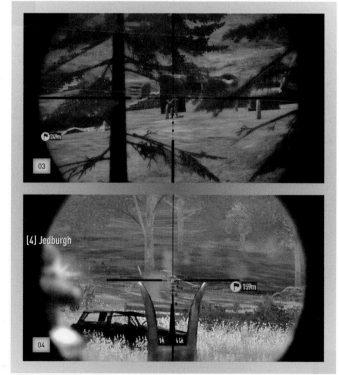

accurate weapon like the Mk17 Mod 0, will often be enough to get the job done in a single burst. **[Screen 01]**

Unit Strengths

It may seem obvious that firing small arms at a heavily armored tank will not be effective and will just be a waste of ammunition. But it is worth remembering that the armored tank will take a similar approach when choosing how to use its weaponry. It will not fire its primary cannon at infantry, even if they are the only enemy forces in the area. This is because the ammunition for the primary cannon is too valuable to the tank's basic purpose, and wasting it on human targets could render the tank useless if an enemy armored vehicle were to join the battle.

This means a tank will only fire at infantry with its machine gun, which makes it much less of a threat to infantry than it is to an APC, for example. Similarly, an AT gunner is a serious threat to an APC, but will be an easy target for enemy snipers or riflemen. This means that the APC will be relying on friendly troops to deal with AT gunners, while the troops rely on the APC for heavy fire support. The table here shows which weapons some of the better equipped vehicles

will use as their first choice against different threats. If one weapon system runs out of ammo, however, they will switch to another. For example, if an AAVP runs out of machine gun ammunition, they'll use grenades against infantry.

	M1A2 Abrams	Type 99	LAV-25	Type 97	AAVP
Vs Infantry	M240 (Coax)	Type-67 II (Coax)	M240 (Coax)	Type-67 II (Coax)	M2 50 Cal
Vs Heavy Tank	120mm Sabot	125mm Sabot	25mm APDS	100mm ATGM	MK19 HEDP
Vs Light Armor	120mm HEAT	125mm HEAT	25mm APHE	30mm AP	MK19 HEDP
Vs 4x4 Vehicle	120mm HEAT	125mm HEAT	25mm APHE	30mm APHE	MK19 HE
Vs Helicopter	M240 (Coax)	Type-67 II (Coax)	25mm APHE	30mm APHE	M2 50 Cal

Stealth Play

Sneaking through areas undetected, or taking the enemy by surprise is vital in some missions and can very often be the best approach. There are a few things you can do that will reduce the likelihood of being spotted. The most important thing to remember is that the quickest way to alert enemies is to fire a weapon without a silencer. For this reason, when starting a stealth mission, you should always check the weapons of every fire team member. Any members without silent weapons should be ordered to hold fire for as long as you are undetected. Fire team members that do have weapons with silencers can be set up to fire on your lead in these situations. **[Screen 02]**

Another thing to remember is that your current stance has a direct effect on the enemy's ability to spot you. If an enemy is looking at you while you're undetected, their vision range is reduced to a percentage of its original range, based on your stance. **[Screen 03]** This means you will be spotted from much further away if you are standing upright, so moving forward while crouching is generally advised. Lastly, you should try to keep your fire team in a tight spread and in either the Vee or Wedge formation. This is another way of reducing your chances of being spotted, as it keeps your fire team members together, making them harder to spot, while giving you a wide spotting range.

Icon	Stance	Effect on enemy spotting range
	Standing	100%
	Crouching	75%
	Prone	50%

GOING PRONE ⓘ

The AI uses a 'miss system' that makes it harder for them to hit player-controlled characters when they're in prone stance. This simulates the greatly reduced target you present while you're prone, by considerably lowering the risk of a bullet hitting you immediately after you've gone prone. This makes prone extremely useful when you've been taken by surprise or are caught in the open, and compensates for you not being able to see through the ground cover in this stance.

Night Vision

The use of Night Vision Goggles during night-time missions can have a great effect on the outcome of engagements. Combat at night reduces your vision in exactly the way you might expect, and the game reflects this by reducing the visible spotting range of the enemies and your fire team members by half. This is negated when Night Vision Goggles are activated, however, bringing the spotting range back up to its standard daytime value. As Spec Ops fire teams, you'll always have Night Vision available to you, and you should use it bring your fire team's spotting range back up to its maximum potential, since there is no downside to using it. **[Screen 04]**

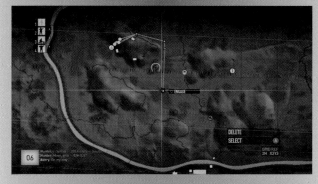

ADVANCED MAP USE

The overview map in Operation Flashpoint: Dragon Rising is a very versatile tool for planning and executing strategies in real time. There are a number of things it allows you to do that may not be obvious until you've spent some time getting accustomed to it.

Chaining Waypoints

The ability to chain waypoints together on the overview map opens up a variety of tactical possibilities that might otherwise be closed to you. You can effectively take full control of your fire team over long distances and execute

complex sequences of commands. On the overview map the target zone is replaced with a very precise pointer in the center of the screen that allows you to select one or more units or point to an area.

At a simple level it can be used for plotting a very specific route for your fire team to take, perhaps to avoid enemy units, while you are too far away from them to direct them normally. Just select the first point you want the fire team to move to and issue the Move command from the radial, and then hold down the Shoot button to add a second Move command to the next point in your desired route. **[Screen 05]** In this way you can direct your squad along a precise route and be sure that they go exactly where you want. When they get there, you can also give them other commands, such as engaging enemies that they have spotted (which would therefore be visible on your map, even though they are not anywhere near being in visual range of them). Ordering your troops to locations you don't have line of sight to gives a massive boost to your ability to issue orders. If you are pinned down, for example, you don't have to stick your head out to issue an order. **[Screen 06]**

Manual Flanking

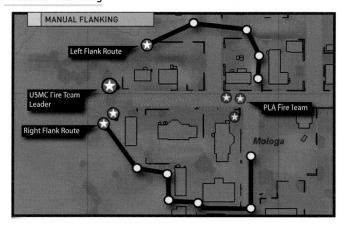

A more advanced use of chaining waypoints is in carrying out very specific flanking commands. If you use the target zone to tell your fire team to flank a particular point, they will always move the same distance away first, before turning in towards the flanking point. This is generally a good enough distance for an effective flanking maneuver, but there are times when taking a wider approach is necessary to avoid detection. Or you simply may not have time for a full, drawn-out flanking procedure and just want your men to flank quickly behind some nearby cover. **[Screen 07]**

On the overview map you can very easily dictate the exact flanking route your fire team should take. This allows you to send one man on a short flank behind cover to the left, while the other two take a much longer approach to take the enemy from behind while you are suppressing them.

Vehicle Control

Using route plotting on the overview map also allows for more complex tactics involving vehicles. If you get your fire team members into a vehicle you can use the map to send them to a location a long distance away from your position. **[Screen 08]**

You can plot their route exactly as you want, whether driving or flying. If they are on board an APC, then it is best to plot a route along any roads that may be in the area, so as to avoid the high number of obstacles in open countryside.

In practical terms, this allows you to flank positions using vehicles, while you take a different approach on foot. It also allows you to plot a route for your fire team to a specific location, and have them lay down suppressive fire on an area using the vehicle's weapons until you get there.

AI SYSTEMS

The AI in Dragon Rising is designed to simulate the ways in which soldiers and fire teams would react to both immediate threats and the information they have about other forces in the area. Here we will outline some of the systems in place that allow the AI to react in a convincing manner to their surroundings and the current state of a given conflict. Note that most of what is described here will apply to both your fire team members and the enemy forces. None of these systems are completely independent, so the action the AI takes will generally result from a combination of these factors.

Perception

The outcome of major engagements is often decided by which side manages to spot the other first. The AI controlling both your fire team members and the enemy units will try to spot threats from as far away as possible, but there are limits in place to ensure the experience is fair and balanced for the player. Knowing the limits of the AI's perception isn't necessary to enjoy the game, but it can help in really pushing your strategies to the extreme of what's possible.

Standard units (both enemy and friendly) have a maximum visual range of 250 meters straight ahead, once they are in a combat state. The visual range can be imagined as a cone, as shown on the diagram here, dropping to 150 meters for peripheral vision on each side. The maximum visual range is reduced by half when units are not in combat and are unaware of any targets or threats. **[Screen 01]**

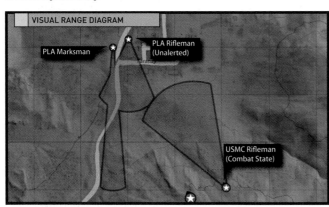

VISUAL RANGE DIAGRAM

PLA Marksman

PLA Rifleman (Unalerted)

USMC Rifleman (Combat State)

Visual range is affected in various ways when on board a vehicle, as shown in the table here. Drivers lose almost half of their spotting range, and their peripheral range is reduced to a quarter of its standard value. Commanders' visual range dead ahead is doubled, but their peripheral vision is again reduced to a quarter. Gunners gain four times the standard visual range dead ahead, bringing their potential spotting range up to 1000 meters, but they lose their peripheral vision entirely as they aim down the sights of the emplaced weapon. **[Screen 02]**

VISUAL RANGE

Position	Effect on Central Range	Effect on Peripheral Range	Effect on Viewing Angle
Driver	0.65	0.65	0.25
Commander	2.0	0.25	0.5
Gunner	4.0	0.0	0.25

Similar modifiers apply to aiming though scoped weapons, with great increases in visual range directly ahead, but at the cost of a dramatic loss of peripheral vision. A scope with a 10x optical zoom capability will give five times the central visual range for a total of 1250 meters, while a 5x zoom gives 625 meters maximum range. Note that these values only apply to spotting enemies while in combat-ready state, and are not related to the ranges from which a unit can accurately make a shot.

Another thing to take into account is that the AI can see vehicles at 2.5 times the range at which they can spot infantry (up to 750m). This is because vehicles are obviously much bigger targets, and easier to pick out. Lastly, all of these values are modified by another value, depending on the time of day, and will be affected by Night Vision Goggles, as shown here. Since the game features a real day-to-night cycle, these values will always be in play. Spotting range is not affected when using Thermal vision, and will at 1.0 at all times of day.

Time of Day	Normal Vision Modifier	Night Vision Modifier
Dawn	0.7	0.9
Day	1.0	1.0
Dusk	0.7	0.9
Night	0.4	0.8

01

02

03

MORALE FACTORS

Factor	Effect Type	Effect Strength
Unit is Behind Cover	Positive	Very Small
Unit is Pinned	Negative	Very Small
Unit is Suppressed	Negative	Very Small
Unit or ally has a Light Wound	Negative	Small
Unit has or ally has a Serious Wound	Negative	Medium
Enemy target has a Light Wound	Positive	Very Small
Enemy target has a Serious Wound	Positive	Small
Enemy target is killed	Positive	Small
Ally is killed	Negative	Large
Ally or allied fire team Fall Back	Negative	Medium
Enemy Falls Back	Positive	Medium

BULLET SENSING   (i)

When you take a shot at an enemy soldier who is not aware of your presence and miss, they will notice the bullet and be sent into an alerted state. For this to happen the bullet must pass within a 3.2 meter radius of the enemy. This 'bullet sensing' zone is a sphere around the enemy's center of mass, so they will notice the bullet even if it goes over their head by a couple of meters.

Morale

The morale of an enemy or friendly unit will be affected by its situation in various ways. If they are experiencing a lot of negative factors, such as friendly deaths or being pinned down in one place for a while, their morale will fall accordingly. If they take out an enemy soldier, or see the enemy fall back, their morale will rise. Here is a list of some of the typical factors that have an effect on morale.

If a unit's morale falls too low, they will be much less effective on the battlefield. They will be more likely to take defensive positions, or even fall back completely. Units will not be operating at 100% of their potential unless their morale is at the maximum. Morale starts at 100%, and may drop during combat, subject to various factors. When outside of combat, morale will be regained slowly at a rate of 0.5% per second, which means it takes 200 seconds (3 minutes 20 seconds) of 'down time' to ensure that morale has been fully regained. This makes the time spent between each engagement highly valuable to your fire team.

Note that this is a complex system that will take other factors into account beyond what is described here. Allies getting wounded or enemies falling back, for example, will cause the morale penalties or bonuses to be applied to the entire fire team, and the strength of the penalty or bonus will depend on how many members of the relevant fire team are injured or killed, or are falling back. **[Screen 03]** The exact morale values gained or lost will also change according to the rank and experience of the Unit in question.

Threat Level

All AI units, including your fire team members, will make an assessment of the forces involved in an engagement before they choose how they should deal with the situation.

They will take into account all enemies within their visual range. They may also account for enemies that have been spotted or engaged by allies in close proximity to them. This first diagram shows a very basic example of how this works. The PLA unit marked 'A' has visual contact with two USMC riflemen and is aware of having two other PLA fire team members backing him up. This means that his side has the advantage in the force assessment, and will look to engage straight away.

The next diagram shows how things look when there are considerably more forces involved in an engagement. Here the PLA unit marked 'A' has two other fire team members in the area, together with an APC. He has visual contact with a four-man USMC fire team. There is also an additional USMC AT gunner in the area that the PLA can't see. From the perspective of the PLA soldier, the APC gives them a great advantage over the known USMC forces, so they will engage. The USMC are aware of the PLA units, but they also take their AT gunner into account, which negates the threat of the enemy APC, leaving them at an advantage in numbers against the smaller PLA fire team.

This last diagram shows the force assessment with a long-range sniper involved, to show how the perception ranges come into play. The sniper's 8X zoom gives him incredible spotting range, and since he is communicating with friendly troops, they can take advantage of this range in their threat assessment.

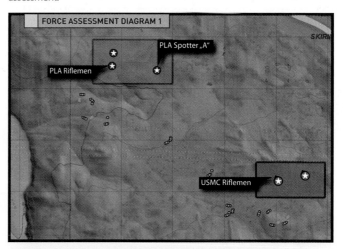

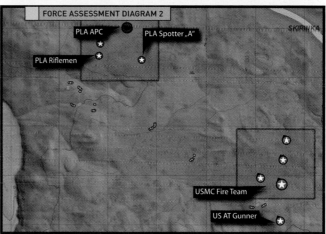

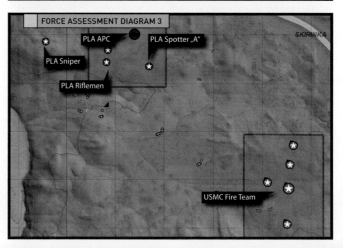

ORDNANCE & EQUIPMENT
CHAPTER 03

The art of war is serious business, and you'll need some serious firepower if you intend to make it out alive. In this chapter we will examine every weapon on both the US and PLA sides of this war. Here, you'll find some important statistics and tips that will help you to fully understand your available arsenal and master its full potential.

BASIC INTEL
CHAPTER 03

In this section we'll explain the basics of the layout and structure of this chapter. There is a large amount of information to absorb, so understanding the layout and what each piece of information means will be vital.

WEAPON LISTINGS

Every weapon (and its variants) in the game has an entry in this chapter. For each entry you will find a statistics table showing all the values for each of the weapon's significant primary attributes. The following sample tables show you what to expect while the accompanying text explains each entry in detail.

Model	Attachment	Magnification	Effective Range
M16A4 Assault Rifle: Basic Model	None	–	200
M16A4 Assault Rifle: CQB	Holographic Reflex Scope	X2	200

WEAPON STATS

Ammunition	5.56 x 45mm FMJ	40 x 46mm HE*	40 x 46mm HEDP*
Max Damage vs Humans	6	20	20
Damage vs Vehicles	1	3	5
Fragmentation Radius	–	7	6
Magazine Capacity	30	1	1
Reload Time	4	3	3
Fire Mode	3-Rnd / Semi	Single	Single
Max Rate of Fire	–	–	–

* Assault version only

Attachments

There are various types of scopes a weapon may be equipped with, and having any of these attached will change the weapon's use and effective range. For weapons that can use different scopes we will state the model name, attachment type, magnification and effective range.

For full details on each of the available optional scope types, see the Assault Rifle Scopes sections for the US and PLA just before a list of their rifles. If a weapon is not equipped with a scope, then you will target using its 'iron sights'.

Magnification

This value indicates the power of magnification the scope can provide. The higher the number, the further away you can sight and target your enemy. Possible values here are X2, X4 and X8. There are set values for basic weaponry, meaning that is the power of the magnification is not scalable.

An entry of 'variable' means the scope has an adjustable zoom that can swing from X2 all the way up to X8 (depending on the scope). Variable scopes are only used on vehicle-mounted weapons. You can adjust the magnification power by clicking Down on the right stick.

Effective Range

This is the maximum distance, in meters, from which you can hit your target using the weapon with the specified attachment. Though the weapon may have a great potential range at which it can hit a target, this value only takes into account the range at which it is likely to do so using a standard aim.

Ammunition

This entry details the physical size of the round your the weapon fires. These measurements, given in mm, are: caliber x case length. The caliber is the diameter of the round. Case length is the length of the case that holds the round. This measurement is for the case only and does not include the length of the projectile.

If only one number is given, then it is the caliber of the round. After the numerical dimensions of the round are acronyms that describe the special properties or type of round the weapon is using. In the example shown here, the acronym is FMJ (Full Metal Jacket). We'll discuss the full list of acronyms after we have covered the rest of the entries in the 'Weapon Stats' table.

Max Damage vs Humans

As you might expect, this is the value of damage that your shot will inflict if you hit a human target. Note that this value is for maximum damage, which means landing a critical hit to a vital body part such as the head. If your shot lands on a minor body part, i.e. an arm or leg, then the damage value will be lower than this maximum value.

Damage vs Vehicles

The value listed here will be used to determine the category or amount of damage a vehicle sustains. Vehicle damage isn't as straightforward as just shoot it and subtract hit points. The amount of damage you do to a vehicle is based on the difference between the value listed in this table, and the vehicle's armor rating. For unarmored and lightly armored vehicles, it can be relatively simple, while heavily armored tanks are more complex, as this example shows.

Vehicle Armor Rating

Vehicle Type	Rating
Unarmored*	0 for all locations on the vehicle
Light Armor	2 for front half of vehicle; 1 for rear of vehicle

*Includes Helicopters

M1A2 Abrams Tank

Hull		Turret	
Location	Rating	Location	Rating
Front	10	Front	10
Side	4	Side	6
Rear	3	Rear	4
Top	4	Top	4
Bottom	3		

Damage falls into three categories for a vehicle, and is represented by warnings on the HUD in the top right of the screen as follows:

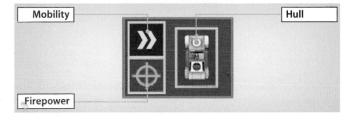

Secondary Damage

One of the two main vehicle systems becomes non-functional (mobility or firepower) or one of the crew or passengers is injured. This also covers the tires being damaged on wheeled vehicles and turrets being damaged on tanks. Secondary damage can be repaired, which means that the damage isn't critical, unless you're in helicopter and the engine is taken out or the pilot is killed. **[Screen 01]**

Destroyed

Both main vehicle systems become non-functional simultaneously, and the vehicle catches fire. You'll hear a warning klaxon and, after a delay of 5 seconds, the ammunition will explode causing the total destruction of the vehicle; however the crew will have time to bail out. This type of damage cannot be repaired. **[Screen 02]**

Catastrophic Damage

The vehicle and its crew is destroyed instantaneously. This type of damage cannot be repaired.

The type of damage your weapon can possibly deal is determined by finding the difference between the Weapons 'Damage vs Vehicle' rating and the vehicle's armor value (above). The possible outcomes are as follows:

Damage Possibilities

Calculation Value	Possible Outcome
0 or less	No Damage
1 – 4	Secondary Damage
5 – 10	Destroyed
> 10	Catastrophic Damage

Let's look at a few examples facing light armor from the rear. From the rear, we see the armor rating is 1. Now consult the entry for your weapon and find the Damage vs Vehicle rating. Finally, subtract that value from 1, which is the vehicle's light armor rating for the rear.

The MEU (SOC) Pistol has a rating of 0. The vehicle has a rating of 1. When we subtract the vehicle's rating of 1 from the MEU's rating of 0, we are left with a value of -1. This result is less than 0, so no damage is sustained. Now a few more examples.

Weapon Rating	Armor Rating	Calculation	Result
M16A4 bullet = 1	Light Armor (Rear) = 1	0	No Damage
M4A1 HE grenade = 7	Light Armor (Rear) = 1	6	Destroyed
C4 Charge = 14	Light Armor (Rear) = 1	13	Catastrophic Damage

The example chart shows that the M16A4 cannot damage a lightly armored vehicle, even from the rear. The M4A1 40 x 46mm HE grenade can destroy a lightly armored vehicle from the rear, and a C4 charge results in catastrophic damage, which means the total destruction of the vehicle and its crew.

Fragmentation Radius

This rating applies to explosive ammunition. It is the diameter range, in meters, that the shrapnel or explosive blast will achieve from the center (ground zero) of the explosion and inflict damage.

Magazine Capacity

Quite simply, this represents the maximum number of rounds that the weapon's clip can hold when full.

Reload Time

This is the total amount of time it takes to eject the current clip (or belt) and inject a fresh one and begin firing again. The greater value here, the longer you'll spend on a reload, so be wary of this when confronting the enemy. Always take cover when faced with long reload times. **[Screen 01]**

Fire Mode

Most of the weapons have multiple fire modes that can be selected by pressing Left on the D-Pad. Pressing repeatedly will cycle through the available modes for the weapon. The modes are as follows.

Full [md] Fully Automatic. Simply pull and hold the trigger down for a non-stop spray of deadly rounds. Firing will continue until you release the trigger or you run out of ammo.

3-Rnd [md] 3-Round Burst. If you pull and hold the trigger down, the weapon will fire three rounds in rapid succession and then cease fire. To fire again, you'll need to release the trigger and then squeeze it once more.

Semi [md] Semi-automatic. Pressing and holding the trigger down will deliver a single shot. To fire another round, release and pull the trigger again. You can continue in this fashion until your clip is empty.

Single [md] A single shot only. As with semi-automatic, pulling and holding the trigger results in one round being fired. However, with this type of weapon, there is no clip to automatically advance the next round meaning you will have to manually reload the next round (if available) to fire the weapon again. **[Screen 02]**

The mode selected will be displayed on screen in the lower right-hand corner just below the equipped weapon icon. This is indicated by the five bullet icons. If all five are highlighted, then fully automatic is selected, while three highlighted icons indicates a 3-round burst. A single highlighted icon means Semi-automatic (or single fire for weapons where this is applicable). **[Screen 03]**

Max Rate of Fire

This rating only applies to fully automatic weapons. This value is the number of rounds per second that can be fired continuously when you squeeze and hold the trigger.

Ammunition Types Explained

Ammunition types is designated in the 'Ammunition' entry of the 'Weapon Stats' table. The designation is made by some rather cryptic acronyms, but read on to discover what all those letters stand for.

AP — Armor Piercing

As the name implies, the armor piercing round is designed to pierce armor. More specifically, any hardened target that would be likely deflect a normal round, including, but not limited to, concrete, steel, ballistic vests, etc. The caliber of the round determines its ability to penetrate a substance. Obviously, the larger the caliber, the more punch the round has, and it will be able to pierce thicker and stronger armor.

The AP round is, at its core, a hardened 'penetrator' round made of hardened steel or some other suitably hard substance. It is shaped and pointed and designed to pierce barriers. It is wrapped in a softer metal jacket (often copper or aluminum). This outer jacket collapses and is destroyed on impact thus preventing a deflection. With the outer jacket destroyed (but not deflected), the inner penetrator round continues forward, penetrates the armor and pierces it.

APDS — Armor Piercing, Discarding Sabot

APFSDS — Armor Piercing, Fin Stabilized, Discarding Sabot

The sabot (in the APDS and APFSDS rounds) is a device used to wrap around a round that is smaller in diameter than the bore it is fired from. The sabot fits snugly into the bore of the weapon, thus centering the round and also allowing for an adequate build-up of propulsive gases to fire the round. Once fired, the sabot falls away as the round travels to the target. The fin stabilized version means that the round itself (not the sabot) has 'fins' at its base (like the fletching or feathers on an arrow) to help stabilize its flight trajectory once the sabot falls away.

APHE — Armor Piercing, High Explosive

This is an AP round with a little something extra; a 'bursting charge' is incorporated behind the penetrator of the AP. The bursting charge is a high explosive that is typically detonated by a delay fuse. The idea here is that the round would pierce the armor, get 'inside' and then detonate, inflicting far more damage than any regular bullet ever could.

ATGM — Anti-Tank Guided Missile

The anti-tank guided missile is just as the name implies [md]; a guided missile designed to take out heavily armored tanks. Early models of this weapon required the soldier to remain stationary after firing to manually use a joystick or radio to input adjustments to the missile trajectory; the soldier was basically the guidance system. Later, more advanced models rely on the radar in the nose of the missile to lock onto and make its way to the target.

FMJ — Full Metal Jacket

The full metal jacket round consists of a soft inner core (typically lead) surrounded by a shell made of a much harder metal. The jacket could be complete, enveloping the inner core 100% or, more often, the rear of the inner core is left exposed. The FMJ offers several advantages over a regular lead round, for example, it allows for much higher muzzle velocities (which means better accuracy) and higher rates of fire.

A particular problem with weapons with a high rate of fire using a lead round is that the bore heats up and could melt the lead rounds. The lead can get deposited on the bore and clog it up, resulting in catastrophic failure [md], known as 'leading the barrel'. An FMJ round alleviates this problem, since the lead is covered in a harder metal. Other advantages are better armor piercing qualities, as they do not expand like softer lead rounds and can withstand some rough handling in the field.

HE — High Explosive

The High Explosive round consists of a very strong steel casing, a bursting charge and a delay fuse. Once ignited, the explosive charge causes the casing to explode and shatter, emitting a deadly spray of pieces of steel (the casing) at high velocity. Most of the damage caused by this type of shell is from the fragments of the casing rather than the blast. Basically, this effect is 'fragmentation'. However, there are rounds that increase this effect with case modifications that are specifically labeled as fragmentation devices such as the HEF rounds (see below).

HEAT — High Explosive, Anti-Tank

The high explosive anti-tank round is a very special round indeed. The warhead is a charged explosive shape which, when in contact with the target, explodes in a predefined direction (into the armor) creating a high velocity metal projectile that punches through the armor. This projectile moves at hypersonic speed (25x the speed of sound). Once the round hits its target, it immediately ignites the projectile that promptly burns through the armor plating as it moves forward. This round is very effective against plain steel, but not so effective against composite and reactive armor.

HEDP — High Explosive, Dual Purpose

The high explosive dual purpose round derives its name from being both high explosive, and armor piercing. It is capable of penetrating the rear, flank, and top armor of some tanks making it a suitable weapon against armored vehicles.

HEF — High Explosive, Fragmentation

High explosive fragmentation rounds are similar to the HE round, but have a larger explosion and a thicker, stronger casing designed to increase the fragmentation effect.

03

Subsonic Rounds

Besides these acronyms, you'll also see that the US Stealth weapons use a 'Subsonic' round. Subsonic simply means slower than the speed of sound. While the speed of sound can vary depending on temperature and humidity, the basic figure of 341 meters per second (1118 f/s) is the general figure used for dry air at a temperature of 15.5 deg C (60 deg Fahrenheit). This means a subsonic round is moving slower than 341 meters per second, thus its report (the sound when it is fired) is quieter and harder to hear than a regular round.

Conversely, a regular round is typically a supersonic round in that it moves faster than the speed of sound with a considerably louder report.

Unguided Rocket

You'll see that some of the weapons fire an 'unguided rocket'. This can be taken at face value and is simply a rocket propelled projectile with no guidance system that you simply point and shoot, so make sure you are accurate with your aim.

US WEAPONRY
CHAPTER 03

TACTICAL

Here you'll find a list of equipment that will be significant in battlefield engagements, but are non-destructive and inflict no damage on the enemy. Instead, these devices are used to aid you in your tactical movements.

M18
SMOKE GRENADE

WEAPON STATS	
Duration	40
Coverage Range	30

Smoke grenades are used to help conceal your movement. Place them strategically between you and the enemy as you advance forward, and your movements will be masked for as long as you are in the smoke. While visibility is reduced as you move through the smoky cloud, you can be sure that the enemy can't target you. [Screen 01] Smoke grenades come in a variety of colors. The colored grenades are a valuable way of letting your team mates (in Co-Op mode) know your location if you are separated from them and they are some distance away.

IR
STROBE GRENADES

WEAPON STATS	
Duration	600
Effective Range	Variable

IR Strobe Grenades flash with a light that is only visible to infrared (night vision or thermal) scopes or goggles. In Co-Op mode, these can prove advantageous for an advance scout. The scout can mark or tag a location with an IR Strobe allowing his team mates to view his location (using night vision or thermal) without alerting nearby enemy forces of his presence. [Screen 02] By targeting or zeroing in on an IR Strobe, a team can easily fire on, or make their way to, the location indicated by the scout.

The effective range of the strobe depends on the power of the night vision device you are using. Note

that you won't find much use for IR Strobes in the regular Single Player Campaign.

CLOSE QUARTERS

The close quarters weaponry listed here are small weapons with limited range. As such, you'll only find yourself using them when you are truly face to face with the enemy.

KA-BAR
COMBAT KNIFE

The tried-and-tested KA-BAR Combat Knife is a USMC soldier's fallback weapon for close and silent encounters. While you may not have to use it very often, it is the undisputed champion of fast stealth kills at close quarters.

WEAPON STATS	
Max Damage vs Humans	12
Damage vs Vehicles	0

MEU (SOC)
PISTOL

The full name of this standard issue pistol is the Marine Expeditionary Unit (Special Operations Capable). It is semi-automatic, magazine fed, single-action, using a .45 ACP (American Colt Pistol) round. The designation of the .45 caliber is in inches and the metric dimensions are 11.43 x 23mm.

The pistol has very poor accuracy, especially when used on the move. When using the iron sights your view will be highly obstructed, and there is a good deal of recoil on the weapon, so you will need to realign your aim after every shot. It also has a slow rate of fire and a very small clip size. These factors make it a last ditch weapon, and mean that you will need to take out your target with the first few shots, or you may very well be in serious trouble.

WEAPON STATS	
Ammunition	.45 FMJ
Effective Range	50
Max Damage vs Humans	5
Damage vs Vehicles	0
Fragmentation Radius	–
Magazine Capacity	7
Reload Time	3
Fire Mode	Semi
Max Rate of Fire	–
Scope Type	–
Scope Magnification	–

03

ASSAULT RIFLE SCOPES

We will go into detail here on the various types of optical scopes and attachments that can be fitted to assault rifles. You won't be able to manually change the scope of your weapon, so you'll need to find a weapon that already has the required attachment equipped. The scopes will be detailed according to the categories used in the game.

TELESCOPIC SCOPE
(MARKSMAN)

As the name implies, this scope acts like a telescope, effectively zooming in by its magnification power (X4 or X8). It is not adjustable (unless specifically listed as such), so the set value listed is the power of the scope. When you sight your target through this scope, the image will be magnified by the specified value allowing you to see further, thus making your aim more accurate over long distances. **[Screen 03]**

This is the most common type of scope, found on most of the Marksman type assault rifles. It is an ACOG scope that generally defaults at X4 magnification, and features range finding markers to help judge the necessary height on long distance shots.

This scope offers no peripheral vision, but its X4 magnification provides a perfect middle ground between the standard reflex sights and the dedicated sniper scopes. This makes any weapon with this scope

equipped highly versatile as both a close quarters weapon and a medium range sniper rifle. Laying down accurate fire over distances of a few hundred meters would be impossible without this scope attached when using a standard assault rifle.

Magnification	Compatible Weapons
X4	M16A4 (Marksman)
	M4A1 (Marksman)
	Mk17 Mod 0 (Marksman)

HOLOGRAPHIC REFLEX SCOPE
(CQB)

This small device doesn't look like a traditional scope. It's a bit smaller and has a square pane of glass to look through. The 'holographic' part of this scope is the electronics embedded in the scope body. These electronics basically draw the crosshairs (targeting reticle) using an internal laser, that you will use to sight your target.

The holographic scope gives you a laser drawn illuminated targeting reticle on the viewfinder of your scope. Since the reticle is illuminated, the operator can keep both eyes open while sighting (the brain will superimpose the image onto the open eye's field of vision). This gives the operator a full field of view with normal depth perception. [Screen 01]

Its holographic technology essentially allows the user to focus their view through the scope without losing their peripheral vision. When using this scope your view will be very slightly blurred in areas that are outside the visual depth of the area you are focusing on.

Magnification	Compatible Weapons
X2	M16A4 (CQB)
	M4A1 (CQB)

RED DOT SIGHT
(ASSAULT) (STEALTH)

This scope is very similar in operation to the holographic scope, the main difference being that it uses a small red dot for aiming instead of the larger reticle of the holographic scope. This type of scope is often referred to as a reflex scope, and provides the standard X2 magnification.

The distinctive red dot that allows for extremely accurate close range aiming is its most notable feature, and is a favorite of Spec Ops marksmen. It sacrifices some of the CQB type's peripheral vision for an increased area of zoomed vision, which is perfect to help line up accurate shots. This scope often is used on stealth weapons, as the center of the red dot is highly visible when using night vision goggles, making it very easy to pick out targets. [Screen 02]

Magnification	Compatible Weapons
X2	M16A4 (Stealth)
	M4A1 (Stealth)
	Mk16 Mod 0 (Assault)
	Mk16 Mod 0 (Stealth)

THERMAL SCOPE
(NIGHT OPS)

The infrared spectral imaging on this scope essentially brings warm areas or objects into sharp contrast against the cooler background of the terrain. This makes identifying and taking out enemy soldiers at night a much simpler task, and even outstrips your night vision goggles for night ops effectiveness. Since warm targets show up as bright white, the scope's black range finding markers are highly visible and easy to use when aiming at a target. Besides the thermal imaging, this scope functions identically to the telescopic marksman scope, including the X4 magnification.

This special scope works off infrared radiation to detect heat radiated from the target. This lets you see the heat profile of your target, thus illuminating them even in a completely dark scenario. [Screen 03]

Magnification	Compatible Weapons
X4	M16A4 (Night Ops)
	M4A1 (Night Ops)
	Mk17 Mod 0 (Night Ops)

RIFLES

You'll find that rifles are the mainstays of your weaponry, and will be the weapons you use most often. They have good range and stopping power, making them an invaluable asset in this war.

Model
M16A4 Assault Rifle
M16A4 Assault Rifle (CQB)
M16A4 Assault Rifle (Marksman)
M16A4 Assault Rifle (Assault)
M16A4 Assault Rifle (Night Ops)
M16A4 Assault Rifle (Stealth)
M4A1 Assault Rifle
M4A1 Assault Rifle (CQB)
M4A1 Assault Rifle (Marksman)
M4A1 Assault Rifle (Assault)
M4A1 Assault Rifle (Night Ops)
M4A1 Assault Rifle (Stealth)
Mk16 Mod 0 Assault Rifle (Assault)
Mk16 Mod 0 Assault Rifle (Stealth)
Mk17 Mod 0 Assault Rifle (Marksman)
Mk17 Mod 0 Assault Rifle (Night Ops)

M16A4
ASSAULT RIFLE

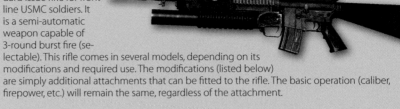

The M16A4 is the standard issue rifle for front line USMC soldiers. It is a semi-automatic weapon capable of 3-round burst fire (selectable). This rifle comes in several models, depending on its modifications and required use. The modifications (listed below) are simply additional attachments that can be fitted to the rifle. The basic operation (caliber, firepower, etc.) will remain the same, regardless of the attachment.

This is a great all-round assault rifle, combining good stopping power with a large capacity and high accuracy on the scoped models. It is favored by USMC fire-teams for mid-range engagements using its 3-round burst setting. This allows you to take out a target in a short, accurate burst of fire from a good distance away.

The assault model of the M16A4 is equipped with an under-slung grenade launcher. The grenade launcher makes use of the low velocity HE and HEDP 40 x 46mm rounds. The considerable range of the grenades make it a powerful tool for taking out large groups of enemies and light or unarmored vehicles. The stealth version of the rifle has a X2 red dot sight attached, and utilizes subsonic rounds and sound suppression to muffle the report of the weapon for low profile engagements.

Model	Attachment	Magnification	Effective Range
M16A4 Assault Rifle: Basic Model	None	–	200
M16A4 Assault Rifle: CQB	Holographic Reflex Scope	X2	200
M16A4 Assault Rifle: Marksman	Telescopic Scope	X4	400
M16A4 Assault Rifle: Assault	Grenade Launcher	–	300 (Grenade Launcher)
M16A4 Assault Rifle: Night Ops	Thermal Scope	X4	400
M16A4 Assault Rifle: Stealth	Red Dot Sight	X2	200

WEAPON STATS			
Ammunition	**5.56 x 45mm FMJ**	**40 x 46mm HE ***	**40 x 46mm HEDP ***
Max Damage vs Humans	6	20	20
Damage vs Vehicles	1	3	5
Fragmentation Radius	–	7	6
Magazine Capacity	30	1	1
Reload Time	4	3	3
Fire Mode	3-Rnd / Semi	Single	Single
Max Rate of Fire	–	–	–

* Assault model only

M4A1
ASSAULT RIFLE

M4A1 is a variant of the M16A2. It is shorter and lighter and has 80% of the same parts as the M16A2, including the same ammunition. A notable difference is the loss of a 3-round burst fire mode in exchange for selectable fully automatic fire. The lack of 3-round burst makes this slightly less effective when engaging single targets at medium range, but the fully automatic fire makes up for this when using the rifle for suppressive fire on enemy positions.

Similar to the M16A4, this basic model has several variants with the addition of optional attachments that make the weapon more suited to specific combat scenarios. With its fully automatic fire and holographic reflex scope, the CQB version offers the best combination of firing speed and accuracy.

Model	Attachment	Magnification	Effective Range
M4A1 Assault Rifle: Basic Model	None	–	200
M4A1 Assault Rifle: CQB	Holographic Reflex Scope	X2	200
M4A1 Assault Rifle: Marksman	Telescopic Scope	X4	400
M4A1 Assault Rifle: Assault	Grenade Launcher	–	300 (Grenade Launcher)
M4A1 Assault Rifle: Night Ops	Thermal Scope	X4	400
M4A1 Assault Rifle: Stealth	Red Dot Sight	X2	200

WEAPON STATS

Ammunition	5.56 x 45mm FMJ	40 x 46mm HE *	40 x 46mm HEDP *
Max Damage vs Humans	6	20	20
Damage vs Vehicles	1	3	5
Fragmentation Radius	–	7	6
Magazine Capacity	30	1	1
Reload Time	4	3	3
Fire Mode	Full / Semi	Single	Single
Max Rate of Fire	15	–	–

* Assault model only

MK16 MOD 0
ASSAULT RIFLE

01

The Mk16 Mod 0 is a modular SOF (Special Operation Forces) combat assault rifle [md] or SCAR. The SCAR comes in two main variations, the SCAR-L or light version, and the SCAR-H or heavy version, with the main difference being the size of the round and magazine that each uses (the SCAR-H uses a larger round with a smaller magazine). The Mk16 Mod 0 is a weapon of the SCAR-L variety.

This stealth variant of the Mk16 Mod 0 utilizes subsonic ammunition and sound suppression to muffle the report of the weapon. This makes it one of the best weapons to use in stealth missions, though the lack of a thermal scope reduces its effectiveness in low visibility conditions. Spec Ops fire-teams will often use the assault model of the Mk16, which offers the excellent combination of the grenade launcher attachment and a red dot scope for precise aiming. [Screen 01]

Model	Attachment	Magnification	Effective Range
Mk16 Mod 0 Assault Rifle: Assault	Grenade Launcher	–	300 (Grenade Launcher)
Mk16 Mod 0 Assault Rifle: Stealth	Red Dot Scope	X2	200

WEAPON STATS

Ammunition	5.56 x 45mm FMJ	40 x 46mm HE*	40 x 46mm HEDP*
Max Damage vs Humans	6	20	20
Damage vs Vehicles	1	3	5
Fragmentation Radius	–	7	6
Magazine Capacity	30	1	1
Reload Time	4	4	4
Fire Mode	Full / Semi	Single	Single
Max Rate of Fire	10	–	–

* Assault model only

MK17 MOD 0
ASSAULT RIFLE

fitted with either a marksman or night ops scope. The Mk16 and Mk17 can also deliver their rounds with slightly higher accuracy than other assault rifles, so they make excellent medium range sniper rifles.

Model	Attachment	Magnification	Effective Range
Mk17 Mod 0 Assault Rifle: Marksman	Telescopic Scope	X4	400
Mk17 Mod 0 Assault Rifle: Night Ops	Thermal Scope	X4	400
WEAPON STATS			
Ammunition		**7.62 x 51mm FMJ**	
Max Damage vs Humans		8	
Damage vs Vehicles		1	
Fragmentation Radius		–	
Magazine Capacity		20	
Reload Time		4	
Fire Mode		Full / Semi	
Max Rate of Fire		10	

This is a SCAR-H (heavy). It is very similar to the Mk16 Mod 0, a SCAR-L, but utilizes more powerful ammunition. The Mk17 is modified for longer range combat, and is the preferred assault rifle of the US Spec Ops teams. Both the marksman and night ops variations are equipped with a X4 telescopic scope, allowing for greater sighting distance, which results in improved accuracy over range.

The extra stopping power is a trade-off for a lower ammunition capacity, but a worthwhile one, which effectively makes this weapon the most deadly assault rifle available when used in short, fully automatic bursts. Similar to the Mk16, the Mk17 doesn't have iron sights, so it will always be

M21
SNIPER RIFLE

Model	Attachment	Magnification	Effective Range
M21 Sniper Rifle	Telescopic Scope	X8	1000
WEAPON STATS			
Ammunition		**7.62 x 51mm FMJ**	
Max Damage vs Humans		12	
Damage vs Vehicles		1	
Fragmentation Radius		–	
Magazine Capacity		20	
Reload Time		4	
Fire Mode		Semi	
Max Rate of Fire		–	

The M21 is a semi-automatic adaptation of the popular M14 rifle. It's equipped with an X8 telescopic scope, enabling superior targeting at long distances. The incredible range of this weapon allows the soldier to destroy his enemy long before his presence is detected. It can be used with devastating accuracy at ranges of over 1 km, though you'll need to go prone and adjust your aim well above the target's perceived height to get optimum results at such extreme ranges.

M82A1
ANTI-MATERIAL RIFLE

an enemy surviving to alert other troops to your presence. It does have a slightly longer reload time than the M21, which equates to a slower rate of fire should you need to take out multiple targets in quick succession.

Model	Attachment	Magnification	Effective Range
M82 Anti-Material Rifle: Basic	Telescopic	X8	1000
M82 Anti-Material Rifle: Night Ops	Thermal	X8	1000
WEAPON STATS			
Ammunition		**12.7 x 99mm FMJ**	
Max Damage vs Humans		16	
Damage vs Vehicles		2	
Fragmentation Radius		–	
Magazine Capacity		10	
Reload Time		5	
Fire Mode		Semi	
Max Rate of Fire		–	

An anti-material weapon is one that is designed to be used against military equipment (material) rather than personnel. The heavy hitting M82 excels at this job with power ammunition, long range, a X8 telescopic scope, and semi-automatic fire. The M82A1 is a SASR (Special Application Scoped Rifle) that is often referred to as the 'light 50' owing to the size of its ammunition. That makes the 12.7mm round .50 in inches, making it a '50 caliber' round.

The M82's rounds are extremely powerful, and will kill any infantry unit in a single shot. This is its primary advantage over the M21 and similar rifles, as the extra stopping power means there's virtually no chance of

MACHINE GUNS

These specialty weapons do one thing, and they do it well; they spray the enemy with lead, metal jacketed lead that is! If you're looking for high rates of fire and a non-stop stream of ammo to pump into your enemy, then one of these MGs is just what you need.

MP5A4
SUB-MACHINE GUN

The MP5A4 is a 9mm sub-machine gun (SMG). It has the fully automatic fire of a larger machine gun while utilizing the cartridge (rounds) of a pistol. This makes it smaller, lighter and more portable than a true machine gun, albeit less powerful. This is best used as a close quarters back-up weapon, and when firing from the hip whilst on the move. It will maintain accuracy in these situations far better than an assault rifle.

WEAPON STATS	
Ammunition	**9 x 19mm FMJ**
Effective Range	150
Max Damage vs Humans	4
Damage vs Vehicles	0
Fragmentation Radius	–
Magazine Capacity	30
Reload Time	3
Fire Mode	Full / Semi
Max Rate of Fire	13

M249 SAW
SQUAD AUTOMATIC WEAPON

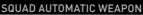

The M249 Light Machine Gun (LMG) is a portable machine gun that combines its high volume of fire with an accuracy and portability that larger machine guns cannot match. A true heavy hitter that can quickly decimate large enemy forces. The substantial ammunition capacity makes it a great weapon for continuous suppressive fire. It is best used from behind cover, while crouching, to offset its relatively poor accuracy. It will be essential for you to master using the iron sights to make effective use of this weapon.

WEAPON STATS	
Ammunition	**5.56 x 45mm FMJ**
Effective Range	200
Max Damage vs Humans	6
Damage vs Vehicles	1
Fragmentation Radius	–
Magazine Capacity	200
Reload Time	8
Fire Mode	Full
Max Rate of Fire	15

MK48 MOD 0
MACHINE GUN

The Mk48 Mod 0 is a variation of the M249 that utilizes a more powerful round. It has a greater range, but a slower rate of fire. It also has a lower ammunition capacity, but it can be just as good for dedicated suppressive fire due to the lower rate of fire making the ammo last longer and the increased stopping power per bullet. It maintains accuracy better than the M249 over longer ranges, and can be a more effective weapon when used on the move. Unlike the M249, using the iron sights in aim mode is not essential with this weapon, as it can be highly accurate when fired from the hip.

WEAPON STATS	
Ammunition	**7.62 x 51mm FMJ**
Effective Range	300
Max Damage vs Humans	8
Damage vs Vehicles	1
Fragmentation Radius	–
Magazine Capacity	100
Reload Time	7
Fire Mode	Full
Max Rate of Fire	11

EXPLOSIVES

You'll often start a mission with some of these explosives. While in the field, you can find more in ammo crates. They aren't listed by individual item, but instead fall under the 'Equipment' category in a crate (or in a fallen soldier's inventory). When you take equipment, make sure to check your current weapon inventory to see if you picked up any extra explosives.

M67
FRAG GRENADE

WEAPON STATS	
Effective Range	40
Max Damage vs Humans	23
Damage vs Vehicles	3
Fragmentation Radius	7

The M67, often referred to as the C13, replaced the familiar Mk2 'pineapple' grenade used in earlier wars. It has a smooth, round body and a 5 second fuse. You can throw a frag grenade up to about 50 meters away with good accuracy once you master the throwing arc. They can be the perfect tool to throw over sandbags or other entrenched positions to reach enemies behind cover. You can also roll them underarm to slide them under vehicles or other obstacles; a normal overarm throw will generally have a high enough arc to use from behind cover.

M14
ANTI-PERSONNEL MINE

WEAPON STATS	
Effective Range	–
Max Damage vs Humans	20
Damage vs Vehicles	3
Fragmentation Radius	7

The M14 is an impact triggered anti-personnel mine. It is designed to be placed on the ground where the unsuspecting enemy will step on it, thus detonating the mine. Once laid and armed, it turns into a very powerful trap, even capable of taking out small or lightly armored vehicles.

M21
ANTI-TANK MINE

WEAPON STATS	
Effective Range	–
Max Damage vs Humans	60
Damage vs Vehicles	9
Fragmentation Radius	10

A very powerful mine designed to destroy armored vehicles. It is specifically used against tanks, as it is capable of causing serious damage to their heavy armor. Its considerable explosive charge will obliterate a soft target (human combatant) if they manage to trip it. These should be placed on roads or places where a tank or APC is likely to pass through.

M18A1
CLAYMORE MINE

WEAPON STATS	
Effective Range	–
Max Damage vs Humans	20
Damage vs Vehicles	5
Fragmentation Radius	20

This mine uses a directional charge, meaning that the charge explodes in one direction, so they are carefully placed, often in high traffic areas, to 'point' toward the area where the enemy is likely to appear. The M18A1 Claymore (in the game) operates in uncontrolled mode, i.e. it does not require the soldier to use a 'clacker' or detonator to set it off, but triggers when the target is nearby. It should be noted that these are not used by the fire-team leader in the Single Player Campaign missions, though other fire-team members have these among their equipment in Co-op mode.

C4
DEMOLITION CHARGE

the detonator. Once the charge is placed, make sure you retreat to a safe distance before detonating the charge remotely. This is an essential tool for completing many Primary Objectives that involve destroying tanks, generators or AAA (anti-air artillery). **[Screen 01]**

This is a powerful charge that must be placed on the target and then manually detonated with

WEAPON STATS	
Effective Range	–
Max Damage vs Humans	25
Damage vs Vehicles	14
Fragmentation Radius	20

EXPLOSIVES - LAUNCHED

There are other ways to launch explosives besides the thrown grenade or the under-slung grenade launchers of the assault rifles. Here we will describe the specifications of the various grenade and rocket launchers the US has in its arsenal.

M32 MGL
MULTIPLE GRENADE LAUNCHER

members using this weapon can easily cover an entire area with explosive fire from a safe distance.

The M32 MGL (Multiple Grenade Launcher) is similar to the under-slung grenade launcher attachment of the assault rifle in that it fires the 40 x 46mm HE and HEDP rounds. It is equipped with a 6-round revolving cylinder (like those found on revolver type handguns) that automatically rotates and chambers the next round after one has been fired. This weapon can be used effectively over great distances. Multiple fire-team

WEAPON STATS		
Ammunition	40 x 46mm HE	40 x 46mm HEDP
Effective Range	300	300
Max Damage vs Humans	20	20
Damage vs Vehicles	3	5
Fragmentation Radius	7	6
Magazine Capacity	6	6
Reload Time	10	10
Fire Mode	Semi	Semi
Max Rate of Fire	–	–
Scope Type	–	–
Scope Magnification	–	–

MK153 SMAW
83MM ROCKET LAUNCHER

The Mk153 SMAW (shoulder-launched multi-purpose assault weapon) is a portable and highly effective anti-armor weapon. It is rather bulky and takes considerable time to ready and deploy, so make sure to ready it from a good cover point before stepping out to take your shot. This weapon can be used to take out all types of vehicles, including heavily armored tanks, and even helicopters if your aim is accurate.

WEAPON STATS		
Ammunition	83mm HEAT	83mm HEF
Effective Range	1000	1000
Max Damage vs Humans	25	25
Damage vs Vehicles	8	5
Fragmentation Radius	7	10
Magazine Capacity	1	1
Reload Time	7	7
Fire Mode	Single	Single
Max Rate of Fire	–	–
Scope Type	Thermal	Thermal
Scope Magnification	x4	x4

GUIDED MISSILES

All the guided missiles are shoulder-mounted attack weapons designed to take out larger and heavily armored vehicles. They utilize a complex targeting system that requires you to lock on to the target, when fired, an on-board guidance system takes the missile to its target. As with other SMAW weapons, they are bulky and take considerable time to ready and deploy, so make sure to ready them from a good cover point. Once ready, acquire your target, ensure a lock, and fire.

The Stinger and Javelin both feature a custom thermal scope with X4 magnification. This makes acquiring and locking on to moving target much easier, especially during night time missions. The Javelin is the strongest missile available to ground troops, and can take out a main battle tank in a single shot. The Sidewinder does not come with a scope equipped, but can track fast moving targets easily, and locks on very quickly. This makes it perfect for taking out attack helicopters.

FGM-148
JAVELIN ANTI-TANK MISSILE

WEAPON STATS	
Effective Range	2500
Max Damage vs Humans	25
Damage vs Vehicles	10
Fragmentation Radius	12
Magazine Capacity	–

WEAPON STATS	
Reload Time	–
Fire Mode	Single
Max Rate of Fire	–
Scope Type	Thermal
Scope Magnification	x4

FIM-92A
STINGER ANTI-AIRCRAFT MISSILE

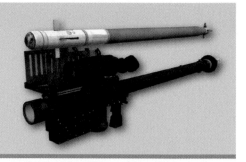

WEAPON STATS		WEAPON STATS	
Effective Range	4500	Reload Time	–
Max Damage vs Humans	25	Fire Mode	Single
Damage vs Vehicles	7	Max Rate of Fire	–
Fragmentation Radius	15	Scope Type	Thermal
Magazine Capacity	–	Scope Magnification	x4

AIM-9L
SIDEWINDER AIR-TO-AIR MISSILE

WEAPON STATS		WEAPON STATS		WEAPON STATS	
Effective Range	6000	Magazine Capacity	–	Max Rate of Fire	–
Max Damage vs Humans	25	Reload Time	–	Scope Type	–
Damage vs Vehicles	8	Fire Mode	Single	Scope Magnification	–
Fragmentation Radius	20				

PLA WEAPONRY
CHAPTER 03

The People's Liberation Army or PLA, is the unified military of the People's Republic of China: they are your enemy in Operation Flashpoint: Dragon Rising. Here you will find all the details of the weaponry they will be using against you and which you can commandeer for your own use.

CLOSE QUARTERS

These are small arms that the PLA will often rely on for short distance, in-your-face encounters.

PLA
COMBAT KNIFE

All the PLA soldiers carry a combat knife, although you'll rarely see them use it. If you're lucky, you'll never see this beast in action. PLA fire-teams will use this in multiplayer modes, where it is a last resort when low on ammo, or a viable option to use when sneaking up on unsuspecting players.

WEAPON STATS	
Max Damage vs Humans	12
Damage vs Vehicles	0

QSZ-92
PISTOL

This is the standard issue 9mm pistol of the PLA. It is slightly less powerful than the MEU (SOC) Pistol used by the US, but it does have a higher magazine capacity. As with the combat knife, this is a back-up weapon that players may be forced to use in multiplayer modes, though it is no match for an assault rifle or a machine gun.

WEAPON STATS	
Ammunition	9 x 19mm FMJ
Effective Range	50
Max Damage vs Humans	4
Damage vs Vehicles	0
Fragmentation Radius	–
Magazine Capacity	15
Reload Time	3
Fire Mode	Semi
Max Rate of Fire	–
Scope Type	–
Scope Magnification	–

ASSAULT RIFLE SCOPES

The assault rifles the PLA use will often be equipped with scopes that are similar in function to those of the US forces. The PLA use a smaller variety of scopes, and finding weapons with the required scope fitted may be a rare occurrence either in equipment crates or on dead bodies. In multiplayer modes, however, PLA players will often have scoped assault rifles in their starting loadouts. The scopes will be detailed according to the categories used in the game.

COMBAT SCOPE
(MARKSMAN)

This is the most common type of scope on PLA weapons. It is found on most of the marksman type assault rifles, and is a very similar ACOG scope to the US equivalent, complete with X4 magnification and range finding markers to help judge the necessary height on long distance shots. This scope drastically reduces peripheral vision to an even more severe degree than any of the US scope types. **[Screen 01]**

Magnification	Compatible Weapons
X4	QBZ-95 (Marksman)
	Type 81-1 (Marksman)

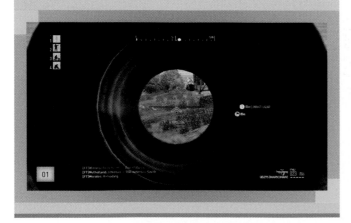

THERMAL SCOPE
(NIGHT OPS)

This scope is functionally the same as the US equivalent, using infrared spectral imaging to bring warm areas or objects into contrast against the darker background. Weapons with this scope fitted are not common, and will usually need to be scavenged from the PLA marksman that was using it after he is killed. It is used on the PLA Type 81-1 **[Screen 02]** rifles in multiplayer modes, and allows PLA snipers to compete on equal terms with the US marksmen.

Magnification	Compatible Weapons
X4	Type 81-1 (Night Ops)
	QBZ95 (Night Ops)

RIFLES

Rifles comprise the majority of the PLA armament. These are plentiful and can be scavenged off dead PLA soldiers or looted from PLA ammo crates. Though they don't quite match up to the US rifles in stopping power, they are just as lethal in the right hands.

Model
QBZ95 Assault Rifle
QBZ95 Assault Rifle (Marksman)
QBZ95 Assault Rifle (Assault)
QBZ95 Assault Rifle (Night Ops)
Type 81-1 Assault Rifle
Type 81-1 Assault Rifle (Marksman)
Type 81-1 Assault Rifle (Assault)
Type 81-1 Assault Rifle (Night Ops)

QBZ-95
ASSAULT RIFLE

This is the basic and most common assault rifle of the PLA forces. It is highly comparable to the M16A4 used by the US. One notable difference is the QBZ-95 supports all 3 modes of fire, fully automatic, 3-round burst, and semi-automatic, while the M16A4 only does 3-round and semi-automatic. As with the M16A4, this weapon comes in several variations depending on the optional equipment attached to it.

The assault model comes with an under-slung grenade launcher that utilizes the 35mm HE and HEDP grenades. These are less powerful than the 40mm grenades used by the US, but still lethal to infantry caught in the blast. The marksman version utilizes a X4 telescopic scope, but is lacking in stopping power compared to US Spec Ops rifles. The basic model has no scope attached, so you must use the iron sights to aim. This is not ideal, because the QBZ-95's iron sights take up a huge amount of your viewing range, and give only a very small reticle with which to sight a target.

Model	Attachment	Magnification	Effective Range
QBZ-95 Assault Rifle: Basic	None	–	200
QBZ-95 Assault Rifle: Marksman	Telescopic Scope	X4	400
QBZ-95 Assault Rifle: Assault	Grenade Launcher	–	300 (Grenade Launcher)
QBZ-95 Assault Rifle: Night Ops	Thermal Scope	X4	400

WEAPON STATS

Ammunition	5.8 x 42mm FMJ	35mm HE*	35mm HEDP*
Max Damage vs Humans	6	20	20
Damage vs Vehicles	1	3	5
Fragmentation Radius	–	6	5
Magazine Capacity	30	1	1
Reload Time	4	3	3
Fire Mode	Full / 3-Rnd / Semi	Single	Single
Max Rate of Fire	10	–	–

* Assault model only

TYPE 81-1
ASSAULT RIFLE

The Type 81-1 is based on the Russian AK-47 Assault Rifle, but with notable improvements in accuracy and operation. Capable of fully automatic or semi-automatic fire, it is comparable to the US Mk17 Mod 0 Assault Rifle. As with the QBZ-95, the Type 81-1 comes in several variations, depending on the optional attachment it comes with. Although not used as frequently as the QBZ-95, this is actually a better all-round weapon, especially the night ops model for Spec Ops missions.

The marksman version of the Type 81-1 is equipped with a X4 telescopic scope, while the night ops version features a thermal scope. The power of the ammunition is unchanged, but the improved sighting of these scopes results in improved long distance shots.

Model	Attachment	Magnification	Effective Range
Type 81-1 Assault Rifle: Basic	None	–	200
Type 81-1 Assault Rifle: Marksman	Telescopic Scope	X4	400
Type 81-1 Assault Rifle: Assault	Grenade Launcher	–	300 (Grenade Launcher)
Type 81-1 Assault Rifle: Night Ops	Thermal Scope	X4	400

WEAPON STATS

Ammunition	7.62 x 39mm FMJ	35mm HE*	35mm HEDP*
Max Damage vs Humans	6	20	20
Damage vs Vehicles	1	3	5
Fragmentation Radius	–	6	5
Magazine Capacity	30	1	1
Reload Time	4	3	3
Fire Mode	Full / Semi	Single	Single
Max Rate of Fire	10	–	–

* Assault model only

QBU-88
SNIPER RIFLE

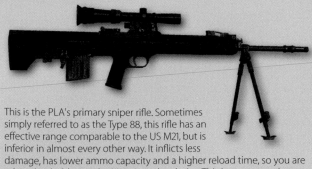

This is the PLA's primary sniper rifle. Sometimes simply referred to as the Type 88, this rifle has an effective range comparable to the US M21, but is inferior in almost every other way. It inflicts less damage, has lower ammo capacity and a higher reload time, so you are advised to hold onto the M21 given the choice. This is not to say that the QBU-88 is ineffective; not at all. When faced with an entrenched PLA sniper, you'll need to be extremely cautious indeed. PLA snipers in multiplayer modes using this weapon can find secluded spots and take out other players from extreme distances.

Model	Attachment	Magnification	Effective Range
QBU-88 Sniper Rifle	Telescopic Scope	X8	1000

WEAPON STATS	
Ammunition	**5.8 x 42mm FMJ**
Max Damage vs Humans	9
Damage vs Vehicles	1
Fragmentation Radius	–
Magazine Capacity	10
Reload Time	5
Fire Mode	Semi
Max Rate of Fire	–

M99
ANTI-MATERIAL RIFLE

The heavy hitting M99 Anti-Material Rifle excels at its job with powerful ammunition, and extremely long range. Its X8 telescopic scope and semi-automatic fire make it a uniquely dangerous threat among PLA weapons. The M99's closest equivalent is the M82 used by the US forces; this weapon has greater ammunition capacity, but is otherwise very similar in use and effectiveness.

Model	Attachment	Magnification	Effective Range
M99 Anti-Material Rifle	Telescopic Scope	X8	1000

WEAPON STATS	
Ammunition	**12.7 x 108mm FMJ**
Max Damage vs Humans	16
Damage vs Vehicles	2
Fragmentation Radius	–
Magazine Capacity	5
Reload Time	5
Fire Mode	Semi
Max Rate of Fire	–

MACHINE GUNS

Like the US, the PLA is also equipped with special fully automatic weapons designed to spray the enemy with a non-stop stream of deadly projectiles.

You can often scavenge these from dead PLA soldiers or grab them from PLA ammo crates.

QCQ-05 SMG
SUB MACHINE GUN

This is a light and accurate sub-machine gun, carried by PLA machine gunners. It uses 5mm rounds, which gives it less stopping power than a basic PLA assault rifle, but with a much higher rate of fire and very quick reload time. Its accuracy will dissipate beyond 100 meters, so it's primarily used as a close combat weapon.

WEAPON STATS	
Ammunition	**5.8 x 42mm FMJ**
Effective Range	150
Max Damage vs Humans	4
Damage vs Vehicles	0
Fragmentation Radius	–
Magazine Capacity	50
Reload Time	3
Fire Mode	Full / Semi
Max Rate of Fire	13

QBB-95 SAW
SQUAD AUTOMATIC WEAPON

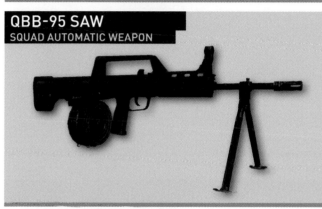

Based on the QBZ-95, this is a light machine gun that uses the same ammunition, but has a higher magazine capacity and firing rate for fully automatic fire. It is often referred to as the Type 95 and as a SAW (Squad Automatic Weapon).

WEAPON STATS	
Ammunition	**5.8 x 42mm FMJ**
Effective Range	200
Max Damage vs Humans	6
Damage vs Vehicles	1
Fragmentation Radius	–
Magazine Capacity	75
Reload Time	4
Fire Mode	Full
Max Rate of Fire	10

TYPE-67 II
MEDIUM MACHINE GUN

This general purpose machine gun sports a moderate magazine capacity and rate of fire. It is often mounted on PLA vehicles as a secondary weapon for the gunner to use against non-armored targets. It is highly comparable to the US Mk48 Mod 0 Machine Gun, with only a smaller magazine capacity holding it back. Its rate of fire and general stopping power is second to none among PLA ballistic weapons.

WEAPON STATS	
Ammunition	**7.62 x 54mm FMJ**
Effective Range	300
Max Damage vs Humans	8
Damage vs Vehicles	1
Fragmentation Radius	–
Magazine Capacity	75
Reload Time	7
Fire Mode	Full
Max Rate of Fire	11

EXPLOSIVES

The PLA's explosive selection is very similar to that of the US forces. They have a full range of grenades and mines available, along with C4 demolition charges. These can be found in the PLA's equipment crates, usually near areas they have set up as outposts.

TYPE 86
FRAG GRENADE

A conventionally designed, plastic bodied grenade that relies on fragmentation for damage. This is effectively the same as the US frag grenade, with the skill of the user being of far greater importance than any minor differences between the types of grenade.

WEAPON STATS	
Effective Range	40
Max Damage vs Humans	23
Damage vs Vehicles	3
Fragmentation Radius	7

TYPE 72
ANTI-PERSONNEL MINE

Another plastic bodied explosive device. As with all land mines, the idea is to place this on the ground, typically in a shallow hole to conceal it. It is detonated by the pressure of someone stepping on it.

WEAPON STATS	
Effective Range	–
Max Damage vs Humans	20
Damage vs Vehicles	3
Fragmentation Radius	7

TM62
ANTI-TANK MINE

The TM62 is a land mine designed to destroy armored vehicles. It is best used against APCs and tanks, though it will also take out off-road vehicles with ease. It is functionally identical to the M2 AT Mine used by the US forces.

WEAPON STATS	
Effective Range	–
Max Damage vs Humans	60
Damage vs Vehicles	9
Fragmentation Radius	10

POMZ-2
CLAYMORE MINE

A stake mounted fragmentation mine. The stake allows the user to stick the mine in the ground and then arm it where unsuspecting enemies will walk into its trigger. It should be noted that these are not used in the Single Player Campaign missions, so you'll only encounter them in multiplayer modes.

WEAPON STATS	
Effective Range	–
Max Damage vs Humans	20
Damage vs Vehicles	5
Fragmentation Radius	20

EXPLOSIVES - LAUNCHED

Besides throwing a grenade at you, or launching one via an under-slung launcher on an assault rifle, the PLA, like the US, have other ways to deliver deadly explosives to their enemy.

PF98
QUEEN BEE ROCKET LAUNCHER

The PF98, or 'Queen Bee', is a 120mm rocket launcher. It is typically deployed as an anti-tank weapon, but is equally devastating against other types of target. It is a shoulder-launched multi-purpose assault weapon (SMAW), and can often be found in PLA equipment crates, or scavenged from dead PLA AT gunners.

WEAPON STATS		
Ammunition	120mm HEAT	120mm HE
Effective Range	1000	1000
Max Damage vs Humans	25	25
Damage vs Vehicles	10	6
Fragmentation Radius	12	18
Magazine Capacity	1	1
Reload Time	11	11
Fire Mode	Single	Single
Max Rate of Fire	–	–
Scope Type	Thermal	Thermal
Scope Magnification	x4	x4

GUIDED MISSILES

All the guided missiles are shoulder-mounted attack weapons designed to take out larger and heavily armored vehicles. They utilize a complex targeting system that acquires a lock on to the target. On firing an on-board guidance system takes the missile to its target. As with other SMAW weapons, they are bulky and take considerable time to ready and deploy.

These are infrared guided missiles, capable of taking out helicopters from a few kilometers away. The QW-2 SAM is used either as a shoulder-mounted weapon, or mounted on vehicles such as the Type 95 SPAAG, and presents a lethal threat to US helicopters. The shoulder mounted version will not fire unless it is locked on to an airborne target.

QW-2
ANTI AIRCRAFT MISSILE

WEAPON STATS	
Effective Range	4500
Max Damage vs Humans	25
Damage vs Vehicles	7
Fragmentation Radius	15
Magazine Capacity	–

WEAPON STATS	
Reload Time	–
Fire Mode	Single
Max Rate of Fire	–
Scope Type	Thermal
Scope Magnification	x4

TY-90
AIR-TO-AIR MISSILE

WEAPON STATS	
Effective Range	4500
Max Damage vs Humans	25
Damage vs Vehicles	7
Fragmentation Radius	20

WEAPON STATS	
Magazine Capacity	–
Reload Time	–
Fire Mode	Single

WEAPON STATS	
Max Rate of Fire	–
Scope Type	Thermal
Scope Magnification	x4

VEHICLES
CHAPTER 03

Here we will provide full details and stats for every single vehicle that can be driven, flown or boarded in Operation Flashpoint: Dragon Rising. Each vehicle's weapon systems will be covered in the same way as the standard infantry weapons.

VEHICLE CONTROL

Here we'll give you the basic Intel you need to successfully board and pilot the various vehicles at your disposal. There are three basic types: light vehicles such as 4x4s or trucks, APCs and helicopters.

The Basics

At any time during the game, you can access the main menu and view the 'Controls' option to see the controller layout for the various positions you can occupy when in a vehicle. Please refer to the Basic Training chapter for a full listing of all the controller configurations.

VEHICLE POSITIONS	
Placement	**Activity**
Driver / Pilot	Drive or Pilot the vehicle to desired locations.
Gunner	Operate the guns of the vehicle.
Commander	Give strategic commands to Driver or Gunner.
Passenger	Along for the ride.

To board a vehicle, approach it and the interaction hand icon becomes available. Interact with the vehicle to board it. Once on board, issue the command 'Mount My Vehicle' to have your men get on board as well. Alternatively, you can stay outside the vehicle, face it, and issue the command 'Enter' to have your men get on board without you. **[Screen 01]**

Once on board, you can press the Interaction button at any time to disembark. If your men are on board without you, issue the command 'Exit' to have them disembark.

You can also press and hold the Switch Seat (Sprint in normal play) button to bring up the seating chart menu. Continue to hold down the button, and you can cycle through the available seating positions even if one of your men is occupying that position (you will swap places).

If you are on board a vehicle, and your men are outside, you can still issue basic infantry commands to them. Moreover, when in a vehicle, you can always access the map to issue long distance commands (commands that are beyond your line of vision).

LIGHT AND ARMORED VEHICLES

Controlling land-based vehicles (Trucks, APCs, etc.) is basically the same regardless of the vehicle you have boarded. The main difference is with the available weaponry of the vehicle, which is of prime concern to the gunner.

Driver

Driving a vehicle is straightforward. Hold the 'Drive Forward' button down, and the vehicle will move forward. As you move, use the left stick to steer. While moving forward, you can use the reverse control to slow your movement. The handbrake can be used as well, but since this locks the vehicle's wheels, it can cause you to spin out uncontrollably, so it's better to rely on reverse.

When driving, you will be presented with a first person viewpoint. If you have difficulty with this view, then click down on the camera stick to change to a third person view. You can cycle through these two viewpoints with repeated clicks of the stick. Other than this, you cannot adjust the camera from the driver's seat. In APCs you can also press left to switch between cockpit view and normal first person perspective. **[Screen 01]**

Gunner

As the gunner, you'll have control of the vehicle's armaments. This is a great position to be in when you have told the driver to move to a specified location and you are expecting resistance. Conversely, you may find it more to your playing style to start as the driver, drive to the required location, then quickly switch to the gunner position to engage the enemy. In this position, you can adjust the camera freely allowing yourself a good view of the area, as well as target any enemy that is present.

If the vehicle has more than one gun, press and hold the Weapon Select button to bring up the weapon menu. You can then cycle through the available weapons, and change which gun you are manning. Once a gun has been selected, you can press and hold the Ammo Select button to bring up the menu for all available ammo. The procedure for selecting a gun and its ammo is identical to the methodology you would use if on foot.

Commander

In this position, the controller layout gives you several valuable commands at your fingertips. With the tap of a button, you can order the driver to move to a location (line of sight) while another button tap will signal the gunner to assault a location (again, line of sight).

This position also allows you free camera control, although line of sight is often blocked by parts of the vehicle depending on which one you have boarded. Some large vehicles, such as main battle tanks, have three main weapons that can be deployed, in which case the commander can operate the third weapon. **[Screen 02]**

Tips and Tricks

If you are outside the vehicle, and your men are on board, you can easily use line of sight or map commands to send your men, vehicle and all, into battle to engage or assault an enemy location.

If you leave your men in the vehicle and you go off on your own, you can call them to you later by ordering them to a location near you. This comes in very handy if you want to go off on a stealth attack or a reconnaissance run and don't want to walk all the way back to where your men are located.

If you want to get a better view of your surroundings, switch to the gunner or commander; both of these positions allow you free control of the camera. Clicking the camera stick in either the commander or gunner location will zoom in for a better view. Click the stick repeatedly to cycle between zoomed and normal perspectives. **[Screen 03]**

You can issue a move command at any time, and from any position in the vehicle. This means that, even as a gunner, you can use the Command menu to tell the driver to move to a desired location. The same is true for engaging or assaulting the enemy [md] no need to switch to the commander position for these tasks.

When in larger, armored vehicles (APCs and tanks), always check for additional weapons when you're the gunner. More often than not, you will be on the smaller coaxial gun when you sign on as the gunner, so make sure to check (via Weapon Select) the availability of the larger cannons that armored vehicles offer. Also make sure to check for additional available ammo types as well for each gun.

HELICOPTER

When in a helicopter, you have the same basic seating positions, but they are termed as follows: pilot, co-pilot, gunner and passenger. The co-pilot and gunner positions operate nearly identically to the commander and gunner positions of a land based vehicle. You can issue orders or fire the main guns in these position; it is the pilot position that becomes interesting.

Pilot

The first thing you need to become accustomed to is flying the helicopter. The right stick (normally used to control the camera) controls the power or thrust and the rudder. The left stick controls the pitch and roll of the helicopter. As you are flying, you can see your speed and altitude displayed on screen (first person view) just below the directional bar located at the top center of the screen. **[Screen 04]**

Power and Rudder
A helicopter flies by pushing downward with air force generated from the top mounted propellers. The faster the propellers turn, the more downward force is generated, thus allowing the chopper to take to the air. You'll use the right stick in the up and down positions to control the power. Press up for more power, and pull down to reduce power.

You control the rudder by pressing the right stick to the left or right; this will rotate the nose of the chopper to the right or left. Use this right to left control to turn right and left.

Pitch and Roll
The left stick controls pitch (forward or rearward tilt) and roll (left or right tilt). Pushing the left stick forward will cause the chopper to pitch forward which is how you'll move. With forward pitch, the air force generated downward by the propellers will propel the chopper forward. The speed of your movement forward is dependent on the angle of the pitch. A slight pitch causes minor movement, while a greater pitch results in faster movement. However, be careful not to allow the pitch to stray beyond 25 degrees to the horizon. Any greater than that and movement and control will be compromised and hard to handle.

Roll, or a tilt to the right or left, will cause a strafing movement to the right or left. If you use a roll in conjunction with a rudder turn, the turn will be executed more sharply and quickly.

On your heads-up display, you'll see several horizontal lines marked at 0 for the center, negative increments (in steps of 5) going up, and positive increments (in steps of 5) going down; these indicate your pitch. **[Screen 05]**

In between these horizontal pitch lines are two other lines that come nearly together in a V shape. This indicates your helicopter. When this line tilts to the right or left (with reference to the pitch line) this indicates a roll in that direction. When the line moves toward one of the pitch lines, this indicates pitch or movement in that direction. A negative marker indicates backward pitch while a positive marker indicates forward pitch.

Flying
You'll have to use both sticks simultaneously to fly a helicopter correctly. Use the power and rudder control, combined with proper pitch and roll to enable you to move forward and make your turns. While you can keep the power at full throttle the entire time, you should develop a lighter touch for rudder, pitch, and roll controls. These are very sensitive, and the lightest of touches is all that is needed to maneuver.

As the pilot, if your chopper is equipped with forward weaponry, you can also fire on enemy targets using the Fire Weapon button. A targeting reticle is displayed in the forward view so that you can align your shots. As with other vehicles, if there is more than one weapon, you can use Weapon Select to change weapons.

Landing
This is by far the trickiest part of flying a helicopter. First you'll want to pick an open area clear of trees and other objects that the propellers could hit. Next, approach the area, and as you are nearly over your landing spot, pull back on the left stick to start backward pitch. This will slow your forward movement. Watch your speed and, as it approaches 0, slowly let your pitch return to neutral.

With the pitch at neutral, all downward force from the propellers is directed straight down. In this position, slowly ease off on the power by pulling back on the right stick. Watch your altitude as you do this, and make sure you don't fall too rapidly. Continue to slowly adjust your power down until you touch ground. Once down, turn off the engine or immediately disembark the chopper.

If you are using the first person view, then rely heavily on the pitch and roll indicators on your heads-up display, as well as the speed and altitude gauges. Keep a neutral roll and move towards 0 pitch for a good landing.

Tips and Tricks

If you get into an uncontrolled spin or turn, switch on the autopilot and let go of the sticks. The autopilot will work to stabilize your flight and return you to a hover at neutral pitch. From there, you are free to turn the autopilot off and try again.

Try switching to the third person view (click down on the right stick) if you are having problems controlling the chopper.

If you're having trouble flying or landing, switch to the co-pilot's seat and order the new pilot to do the job for you. **[Screen 06]**

03

US VEHICLES

US vehicles offer far more than just a means of transport. They are also rolling armaments capable of laying down some serious firepower. Here we will show you the stats of the heavy arms the US forces will bring to bear.

M1A2 ABRAMS
MAIN BATTLE TANK

This fearsome tank is the most powerful land unit of the US military. It represents a deadly threat to any land-based enemy unit in the field. Though extremely heavily armored, it is still vulnerable to anti-tank explosive weapons, especially from the rear. The M1A2's main cannon fires 120mm high explosive rounds capable of destroying buildings or the most heavily armored vehicles. **[Screen 01]** It is also equipped with two powerful machine guns to allow for infantry suppression.

CREW POSITIONS	VIEW MODES	WEAPONS	TOTAL AMMO
Driver	normal, night	none	–
Commander	normal, thermal	M2HB 12.7mm HMG	900
Gunner	normal, thermal	120mm Main Cannon	41
		M240 7.62mm (Coax)	7200

CHARACTERISTICS

Drive Type	Tracked	Off-Road Speed	48.28
Amphibious	no	Power	1500 @ 3000 rpm
Weight	64 tons	Torque	3950 lb/ft @ 1k rpm
Road Speed	67.6		

ARMOR RATING

Hull		Turret	
Location	Rating	Location	Rating
Front	10	Front	10
Side	4	Side	6
Rear	3	Rear	4
Top	4	Top	4
Bottom	3		

01

AAVP7A1 AMTRAK
AMPHIBIOUS ASSAULT VEHICLE

This is a highly versatile armored vehicle. It can be deployed as a marine vehicle to deliver troops to land en masse, which makes it a key component in any offshore invasion strategy. Its primary weapon is the Mk19 Grenade Launcher, and it also sports the same '50 caliber' machine gun as the M1A2 Abrams tank, though the AAVP7A1 version can store more ammunition. This combination of weapons makes it perfect for advancing assaults or attacking well fortified enemy positions.

The AAVP7A1 also comes equipped with 81mm smoke bombs, which will disperse an extremely large amount of smoke across are a wide area. This is the perfect aid for covering the force's approach during beach landings.

CREW POSITIONS	VIEW MODES	WEAPONS	TOTAL AMMO
Driver	normal, night	none	–
Gunner	normal, thermal	M2HB 0.50 Cal	1000
		Mk19 Grenade Launcher	768
Commander	normal, thermal	81mm Smoke Bombs	16

CHARACTERISTICS

Drive Type	Tracked	Off-Road Speed	40/15
Amphibious	Yes	Power	400 @ 2800 rpm
Weight	25 tons	Torque	825 ft/lb @ 2050 rpm
Road Speed	72 kph	Passengers	13

ARMOR RATING

Hull		Turret	
Location	Rating	Location	Rating
Front	2	Front	1
Side	1	Side	1
Rear	1	Rear	1
Top	1	Top	1
Bottom	1		

LAV-25 APC
ARMORED PERSONNEL CARRIER

As the name suggests, this is a heavily armored vehicle that is used to transport troops into battle. While it cannot carry as many troops as some other APC types, it is lightweight and armed with some seriously heavy weaponry. Its 25mm chain gun makes it a deadly threat to infantry and the extra M240s give it the ability to attack targets in multiple directions simultaneously. [Screen 02]

CREW POSITIONS	VIEW MODES	WEAPONS	TOTAL AMMO
Driver	normal, night	none	–
Commander	normal, thermal	M240 (Pintle)	600
Gunner	normal, thermal	25mm Bushmaster	630
		M240 (Coax)	1600

CHARACTERISTICS

Drive Type	Tracked	Off-Road Speed	40/15
Amphibious	Yes	Power	400 @ 2800 rpm
Weight	25 tons	Torque	825 ft/lb @ 2050 rpm
Road Speed	72 kph	Passengers	4

ARMOR RATING

Hull		Turret	
Location	**Rating**	**Location**	**Rating**
Front	2	Front	1
Side	1	Side	1
Rear	1	Rear	1
Top	1	Top	1
Bottom	1		

02

M1025 HMMWV
ARMORED ARMAMENT CARRIER

The HMMWV stands for high mobility multi-purpose wheeled vehicle. It comes in many different configurations to suit various purposes, such as cargo transport and an ambulance service. The armored armament carrier version is the only one that sports mounted weapons. [Screen 03] The HMMWV can be equipped with either the M2 machine gun or the Mk19 Grenade Launcher, but not both together.

CREW POSITIONS	VIEW MODES	WEAPONS	TOTAL AMMO
Driver	normal	none	–
Commander	normal	none	–
Gunner (M2HB Variant only)	normal	M2HB Heavy Machine Gun	600
Gunner (Mk19 Variant only)	normal	Mk19 Grenade Launcher	180

CHARACTERISTICS

Drive Type	4x4
Amphibious	no
Weight	3.5 tons
Road Speed	100
Off-Road Speed	60
Power	150 @ 3600 rpm
Steering	Front
Passengers (AAC Variant)	1
Passengers (Troop Carrier Variant)	6

ARMOR RATING

Hull	
Location	**Rating**
Front	1
Side	1
Rear	1
Top	1
Bottom	1

03

M939A2
TROOP TRANSPORT TRUCK

The M939A2 comes in three variants: troop transport, cargo carrier and tanker truck. The troop transport version is the one you'll see in Operation Flashpoint: Dragon Rising. **[Screen 01]** This is the US army's primary troop and cargo carrier, but does not feature any weapons or offensive capability and is not an armored vehicle.

CREW POSITIONS	VIEW MODES	WEAPONS	TOTAL AMMO
Driver	normal	none	–
Commander	normal	none	–
CHARACTERISTICS			
Drive Type		6x6	
Amphibious		no	
Weight		12.5 tons	
Road Speed		80	
Off-Road Speed		40	
Power		240 @ 2100 rpm	
Steering		Front	
Passengers (Transport variant only)		15	

01

DPV LIGHT BUGGY
DESERT PATROL VEHICLE

This is a high mobility vehicle that looks like a heavily armed buggy. It is lightly armored, but capable of high speeds, which makes it a hard target to hit. It is the speed and extreme off-road capabilities that make this vehicle such a valuable asset in missions where reaching key positions quickly is of vital importance. **[Screen 02]**

CREW POSITIONS	VIEW MODES	WEAPONS	TOTAL AMMO
Driver	normal	none	–
Commander	normal	M240 Machine Gun	600
Gunner	normal	M2HB Heavy Machine Gun	300
CHARACTERISTICS			
Drive Type		4x4	
Amphibious		no	
Weight		2 tons	
Road Speed		97 kph	
Off-Road Speed		97 kph	
Power		125	
Steering		Front	

02

SURC
PT BOAT

The SURC (or small unit riverine craft) is the US navy's primary patrol boat. There is a Mk19 Fully Automatic Grenade Launcher mounted on the SURC's aft, which is operated by the primary gunner. The SURC also features two M240 Machine Guns mounted on external pintles at the bow. The vehicle's secondary gunners can make use of these powerful machine guns. **[Screen 03]**

CREW POSITIONS	VIEW MODES	WEAPONS	TOTAL AMMO
Pilot	normal	none	–
Commander	normal	none	–
Gunner1	normal	Mk19 Grenade Launcher	180
Gunner2	normal	M240 Machine Gun	600
Gunner3	normal	M240 Machine Gun	600
CHARACTERISTICS			
Drive Type	Water Jet		
Weight	4.5 tons		
Speed	70 kph		

03

AH-6J LITTLE BIRD
ATTACK HELICOPTER

The 'Little Bird' is a Spec Ops attack helicopter, modified for stealth missions. It features a LAU-68 rocket pod, which fires Hydra 70 rockets with high explosive warheads. **[Screen 04]** It is an extremely capable offensive unit, and can be armed with Hellfire anti-tank missiles, or air-to-air Stinger missiles with a pair of M34 Mini-guns.

CREW POSITIONS	VIEW MODES	WEAPONS	TOTAL AMMO
Pilot	normal	LAU-68 70mm rocket pods	14
Pilot		M134 mini-guns	10000
Co-Pilot	normal	none	–
CHARACTERISTICS			
Drive Type	Rotary		
Weight	1.5 tons		
Cruise Speed	240 kph		
Max Dive Speed	280 kph		
Ceiling	500 m		
Countermeasures	yes		
Thermal	no		
Laser Designator	no		

04

AH-1Z
ATTACK HELICOPTER

The AH-1Z (also known as the 'Viper') is the newest and most impressive twin-engine attack helicopter in the US Marine Corps. It is built for speed (with a max speed of 255 mph/411 km/h) and armament, and fires the same Hydra 70 rockets as the Little Bird, but with added AIM-9 Sidewinder air-to-air capability. It also features a 20mm Gatling gun for low-flying infantry suppression. **[Screen 01]**

CREW POSITIONS	VIEW MODES	WEAPONS	TOTAL AMMO
Pilot	normal	LAU-61 70mm rocket pods	76
Pilot		AIM-9L Sidewinder	2
Gunner	normal, thermal	20mm M9/ Gatling Gun	750

CHARACTERISTICS	
Drive Type	Rotary
Weight	7 tons
Cruise Speed	260 kph
Max Dive Speed	400 kph
Ceiling	500 m
Countermeasures	18 flare
Thermal	yes
Laser Designator	yes

01

MH-60S
TRANSPORT HELICOPTER

The MH-60S is a transport helicopter, and is most often used for insertion and extraction purposes. Though it is armed with M134 door guns, it is not an offensive unit and, as such, the area must be clear of all anti-air threats for it to be deployed safely. **[Screen 02]** The MH-60S comes equipped either with two M134 Mini-guns, or two M2HB Machine Guns, one on each side door. The primary gunners use these to cover extractions in areas where there is infantry presence on the ground.

CREW POSITIONS	VIEW MODES	WEAPONS	TOTAL AMMO
Pilot	normal	none	–
Co-pilot	normal	none	–
Gunner1	normal	M134 mini-gun	5000
Gunner2	normal	M134 mini-gun	5000

CHARACTERISTICS	
Drive Type	Rotary
Weight	8 tons
Cruise Speed	260 kph
Max Dive Speed	300 kph
Ceiling	500 m
Countermeasures	24 flare
Thermal	no
Laser Designator	no

02

PLA VEHICLES

The PLA have their own selection of combat-ready vehicles. Most of the PLA's arsenal is custom built by Chinese contractors to compete with (and in some cases exceed) the specifications of each vehicle's US and Russian equivalent. These are serious ordnance, and not to be taken lightly.

ZTZ-99 TYPE 99
MAIN BATTLE TANK

This is the PLA's biggest gun as far as land vehicles are concerned. The ZTZ-99 (usually referred to as the 'Type 99') is capable of competing with the best that US battle tanks have to offer in terms of firepower, and can use a large variety of different shells to make it a highly versatile threat. It is not quite as well armored as the M1A2 Abrams, but is still capable of withstanding more punishment than most other land vehicles. **[Screen 03]**

CREW POSITIONS	VIEW MODES	WEAPONS	TOTAL AMMO
Driver	normal, night	none	–
Commander	normal, thermal	QJC-88 12.7mm Heavy Machine Gun	200
Gunner	normal, thermal	125mm Main Cannon	30
		Type 67 II 7.62mm Machine Gun (Coax)	1750

CHARACTERISTICS

Drive Type	Tracked	Off-Road Speed	60
Amphibious	no	Power	1500
Weight	52 tons	Torque	22.78 p/w
Road Speed	80		

ARMOR RATING

Hull		Turret	
Location	Rating	Location	Rating
Front	7	Front	8
Side	4	Side	6
Rear	4	Rear	4
Top	4	Top	4
Bottom	2		

03

TYPE 89A
SP TANK DESTROYER

This is a 6x-wheeled, highly mobile attack vehicle. Its primary purpose is as a 'tank destroyer', and it uses a 105mm smooth bore cannon to get the job done. This vehicle is lethal to tanks, as even the M1A2 Abrams' composite armor cannot withstand the Type 89's main cannon fire. Air-to-ground rockets are recommended to combat the Type 89A.[Screen 01]

CREW POSITIONS	VIEW MODES	WEAPONS	TOTAL AMMO
Driver	normal, night	none	–
Commander	normal, thermal	QJC-88 12.7mm Heavy Machine Gun	300
Gunner	normal, thermal	105mm Main Cannon	40
		Type 67 II 7.62mm Machine Gun (Coax)	2000

CHARACTERISTICS

Drive Type	6-Wheeled	Off-Road Speed	40
Amphibious	no	Power	320 @ 2500
Weight	19 tons	Steering	2 Front
Road Speed	80		

ARMOR RATING

Hull		Turret	
Location	Rating	Location	Rating
Front	1	Front	1
Side	1	Side	1
Rear	1	Rear	1
Top	1	Top	1
Bottom	1		

01

ZBD97 TYPE 97
INFANTRY FIGHTING VEHICLE

This tank is adapted to take on infantry squads, and is nicknamed the 'Type 97', in keeping with other PLA vehicle names. It is tread-driven like the Type 95 tank, but is larger and more heavily armored. Its main cannon is a threat to all land vehicles, and the 30mm autocannon is an extremely powerful anti-infantry weapon. [Screen 02]

CREW POSITIONS	VIEW MODES	WEAPONS	TOTAL AMMO
Driver	normal, night	none	–
Commander	normal, thermal	none	–
Gunner	normal, thermal	100mm Main Cannon	39
		30mm autocannon	1000

CHARACTERISTICS

Drive Type	Tracked	Off-Road Speed	40/10
Amphibious	Yes	Power	360
Weight	10 tons	Torque	–
Road Speed	60	Passengers	7

ARMOR RATING

Hull		Turret	
Location	Rating	Location	Rating
Front	2	Front	2
Side	1	Side	1
Rear	1	Rear	1
Top	1	Top	1
Bottom	1		

02

TYPE 92 WZ551A
WHEELED APC

The Type 92 is the newest variant of the WZ551 armored personnel carrier. It is highly comparable to the LAV-25, with the same weapon types, but it is based on a 6x6 design. The Type 92 is slower than the LAV-25, but can carry more passengers (up to a maximum of 9). **[Screen 03]**

CREW POSITIONS	VIEW MODES	WEAPONS	TOTAL AMMO
Driver	normal, night	none	–
Commander	normal, thermal	none	–
Gunner	normal, thermal	25mm autocannon	480
		Type 67 II 7.62mm Machine Gun (Coax)	1000

CHARACTERISTICS			
Drive Type	2 Front, 6-Wheeled	Off-Road Speed	45
Amphibious	Yes	Power	40/10
Weight	13 tons	Torque	–
Road Speed	85	Passengers	9

ARMOR RATING			
Hull		**Turret**	
Location	Rating	Location	Rating
Front	2	Front	1
Side	1	Side	1
Rear	1	Rear	1
Top	1	Top	1
Bottom	1		

03

TYPE 95 SPAAG
SP ANTI-AIRCRAFT ARTILLERY

The Type 95 is a light tank, designed purely as an anti-aircraft vehicle. This makes the Type 95 perhaps the PLA's most important defensive unit owing to the reliance of the US on air strikes to gain tactical advantages. It is armed with four QW-2 SAM infrared homing missiles and 25mm autocannons to defend the unit from infantry threats. **[Screen 04]**

CREW POSITIONS	VIEW MODES	WEAPONS	TOTAL AMMO
Driver	normal, night	none	–
Commander	normal, thermal	none	–
Gunner	normal, thermal	25mm autocannon	4000
		QW-2 Surface-to-Air Missiles	4

CHARACTERISTICS			
Drive Type	Tracked	Off-Road Speed	35
Amphibious	No	Power	320
Weight	23 tons	Torque	–
Road Speed	50		

ARMOR RATING			
Hull		**Turret**	
Location	Rating	Location	Rating
Front	2	Front	1
Side	1	Side	1
Rear	1	Rear	1
Top	1	Top	1
Bottom	1		

04

BJ2022
OFF-ROAD VEHICLE

The BJ2022 can come is many varieties, and is a very adaptable vehicle. It is a 4X4 vehicle, comparable to the US HMMWV. It comes in three primary versions, standard, heavy machine gun and grenade launcher. [Screen 01] The standard version does not have a mounted weapon fitted. All versions of the BJ2022 are extremely valuable for covering distance between engagements and heading off-road to scout the terrain.

CREW POSITIONS	VIEW MODES	WEAPONS	TOTAL AMMO
Driver	normal	none	–
Commander	normal	none	–
Gunner (QJC-88 variant only)	normal	QJC-88 12.7mm Heavy Machine Gun	600
Gunner (LG3 variant only)	normal	LG3 Grenade Launcher	180

CHARACTERISTICS			
Drive Type	4x4	Power	100kW @ 3600
Amphibious	No	Torque	313Nm @ 2000
Weight	2 tons	Steering	1 Front
Road Speed	150	Passengers (Standard variant)	7
Off-Road Speed	100	Passengers (QJC-88 and LG3 variants)	4

01

SX2190
TRANSPORT TRUCK

Another highly versatile vehicle, the SX2190 is one of the PLA's main workhorses. It is used for many purposes, but the four types seen in Dragon Rising are: troop transport, fuel truck, cargo truck and missile platform. The transport truck version is the most important one to look out for in combat situations, as it could be carrying up to 22 well armed passengers. The missile platform version represents a serious anti-naval threat, and as such is often the US fire-team's primary target in missions where naval support is vital. [Screen 02]

CREW POSITIONS	VIEW MODES	WEAPONS	TOTAL AMMO
Driver	normal	none	–
Commander	normal	none	–

CHARACTERISTICS			
Drive Type	6x6	Off-Road Speed	40
Amphibious	No	Power	–
Weight	15 tons	Torque	206kW @ 2,400r/min
Road Speed	80	Passengers (Transport variant)	22

02

FAV
FAST ACTION VEHICLE

This is the PLA's equivalent to the DPV; an extremely fast and mobile unit with supreme off-road capability. **[Screen 03]** It is well armed with heavy machine guns, which give it amazing effective combat range when combined with its mobility. Its primary use is to get to mission-critical locations quickly without the need for a high profile aerial insertion, and it also makes a great mobile weapons platform.

CREW POSITIONS	VIEW MODES	WEAPONS	TOTAL AMMO
Driver	normal	none	–
Commander	normal	Type 67 II 7.62mm Machine Gun	450
Gunner	normal	QJC-88 12.7mm Heavy Machine Gun	300

CHARACTERISTICS			
Drive Type	4x4	Off-Road Speed	80
Amphibious	No	Power	85
Weight	2 tons	Steering	1 Front
Road Speed	140		

03

PTBR
PT BOAT

The PLA's primary shallow water patrol vehicle, the PTBR is well armed and fast moving. Patrol squads have access to three powerful weapons; a QJC-88 Heavy Machine Gun at the bow, an LG3 Grenade Launcher at the port aft, and a Type 67 II GPMG at the starboard aft. The PTBR is a deadly addition to the PLA's arsenal in any engagement near to water. **[Screen 04]**

CREW POSITIONS	VIEW MODES	WEAPONS	TOTAL AMMO
Pilot	normal	none	–
Gunner1	normal	QJC-88 12.7mm Heavy Machine Gun	600
Gunner2	normal	LG3 Grenade Launcher	180
Gunner3	normal	Type 67 II 7.62 Machine Gun	450

CHARACTERISTICS			
Drive Type	3x Outboard	Speed	120
Weight	4 tons	Passengers	6

04

MI-171
TRANSPORT HELICOPTER

The Mi-171 in two versions, the Mi-171, which has no weapons equipped, and the Mi-171V5 armed variant. The armed variant features HF25 rocket pods, much like the Z-10, which makes it uniquely well armed for a transport helicopter. Both versions of the Mi-171 can carry a maximum of 19 passengers. [Screen 01]

CREW POSITIONS	VIEW MODES	WEAPONS	TOTAL AMMO
Pilot (Armed variant only)	normal	HF25 57mm rocket pods	132
Co-pilot	normal	none	–

CHARACTERISTICS			
Drive Type	Rotary	Ceiling	500 m
Weight	10 tons	Countermeasures	12 flare
Cruise Speed	240 kph	Passengers	19
Max Dive Speed	260 kph		

01

Z-10
ATTACK HELICOPTER

The PLA make extensive use of the Z-10 to patrol their captured territory. The Z-10 is comparable to the US AH-1Z in terms of speed and maneuverability. It is armed with both air-to-ground rockets and air-to-air missiles, as well as a 30mm chin cannon. This combination of weapons gives it the ability to enter virtually any combat zone as a serious threat. [Screen 02]

CREW POSITIONS	VIEW MODES	WEAPONS	TOTAL AMMO
Pilot	normal	HF25 57mm Rocket Pods	44
		TY-90 Air-to-Air Missiles	8
Gunner	normal, thermal	30mm autocannon	250

CHARACTERISTICS			
Drive Type	Rotary	Ceiling	500 m
Weight	6 tons	Countermeasures	18 flare
Cruise Speed	260 kph	Passengers	–
Max Dive Speed	400 kph		

02

US VEHICLE WEAPONS

120MM M256A1
MAIN CANNON

This is the very impressive main cannon of the US M1A2 Abrams tank. This weapon is capable of destroying most targets in one shot, including heavily armored units. The gunner takes control of this weapon, and also has control of the turret's directional aiming independently of the direction the tank is facing.

WEAPON STATS

Ammunition	120mm APFSDS	120mm HEAT
Effective Range	1500	1500
Max Damage vs Humans	30	25
Damage vs Vehicles	14	10
Fragmentation Radius	4	18
Magazine Capacity	–	–
Reload Time	7	7
Fire Mode	Single	Single
Max Rate of Fire	–	–
Scope Type	Thermal	Thermal
Scope Magnification	Variable	Variable

M240
MACHINE GUN (COAX)

The M240 Machine Gun is a coaxial weapon, which means it is a secondary weapon mounted alongside a heavier, more powerful primary weapon such as the main cannon of a tank. This weapon is at the tank commander's disposal, offering the main gunner support on his blind side.

WEAPON STATS

Ammunition	7.62 x 51mm FMJ
Effective Range	1000
Max Damage vs Humans	8
Damage vs Vehicles	1
Fragmentation Radius	–
Magazine Capacity	100
Reload Time	3
Fire Mode	Full
Max Rate of Fire	5
Scope Type	–
Scope Magnification	–

M2HB
HEAVY MACHINE GUN

This heavy machine gun utilizes a 12.7mm caliber round, which, in inches is .50 or 50 caliber. This earns it the nickname of the '50 cal'. It is a heavy, vehicle-mounted weapon with a rather slow rate of fire (compared to other machine guns). The gunner can use this weapon instead of the main cannon to suppress infantry units.

WEAPON STATS

Ammunition	12.7 x 99mm FMJ
Effective Range	1000
Max Damage vs Humans	10
Damage vs Vehicles	1
Fragmentation Radius	–
Magazine Capacity	200
Reload Time	3
Fire Mode	Full
Max Rate of Fire	5
Scope Type	–
Scope Magnification	–

MK19
GRENADE LAUNCHER

The Mk19 is a fully automatic grenade launcher capable of firing five 40mm HE or HEDP grenades per second. The air-cooled design ensures it will not 'cook off' during sustained instances of fire. When a weapon 'cooks off' it becomes so hot that the ammunition explodes inside the weapon, which is not a good thing.

WEAPON STATS

Ammunition	40 x 53mm HE	40 x 53mm HEDP
Effective Range	900	900
Max Damage vs Humans	20	20
Damage vs Vehicles	3	5
Fragmentation Radius	7	6
Magazine Capacity	96	96
Reload Time	4	4
Fire Mode	Full	Full
Max Rate of Fire	5	5
Scope Type	–	–
Scope Magnification	–	–

03

25MM M242
BUSHMASTER CHAIN GUN

This is a high-powered, chain-fed autocannon, capable of both semi-automatic and fully automatic firing modes. It is generally mounted on the LAV-25 APC and the M2A3 Bradley tank. It is effective against aerial targets such as helicopters, and can easily suppress infantry units, even in heavily fortified positions.

WEAPON STATS

Ammunition	25mm APDS	25mm APHE
Effective Range	1500	1500
Max Damage vs Humans	20	20
Damage vs Vehicles	6	5
Fragmentation Radius	1	4
Magazine Capacity	60	150
Reload Time	3	3
Fire Mode	Full	Full
Max Rate of Fire	3	3
Scope Type	Thermal	Thermal
Scope Magnification	Variable	Variable

LAU-68
ROCKET POD

The LAU-68 is identical to the LAU-61, apart from its lower ammo capacity. You'll find this one mounted on the AH-6J 'Little Bird' attack helicopter. It fires Hydra 70 rockets, with high explosive, impact-detonating warheads.

WEAPON STATS

Ammunition	70mm unguided rocket
Effective Range	1000
Max Damage vs Humans	20
Damage vs Vehicles	8
Fragmentation Radius	14
Magazine Capacity	7
Reload Time	–
Fire Mode	Single
Max Rate of Fire	–
Scope Type	–
Scope Magnification	–

M134
MINI-GUN

The M134 Mini-gun is a Gatling gun, which utilizes six rotating barrels to deliver an extremely high rate of fire. It is called 'mini' because it is smaller and utilizes less powerful rounds than larger Gatling guns such as the Vulcan.

WEAPON STATS

Ammunition	7.62 x 51mm FMJ
Effective Range	900
Max Damage vs Humans	8
Damage vs Vehicles	1
Fragmentation Radius	–
Magazine Capacity	5000
Reload Time	–
Fire Mode	Full
Max Rate of Fire	15
Scope Type	–
Scope Magnification	–

LAU-61
ROCKET POD

This is an aircraft mounted rocket launcher or 'pod' that launches Hydra 70 rockets. This one is mounted on the AH-1Z attack chopper, and is a higher capacity (19 shot) version of the LAU-68 found on the Little Bird. Though the missiles are unguided, they are still a lethal threat to slow moving tanks.

WEAPON STATS

Ammunition	70mm unguided rocket
Effective Range	1000
Max Damage vs Humans	20
Damage vs Vehicles	8
Fragmentation Radius	14
Magazine Capacity	19
Reload Time	–
Fire Mode	Single
Max Rate of Fire	–
Scope Type	–
Scope Magnification	–

PLA VEHICLE WEAPONS

125MM
MAIN CANNON

The Type 99's 125mm main cannon is a highly destructive weapon, capable of being used at high precision over incredible distances. It can fire a variety of different rounds, depending on the result required. Some offer high armor penetration, while others will have a larger blast radius.

WEAPON STATS

Ammunition	125mm APFSDS	125mm ATGM	125mm HEF	125mm HEAT
Effective Range	1500	4500	1500	1500
Max Damage vs Humans	30	25	25	25
Damage vs Vehicles	13	10	7	10
Fragmentation Radius	4	12	22	16
Magazine Capacity	–	–	–	–
Reload Time8	6	6	6	6
Fire Mode	Single	Single	Single	Single
Max Rate of Fire	–	–	–	–
Scope Type	Thermal	Thermal	Thermal	Thermal
Scope Magnification	Variable	Variable	Variable	Variable

105MM
MAIN CANNON (TYPE 89A)

This is the main cannon of the ZSD-89 or Type 89 PLA APC. It offers almost the same variety of possible rounds as the Type 99's main cannon, with very similar results in firepower.

WEAPON STATS

Ammunition	105mm APFSDS	105mm ATGM	105mm HEF	105mm HEAT
Effective Range	1500	4500	1500	1500
Max Damage vs Humans	30	25	25	25
Damage vs Vehicles	11	9	6	9
Fragmentation Radius	3.5	10	20	14
Magazine Capacity	–	–	–	–
Reload Time8	8	8	8	8
Fire Mode	Single	Single	Single	Single
Max Rate of Fire	–	–	–	–
Scope Type	Thermal	Thermal	Thermal	Thermal
Scope Magnification	Variable	Variable	Variable	Variable

TYPE-67 II
MACHINE GUN (COAX)

This coaxial, or secondary machine gun is mounted on vehicles alongside a larger, primary cannon type weapon. This is operated by the main gunner when dealing with infantry threats, and has a high ammunition count for prolonged firing.

WEAPON STATS

Ammunition	7.62x 54mm FMJ
Effective Range	1000
Max Damage vs Humans	8
Damage vs Vehicles	1
Fragmentation Radius	–
Magazine Capacity	250
Reload Time	3
Fire Mode	Full
Max Rate of Fire	5
Scope Type	–
Scope Magnification	-

QJC-88 HMG
HEAVY MACHINE GUN

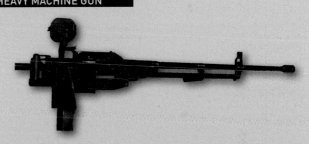

This emplaced, or secondary pintle-mounted machine gun is used on tanks alongside their main cannon. This weapon is usually operated by the commander to aim at closer targets that the main cannon would not fire at so effectively, though it is also a highly effective long range machine gun.

WEAPON STATS

Ammunition	12.7x108mm FMJ
Effective Range	1000
Max Damage vs Humans	8
Damage vs Vehicles	2
Fragmentation Radius	–
Magazine Capacity	100
Reload Time	3
Fire Mode	Full
Max Rate of Fire	5
Scope Type	–
Scope Magnification	–

100MM MAIN CANNON
(TYPE 97)

This is the primary cannon of the Type 97 PLA tank. This cannon uses high impact rounds with a large blast radius. As with the larger cannons of other PLA tanks, this cannon has ATGM and HEF options for incredible anti-tank range or a large fragmentation radius for infantry threats.

WEAPON STATS

Ammunition	100mm ATGM	100mm HEF
Effective Range	4500	1500
Max Damage vs Humans	25	25
Damage vs Vehicles	9	6
Fragmentation Radius	10	20
Magazine Capacity	–	–
Reload Time	7	7
Fire Mode	Single	Single
Max Rate of Fire	–	–
Scope Type	Thermal	Thermal
Scope Magnification	Variable	Variable

30MM AUTOCANNON
(TYPE 97)

This is the secondary cannon of the ZBD-97 or Type 97 tank. Though it uses much smaller rounds than the main cannon, this is still a highly effective anti-armor weapon.

WEAPON STATS

Ammunition	30mm AP	30mm APHE
Effective Range	1500	1500
Max Damage vs Humans	20	20
Damage vs Vehicles	7	6
Fragmentation Radius	1	5
Magazine Capacity	250	250
Reload Time	3	3
Fire Mode	Full	Full
Max Rate of Fire	3	3
Scope Type	Thermal	Thermal
Scope Magnification	Variable	Variable

25MM AUTOCANNON
(TYPE 92)

This is the primary cannon or big gun, of the Type 92, 6-wheeled APC. It offers a similar high fragmentation threat to the Type 97's secondary cannon.

WEAPON STATS

Ammunition	25mm AP	25mm APHE
Effective Range	1500	1500
Max Damage vs Humans	20	20
Damage vs Vehicles	6	5
Fragmentation Radius	1	4
Magazine Capacity	120	120
Reload Time	3	3
Fire Mode	Full	Full
Max Rate of Fire	3	3
Scope Type	Thermal	Thermal
Scope Magnification	Variable	Variable

25MM AUTOCANNON
(TYPE 95)

This is the main cannon of the Type 95, tread driven armored tank used by the PLA. It uses exploding, armor piercing rounds to take out enemy vehicles with a relatively high rate of fire.

WEAPON STATS

Ammunition	25mm APHE
Effective Range	1500
Max Damage vs Humans	20
Damage vs Vehicles	5
Fragmentation Radius	4
Magazine Capacity	999
Reload Time	–
Fire Mode	Full
Max Rate of Fire	20
Scope Type	Thermal
Scope Magnification	Variable

LG3
GRENADE LAUNCHER

This vehicle-mounted, fully automatic grenade launcher is capable of firing 5x40mm HE or HEDP grenades per second. A truly deadly and fierce weapon that is sometimes mounted on the BJ2022.

WEAPON STATS

Ammunition	40 x 53mm HE	40 x 53mm HEDP
Effective Range	900	900
Max Damage vs Humans	20	20
Damage vs Vehicles	3	5
Fragmentation Radius	7	6
Magazine Capacity	30	30
Reload Time	4	4
Fire Mode	Full	Full
Max Rate of Fire	5	5
Scope Type	–	–
Scope Magnification	–	–

HF-25
ROCKET POD

These rocket pods (launchers) can be found mounted on the PLA's various attack helicopters. They are unguided air-to-ground rockets used to eliminate slow moving targets or strike fortified enemy positions.

WEAPON STATS	
Ammunition	57mm Unguided Rocket
Effective Range	1000
Max Damage vs Humans	20
Damage vs Vehicles	7
Fragmentation Radius	12
Magazine Capacity	22
Reload Time	–
Fire Mode	Single
Max Rate of Fire	–
Scope Type	–
Scope Magnification	–

30MM
AUTOCANNON (Z-10)

This is the main chin cannon of the PLA's WZ-10 attack helicopter. It is designed to take out armored vehicles, but is equally effective against enemy infantry, making a patrolling Z-10 a very dangerous foe.

WEAPON STATS	
Ammunition	30mm APHE
Effective Range	1500
Max Damage vs Humans	20
Damage vs Vehicles	6
Fragmentation Radius	5
Magazine Capacity	250
Reload Time	–
Fire Mode	Full
Max Rate of Fire	6
Scope Type	Thermal
Scope Magnification	Variable

MISSION BRIEFING
CHAPTER 04

Operation Flashpoint: Dragon Rising presents you with a highly realistic first person combat simulation. From the detailed weapon and vehicle make-up, to the incredible enemy and team-mate AI, this gaming experience is truly intense. Faced with 11 missions, this campaign is not easy to get through, but by following the expert advice within this Mission Briefing, your chances of survival are all but guaranteed. Read on to find out how the pros tackle the PLA and beat them into submission!

ELEMENTS OF THE MISSION BRIEFING
CHAPTER 04

In this chapter you'll find the full and detailed walkthrough for each and every Campaign Mission in Operation Flashpoint: Dragon Rising. Each mission entry will give you in-depth information concerning your objectives, available weaponry, detailed maps, and Intel on how you should proceed in order to be successful. The information will be presented as follows:

① Mission Title and Briefing
Here you'll see the full title of the mission as well as some text giving you a brief overview of your objectives.

② Mission Objectives
Listed here are the Primary, Secondary, and any Bonus Objectives for the mission. All Primary objectives need to be completed in order to succeed with the mission. Secondary and Bonus Objectives are extra challenges to you that will often unlock an Achievement or Trophy.

③ Weapons & Vehicles
Here you will find a list of all weapons and vehicles used in the mission by both the US and the PLA. It should be noted that, on occasion, some vehicles are off-screen and not available to the player, but instead lend supporting fire in the form of Fire Missions.

④ Mission Overview Map
This map shows the entire area of the mission and shows the planned RV route through the mission. The RV points listed on the map will be referenced in the walkthrough text below.

⑤ Equipment & Vehicles Map
This special map shows the location and inventory contents of all ammo crates in the mission area. Also detailed are emplaced weapon and vehicle locations. The overview text gives you a general rundown of the equipment and vehicles in the area and a few pointers on how to utilize what is available.

⑥ Mission Walkthrough
Finally you come to the brunt of the matter. The walkthrough will utilize zoomed maps so you get a closer look at certain areas, and will give text guidance on how you should proceed. Each text entry is preceded by an RV (Rendezvous) point as shown on the overview map. By looking at the overview map and finding the RV points, you will always know where you are, where you should go, and what you should do to be successful.

GENERAL TIPS

RV Points

The overview map for each area shows the suggested route you should take. However, this is a free roaming environment, and you can always opt to take a different route. In some cases, taking an obscure route can keep you out of harm's way so that you avoid combat entirely. When faced with a difficult situation, you may want to pursue the less traveled road, especially if a particular mission is giving you trouble. Simply find a route through the woods or around the aggressors, and you can often skirt combat and disaster entirely.

It should be noted that, while you are free to roam, there are limitations. Should you travel too far off the beaten path, and so go far away from the direction of your objectives, the game will warn you that you are too far out. If you continue to stray and do not attempt to get back close to your objective, the mission will fail as you will be considered AWOL (Absent Without Leave). .

Checkpoints

This walkthrough is based on the Normal difficulty setting, and you are highly advised to play through the game the first time on Normal. At that difficulty level, you are given far more on-screen indicators and far more checkpoints to save your progress. Proper utilization of checkpoints is crucial if you wish to succeed. Once you have triggered a checkpoint you can reload manually at any time to try a particular area again with a different strategy, or simply reload if you have been killed. On a first pass through the game, checkpoints will be a very welcome sight indeed.

Achievements and Trophies

At key points within the walkthrough you will see notifications that it is possible to unlock an Achievement or Trophy at that point in the mission. Pay attention to these so that you fully understand what must happen in order to unlock the specified item. If you are having trouble with any of the Achievements or Trophies, then please refer to the Extras chapter where you'll find a full guide detailing how to unlock each and every one of them.

Get Creative

This walkthrough is laid out to take you through each mission as it was designed to be played on the most basic level. You will be guided through each area, and shown how to confront the enemy whenever they appear. However, as mentioned before, this is a free roaming experience: so feel free to break away and try to do things a bit differently so that you find your own playing style.

Many confrontations are not required, so you may just want to skip them. Further, many of the friendly vehicles that are normally driven by friendly USMC teams can be taken over for your own use, which will drastically change the dynamics of the mission. When you see a friendly vehicle, don't hesitate to experiment and take control of it to see how that changes the mission **[Screen 01]**.

Use Your Map

The map can be one of your most useful and powerful tools. Not only does it show the lay of the land, but it will also display any PLA enemies, vehicles, and objective points that have been spotted. In using the map, you can see where you are going, what your are facing, and can even give your men long range orders that line of sight simply can't cover. Further, via the map, you can stack orders so that it is possible to give your men a chain of commands that they will execute in sequential order. Effective use of the map can often mean the difference between success and failure.

Recon the Area

When you are approaching a new area where the PLA may be present, it is always helpful to use your binoculars to scan ahead and see what awaits you **[Screen 02]**. This is best done from high lookout points such as a hill or mountain. When you look ahead and spot an enemy, they will show up on your map, which makes it far easier to track the enemy and know what you are walking into. Never walk into an area blind if you can help it! Make use of your binoculars to scout forward areas, which in turn will make your map (due to PLA icons showing up) all the more useful.

Send in the Scouts

In some situations, you may not be able to see what lies ahead. In these cases it may prove helpful to send one of your men forward to scout the area. By selecting just one man and then using the map and the Move command, you can send him ahead to scout the area and spot any PLA trouble. In doing this, he'll often spot PLA causing them to appear on the map making planning your own route far easier. Should your scout encounter the enemy and be pinned down, make haste to come to his aid with suppressing fire so that he can fall back and rejoin your team.

Don't Die!

You have a Medic with you in every mission. You should strive to protect him as he can fully heal you if you are hurt. When you are shot and bleeding out, you can use your Field Dressing to stop the bleeding and save your own life, but often you will have sustained damage to an arm (which affects your ability to aim) or damage to a leg (which will take away your ability to sprint). If you use the command radial to call the Medic to you, he will use his Medical Kit to fully heal you thus giving you a new lease of life.

A Medic can even pull you back from death's door if you are incapacitated. In that case, you will find yourself lying on the ground and bleeding out with only one command available: Medic **[Screen 03]**. Call him immediately, and if he makes it in time, you'll be fully revived. Don't underestimate the usefulness of your Medic; rely on him as often as needed to ensure your success.

DRAGON RISING
MISSION 01

The Dragon Rising mission has two main sections that can be completed in any order. The southern section of the island hides the main objective, which is to destroy the radar. The northern side of the island has three Secondary Objective targets, 2 x SAM Missile launchers and a Sunburn anti-ship system.

Equipment and Vehicles

At the start of the mission at RV1, there is an ammo crate you can raid for a Marksman that will come in handy later in the mission, and don't overlook the abandoned vehicles you can use in the south. To the north, you'll find a powerful Javelin Missile as well as an abandoned PLA vehicle that you can commandeer for your own use if need be. To the west, you'll find an assortment of long-range weapons. The M82 Sniper rifle being the superior choice for tackling the western SAM site. And don't overlook the abandoned PLA chopper on the western coast, which you can use for the Bonus Objective.

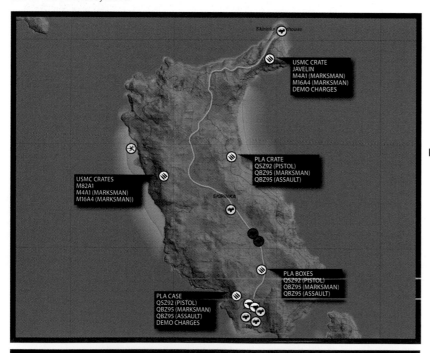

MISSION WEAPONS AND VEHICLES

Item	US
Weapons	US Knife
	MEU (SOC) Pistol
	MP5A4 Sub-Machine Gun
	M16A4 Assault Rifle (Marksman)
	M4A1 Assault Rifle (Marksman)
	Mk17 Mod 0 Assault Rifle (Marksman)
	Mk16 Mod 0 Assault Rifle (Assault)
	M249 Light Machine Gun
	Mk48 Mod 0 Medium Machine Gun
	M21 Sniper Rifle
	M107 Anti Material Rifle
	US Fragmentation Grenade
	US Smoke Grenade
	US Coloured Smoke Grenade Red
	US Coloured Smoke Grenade Yellow
	US Claymore
	US Anti Personnel Mine
	US Anti Tank Mine
	US Demolition Charge
	IR Stobe
	FGM-148 Javelin Guided Anti-Tank Missile
	SMAW Rocket Launcher
Vehicles	MH-60S

Item	PLA
Weapons	PLA Knife
	QSZ92 Pistol
	QBZ95 Assault Rifle
	QBZ95 Assault Rifle (Marksman)
	QBZ95 Assault Rifle (Assault)
	Type 81-1 Assault Rifle (Marksman)
	QBB95 Light Machine Gun
	Type 67-II Medium Machine Gun
	PLA Fragmentation Grenade
	PLA Smoke Grenade
	PLA Coloured Smoke Grenade Red
	PLA Anti Personnel Mine
	Field Dressing PLA
	PF98 Queen Bee Rocket Launcher
Vehicles	Type 97 Infantry Fighting Vehicle
	BJS2022 with HMG
	Mi-171 Transport
	SX2190 Missile Launcher
Emplacements	QJC 88 Heavy Machine Gun *

* Tall mount

Primary Objectives	Secondary Objectives	Bonus Objectives
Destroy Early Warning Radar	Destroy Surface-to-Air Missiles	Skirinka Island Tour
Secure Landing Zone	Destroy Sunburn anti-ship system	
Extract by Helicopter	Destroy Surface-to-Air Missiles	

OBJECTIVE OVERVIEW

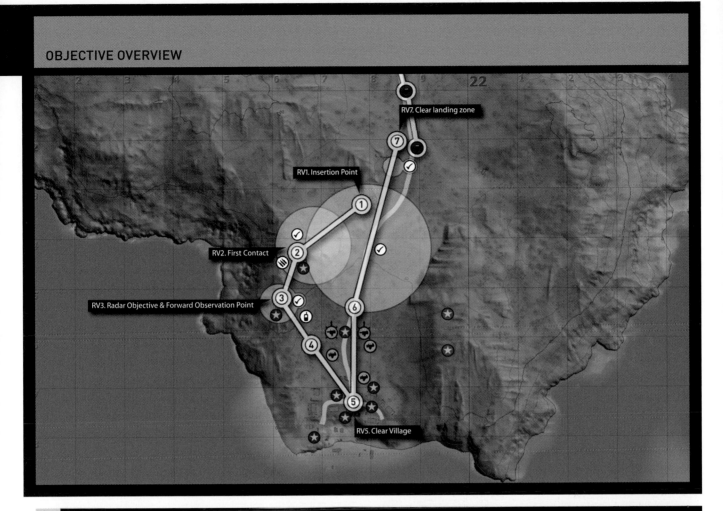

RV7. Clear landing zone

RV1. Insertion Point

RV2. First Contact

RV3. Radar Objective & Forward Observation Point

RV5. Clear Village

PRIMARY MISSION OBJECTIVES

1   Once the opening speech is over, you'll have control of your character. You are the leader of a four-man Fire Team codenamed Saber 2 and, as the leader, it is your job to lead your men into combat. You find yourself in an open area after being dropped off by helicopter. This initial area is free of enemy presence, and is a great distance away from the nearest enemy. Because of this, you can safely fire your weapons here and the enemy will not be alerted to your presence. Now is a good time to familiarize yourself with the controls of the game, and even fire off a few rounds if you like. Be mindful of this starting area, as it is the LZ that will also be used to extract you at the end of the mission.

In this area you'll find a small, unmanned defensive position consisting of sandbags and camouflage netting. At that position, you'll also find your first set of ammo crates **[Screen 01]**. Approach these crates, and the interaction Hand icon will appear. Interact with the crates, and a menu will appear on screen showing you the contents of the crates. The QBZ-95 Marksman rifle is a great choice here. The scope on that rifle will allow you to zoom in from a distance and snipe the upcoming enemies in relative safety.

2   When you're ready, begin your mission by following the RV Marker. This small yellow flag that appears on screen will show you your suggested route to your next objective. By following RV Markers, you'll always know where to go next. The current RV Marker will lead you to a small abandoned building surrounded by a crumbling wall. Have your men follow you to this location. You can either walk around the wall or climb over it. If you choose to climb over it, pick a low spot in the wall and approach it. Once you are near, the interaction Hand icon will appear. Interact with the wall to get over it.

Now that you are here, your first enemy encounter is fast approaching. To the South, a new RV Marker will have spawned, and you'll soon see two enemy PLA soldiers coming round the building in the distance. The PLA soldiers will take cover behind some sandbags and begin attacking you.

Quickly issue the command to have your men lay down Suppressing Fire on the PLAs' location. While your men are doing this, go to the right and make your way south through the woods and flank the enemy soldiers. Make sure you stay far enough into the woods to avoid being detected. Once you are slightly south of the enemy, make your way up and behind them and take

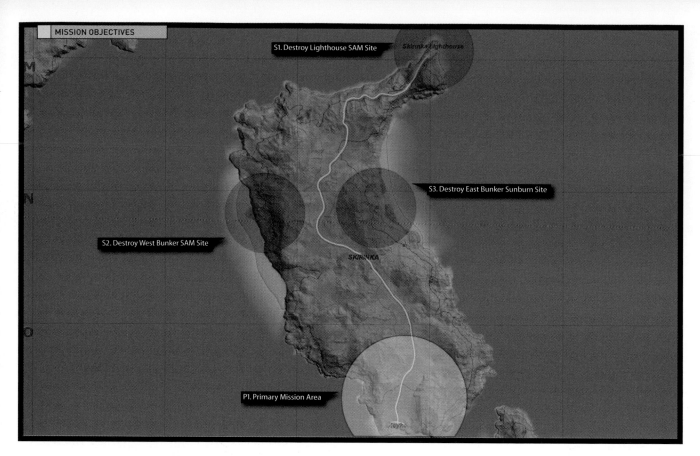

S1. Destroy Lighthouse SAM Site

Skirinka Lighthouse

S3. Destroy East Bunker Sunburn Site

S2. Destroy West Bunker SAM Site

SKIRINKA

P1. Primary Mission Area

Toyru

them out. Do this correctly, and you'll easily eliminate the enemy before they know what's hit them. As you are flanking the enemy, it is possible your men will kill them from a distance, which is also a welcome outcome.

Now that the enemy is disposed of, make sure you check their bodies for equipment and ammo. Approach a fallen PLA soldier and look down at him. The interaction Hand icon will appear. Interacting with the fallen PLA will open a menu identical to the one you saw at the ammo crate. As with the ammo crate, you can pick and choose what you want to take. It's a good idea to take all ammo and equipment. Also in this area is a checkpoint that will automatically fire once the PLA soldiers are down, so, if things go awry, you can always restart from here.

③ Destroy Early Warning Radar

You're close to your first objective now, the enemy radar station. The objective is guarded by more PLA soldiers. You'll need to take them out before you can destroy the radar. When you're ready, have your men fall in behind you in a Wedge formation. Switch over to the QBZ-95 Marksman rifle. Head south and to the right of the camouflage netting you'll see ahead. Move just past the netting to the top of the hill and look down to the south.

Immediately zoom in with the Marksman rifle and aim for the small building in the distance **[Screen 01]**. There you'll see the PLA soldiers come from round the back. If you're quick, you can easily snipe them all as they come milling out, before they get a chance to take a shot at you. While you are firing on the PLA, issue the command to your men to engage the area you are firing on. This will cause them to move forward and attack, making this firefight all the shorter.

If you don't have the QBZ-95, or you just want something a little more flashy, then switch to the Mk16 Assault Rifle you started with, or the QBZ-95 Assault Rifle. Both of these have an underslung grenade launcher. Equip the Assault Rifle and then change your ammo type to the grenades. Adjust your aim so that the arc of the grenade will reach your targets, and then let them rip. You'll notice an explosive barrel near the small building. Hitting it will cause it

to detonate and destroy the building, eliminating it as a cover point for the PLA **[Screen 02]**.

Lay down a few grenades and your enemy will soon be vanquished. It should be noted that, if you opt for the grenades, don't tell your men to engage or assault the area. Instead, have them stay near you and use suppressing fire – you wouldn't want your men running into the splash of one of your grenades!

Once the PLA have been killed, have your men fall back to a safe distance – 30 to 40 meters will do it. Now approach the radar station. When you are near, a small tutorial will play out. When it's over, switch your weapon to the C4 charges. Get close to the radar station and lay a charge. Now retreat to a safe distance and rejoin your men. Once clear, detonate the charge, thus destroying the radar and completing the first Primary Objective.

ACHIEVEMENT / TROPHY

Without Warning. Destroying the radar will grant you an Achievement for the 360 or a Trophy for the PS3.

When the radar has been destroyed, you'll receive a radio communication informing you that, with the radar down, US forces can now provide you with Artillery Strikes. To summon an Artillery Strike, you'll need to press the "Call Combat Support" button. There are several options to choose from, depending on how you want the strike to play out. In this mission, you've only got one Artillery Strike to call in. Once you use it, that's it; so use it wisely.

PRO TIP!

If you plan on tackling the Secondary Objectives in this Mission, save your Artillery Strike for use on those. Do not use it now!

(4) Now that the radar is down, command wants you to take up an overwatch position on the village below, where there is a strong PLA presence. The USMC is assaulting the PLA from the east, and command wants you to lend a hand in eradicating the PLA from the village. There are 20 PLA soldiers in total to deal with. All you need do is kill at least 16 of them and the USMC will mop up the rest.

One option here is to call in an Artillery Strike on the brunt of the PLA. This is a very powerful option that makes dealing with this part of the mission a breeze. However, if you plan on going after the Secondary Objectives, it's strongly suggested that you save the Artillery Strike for later. You'll find having the Artillery Strike for the Secondary Objectives will make your life a lot easier.

ACHIEVEMENT / TROPHY

Hard Rain - Calling in an Artillery Strike for the first time will grant you an Achievement for the 360 or a Trophy for the PS3.

Make your decision on whether or not to use the Artillery Strike. Then, when ready, head down the slope and through the trees to the east. Near the road is a small outpost with a PLA soldier and an emplaced machine gun **[Screen 03]**. Use the trees for cover and ease up close until you can sight him with your rifle. Take him out quickly and then prepare to enter the village, which is now due south.

(5) In the south-west corner of the village is a building **[Screen 04]**. Move towards it, and once you can see it, order your men to enter the building. Follow them in. Once inside, use the building for cover and attack the PLA forces through the doorways and windows. Check your map often to see where the PLA soldiers are located. When you have killed the soldiers closest to your location, move east to the next building. Continue using the buildings for cover and check your map frequently. If a PLA soldier is hiding round a corner, have one of your men flank him to the right or left to draw him out so that you can get a clean shot.

(6) After you have killed the requisite 16 PLA soldiers, the USMC will move in and finish the job. When the USMC begin to move in, go ahead and scavenge the fallen PLA soldiers for inventory. Once that is done, head north. You'll find an off-road vehicle just south of the enemy emplacement you attacked prior to entering the village. Board the vehicle as the driver and order your men aboard as well. Now head north up the dirt road toward the LZ, where you started this mission.

(7) **Secure Landing Zone / Extract by Helicopter**
As you get close to the LZ, you'll cross a checkpoint and will be informed that PLA vehicles are heading your way. Stop your vehicle immediately and disembark. Two PLA vehicles are coming with three soldiers in each: a driver, passenger, and gunner. If you attempt to stay in your own vehicle, you'll be a very easy target for the opposing vehicle gunners, so disembark and head west to take cover amongst the low walls and trees of a ruined building that you'll find just off the road.

Hold your ground, making sure you use the low walls for cover – crouching is best here. Look at your map to see where the vehicles are located, and then order your men to engage them. As your men do so, lend them supporting fire from your cover point. When attacking the vehicles, always go for the gunner in the rear first, as he is your most dangerous opponent in this confrontation. Once he is down, try to take out the driver so as to stop the vehicle in its tracks, and then follow up by finishing off the passenger. Once all six men are down, the LZ will be secure and your evac helicopter will fly in and land. At this point, you can board the helicopter with your men and end this mission or you can continue to the north to tackle the Secondary Objectives **[Screen 05]**.

SECONDARY OBJECTIVE 1: SAM AT THE LIGHTHOUSE

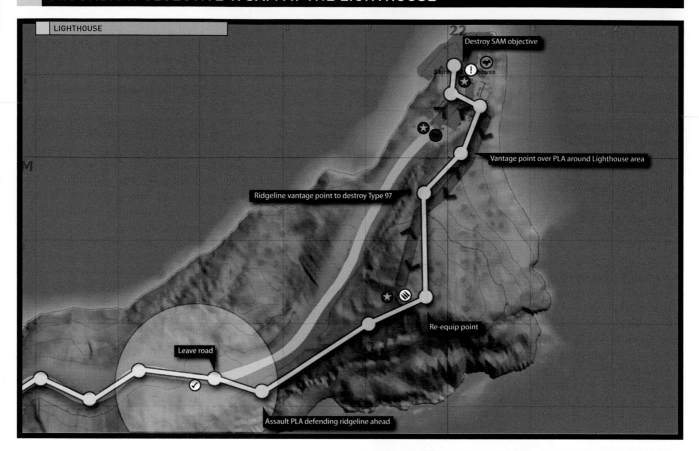

LIGHTHOUSE

Destroy SAM objective

Vantage point over PLA around Lighthouse area

Ridgeline vantage point to destroy Type 97

Re-equip point

Leave road

Assault PLA defending ridgeline ahead

(1) From the LZ where you finished your Primary Objective, board one of the vehicles in the area and follow the road north. Stick to the road and drive as fast as you dare. Along the way, you may encounter a few PLA soldiers who will fire upon you, but you can simply ignore them and keep driving north. Your goal here is to reach the checkpoint which is a long way off to the north, just south of the objective. Once you reach the checkpoint, you're assured of restarting your game from there if something should go wrong.

(2) From the checkpoint, disembark from the vehicle. There are a couple of options at this point. The easiest thing to do here is to leave your men in the vehicle and then head north alone. As you get close to the steep hill on your right, you'll be attacked by the PLA soldiers in the distance. As soon as you can see them, switch to your Assault Rifle and use the under-slung grenade launcher. The distance between you and your enemy is significant, but by aiming high so that you fire a long, arcing shot, you can easily take out the opposing forces from where you stand [Screen 01]. After you have killed the first three soldiers, hold your ground and wait for the patrol to arrive. When they are on the scene, again resort to high arcing grenade shots to take them out. When they are all dead, head up the slope they were protecting.

(3) **Destroy Surface-to-Air Missiles #1**
At the top of the hill you'll find a ruined tower. Inside the open ruins is a pile of ammo crates. Interact with them and grab a new scoped rifle and, most importantly, the Javelin Missile launcher. Once you have the launcher, switch it to your secondary slot and re-equip the scoped rifle.

PRO TIP! (i)

Save the Javelin for the next objective. Do not use it here!

01

Now you need to take out the SAM that is located near the lighthouse. If you saved your Artillery Strike from the Primary Objective, then this is a stroll in the park. Head east towards the sea. As you do, equip the Binoculars to get a better view of the distant village. When you are close to the cliff edge, head north until you can just see the village. Keep an eye out for enemy patrols, and if any PLA show up, cut them down.

When you are close enough to see the village, peer through the Binoculars toward the north. Just below the lighthouse you'll see the SAM Missile launcher. As soon as you can see it, call in an Artillery Strike. The best choice here is a Barrage Strike [Screen 02]. When the strike commences, enjoy the show and listen carefully to the radio reports. You'll soon hear that the SAM has been destroyed, thus completing this Secondary Objective.

At this point you are free to return to your men, or you can head down to the lighthouse. There is a checkpoint there, so this is worthwhile. In the lighthouse area is a Type-97 armored vehicle that you can destroy. If you wish to

do this, stick close to the eastern cliff edge near the sea and head down into the encampment below. Once you are there, move to the largest building near the southern edge of the compound. Do not enter the building, but instead get close to the wall and use it for cover.

Head to your right (the north) making sure you stick close to the wall. The Artillery Strike will have killed all the PLA in the northern part of the lighthouse encampment, so no need to worry about a surprise attack from that direction. Circle round the building until you can see to the south. Ahead you'll see the armored vehicle. Just past that, and further south (and slightly to the right), is a defensive position occupied by more PLA soldiers. Your goal at this point is to stay close to the building you are near and run to the rear of the armored vehicle. Once there, plant a C4 charge and then make a hasty retreat back the way you came **[Screen 03]**. When you are on the other side of the building, detonate the C4 to destroy the armored vehicle.

As you attempt this, the PLA occupying the defensive position just past the armored vehicle may spot you and fire at you. If this happens, crouch down to make yourself less of a target, but move quickly to plant the C4. If you're quick, you can ignore the PLA, plant the C4, and make a safe retreat without ever being hit. With the armored vehicle down, return the way you came and make your way back to the vehicle with your men.

Alternative Strategies

At the start of this objective, have your men disembark the vehicle and follow you in a column formation. Head towards the sea to the east. You'll soon encounter a sloping cliff edge. Leave the road and head down the slope to about halfway, then turn north and make your way to the large hill where the PLA are stationed. As you get close, have your men flank left while you head to the right. Once the PLA spot you, keep them under constant fire.

Order your men to suppress or engage the PLA. If you use your map, you can pick a single PLA soldier and have your men assault him. Stay low, and keep the PLA pinned down with gunfire as you move close enough to deliver a deadly shot. You can also opt for grenades here if your men aren't too close to the PLA.

As soon as the PLA are down, have your men regroup to you, and again use a Column formation as you head up the hill to the ruined tower. Once in the tower, pillage the ammo crates for a new scoped rifle and the Javelin Missile launcher.

Now head east to the cliff edge and then follow the edge north and into the lighthouse encampment. Adopt a Wedge formation as you slowly ease into the encampment. Take out any PLA you can from a distance, and make your way to the buildings for cover. Keep an eye on your map to check where your enemy is located and have your men flank any PLA that are using the buildings for cover. Once you've cleared the northern end of the encampment, use your C4 to blow the SAM.

Now you can leave the encampment or use your C4 or Javelin to take out the armored vehicle. However, if you plan on aiming for either of the other two Secondary Objectives, you should opt for the C4 and save the Javelin. Having the Javelin for the next objective will make things a lot easier.

When ready, backtrack the way you came to your vehicle. It should be noted that you don't have to kill the PLA in the defensive position at the southern end of the encampment (just past the armored vehicle). Ignore these PLA, unless you just want more combat, and leave as you entered, after destroying the SAM and the armored vehicle.

SECONDARY OBJECTIVE 2: SUNBURN ON THE EAST BUNKER

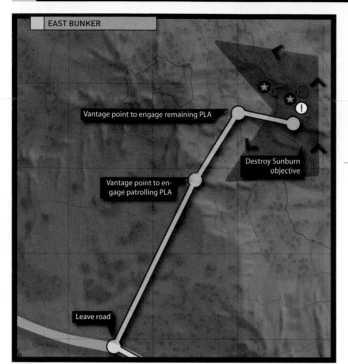

EAST BUNKER

Vantage point to engage remaining PLA

Destroy Sunburn objective

Vantage point to engage patrolling PLA

Leave road

① **Destroy Sunburn anti-ship System**
It's best to tackle this objective after you have finished the SAM objective at the Lighthouse. After that objective is down, you'll need to head south to reach the East Bunker where the Sunburn Missile launcher is located. From the checkpoint in the road you reached at the start of the Lighthouse objective, head up the sloping hills to the south. You can walk, but it's easier and faster to drive the off-road vehicle. Your goal is to make your way to the Sunburn Missile site.

Once you get close, stop the vehicle and leave your men in it. If you kept the Javelin Missile launcher from the Lighthouse objective, now is the time to

use it. While crouching, ease forward until you can just see the Sunburn Missile. Now equip the Javelin and lock-on to the Sunburn **[Screen 01]**. Once you achieve a lock, fire your Missile and destroy the Sunburn. That will complete this objective, and you can now make a hasty retreat back to your vehicle. Once in the vehicle, head east and make your way back to the road.

It should be noted that there is a checkpoint down at the Sunburn site if you wish to trigger it, but if you have used the Javelin for an easy win, there is no need to engage the PLA just to trigger the checkpoint. Instead, make your way to the next Secondary Objective, where a checkpoint awaits you.

Alternative Strategies

If you don't have the Javelin Missile launcher, then you'll need a more hands-on approach. In the encampment around the Sunburn Missile you'll see on old concrete bunker around which the PLA are encamped. Have your men follow you in a Wedge formation, until you are just close enough to see the bunker. Command your men to lay down suppressing fire on the bunker and the sandbag defensive position. As they do so, this will pin the PLA allowing you to use a scoped rifle to pick the enemy off one at a time. Use this suppressing and sniper approach until all the PLA are dead, then make your way down to the Sunburn Missile. One C4 charge is all it takes to destroy it and complete this objective. By taking this hands-on approach, you'll also trigger the checkpoint.

SECONDARY OBJECTIVE 3: SAM ON THE WEST BUNKER

① After you leave the road, make your way directly to the checkpoint. After it is triggered, your game will be saved, which means that your previous accomplishment with the other two Secondary Objectives is locked. From the checkpoint, have your men adopt a Column formation and follow you south to find the remains of a building, amongst which you'll find a stash of ammo crates. Stock up here on ammo and, in particular, grab the Model 82A1 scoped rifle.

Accomplishing this objective will take careful planning and proper placement. Once the new rifle is yours, head north to a small ridge. As you get close, open the map and order your men to flank left on the bunker located in the beach encampment down below. Watch the map, and give your men time to get down into position. From the lower ground, they can use the trees for cover as they move in toward the encampment.

② **RV2: Destroy Surface-to-Air Missiles #2**
When your men are close to the encampment below, set yourself up on this small ridge overlooking the encampment. Zoom in with your scope and begin picking off the PLA forces down below **[Screen 02]**. As you are doing this, be wary of being flanked by the PLA patrol team that walks this ridge. Should they get close, fall back to the ruins and take them out with close-quarters combat.

After you have sniped all the PLA you can see, make your way cautiously down the slope toward the encampment. You'll encounter more enemy as you do so. Make sure you stay in a crouch as you move and snipe the enemy as

quickly as possible. If need be, lie prone on the ground and order your men (via the map) to assault any PLA that have you pinned down. If PLA fire is too heavy, make a hasty retreat back to the ruins, and then follow your men's path down to lower ground and assault the remaining PLA forces from that vantage point. After the enemy has been eradicated, use your C4 to blow the SAM and complete this objective.

There is a checkpoint here in the encampment, so after you have blown the SAM Missiles, make sure you trigger it to save your progress.

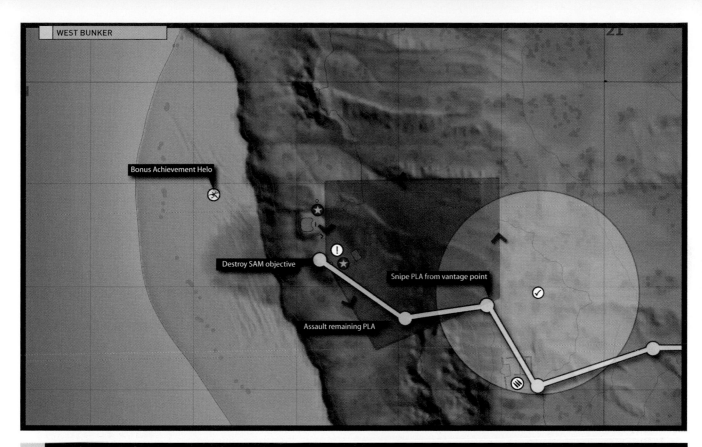

WEST BUNKER

Bonus Achievement Helo

Destroy SAM objective

Snipe PLA from vantage point

Assault remaining PLA

BONUS MISSION OBJECTIVES

After you have completed Objective 3 and destroyed the SAM on the West Bunker, you will be very close to a Helicopter that you can use to unlock an Achievement **[Screen 03]**. From the West Bunker, head west to the beach to find the chopper. Get near it and enter it as you would any vehicle. Order your men aboard with you, and then take to the air. The goal here is to follow the coast and fly completely around the island. Refer to the map above to view the route you must take in order to complete this Achievement. It should be noted that it doesn't matter if you fly clockwise or counterclockwise. Simply complete the circuit in your desired fashion and you'll unlock this Achievement.

ACHIEVEMENT / TROPHY

Skirinka Island Tour: Completing the circle around the island's coast will grant you an Achievement for the 360 or a Trophy for the PS3.

Once you've accomplished all of the Secondary Objectives, or accomplished as many as you care to, head back to the waiting Helicopter at the LZ. Board it with your men, and this mission is complete.

03

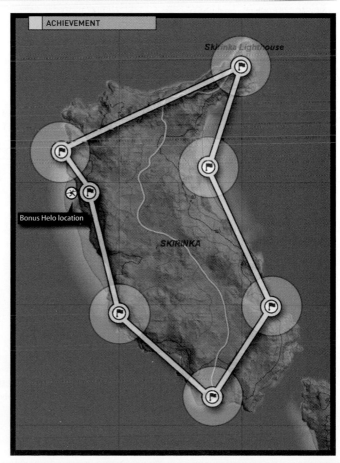
ACHIEVEMENT

Skirinka Lighthouse

Bonus Helo location

SKIRINKA

BLINDING THE DRAGON
MISSION 02

This mission is about a mix of stealth and hit-and-fade tactics; putting the PLA off their guard and eliminating them, using superior firepower and positioning. The first part of the mission sees you infiltrate PLA territory and eliminate the Sunburn site, then moving up to the foothills of the mountains to the east to eliminate a key Radar site before breaking contact and moving to your exit position.

Equipment and Vehicles

When you start this mission, you'll find an ammo crate at RV1 that contains an M4A1 Marksman which is a nice compliment to the Mk17 for long-range combat in the upcoming areas. To the far north of RV1 you'll see an abandoned PLA Truck. This vehicle doesn't figure in the mission, and it's heavily guarded by four PLA soldiers, which means you're almost bound to be spotted if you go after it. During regular play, ignore it, but on a replay you may want to experiment with it if you're curious or looking for something different. During the mission proper, you'll come across ammo crates at the Sunburn site and the village (Commander Bonus Objective) that you can use to resupply your inventory if needed.

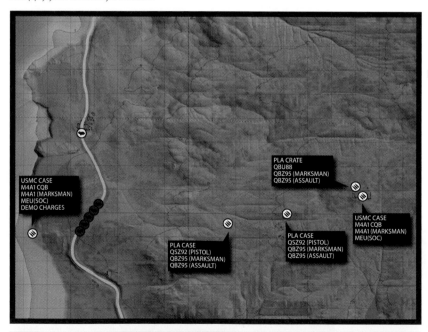

USMC CASE
M4A1 CQB
M4A1 (MARKSMAN)
MEU(SOC)
DEMO CHARGES

PLA CASE
QSZ92 (PISTOL)
QBZ95 (MARKSMAN)
QBZ95 (ASSAULT)

PLA CASE
QSZ92 (PISTOL)
QBZ95 (MARKSMAN)
QBZ95 (ASSAULT)

USMC CASE
M4A1 CQB
M4A1 (MARKSMAN)
MEU(SOC)

PLA CRATE
QBU88
QBZ95 (MARKSMAN)
QBZ95 (ASSAULT)

MISSION WEAPONS AND VEHICLES

Item	US
Weapons	US Knife
	MEU (SOC) Pistol
	MP5A4 Sub-Machine Gun
	M4A1 Assault Rifle (CQB)
	M4A1 Assault Rifle (Marksman)
	M4A1 Assault Rifle (Stealth)
	Mk16 Mod 0 Assault Rifle (Assault)
	Mk17 Mod 0 Assault Rifle (Night Ops)
	Mk48 Mod 0 Medium Machine Gun
	M21 Sniper Rifle
	US Fragmentation Grenade
	US Smoke Grenade
	US Coloured Smoke Grenade Red
	US Claymore
	US Demolition Charge
	IR Stobe
Vehicles	SURC Boat
	AH-1Z Ground Attack

Item	PLA
Weapons	PLA Knife
	QSZ92 Pistol
	QCW05 Sub-Machine Gun
	QBZ95 Assault Rifle
	QBZ95 Assault Rifle (Marksman)
	QBZ95 Assault Rifle (Assault)
	QBZ95 Assault Rifle (Night Ops)
	Type 81-1 Assault Rifle
	Type 81-1 Assault Rifle (Assault)
	QBB95 Light Machine Gun
	PLA Fragmentation Grenade
	PLA Smoke Grenade
	PLA Coloured Smoke Grenade Red
	PLA Claymore Mine
	PLA Anti Personnel Mine
	PLA Anti Tank Mine
	Field Dressing PLA
	QW-2 SAM Anti Aircraft Homing Missile
Vehicles	Type 95 Anti-Aircraft Artillery
	BJS2022 with HMG
	SX2190 Truck
	SX2190 Cargo Truck
	Z-10 Attack
	Mi-171 Transport
	SX2190 Missile Launcher
Emplacements	QJC 88 Heavy Machine Gun *

* Tall mount

Primary Objectives	Secondary Objectives	Bonus Objectives
Destroy Sunburn Site	Remain Undetected by PLA forces	Eliminate PLA commander
Disable Air Defenses	Reach Flanking Position	
Proceed to Overwatch		

OBJECTIVE OVERVIEW

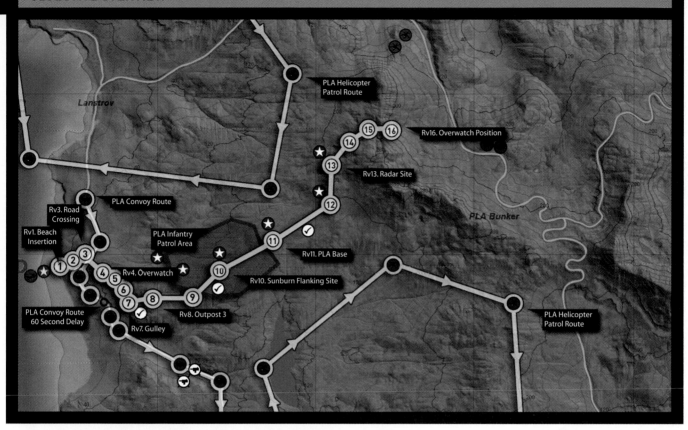

PLA Suspicion

Because this mission takes place before any major USMC activities on the island, the PLA forces are not expecting any enemy forces to be present. The element of surprise will give you a great advantage. To improve your stealth, simply follow these tips:

• Keeping crouched down lowers your profile and makes both you and your fire-team less easy to see when moving around.

• Keeping your team in Fire on My Lead or Return Fire, allows you to maneuver them without engaging any PLA before you want them to.

• Always scope out an upcoming area using your thermal scope and binoculars so that you can track enemy movements before engaging with them. Spotting the enemy from a distance will cause them to appear on your Radar.

If you become suspected by any PLA forces, you have 25 seconds to become unidentified (moving out of sight behind cover, or into gullies, is best in these situations), before the PLA have a chance to raise the alarm. You'll know you are suspected when you hear the message: They're searching for us. When you hear this, look quickly for a place to hide. If you are successful in hiding, you'll hear the message: We've lost them, and you can go back to your mission.

If you are spotted, you'll hear the message: They know we're here, which indicates that nearby PLA forces have been alerted, thus increasing the mission's difficulty. If this happens, a PLA attack helicopter will be sent to your last known position. It will try to track you down and take you out, but if you keep out of harm's way, the chopper will fly off back to base. When you hear the message: They know we're here, immediately seek cover when the attack chopper is on its way. If it finds you out in the open, it will attack!

PLA Detection

When engaging certain enemies or completing objectives (or when first fully identified by the PLA), the PLA will send an armed response unit to the relevant location in the form of one of a pair of WZ-10 attack helicopters. The helicopters will be sent out if:

• One of the guards of the Sunburn site is killed

• The Sunburn is destroyed

• One of the PLA at the PLA base has been killed

• The player is fully identified by the PLA (as described above in PLA Suspicion)

The helicopter will move into the area and then act as a weapons platform against any USMC units which it can identify. If no enemy units are identified after 30 seconds the helicopter will move back out to its patrol route, deploying flares against any possible SAM attack. If engaged, the helicopters will often turn on their aggressors and attempt to eliminate them, attacking any USMC units for 60 seconds.

Going prone or hiding in any convenient buildings or clump of trees will help you avoid this significant threat when it appears. Always seek cover when the PLA attack chopper comes on scene and never engage it. The chopper is heavily armored, and trying to take it down with rifles is an extremely bad idea, considering the power of the chopper's weaponry.

① During this mission, your team is codenamed Saber 2. Another friendly fire-team is with you on this mission, and they are codenamed Saber 3. Start the mission by raiding the ammo crates in the area; the M4A1 Marksman is a good choice. Now follow the RV markers on screen. The goal is to head east and go round the PLA guard's hut by the road. Give the hut a wide berth and make your way to the game checkpoint indicated on the map at RV7.

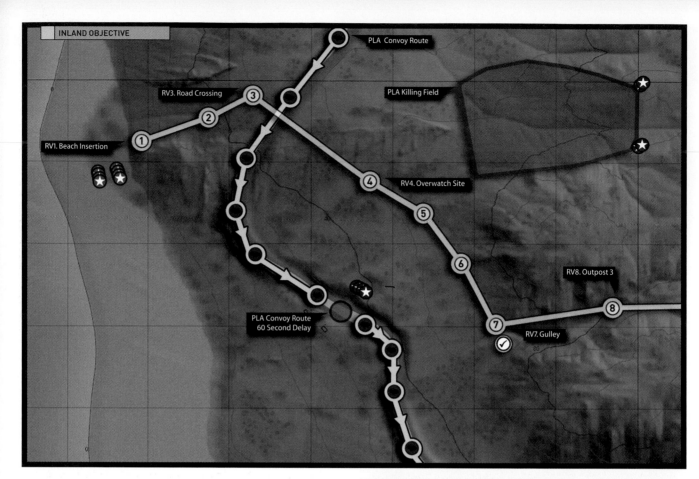

INLAND OBJECTIVE

PLA Convoy Route

RV3. Road Crossing

PLA Killing Field

RV1. Beach Insertion

RV4. Overwatch Site

RV8. Outpost 3

PLA Convoy Route
60 Second Delay

RV7. Gulley

If you stay far enough away from the PLA forces, they'll never see you. As you are making your way to the checkpoint, have your men follow you in a tight formation, and make sure they only fire on your lead. Staying in a crouch position is also a good idea. As you are following the RV markers, Saber 3 will take up an overwatch position at RV4. Leave them there and continue onward to RV7.

The goal is to remain undetected by the PLA at the guard's hut and in the convoy. Remaining undetected is not only a good idea, but also one of your Secondary Objectives. However, you could engage the PLA and the convoy at the guard's hut if you so desire, but it is not recommended [Screen 01].

The convoy consists of five vehicles: a PLA armed light vehicle and four PLA cargo trucks. While not so dangerous on their own, they can spot you and call in additional forces to your position. Besides the convoy, there are also four PLA soldiers at the guard's hut.

If engaged, the convoy vehicles will try to avoid contact, going across country and speeding out of the combat zone. If any of the vehicles becomes immobilized, then the driver will dismount and defend his vehicle.

It's best to avoid the convoy altogether as the benefits gained by eliminating it are worth less than the alarm and ammo usage it would take to fully neutralize the convoy and any alerted PLA troops. Not to mention that being detected at this point will cause you to fail one of the Secondary Objectives. The main weaponry of the PLA soldiers here is the QBZ95, in both primary and assault variations, as well as equipment like mines and grenades. This means that if you scavenge the soldiers, should you kill them, this won't net you any significant inventory.

(7) Once you've made it to RV7, move carefully up the riverbed. As before, have your men follow you in a tight formation and have them only fire on your lead. While you are traversing the river bed, Saber 3 will take the opportunity to move north-east and inland to set up an overwatch position over the Sunburn site. If you haven't been spotted by this point, you will have successfully moved inland undetected, thus completing one of your Secondary Objectives. The area you now move into is lightly guarded, but

01

the PLA have set up a lookout where the gulley opens up some 50 meters down the RV route.

The low scrub and rocks provide good cover to your left and a better vantage point from which to observe the outpost, but if you want to circumvent the guard post, move south then east under the brow of the hill or risk being spotted at such close range.

(8) **Remain Undetected By PLA Forces**
When you reach the lookout at RV8, you'll complete the Secondary Objective of remaining undetected (assuming you weren't spotted prior to this). At RV8, there are various ways of eliminating the PLA soldiers in the lookout, but a good way of making this engagement a lot easier is to get the guard to leave the emplacement. To achieve this, injure but don't kill the more exposed guard in order to draw the second one outside. When he comes out, eliminate him as he goes to the aid of his fellow soldier. With them both out in the open, you can easily finish them off from a distance [Screen 02].

Once you have dealt with the PLA here, continue onward to RV9, which is further to the east. The next area is mostly clear of PLA (if you have kept

SUNBURN

Primary Objective 2
Eliminate Sunburn

SP1. Plant Demolition Charge

SP2. Retreat To Safe Distance!

PLA Infantry Reaction Force

RV10. Sunburn Flanking Site

04

out of contact with the PLA), but remain stealthy so as to avoid the smaller fortified PLA emplacement to the north and any PLA patrols which may be in the area. Again, have your men follow you in a tight formation, and make sure they only fire on your lead.

While navigating this more open terrain, Saber 3 will be in a position to spot the site of the Sunburn launcher and mark out a good location from where to flank the objective. The RV route leads you through the best cover before finishing at a two-story building overlooking the Sunburn site.

Alternate Strategies for RV7 & RV8

You'll now need to head further east up the dry river bed. Ahead is a guard's hut, so it is best to get on the south ridge (right side) of the river bed [Screen 03]. Climb the hill there and stay away from the guard's hut, thus missing that engagement. As you are moving up the ridge, watch the southern sky for a PLA helicopter to fly by. As soon as you see it, drop to a crouch position and sit still while it passes. When it is gone, continue forward to a large clump of trees. Past the trees is a small gulley. Get in the gulley and head north toward the building near the Sunburn site.

10 Reach Flanking Position / Destroy Sunburn Site
To the south of the Sunburn site is a small selection of farm buildings. While open to the south, the farmhouse building and the fenced area to the north provide an ideal location from which to attack the Sunburn site. When you arrive at this location, RV10, there is a checkpoint, and you'll also clear the Secondary Objective of Flanking the Sunburn site. If you arrive before Saber 3 have taken up their position, lie low and wait for them to radio you that they are ready.

The second story of the farmhouse building provides a good vantage point over the Sunburn site, while the hay bales to the north make a good staging-point for a closer-range assault. Given that there is little cover to the west and east of the Sunburn site, this location is the best one for long-range combat, especially with the increased detection range afforded by your scoped weapons.

Enter the building and have your men halt. Inside the building, go to the second floor where there is a window overlooking the Sunburn to the north. Prepare your M4A1 Marksman and get the enemy ahead in its sights. Once both teams are in position, Saber 3 will start the assault on the Sunburn from

01

02

03

Be aware that, once one of the Sunburn guards has been killed, the PLA will become alerted to your presence and send an armed response in the form of a WZ-10 attack helicopter. If it arrives before you have taken the Sunburn site, you will need to find cover quickly to avoid its attacks.

After PLA guards have been downed, move in quickly to plant a C4 charge, as another small force of PLA soldiers will be moving in to investigate from the west. Retreat to a safe distance before detonating the explosive. Find a suitable location to lie low, or quickly advance east as the second PLA helicopter moves in to investigate the disruption. Once the Sunburn is destroyed a checkpoint will be triggered and you will gain an Artillery Strike.

Alternate Strategies for RV10

As before, enter and take up position on the second floor. When Saber 3 is ready, have your men launch an assault on the Sunburn site, while you snipe the PLA forces from the second-floor window. When the PLA are all dead, have your men move fast to the north where there is a large clump of trees. Immediately run to the Sunburn, plant the C4, and then follow your men. When you have destroyed the Sunburn, you will be given an Artillery Strike.

There is an ammo crate next to a tent, if you want to grab a new weapon **[Screen 02]**. Run quickly to your men and continue deep into the trees and then crouch down or go prone. Detonate the C4 and the Sunburn is history, thus completing the objective. Now check your map and work your way to the checkpoint to the east to save your progress. At this point, you can attack the village as an attempt on the Bonus Mission Objective, or you can continue on to the last Primary Objective. If you want to attack the village, see the RV11.

> **PRO TIP!**   (i)
>
> You can use the Artillery Strike on the village to make that objective easier, but it's best to save it for the last Primary Objective and gain an easy win.

(11) **Eliminate PLA Commander**

At RV11, you'll encounter a PLA base with quite a few soldiers. Of immediate interest is the base Commander. Eliminating him will complete your Bonus Objective. Entering the base and engaging the PLA here is completely optional.

After the Sunburn was destroyed, Saber gave you access to ship-to-shore artillery support. You'll only have one Artillery Strike in this mission, so think strategically when deciding which target to use it on. The PLA base at RV11 is a temping target. However, the base does contain some useful ammo crates and good defensive positions (the buildings in particular) should you find yourself pinned down by PLA forces. If you use the Artillery Strike on the base, the ammo crates and many of the buildings will be destroyed, robbing you of cover as well as ammo replenishment **[Screen 03]**.

the north, drawing much of the PLA's attention and firepower. Once combat is underway, have your men assault the Sunburn site, while you snipe the PLA forces from the second-floor window **[Screen 01]**.

COMMANDER

PLA Control Area

SP7. Move to RV

PLA Chopper Attack

SP4. Eliminate PLA in Building and Emplacement

SP6. Rendezvous with Team

SP3. Eliminate PLA near Sam

Bonus Objective Eliminate PLA C.O.

SP5. Rearm at Ammo Crates

SP1. Eliminate Commander

04

SP2. Enter Building

04

05

The forces at the base can be dispatched by you and your team, owing to your superior weaponry and the element of surprise. So saving the strike and opting for a direct assault is worth the risk. If you save the strike, then you can use it against the PLA forces guarding the Radar site later on in the mission.

When you attack the PLA Base, there are some important points to consider. The base is lightly guarded, but it does contain a number of explosive objects, such as fuel canisters and stacks of artillery shells. While these can be used to eliminate enemies within the base, they will also eliminate the ammo supplies which are available for you to use, so watch your fire carefully [Screen 04].

The best route through the base is to advance from the east. As you advance, keep an eye on the windows of the house with the outside staircase, as the PLA commander is usually in this building. Eliminating him will earn you the Bonus Objective. Move into this building, while sending your team through the east gate. From this vantage point you can eliminate PLA within the courtyard while your fire-team acts as spotters, destroying enemies from close range.

When the PLA in the courtyard and those next to the SAM have been eliminated, move in to tackle others in the concrete emplacements to the north-east

and south-west. Watch out for any units who may move in from the east in reaction to your attack as you join up with your team. Rearm from any intact ammo crates you find before continuing west towards the PLA air defense site.

Alternate Strategies for RV11

There is a checkpoint east of the PLA Base. Check the map and make your way there, making sure you give the Base a wide berth so that you avoid being spotted. As always, have your men follow you in a tight formation and make sure they only fire on your lead.

From the checkpoint, you'll be east of the Base and hiding behind a stack of logs. To take the Base and kill the Commander, you could use an Artillery Strike, but that will make the final objective all the more difficult. Since you are at a checkpoint, it's best to just attack the Base and save the Artillery Strike.

Before moving in, use the binoculars to scan the Base. This will make the PLA soldiers show up on your map. Now, facing the Base, get your men to attack the northern end while you head to the south [Screen 05]. Kill the PLA you encounter and make your way into the first building you come to. In the

building, check your map and order your men to engage the PLA. They will draw the PLA's attention while you circle round and take the PLA out. Use the buildings to your advantage as you go through the village and you'll soon destroy all the PLA, including the commander.

12. Engage the PLA Base, or move around it, and make your way to the checkpoint indicated on the map. This is east of the Base. From this checkpoint, head further east toward the SAM site. Use the trees in the area for cover and you can advance safely most of the way up into the foothills.

If you are spotted by any of the PLA forces as you move into the foothills, only two of the four fire-teams in the area will move down to engage you [Screen 01]. If they attack, they can be easily eliminated from long range, but the tree cover to the north makes spotting units from that direction more difficult, so keep a careful eye on it.

Both the SAM and Radar sites are positioned on the crests of hills in flat, paved areas cleared of trees. The Radar site is placed near old mining relics and tall metal pylons, making it easy to spot when in range.

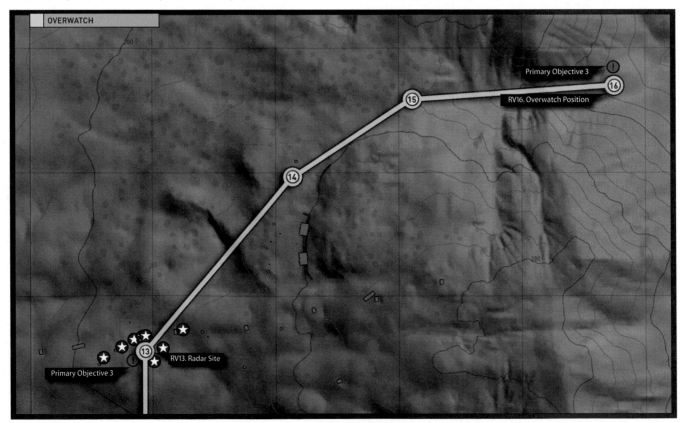

The best approach is to move close to the units guarding the SAM site from the south or flank wide and attack from the west. Using fragmentation grenades and your superior equipment, you can easily eliminate the PLA here before setting your sights on the second Primary Objective: the Radar site.

13 Disable Air Defenses / Proceed to Overwatch
In order to disable the PLA's air defensive network in the area, this mobile Radar site has to be eliminated. Effectively blinded, the SAM and AAA positions will be ineffective against a USMC aerial assault. With most of the PLA forces hopefully eliminated in your initial assault at RV12, the Radar

should also fall easily to a direct attack. Come in from the south and have your men flank left as you move round to the right (east). Attack in unison with your men, and the PLA will fall. When they are dead, place a C4 charge on the Radar, move away to a safe distance and detonate it.

With the Radar down, you have completed the second Primary Objective of disabling the PLA's air defense. Now, all you need to do is follow the RV markers 14-16 to a new overwatch position. When you reach RV16, you'll have completed your last Primary Objective and the mission will end.

Alternate Strategies for RV12 & RV13

From the checkpoint, head due east into the trees ahead. To the north is a SAM site. You can attack it if you like, but it isn't necessary, since the Primary Objective is the Radar, which will disable the SAM, so no need to actually destroy the SAM. Instead, go due east and ignore the SAM site. Make sure you give the site a wide berth so the PLA soldiers there don't spot you. While you are traveling, have your men follow you in a tight formation and make sure they only fire on your lead.

After you have gone far enough east, you'll come to a small mountain. To the north-east is a wooden tower, which you should make your way to. Once there, head north-west, following the other wooden towers on the mountain. Make your way to the fourth tower down. From your new vantage point, look down and spot where the Radar site is [Screen 02]. Equip the binoculars to get a better view of your target, and call in an Artillery Strike to take it out. The Artillery Strike will destroy the Radar, thereby completing the objective. Now turn and head north over the mountain to the overwatch location, where this mission will end.

If you don't have the Artillery Strike, then have your men flank left as you move in from the right. Use long range fire from afar to take out the PLA forces as your men move in. As soon as they are dead, plant C4 on the Radar and retreat. Blow the Radar and then make your way to the overwatch position to end the mission.

ACHIEVEMENT / TROPHY

Saber Beats SAM: Destroying the Radar will disable the SAM site and award you an Achievement for the 360 or a Trophy for the PS3.

UNITED WE STAND
MISSION 03

This is the first infantry mission in which you take the role of Hunter, a fire-team leader of Dagger One Bravo. In this mission you are the main assault force of the USMC on the main island of Skira. The success of this mission will give the USMC a foothold on the island and allow them to land heavy armor and logistics.

Equipment and Vehicles

Looking at the map, you'll see that ammo crates are rather scarce in this mission with only two available. You'll find one behind the farmhouse at RV3, and this one you should definitely go through in order to grab the Queen Bee. The other crate is at the end of the mission at RV10. With ammo crates so far and few between, you'll need to be conservative with your ammo, or rely on scavenging fallen PLA soldiers for their weaponry. The PLA in this mission actually carry decent weapons in some areas, and you can easily get a Queen Bee from an AT soldier, a QW-2 AA missile from an AA soldier or a Type 81-1 Marksman rifle from a PLA spotter (as detailed later in the Mission Briefing).

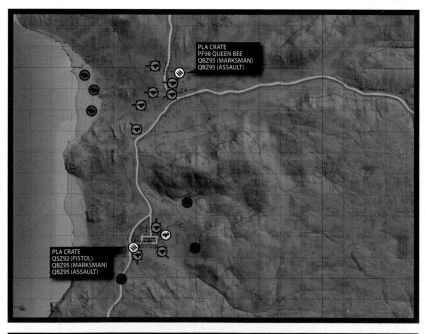

PLA CRATE
PF98 QUEEN BEE
QBZ95 (MARKSMAN)
QBZ95 (ASSAULT)

PLA CRATE
QSZ92 (PISTOL)
QBZ95 (MARKSMAN)
QBZ95 (ASSAULT)

MISSION WEAPONS AND VEHICLES

Item	US
Weapons	US Knife
	MEU (SOC) Pistol
	MP5A4 Sub-Machine Gun
	M16A4 Assault Rifle
	M16A4 Assault Rifle (Marksman)
	M16A4 Assault Rifle (Assault)
	M249 Light Machine Gun
	M21 Sniper Rifle
	US Fragmentation Grenade
	US Smoke Grenade
	US Coloured Smoke Grenade Red
	US Coloured Smoke Grenade Yellow
	US Claymore
	US Anti Personnel Mine
	IR Stobe
	SMAW Rocket Launcher
	M16A4CQB Assault Rifle
Vehicles	AAVP7A1
	AH-1Z Ground Attack
	MH-60S

Item	PLA
Weapons	PLA Knife
	QSZ92 Pistol
	QBZ95 Assault Rifle
	QBZ95 Assault Rifle (Marksman)
	QBZ95 Assault Rifle (Assault)
	Type 81-1 Assault Rifle (Marksman)
	QBB95 Light Machine Gun
	Type 67-II Medium Machine Gun
	PLA Fragmentation Grenade
	PLA Smoke Grenade
	PLA Coloured Smoke Grenade Red
	PLA Anti Personnel Mine
	Field Dressing PLA
	PF98 Queen Bee Rocket Launcher
	QW-2 SAM Anti Aircraft Homing Missile
Vehicles	Type 97 Infantry Fighting Vehicle
	BJS2022 with HMG
Emplacements	QJC 88 Heavy Machine Gun *

* Tall mount

Primary Objectives	Secondary Objectives	Bonus Objectives
Secure Beachhead	Eliminate PLA Anti-Tank Teams	Destroy PLA Armor
Eliminate PLA Spotter Team		
Eliminate PLA Anti-Air Teams		

OBJECTIVE OVERVIEW

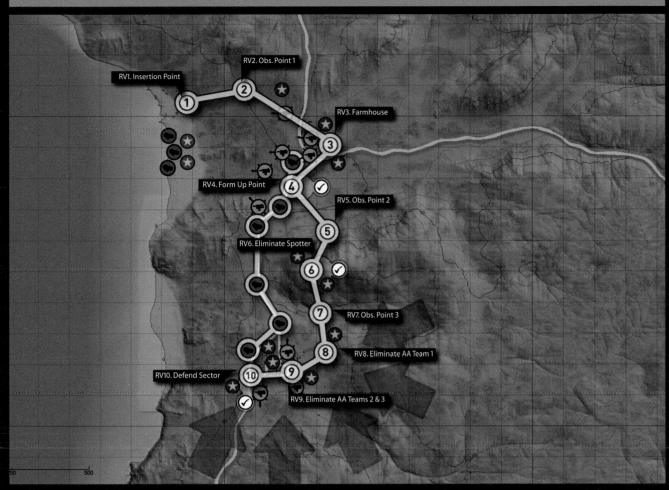

RV1. Insertion Point
RV2. Obs. Point 1
RV3. Farmhouse
RV4. Form Up Point
RV5. Obs. Point 2
RV6. Eliminate Spotter
RV7. Obs. Point 3
RV8. Eliminate AA Team 1
RV9. Eliminate AA Teams 2 & 3
RV10. Defend Sector

MISSION OBJECTIVES

One excellent method of attack is to have your men lay down suppressing fire while you push into the clump of trees. There is a pile of logs ahead you can use for cover. Once you are behind the logs, use the map and get your men to engage the AT soldiers while you lend them supporting fire from your cover location. A good option is to use a grenade, should the opportunity present itself.

When the first AT soldier is down, check his inventory and grab the Queen Bee rocket launcher. Remember that the AT teams are two-man teams, which means that there is one more PLA soldier in the immediate area. Check your map to see where he is and then have your men engage him.

SEQUENCE BREAKING!

It should be noted that, from the beach, you can actually run up to one of the AAVPs and board it if you like. You can also break the intended sequence of the game by heading directly east toward the radio tower and engaging the PLA there. This will allow you skip the next series of encounters and launch right into the second Primary Objective.

(2) As you start the mission, you will be asked to eliminate a PLA Anti-tank team (three teams of two soldiers) on the left flank. This is a Secondary Objective, but by carrying it out you will ensure that some of the AAVPs will make it off the beach and help you secure the beachhead [**Screen 01**].

From RV1 at the beach, head north toward the clump of trees ahead where RV2 is located. Have your men follow you in a wedge pattern. As soon as you are directly across from the trees, move toward them and engage the PLA.

(3) Eliminate PLA Anti-tank Teams / Destroy PLA Armor
With the first AT team down, head south through the trees toward RV3. As you make your way through the trees you will be able to see the burnt-out Type-97 and the second AT team using it as cover. They are also using

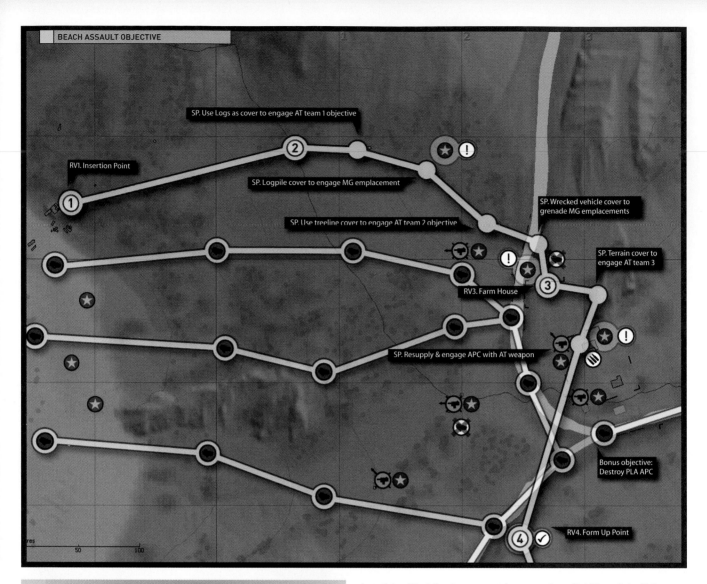

SP. Use Logs as cover to engage AT team 1 objective

RV1. Insertion Point

SP. Logpile cover to engage MG emplacement

SP. Wrecked vehicle cover to grenade MG emplacements

SP. Use treeline cover to engage AT team 2 objective

SP. Terrain cover to engage AT team 3

RV3. Farm House

SP. Resupply & engage APC with AT weapon

Bonus objective: Destroy PLA APC

RV4. Form Up Point

50   100

01

the ruined walls at the side of the road for cover. With the trees as your cover, get your fire-team to suppress the AT team while you break cover and head towards the nearest ruined wall. The second AT team is usually set up near the burning remains of the PLA Tank **[Screen 01]**.

Have your men attack or engage the AT team ahead. Lend support with short bursts of fire. Quickly target and kill the two PLA soldiers and then take up a position behind the burnt-out tank. The tank will provide you with cover from the sizeable force located near the farmhouse to the west.

When you're ready, have your men attack the PLA near the farmhouse. Support them with suppressing fire, or use the Queen Bee to take the PLA out. The

last of the AT soldiers is amongst the enemy here. By killing all the PLA near the farmhouse, you will also eliminate the third AT team and your Secondary Objective will then be completed.

While you are attacking the farmhouse, the US AAVPs will move into position and lend you support. If you are having a tough time here, then remain behind the tank for cover and wait for the AAVPs to arrive, making the battle less difficult. When all the PLA are dead, it's time to move to the form-up point at RV4.

ACHIEVEMENT / TROPHY

Get Creative: If you're quick, you can reach the farmhouse and find a PLA APC. Destroy it with a Queen Bee and unlock an Achievement for the 360 or a Trophy for the PS3.

A note about the PLA Armor Bonus Objective.

If you take too long to reach the farmhouse, the US AAVPs will destroy the PLA APC for you and you'll miss this Achievement/Trophy. In fact, if the AAVPs are not destroyed by the PLA AT teams, they will move in quickly and will almost certainly destroy the PLA APC before you get a sniff at it.

If you are having a hard time with this Bonus Objective, consider restarting the mission and staying back at the beach for a while. This means that one or two of the AAVPs will be destroyed, but it also means you'll be able to take out the PLA APC on your own (using a Queen Bee) and achieve the Bonus Objective **[Screen 02]**.

04

In the end however, it's far more sensible to protect the AAVPs so that they survive and can then help you with the ending-the-mission objectives in the village. Missing the Bonus Objective here is a price worth paying to keep the AAVPs alive for the end of the mission.

(4) Once the farmhouse is clear you will all hear the command 'All Daggers form up'. When this happens, the US forces will form up on the road leading to the village. This is your cue to make your way quickly over to RV4.

When the US Convoy is forming up you will see a PLA mortar strike on the road in front of you, then, 60 seconds later, the next strike will take out the lead AAVP **[Screen 03]**. This is when you will be given your next objective: Eliminate PLA Spotter Team.

You will have four minutes between critical strikes on the US Convoy (the remaining AAVPs and US Infantry). If the mortars manage to destroy or kill three targets then you will have failed the Eliminate PLA Spotter Team objective. This gives you a window of eight minutes to get up the hill to the Radio Mast and eliminate the PLA Spotter Team.

(6) **Eliminate PLA Spotter Team**
From RV4, use your binoculars to spy a pair of PLA soldiers on a hill to the south. Get your men to attack them. While your men are doing this, head south to RV5 and then into the trees ahead. As soon as you are in the trees, turn and make your way south up the hill toward the large radio antenna.

As you are going up the hill, equip the Frag Grenade. When you are near the top, get into the crouch position and ease your way up over the hill until you can see the base of the antenna. There are three PLA soldiers here. Two of them will be directly ahead and bunched up **[Screen 04]**. One well thrown Frag Grenade will take out the first two in one go. Now circle round and take out the third. The third PLA soldier has a high-powered Type 81-1 Marksman Rifle which you may want to take. After you have eliminated the three PLA near the radio tower, go and help your men with the last two PLA spotters, making sure you trigger the available checkpoint in this area.

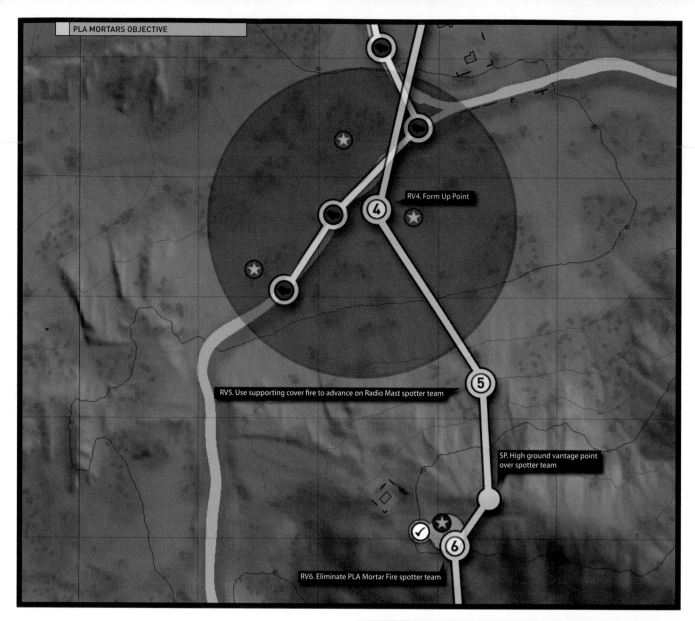

PLA MORTARS OBJECTIVE

RV4. Form Up Point

RV5. Use supporting cover fire to advance on Radio Mast spotter team

SP. High ground vantage point over spotter team

RV6. Eliminate PLA Mortar Fire spotter team

Once this is done, you'll need to leave the area. However, before you go, there is one thing more you can do to make the upcoming encounters a little more manageable. Before you leave the hillside to search for the PLA AA teams, go to the right of the Radio Mast, where you can see the front right side of the village and a sandbag emplacement. There are several PLA soldiers grouped together there. Equip the Queen Bee (the one that you looted from the AT soldier or got from the ammo crate behind the farmhouse); you should have at least two rounds left.

Aim slightly high at the sandbag emplacement and kill the PLA soldiers located there **[Screen 01]**. Taking them out now means not having to worry about them spotting and firing on you later in the village. However, only do this if you have two rounds or more for the Queen Bee! You'll want at least one round for later in the village. It will make it much easier for you to take out the second AA team.

01

(8) After you have taken out the PLA Spotters, a Hydra US Close Air Support attack helicopter (CAS) will inform Dagger that the PLA have hidden anti-air teams around the village. You are then tasked to seek out and eliminate them. You have approximately 10 minutes to search and eliminate three two-man AA teams. If the CAS helicopter is shot down by any of these AA teams, you will have failed the mission.

Next you need to head down into the village below to take out three AA teams. The first is to the east of the village near a small shack. There are two soldiers

per team. Before heading down, it's a good idea to use your binoculars to scan the village thoroughly. This will cause the PLA soldiers to appear on your map, which can prove helpful.

Start by having your men flank left of the small shack as you move forward. The two PLAs here are split up, one at the rear of the shack, the other at the front. If you have the Marksman Rifle from the previous area, take out the PLA soldier at the rear from long distance as your men move in. Once the soldier

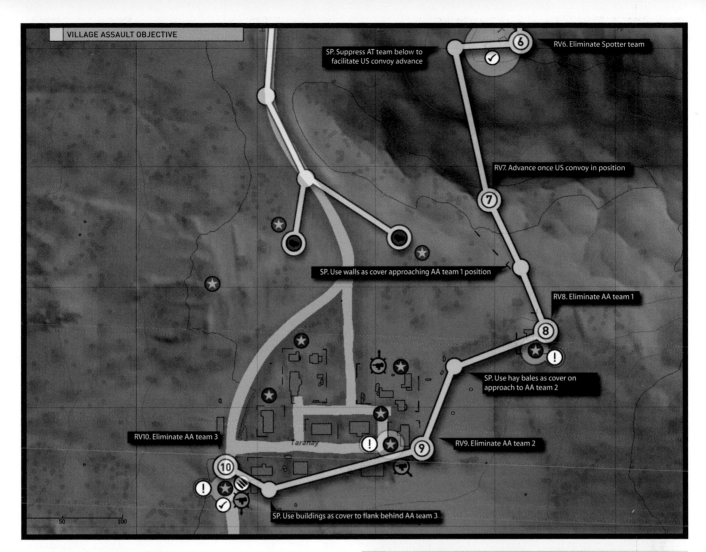

VILLAGE ASSAULT OBJECTIVE

SP. Suppress AT team below to facilitate US convoy advance

RV6. Eliminate Spotter team

RV7. Advance once US convoy in position

SP. Use walls as cover approaching AA team 1 position

RV8. Eliminate AA team 1

SP. Use hay bales as cover on approach to AA team 2

RV10. Eliminate AA team 3

RV9. Eliminate AA team 2

Taranay

SP. Use buildings as cover to flank behind AA team 3

at the rear is down, approach the shack and ready your weapon. Open the door and you'll see the second PLA through the shack, guarding the front door **[Screen 02]**. If you act quickly and shoot him in the head, you'll kill him instantly before he can react. With him down, the first AA team is history.

Now, switch to the Queen Bee you looted earlier from the farmhouse and then enter the shack. Look out of the front door of the shack to the SW and you'll see the next AA team at RV9 looking off into the distance. You can take them both out easily with one Queen Bee rocket. Otherwise, have your men attack them while you fire from the shack.

With the second AA team down, hold your position at the shack while the US AAVPs move into the area and attack the PLA. There is a considerable force in this village, so use the low wall for cover and take out any PLA who get close. Check your map frequently. As soon as the area to the south is clear of PLA, you're ready to move.

Go out through the back door of the shack and head south on a path perpendicular to the village **[Screen 03]**. On reaching the far southern edge of the village, turn and head west towards the last AA team. View your map and have your men attack the team as you sneak up from behind. More often than not the team is in a building at the western end of the village and you can come in through the back door and surprise them. When the last AA team has been eliminated you will get a radio message from control informing you that Hydra One (CAS) is inbound. Elimination of this last AA team will also complete one of your Primary Objectives.

10 Secure Beachhead
Once the remaining PLA force have been eliminated or have fled the village you will be informed that a PLA counter-attack is imminent and that your next objective is to hold the south-west section of the village and the

02

03

road leading to the airfield. This is when a checkpoint save becomes available, so make sure you trigger it.

If the AAVP you were told to protect against the AT teams at the start of the mission has not been destroyed, then it will come in and assist you with holding this sector, while the remaining US fire-teams and AAVP will take up strategic positions in the village to cover the north-east, east and south-east sides of the village **[Screen 01]**. Hydra One will remain in the air for about five minutes until they have to RTB (return to base).

You have two to three minutes before the PLA counter-attack begins. Start by having your Engineer man the stationary gun behind the sandbag. Now tell your two other men to defend the Engineer. There is an ammo crate nearby that you can raid for a Marksman Rifle, if you don't have a long-range weapon.

It's now all about survival. Watch the southern horizon and keep checking your map. PLA will come over the hill a long way to the south. Your men will make a good job of taking them out and the AAVP (if it survived) will do an excellent job destroying the encroaching PLA **[Screen 02]**. However, the PLA coming over the hill have Queen Bees, which they will use to destroy the AAVP. If it goes down, then defending your sector gets somewhat harder. It should be noted that you can mount the APC if you want to and use its guns, but it's safer to stay on foot.

Because of this, you may want to check the hill occasionally with a scope weapon and try to identify any PLA in possession of a Queen Bee. If you identify one, take him out immediately with long-range fire before he can destroy the AAVP.

As well as coming over the southern hill, groups of PLA will come through the woods on the western side of the road **[Screen 03]**. You'll need to check your map frequently to spot them moving in, or they'll easily get close and overtake you. A long-range rifle is excellent for taking them out as they come through the trees. When moving in from the woods, the PLA always take the same path, so it's possible to lay mines in the path and take them out before

they reach you. However, even with mines, you should always be prepared to take on the PLA yourself to make sure they don't make it to your position. The PLA who come through the woods will be running, and they move fast, so never neglect them.

PRO TIP!

Once you know the route the PLA use to come in on the west side of the road, you can lay mines in their path to give them a nasty surprise.

The rest of the village will be protected by the other USMC soldiers (especially at the northern and eastern edges), so all you need to do is concentrate on your southern position. Once the first wave has hit the village, a second wave of two vehicles armed with HMGs will come in about two minutes later, arriving from the south road and the north-east corner.

The enemy vehicles pose some threat if the AAVPs are not around to protect you, as they have a 12.7mm HMG positioned on the back. Hydra One (CAS), if still around at this point, is generally very effective at eliminating

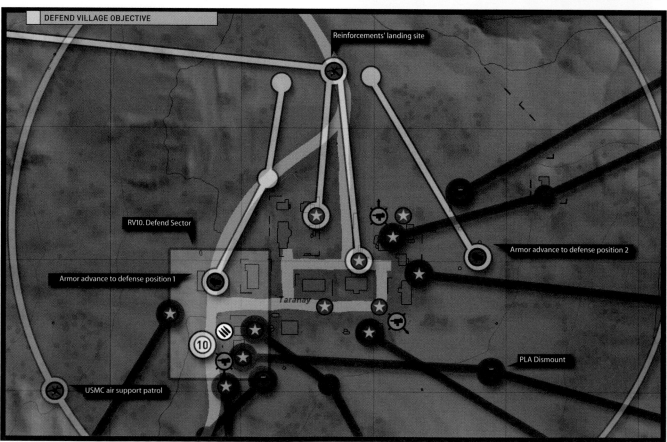

DEFEND VILLAGE OBJECTIVE

Reinforcements' landing site

RV10. Defend Sector

Armor advance to defense position 2

Armor advance to defense position 1

Taranay

PLA Dismount

USMC air support patrol

04

vehicles **[Screen 04]**. After two to three minutes a third wave will spawn and attack the village from the east, south and south-east.

If any of the other US fire-teams are unable to hold their sectors, then you will be informed by radio that the enemy have breached either the north or east sectors of the village, so listen out for these radio messages and watch your back. However, even if the other teams are breached, don't abandon your southern post. Just stay where you are and keep a ready eye on the map to make sure no PLA make it inside the village and flank you. If at any point the US forces drop below seven or eight men, then a reinforcement helicopter will come in and drop off two new fire-teams. The replacements will always move to a breached sector and try to shore it up and repel the PLA there.

Guard your southern sector and protect your AAVP as best you can with long-range fire. Keep a close eye on the woods on the western side of the road for PLA coming in from that area. Just remember: your primary goal here is to hold your ground and survive the counter-attack. If you repel all encroaching PLA and survive three waves of this counter-attack, your mission will be complete and you will also achieve your Primary Objective: Secure Beachhead.

ACHIEVEMENT / TROPHY

Tide's Out – When you have successfully defended the village, you will unlock this Achievement for the 360 or a Trophy for the PS3.

EAGLE OFFENSE
MISSION 04

Eagle Offense is an 'Infantry Storming Objective' mission which consists of three main elements. The first is the route to the airfield where the player and his fire-team must clear the way to the airfield for the USMC Convoy by destroying incoming PLA APCs.

The second part involves a fierce firefight inside the airfield against well dug-in PLA units within a time constraint.

The third presents the player with the challenge of a heavy flow of PLA vehicles coming in from the east to retake the airfield. The player must defend the site until help arrives in the form of a AH-1Z.

Equipment and Vehicles

Most of the ammo crates are located at the airfield, a heavily fortified area. However, you can find one ammo crate near RV4 that you can easily pillage if you're running low on ammo. The crates in the airfield are more difficult to access, as the PLA presence there is very high. With ammo being a bit hard to come by in the airfield, you'd better be conservative with your weaponry as you push into the airfield. Looking at the map, you'll see there are some emplaced AGLs (Automatic Grenade Launchers) that are fun to use if you have the time and inclination; in particular the AGL at RV3 will come in handy against the PLA in the ruins to the south.

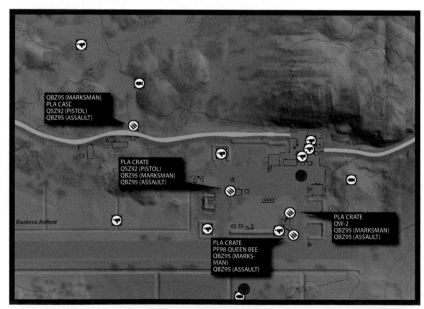

MISSION WEAPONS AND VEHICLES

Item	US
Weapons	US Knife
	MEU (SOC) Pistol
	MP5A4 Sub-Machine Gun
	M16A4 Assault Rifle
	M16A4 Assault Rifle (Marksman)
	M16A4 Assault Rifle (Assault)
	M4A1 Assault Rifle
	M4A1 Assault Rifle (Marksman)
	M249 Light Machine Gun
	Mk48 Mod 0 Medium Machine Gun
	US Fragmentation Grenade
	US Smoke Grenade
	US Coloured Smoke Grenade Red
	US Anti Personnel Mine
	US Anti Tank Mine
	US Demolition Charge
	IR Stobe
	FGM-148 Javelin Guided Anti-Tank Missile
	SMAW Rocket Launcher
Vehicles	AAVP7A1
	M1025 HMMWV with Machinegun
	AH-1Z Ground Attack
Emplacements	M2 .50 Calibre Heavy Machine Gun *

Item	PLA
Weapons	PLA Knife
	QSZ92 Pistol
	QCW05 Sub-Machine Gun
	QBZ95 Assault Rifle
	QBZ95 Assault Rifle (Marksman)
	QBZ95 Assault Rifle (Assault)
	QBB95 Light Machine Gun
	Type 67-II Medium Machine Gun
	PLA Fragmentation Grenade
	PLA Smoke Grenade
	PLA Coloured Smoke Grenade Red
	PLA Claymore Mine
	PLA Anti Personnel Mine
	PLA Anti Tank Mine
	Field Dressing PLA
	PF98 Queen Bee Rocket Launcher
	QW-2 SAM Anti Aircraft Homing Missile
Vehicles	Type 97 Infantry Fighting Vehicle
	BJS2022 with HMG
	Z-10 Attack
	Mi-171 Transport
Emplacements	QJC 88 Heavy Machine Gun *
	LG-3 Auto Grenade Launcher *

* Tall mount

Primary Objectives	Secondary Objectives	Bonus Objectives
Destroy or Incapacitate two PLA Type 97 APCs	Fire Mortars on PLA Position in Ruins	Destroy or Incapacitate PLA Transport Helicopter
Take Control of the Control Tower	Fire CAS on Incoming PLA Reinforcement Vehicles	
Hold the Control Tower Against Oncoming PLA Reinforcements	Destroy or incapacitate PLA Attack Helicopter	

OBJECTIVE OVERVIEW

RV2. Destroy PLA Armor

RV3. Recon Position

RV4. Join Convoy

RV5. Battle for the Airfield

RV6. Take Control Tower and Defend Airfield

Raskova Airfield

04

MISSION OBJECTIVES

① In this part of the mission the player and his fire-team find themselves alone, without the support of the rest of the USMC forces. They need to make their own way to the airfield and, en route, destroy any PLA Armor that could inflict casualties on the convoy.

② Destroy or Incapacitate 2 PLA Type 97 APCs / Destroy or Incapacitate PLA Transport Helicopter

The PLA conceal two Type 97s in the terrain to the area west of the airfield. The player must engage them quickly, as these are lethal to the USMC convoy and can destroy it in a matter of minutes. The USMC AAVPs will hold fire until the objective is completed (when the two Type 97s are destroyed or incapacitated). Failing this objective will fail the mission. You will fail this mission if you and your fire-team are killed, or 8 or more of the US convoy are killed, so you'll have to move quickly before the PLA tanks can engage the convoy.

At the start of the mission, open the map and you'll see an emplaced gun to the southeast. Order your men to attack it. As they are doing so, equip the SMAW in your inventory, and then head east to a small hill. Get to the top of the hill, go to the far side, look down and you'll see the PLA APCs **[Screen 01]**. Use the SMAW to take out the rear APC, then immediately back up and reload. Don't stay exposed in the open for long, especially to reload, as the second PLA APC will be quick to sight and fire on you. Once you have reloaded

your SMAW, approach the hilltop once more and target the last tank. Destroy the second tank and you're done with your first Primary Objective.

Once the tanks are down, move down from the hill you are on and into the field below. Have your men regroup on you (Follow Me). As you make your way to the next objective point, a Transport Helicopter will fly overhead from the south; this is your Bonus Objective. If you wish to complete this objec-

01

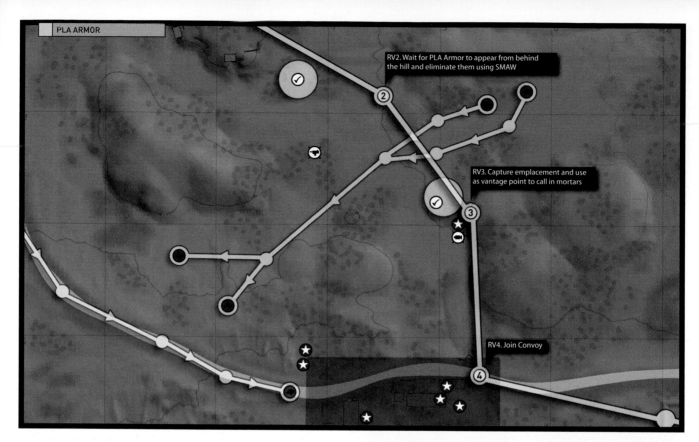

PLA ARMOR

RV2. Wait for PLA Armor to appear from behind the hill and eliminate them using SMAW

RV3. Capture emplacement and use as vantage point to call in mortars

RV4. Join Convoy

tive, you can take the chopper out with your Assault Rifle. Using the SMAW is also an option, but the chopper is fast and the SMAW is not guided, so it's best to use your Assault Rifle **[Screen 01]**. If you are quick to fire, this Bonus Objective will be yours. You only get one shot at this, so aim accurately. Once the chopper is down and your men are with you, move on to the next area. Remember that you alone must take the chopper out; it won't count if your men do it, so order them to hold fire to allow you to take out the chopper.

ACHIEVEMENT / TROPHY

Hip Shooter: Destroying the PLA Transport Chopper will unlock this Achievement for the 360 or the Trophy for the PS3.

③ Fire Mortars on PLA Position in Ruins

There are some ruins to the west of the airfield in which the PLA have set up a position that strongly opposes the USMC convoy, and is stopping it from safely advancing into the airfield.

Your job is to recon that position and choose its strongest location (the one most heavily fortified with PLA soldiers). While you are still in the field near the PLA APCs you just destroyed and not at RV3, equip the binoculars and survey the ruins. You'll have to move a little closer, but don't enter RV3 just yet. As you do this, it is best to order your fire-team to hold their fire or Fire on Your Lead so they don't start shooting and thus alert the PLA to your presence).

Make your way over a small hill to the southeast and at the top the hill you'll see a PLA solider manning an emplaced Grenade Launcher. Take him out quickly and then take cover behind the sandbags. You'll soon get a radio message that you can call in a Mortar Strike. Peek over the sandbags at the ruined buildings to the south. You'll call the Mortar Strike in the same way as you would an Air Strike. Target a building with PLA soldiers and call the strike. Calling the strike completes your first Secondary Objective **[Screen 02]**.

Remember that you don't have to call in the Mortar Strike, and can simply move to the east instead. If you do this, the mortars will be reassigned for other use (meaning you don't get to use them) and you'll fail this Secondary Objective.

During the entire time the USMC will stay a good distance up the road and wait for you to call down the mortars. Once the strike has been called, the

convoy will begin moving, so make sure your aim is true and away from the road when calling the strike, or your mortars could hit the convoy. If you fail this objective by moving out of the area (and don't call the strike), the vehicles will resume their advance to the airfield, tackling any PLA resistance in the ruins. If you fail, the mortars will be reassigned to another task and you will not be able to save them to use later. It's all or nothing here, so call the strike and take out the PLA to the south before moving on to RV4.

⑤ Take Control of the Control Tower

Make your way south to RV4 where you'll rejoin the convoy. Travel the road with the convoy, and stay behind the AAVPs and use them as cover as you advance. En route to RV5, you'll learn that you must now enter the airfield and take over the Control Tower at RV6.

Once in the airfield, the USMC convoy deploys in a pincer move and Infantry Units riding the AAVPs disembark and assault designated locations within the airfield zone. Try to avoid firing on friendly units and keep your head down. The PLA are well dug-in in buildings and fortified positions.

You'll enter the airfield from the northwestern corner, and can dig-in in a fortified concrete position in a ditch area that provides excellent cover. One of the AAVPs will move further into the airfield and can provide you with good cover and a vantage point over dangerous areas. Your objective: reach the Control Tower at RV6.

The fight to the Control Tower may be a hard one, and you will have to make good use of cover and remain mindful of your flanking. Keeping the Medic alive may be the difference between life and death, and making sure buildings are empty when entering them can keep you from dying at the hands of a hidden PLA soldier.

There is a PLA ammunition crate at the side of one of the buildings in the center of the airfield if you need to restock. However, firing on the red barrels next to that building may prove useful in eliminating some of the PLA inside, but it will also destroy the ammo crates **[Screen 03]**.

Once a member of the USMC enters the airfield area, a timer is triggered that gives you 6 minutes and 20 seconds to gain control of the tower. The PLA will begin firing mortars on the airfield at this point. The first mortar will fall in open terrain outside the airfield due west approximately 5 seconds after a USMC member enters the airfield and the timer starts.

Two minutes later, the second mortar is dropped (all are in the form of a barrage) a little closer to the USMC vehicles positioned on the outskirts of the airfield.

Two minutes and 40 seconds later, a third mortar barrage is dropped which this time hits and destroys one AAVP. When this happens, you'll be told to achieve the objective more quickly.

A mere 8 seconds later the fourth mortar drops which destroys another AAVP. You'll then get another radio communication which makes it very clear that if you don't hurry and take control of the tower, the mission will fail. When it gets this late into the mission, the checkpoint in the Control Tower will turn off.

Finally, after 1 minute and 20 seconds after the last radio communication, the fifth and final PLA mortar will drop and destroy the third AAVP. If this happens, the mission fails.

Alternate Strategies for RV5

There is a checkpoint just outside the airfield, so go through it once you arrive at the airfield to save your progress. One of the easiest ways to tackle this objective (Secure the Control Tower) is to find a vehicle. Enter the ve-

04

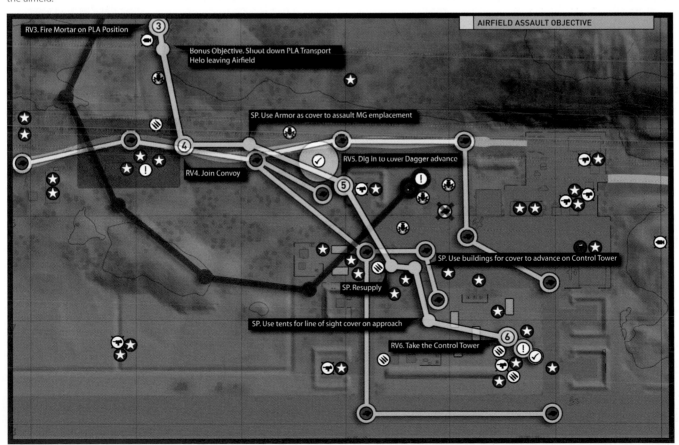

AIRFIELD ASSAULT OBJECTIVE

RV3. Fire Mortar on PLA Position
Bonus Objective. Shoot down PLA Transport Helo leaving Airfield
SP. Use Armor as cover to assault MG emplacement
RV5. Dig In to cover Dagger advance
RV4. Join Convoy
SP. Use buildings for cover to advance on Control Tower
SP. Resupply
SP. Use tents for line of sight cover on approach
RV6. Take the Control Tower

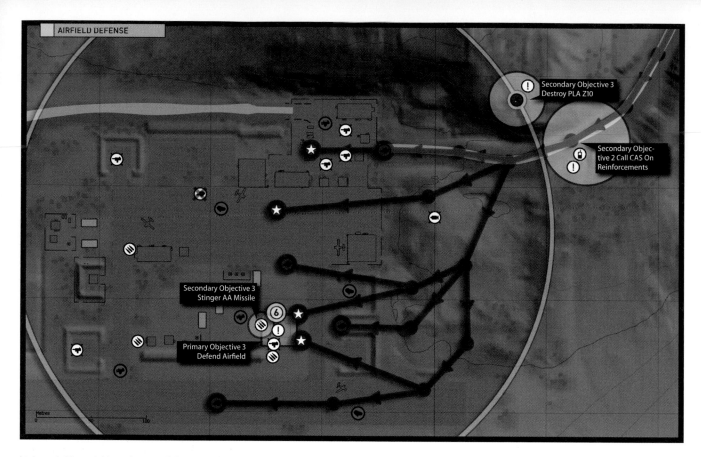

Secondary Objective 3
Destroy PLA Z10

Secondary Objective 2 Call CAS On Reinforcements

Secondary Objective 3
Stinger AA Missile

Primary Objective 3
Defend Airfield

hicle and drive quickly to the rear of the Control Tower; it's best to approach it from the east when you do this. Once there, you'll have to deal with two PLAs manning an emplaced gun at a sandbag location behind the Control Tower. They will be facing west, so dispatch them quickly. Run them over with your vehicle to achieve the fastest kill! **[Screen 01]**

Now go through the door and kill the PLA soldier on the ground floor. Now make your way to the stairs where you can sight and shoot a second PLA soldier from the stairs; he is on the second floor near a west-facing window. Now make your way up the last set of stairs from the second floor to the roof, and kill the PLA soldier there. This will secure the building and complete the second Primary Objective.

If you can't find a vehicle, then follow the road to the easternmost edge of the airfield and enter the building there **[Screen 02]**. You'll encounter some PLA inside, so take them out. You're now directly across from the Control Tower, so take out the PLA guarding it with ranged fire, and use the building for cover. Once the guards are down, enter the building, kill the three PLA there if they are still alive, and the tower is yours.

⑥ Hold the Control Tower Against Oncoming PLA Reinforcements / Fire CAS on Incoming PLA Reinforcement Vehicles / Destroy or Incapacitate PLA Attack Helicopter

Now that you are in control of the tower, you must not leave the tower for the PLA to claim. The mission will fail if too many PLA enter the tower and there is no USMC soldier left to defend it. To avoid this, order your men to defend the tower's position. There is a checkpoint in the tower, so make sure you trigger it.

Once the Control Tower is taken, the PLA reinforcements will launch their attack on the airfield with PLA Type 97s and Infantry Units. The attacking PLA APCs will come down the road from the east in waves of one vehicle initially and then, after 70 seconds two others, another two after another 70 seconds and then one more vehicle after a further 70 seconds **[Screen 03]**.

Each of these vehicles carries a PLA fire-team that disembarks the vehicle when it reaches a specific area outside the airfield. The vehicle then moves on to resume its attack and enter the airfield. The Infantry Unit will generally move into the airfield to launch a direct assault the Control Tower.

In this part of the mission, if the USMC sustains too many casualties (the AAVP and the entire fire-team are killed) additional USMC forces will be sent in to replace them. Replacements consist of one AAVP and a fire-team. The additional reinforcements can mount up to two AAVPs and two fire-teams in total, replacing two AAVPs and two fire-teams killed in the battle.

Once the PLA APCs start coming down the eastern road, make your way to the top of the tower and watch them (all you need do is see them). This will cause you to radio in the approaching enemy and net you the use of an Air Strike in the form of four Air-to-Ground small missiles on designated targets.

It is best to designate targets for the Air Strike from the roof of the Control Tower, as the roof provides the best vantage point. However, it is also the

most exposed to the enemy, so you will need to keep your head down as much as possible.

To call the Air Strike, simply look at your target (line of sight or through the scope of your weapon) and designate the target as you would with any other Air Strike. This strike is a small missile that takes several seconds to deploy. Furthermore, the missile will not move with a moving vehicle, but will instead land at the exact spot you have designated enabling the PLA APC to move out of range of the incoming missile. To avoid this, wait for the APC to stop and unload the fire-team it is carrying. Once it stops, immediately call the strike and, if you act quickly, the missile will destroy the APC and the disembarking PLA simultaneously. Once you call your first Air Strike, you will complete the second Secondary Objective **[Screen 04]**.

ACHIEVEMENT / TROPHY

Shock and Awe- Calling an Air-Strike for the first time will grant you an achievement for the 360 or Trophy for the PS3

As you are dealing with the encroaching APCs and PLA soldiers, another threat will arise: a PLA attack chopper. This Attack Helicopter will make its way to the airfield to aid the PLA reinforcements. This chopper can wreak havoc among the USMC vehicles and infantry, and could even destroy the Control Tower, killing both you and your fire-team inside. Once you learn of the incoming chopper, make your way to the first floor of the tower to the ammo crates there, and take the Singer AA Missile.

PRO TIP! ⓘ

The PLA attack chopper can destroy the tower killing you and your men, so make taking it out a priority as soon as you learn it is approaching.

Once you have the AA Missile, exit via the front entrance and cross to the tent. Take cover there, and let your fire-team deal with the incoming PLA APCs. Ready the AA Missile and look to the eastern sky. The helicopter is marked by an icon, making it easy to find. Once the helicopter is visible, aim the Stinger at it and a small, square lock will appear on the chopper.

Keep the scope trained on the chopper until you get a full lock as indicated by a diamond shape around the square reticle. Once you get this full lock, fire the missile! **[Screen 05]** The missile is guided, so once it is locked and away, it will track and destroy the chopper in seconds. Once the helicopter is destroyed, you will have completed the third Secondary Objective.

This also triggers the earlier arrival of the USMC AH-1Z. The AH-1Z is scheduled to arrive at a specific point in the mission, but the completion of the third Secondary Objective rewards the player with an earlier arrival and completion of the mission. Once the AH-1Z arrives at the airfield, the morale of the PLA reinforcements cracks, and they start fleeing from the airfield with the AH-1Z in pursuit. The airfield is taken by the USMC forces, and the mission is accomplished..

With the PLA chopper down, go back to the first floor and use the windows to pick off the encroaching PLA soldiers. Take them out fast, and use any Air Strikes you have left. Destroying the enemy attack chopper quickly will free the USMC AH-1Zs to come in early, so you only need hold out for a short while before the AH-1Zs arrive to push back the PLA and end the mission.

ACHIEVEMENT / TROPHY

Runway Relief: When you successfully complete the mission, you'll unlock this Achievement for the 360 or Trophy for the PS3.

Notes About RV6

There is a checkpoint inside the Control Tower that you should trigger once you arrive. However, it is possible to miss it as you storm through the tower taking out the PLA. In fact, you can even get all the way to the roof and trigger the incoming PLA APCs and attack the chopper before you realize you need to trigger the checkpoint. In this event, you can save the game in a bad position such that the chopper is already on top of you, and is able to destroy the tower before you can even reach the Stinger Missile in the crate. You should therefore ensure you trigger the checkpoint as soon as you have control of the tower (as indicated by the on-screen message). Once the checkpoint has been triggered, go back to the roof and spot the incoming APCs and continue the mission as described earlier.

02

03

04

05

POWDER TRAIL
MISSION 05

Powder Trail is a daring raid through enemy lines to locate and extract a helicopter crew shot down during air operations supporting the capture of Raskova Airfield. While PLA forces are in the process of withdrawing from the southwest of Skira and regrouping behind defensive lines, the USMC has a short window in which to rush in and retrieve the downed crew.

Equipment and Vehicles

You will find this mission has a large number of ammo crates thus allowing you to cut loose if you like. The ammo crate in Echo One's area holds a SMAW an M4A1 Marksman Rifle, both of which can make your first firefight much easier. There are ammo crates at RV4, RV6, and RV7, all of which are fairly close together, making it easy to stay well armed when confronting the PLA. You'll also find ammo crates at RV9 and RV11 as you make your way to the village. With such plentiful ammo, you can certainly afford to go full throttle against the PLA, but don't forget that the village at RV12 presents quite a challenge, so don't get too carefree on your way there. Make sure to pillage the crates at RV11 if you are low on ammo before you enter the village.

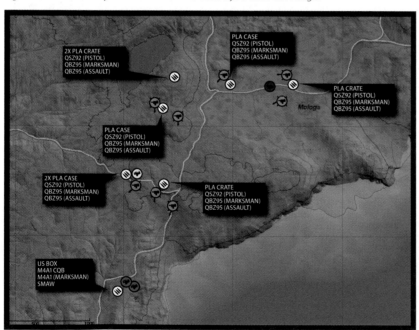

MISSION WEAPONS AND VEHICLES

Item	US
Weapons	US Knife
	MEU (SOC) Pistol
	MP5A4 Sub-Machine Gun
	M16A4 Assault Rifle
	M16A4 Assault Rifle (Assault)
	M4A1 Assault Rifle
	M4A1 Assault Rifle (CQB)
	M4A1 Assault Rifle (Marksman)
	M4A1A Assault Rifle
	M249 Light Machine Gun
	Mk48 Mod 0 Medium Machine Gun
	M21 Sniper Rifle
	US Fragmentation Grenade
	US Smoke Grenade
	US Coloured Smoke Grenade Red
	US Anti Personnel Mine
	US Anti Tank Mine
	US Demolition Charge
	IR Stobe
	SMAW Rocket Launcher
Vehicles	M1025 HMMWV with Machinegun
	AH-6J Attack
	AH-1Z Ground Attack
	MH-60S

Item	PLA
Weapons	PLA Knife
	QSZ92 Pistol
	QCW05 Sub-Machine Gun
	QBZ95 Assault Rifle
	QBZ95 Assault Rifle (Marksman)
	QBZ95 Assault Rifle (Assault)
	Type 81-1 Assault Rifle (Marksman)
	Type 81-1 Assault Rifle (Assault)
	QBB95 Light Machine Gun
	Type 67-II Medium Machine Gun
	QBU88 Sniper Rifle
	PLA Fragmentation Grenade
	PLA Smoke Grenade
	PLA Coloured Smoke Grenade Red
	PLA Claymore Mine
	PLA Anti Personnel Mine
	PLA Anti Tank Mine
	Field Dressing PLA
	PF98 Queen Bee Rocket Launcher
Vehicles	Type 92 WZ551A APC
	Type 95 Anti-Aircraft Artillery
	BJS2022
	SX2190 Truck
	Z-10 Attack
	Mi-171 Transport
Emplacements	QJC 88 Heavy Machine Gun *

* Tall mount

Primary Objectives	Secondary Objectives	Bonus Objectives
Search for Downed Crew	Support Recon Team Dagger One Echo	Destroy PLA Armored Units near Mologa
Rescue Helicopter Crew	Search Last Known Position of Helicopter	
Safely Extract Helicopter Crew	Destroy AA Site	

OBJECTIVE OVERVIEW

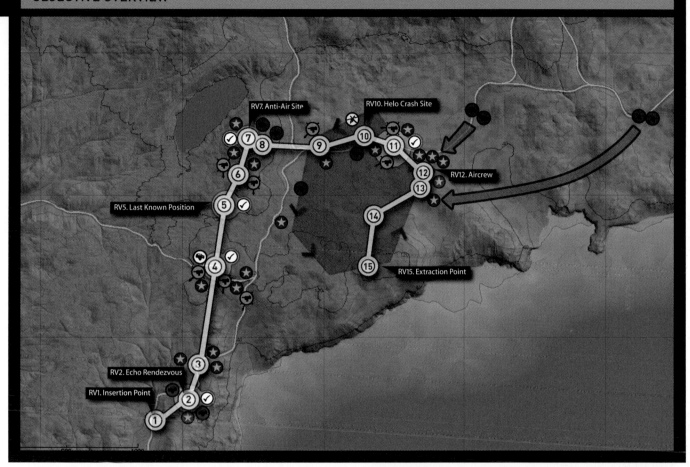

RV7. Anti-Air Site

RV10. Helo Crash Site

RV12. Aircrew

RV5. Last Known Position

RV15. Extraction Point

RV2. Echo Rendezvous

RV1. Insertion Point

PRIMARY MISSION OBJECTIVES

(1) As the insertion transport peels away, your first task is to combine forces with a second USMC fire-team already active in the field, Dagger One Echo. They await with light armor support concealed in a copse of trees 250 meters east, but their position has been compromised by PLA recon elements. Take your team and make haste to reach Echo to bolster their defenses.

PRO TIP! (i)

You start with a SMAW in your inventory, and a second will soon appear in another ammo crate. Make sure to save at least 2 SMAW Rockets for the end of the mission, as they will make it much easier for you!

(2) Support Recon Team Dagger One Echo

You have two choices at this point; either run straight to Echo where they are dug-in at the trees, or head north east to flank the 3 PLA fire-teams that are moving in. The best approach is to flank the PLA. There are 3 fire-teams ahead, each consisting of 3 PLA soldiers. Once you cross the road on your north eastern route, you'll come to the first PLA team near some trees. Stay crouched down as you advance and order your men to assault the PLA team. Use the trees for cover as you move, and take the PLA out [Screen 01].

PRO TIP! (i)

There is an M4A1 Marksman Rifle in the ammo crate next to Echo squad. It's long range and scope will make the next firefight a bit easier.

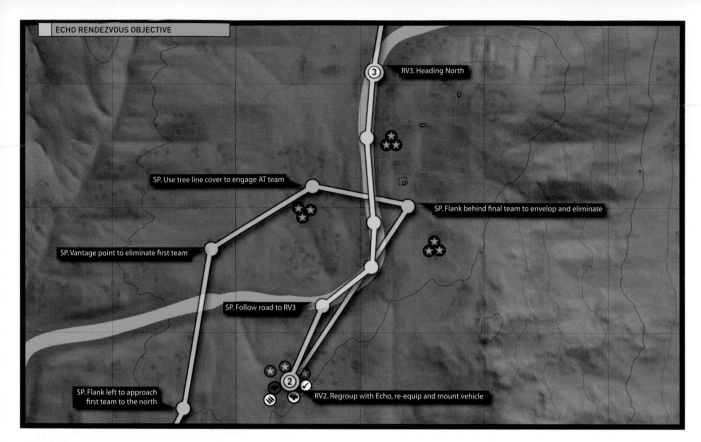

ECHO RENDEZVOUS OBJECTIVE

RV3. Heading North

SP. Use tree line cover to engage AT team

SP. Flank behind final team to envelop and eliminate

SP. Vantage point to eliminate first team

SP. Follow road to RV3

SP. Flank left to approach first team to the north

RV2. Regroup with Echo, re-equip and mount vehicle

Once the first PLA team is down, you should concentrate on the next team that is furthest to the north. That team has an AT Gunner with them and, if they get close to Echo's location, he will destroy the vehicles there, making the rest of the mission very slow going. Use the tree line where the first PLA team was located, and have your men engage the PLA team to the north. That team will storm down the road, so hold your ground and pick them off as they get close.

Once the second PLA team is down, check your map to find the location of the final team. Have your men attach them as you move round north of the team and flank their rear. Stay crouched down as you pursue them and you will easily get behind them, as their attention will be on Echo to the south. Take them all out quickly, and then you can rendezvous with Echo at RV2, thereby completing the first Secondary Objective.

When you reach RV2, you'll trigger a checkpoint and receive new intel that will have you doing recon on a possible location for the missing US chopper. Before you move out, raid the ammo crate here. Grabbing the M4A1 Marksman is a great choice, and make sure to replenish your SMAW if you have used it before this point. When you are ready, enter the empty vehicle and wait for Echo team to board their own vehicle. They will soon move forward, so follow them to RV3 **[Screen 01]**.

4 **Search for the Downed Crew**

At this stage the only clue you have to the location of the missing crew is their last signal before they went down at the relayed grid coordinates about 1.4 km north. Reconnaissance of that position will require you to breach enemy lines. The PLA have set up fortifications along a strategic road junction at the merger of two main access routes from the southwest of the island.

Drive through RV3, and continue off-road to the north where you will see the PLA fortifications silhouetted along the ridge ahead, backed by ominous distant AA tracer fire. Dagger One Echo will divert up the slope to the west, looking to flank the defenses and avoid the incoming MG fire. At this point you could elect to follow Echo as they skirt the tree line to attack the enemy from the left. Alternatively, branch right and hit the right hand side of the defensive line from the southern road, trapping the PLA in a pincer movement. In either case, be very wary of the machine gun emplacements, which can bring a halt to your vehicle very quickly.

PRO TIP!

Monitor Echo closely. The longer you can keep them close and combat-effective, the more assistance you will gain from their presence as the mission unfolds.

By far the best approach is to proceed slowly and follow Echo team. They will soon turn west to flank some emplaced gunners. Once this happens, move ahead, speed up and pass Echo team. Pass the emplaced gunner on the western side of the encampment and park your vehicle behind the building just behind the gunner **[Screen 02]**. Disembark your vehicle and quickly have your men engage the two PLA soldiers at the closest emplaced gun. From there, move forward and engage the next two PLA soldiers at the second gun emplacement. Take them out quickly and, when they are dead, a checkpoint will become available that you can trigger to save your progress. If you did this quickly, then Echo team will be in good shape to move on with you.

As you are assaulting the encampment, be aware that a PLA attack chopper will often fly overhead and bombard your location. When you see the chop-

per moving in, scramble for cover, as the attack chopper may target and destroy your vehicle. Don't worry if this happens, because there is another empty vehicle in the encampment that you can commandeer. When you're ready, enter your vehicle once more and head to RV5.

PRO TIP! (i)

Be careful not to venture too far east at this point. The closer you get to the road on that side, the more likely you are to attract the attention of the PLA attack chopper patrolling the area.

⑤ Search Last Known Position of Helicopter

Head to RV5, where you will encounter another checkpoint and two small buildings. You'll approach the buildings from the south as you near RV5. Stop just south of the small buildings, and disembark your vehicle. Once you are out, slowly make your way to RV5 and the checkpoint. By going on foot, you'll avoid attracting fire that could damage or even destroy your vehicle. Ease up between the buildings and you'll receive a radio communication.

As the message is playing, sneak between the buildings and lie down on the ground facing south. There are two emplaced gunners up ahead at the base of a hill **[Screen 03]**. Use the M4A1 Marksman and target each gunner and take them out (use single shot fire mode for greater accuracy). Once they are dead, return to your men and huddle behind the buildings as you try to remain undetected by the circling PLA chopper and AT gunners to the south.

When the message is complete, you will receive an Artillery Strike, and be tasked with the optional assignment of taking out the Anti-Air site on top of the hill to the south. The AA site is heavily fortified, so it will be a challenging mission. You can use the Artillery Strike on the AA site to soften the PLA up, but it's best to save the strike for the end of the mission where it will prove far more valuable.

PRO TIP! (i)

You'll receive an Artillery Strike here that you could use on the AA site ahead, but save the strike for the end of the mission where it will make life a lot easier.

04

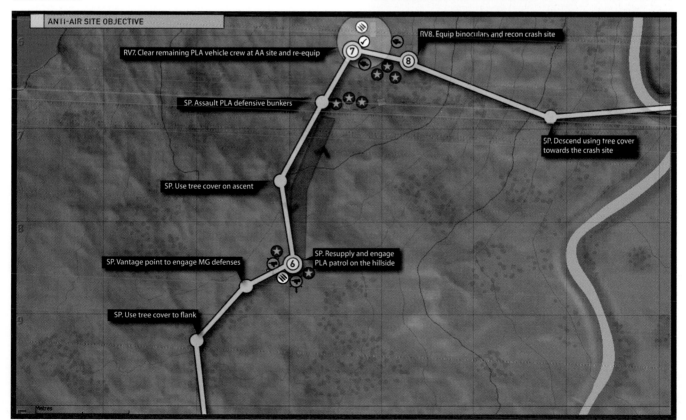

ANTI-AIR SITE OBJECTIVE

RV8. Equip binoculars and recon crash site

RV7. Clear remaining PLA vehicle crew at AA site and re-equip

SP. Assault PLA defensive bunkers

SP. Descend using tree cover towards the crash site

SP. Use tree cover on ascent

SP. Resupply and engage PLA patrol on the hillside

SP. Vantage point to engage MG defenses

SP. Use tree cover to flank

Metres

01

fly around the area harassing you for fear of AA retaliation, so it will now leave the area and head east to safety. This will make things much easier from now on. Moreover, with the AA site down, your evac chopper at the end of the mission will reach you more quickly, making your evacuation faster and less risky. Finally, by clearing the AA site, you will have opened a checkpoint there that you can use to save your progress. All-in-all, taking out the AA site is a very good decision!

(8) RV8 is on the eastern slope of the hill of the AA site. Go there, equip the binoculars and scan the area below and to the east. You'll see the crashed chopper in the distance. Continue scanning the area, especially the tents near the trees, to spot the PLA soldiers in the area. You will receive a radio message during this recon and, as the communication is playing out, a PLA truck will start heading up the road from the east. This truck is carrying PLA soldiers that will reinforce the other PLA in the area, so it's a good idea to take it out while it is on the road.

Use your binoculars and find the burning PLA tank that is on the road. The PLA truck will come past it soon. Look just west of the tank, and use the range finder in your binoculars to find a distance of 140 meters west of the burning PLA tank. The easiest way to do this is to first range the tank, then range again to the west. So if the tank ranges out at 500 meters away, then you need to find the spot that is 360 meters away on the road. Once you find that spot, equip your SMAW, but make sure you are using HEF rounds! You'll need to save the HEAT rounds for later!

Now ready the weapon and sight the approaching PLA truck. Your goal is to wait until the truck reaches that spot 140 meters west of the tank you just located, and then take it out with a SMAW Rocket. This is a long shot, so you'll need to adjust your aim slightly high. Use the second horizontal line below dead center on your crosshairs for this target **[Screen 02]**. At this distance (360 to 400 meters), the second lower line is the sweet spot. Position the line over the middle of the vehicle and fire.

If you do this correctly, the SMAW rocket will stop the PLA truck and all the soldiers will immediately disembark. This keeps them far away from the immediate area and gives you time to move forward. Destroying the truck will often demoralize the PLA soldiers, and they will run off. As the soldiers disembark, don't hesitate to hit them with your last HEF SMAW rocket if you

(6) Once you are ready, board your vehicle and head south toward the house up ahead on the right. Park behind it and then disembark the vehicle. Order your men to defend the house, and then enter it yourself. Go to a north-facing window and use the M4A1 Marksman on the PLA who will soon be assaulting your position. There are quite a few PLA, and they are persistent. Use the building for cover as you reload, and continually pick off the enemy as they approach **[Screen 01]**. If you aim accurately and consistently you will soon wipe out the advancing PLA forces. Once you have eliminated the majority of the PLA forces, have your men move forward and assault the any remaining PLA while you cover your men from your position with ranged fire. Once all of the PLA have been destroyed, board your vehicle and drive up to the AA site at RV7.

(7) Destroy AA Site

With all the PLA dead and no one to man the AA site, it is effectively offline and ineffective. There is no need to actually destroy the AA vehicles here; simply eliminating the team manning them will suffice. If you do want to destroy the vehicles just for fun, it will require the use of your SMAW, and you're better off saving those rounds for later.

By killing all the PLA here and thus rendering the AA site ineffective, you have removed the PLA attack chopper's safety blanket, and it can no longer

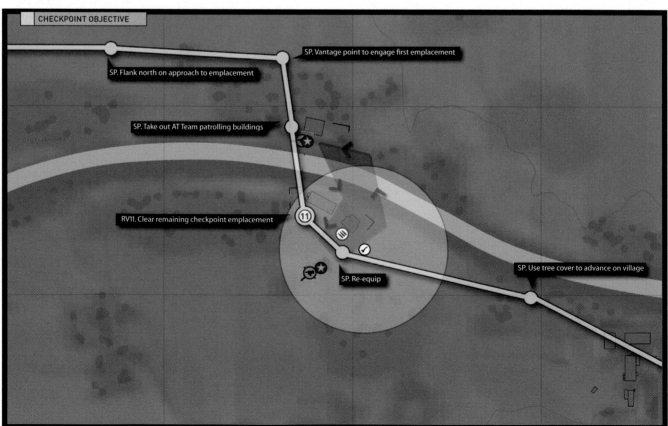

wish. You could use a HEAT rocket here if you like to destroy the incoming truck, but that will leave you with only one HEAT Rocket, and you'll really need them both at the end of this mission!

As you are doing this, Echo will often run down to engage the foot soldiers who will be making their way to your location by now. Equip your Marksman Rifle and ease down the hill a few meters. Take up position, and sight the PLA from a distance. Take them all out as they approach. Once they have been killed, enter your vehicle (if you still have it) and head down the hill toward the PLA encampment below at RV9. If you took out the PLA truck earlier with your SMAW, there won't be many PLA left here. Park your vehicle outside the encampment, and then engage any PLA there. Once they are dead, raid the ammo crate here if you like, then get back in your vehicle and head over to the burning remains of the downed chopper at RV10 **[Screen 03]**.

(11)　At the chopper, you will receive another radio communication informing you that the downed chopper team is inside the village and pinned down. This means they survived the crash and are fighting the PLA.

Important: after the radio communication with Saber 2, this mission will be timed, and you now have 50 minutes to reach the downed chopper crew, or their position will be overrun and you'll lose them.

From the chopper, head southeast toward RV11, which is a PLA checkpoint. There are two emplaced gunners (one on each side of the road) and AT gunners to contend with. It's best to leave your vehicle as you make your approach, as the vehicle will attack the AT gunner's rocket attacks. On foot, head toward the burning wreckage of a PLA tank. Keep the wrecked tank between you and the emplaced gunner on the left side of the road as you advance **[Screen 04]**.

Once you are behind it, have your men attack the area, and then peek out from the left side of the tank and take out the emplaced gunner ahead of you. Now scan the area ahead for more PLA soldiers and take them out from a distance. Once you have most of them down, head to the right side of the road and dispatch the emplaced gunner there. Check your map for any remaining PLA in the area and mop them up. Once they are down, use the checkpoint here, and re-supply at the ammo crate if you want to.

(12)　**Rescue Helicopter Crew / Safely Extract Helicopter Crew**
It's now time to head into the village and rescue the downed crew. Get to the village and follow the main road in; you'll be heading south down this road. As you move, you'll encounter a PLA fire-team attacking the building with the chopper crew inside. Take out this fire-team to the west quickly, and then have your men lay down suppressing fire to the northeast where three more PLA fire-teams are located. As they do so, enter the building where the

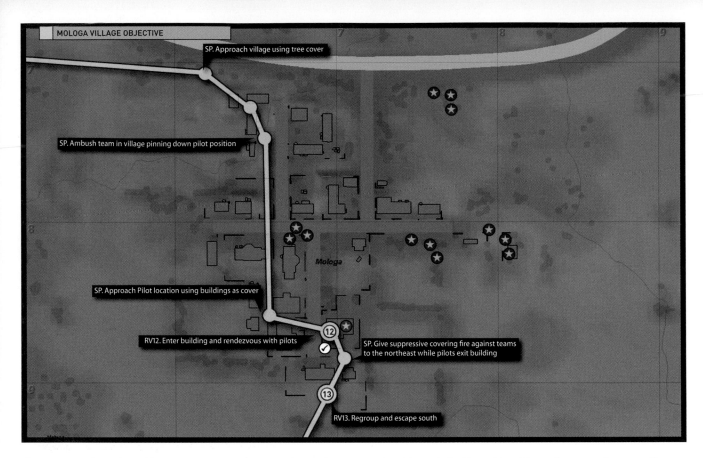

SP. Approach village using tree cover

SP. Ambush team in village pinning down pilot position

SP. Approach Pilot location using buildings as cover

RV12. Enter building and rendezvous with pilots

SP. Give suppressive covering fire against teams to the northeast while pilots exit building

RV13. Regroup and escape south

Mologa

chopper crew is located. Quickly equip the SMAW with HEAT rockets and then trigger the checkpoint.

Have the chopper crew follow you to RV13 at the southern edge of the village. Take up a position behind the building there, and wait for the first transport chopper to come in. Once it flies over the building and begins to hover, destroy it with a HEAT rocket. Note, you must use a HEAT rocket here as the HEF rockets will only down the chopper, but not destroy it. The crew on board can often survive the fall, so make sure to use your HEAT rounds **[Screen 01]**. OK, you could just ignore the choppers and make a run for it using suppressing fire to slow the PLA down, but the PLA choppers' drop-off is rapid and persistent, so it is in your best interest to take them out in the air if at all possible.

Once the first chopper is down, have the crew and your men group on you in a tight spread as you reload another HEAT round. A second transport chopper will come in from the east. Let it fly overhead and, once it slows to the west, shoot it down with the SMAW. Now order your men and the crew to move fast to RV14 to the southwest. Hold your position as they move, and two PLA armored vehicles will soon show up. If you saved your Artillery Strike from earlier in the mission, now is the time to use it. Call the strike in on the westernmost vehicle. Once you've called it in, run after your men and don't look back. Move as quickly as possible to the extraction point at RV15 to end the mission **[Screen 02]**.

ACHIEVEMENT / TROPHY

Sandman's Saviors: successfully extracting the downed chopper crew will unlock this Achievement for the 360 or Trophy for the PS3.

Alternative Strategies for RV12

From RV11, you've only got 50 minutes to retrieve the chopper team and get them to the evac site. If you've been moving quickly, you can take your time to go through the village to eliminate the PLA present. There are four fire-teams to deal with, and often the last few PLA will run away if you have killed the rest. Quickly move in and out between the buildings and have your men

engage and assault the PLA with you. The reinforcement choppers will come in approximately 5 minutes after you have assaulted the PLA in the village.

When it is close to time for their arrival, have your men suppress any remaining PLA while you head to the south end of the village and ready your SMAW with HEAT rockets. Destroy the two choppers as they come in, and then grab

the chopper crew and trip the checkpoint. Now all you have to worry about are the PLA armored vehicles, but they are easily skirted if you take a southern route and head into the trees as you make your way to the evac point.

If you don't have two HEAT rockets for your SMAW, you can effectively eliminate the incoming choppers with HEF rockets. The trick here is to hit them while they are high in the sky, so that the fall will kill the PLA inside. If the chopper isn't high enough, the PLA will survive the fall and become a problem for you. The choppers will come in from the east and, with a little practice, you can lead them as they come in (and they come in fast) and hit them head on with an HEF rocket [**Screen 03**].

As they approach from the east, they will be high enough for the fall to kill the soldiers. If you wait until they come in and hover, the chopper will be too low. If you're going to try using the HEF rockets, it is best to go and rescue the chopper crew first to trigger the checkpoint. Once you have saved your game, you're free to reload your last checkpoint as many times as it takes to get a good HEF shot in on the incoming choppers. The easiest way is to track a chopper for a HEF shot by getting directly in its path, forcing it to fly overhead. Just go ahead of it slightly and fire your HEF rocket so that it

intercepts the chopper. The first chopper is the harder of the two to track, so if you have at least one HEAT rocket, use it on the first chopper, then stand in the path of the second chopper and lead it with the HEF rocket.

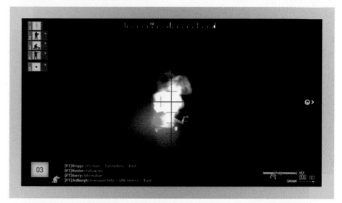

BONUS OBJECTIVE AT RV12: DESTROY PLA ARMORED UNITS NEAR MOLOGA

If you have two HEAT rockets, use one on the first transport chopper and then switch to HEF. Lead the second chopper as it comes in, and take it down with a HEF and then switch back to HFAT. Now call an Artillery Strike on the westernmost armored vehicle as you order your men and the chopper crew to advance rapidly to RV14.

Now use the buildings for cover and sneak up on the last armored vehicle and take it out with the HEAT rocket [**Screen 04**]. If you have two HEAT rockets, use one on the first transport chopper and then switch to HEF. Lead the second chopper as it comes in, and take it down with a HEF and then switch back to HEAT. Now call an Artillery Strike on the westernmost armored vehicle as you order your men and the chopper crew to advance rapidly to RV14.

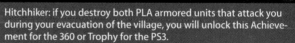

ACHIEVEMENT / TROPHY

Hitchhiker: if you destroy both PLA armored units that attack you during your evacuation of the village, you will unlock this Achievement for the 360 or Trophy for the PS3.

If you plan on going for the Bonus Objective, then you'll have to save at least one HEAT rocket for your SMAW; the HEF will simply not take out the armored vehicles. This means that even if you have both HEAT rockets, you'll have to take out one of the choppers with an HEF. In this case, it's best to trigger the checkpoint, then get into position at the southern end of the village.

HIP SHOT
MISSION 06

This mission comprises two separate parts; accessing and destroying the generator, and your retreat to the landing zone, and extraction. Hip Shot is set at night and under cover of darkness so that your Spec Ops Team can sneak past or stealth kill the majority of the PLA forces outside the fuel depot. After the generator is destroyed however, the PLA will seek you out aggressively and extraction is your only hope of survival.

Equipment and Vehicles

When you look at this equipment map, you will immediately notice that there is only one ammo crate on it; your first clue that something is different here. What kind of mission would supply you with so little ammunition? A stealth mission of course! In this mission, your objective is to lay low, use stealth and not rely heavily on fire from your weapons. You and your team start the mission with silenced weapons that make minimal noise and, if you stay true to the path of the stealthy, you will need very little ammo for this mission; the inventory you start with will be more than enough. However, if you want to raid the ammo crate, it is at the southwestern corner of the compound near a parked off-road vehicle.

PLA CRATE
QSZ92
QBZ95 (MARKSMAN)
QBZ95 (ASSAULT)

Fuel Depot

Primary Objectives	Secondary Objectives	Bonus Objectives
Destroy Fuel Depot Generator	Get into Position for Diversionary Strike	Destroy all the PLA Fuel Trucks
Rendezvous with Team at Extraction Point		

MISSION WEAPONS AND VEHICLES

Item	US
Weapons	US Knife
	MEU (SOC) Pistol
	MP5A4 Sub-Machine Gun
	M16A4 Assault Rifle (Stealth)
	M4A1 Assault Rifle (Stealth)
	Mk17 Mod 0 Assault Rifle (Marksman)
	Mk16 Mod 0 Assault Rifle (Assault)
	Mk16 Mod 0 Assault Rifle (Stealth)
	Mk48 Mod 0 Medium Machine Gun
	US Fragmentation Grenade
	US Smoke Grenade
	US Coloured Smoke Grenade Red
	US Anti Personnel Mine
	US Anti Tank Mine
	US Demolition Charge
	IR Stobe
Vehicles	MH-60S

Item	PLA
Weapons	PLA Knife
	QSZ92 Pistol
	QCW05 Sub-Machine Gun
	QBZ95 Assault Rifle
	QBZ95 Assault Rifle (Marksman)
	QBZ95 Assault Rifle (Assault)
	Type 81-1 Assault Rifle (Marksman)
	Type 81-1 Assault Rifle (Assault)
	QBB95 Light Machine Gun
	PLA Fragmentation Grenade
	PLA Smoke Grenade
	PLA Coloured Smoke Grenade Red
	PLA Anti Personnel Mine
	PLA Anti Tank Mine
	Field Dressing PLA
	PF98 Queen Bee Rocket Launcher
Vehicles	BJS2022
	BJS2022 with HMG
	SX2190 Fuel Tanker
	Fast Attack Vehicle
	Mi-171 Transport
	Mi-171V5 Ground Attack

OBJECTIVE OVERVIEW

RV7. Clear LZ of PLA troops for extraction

RV2. Use tree cover to pass behind PLA lookout post

Insertion point

RV1. Observe PLA vehicle

RV3. Observe Patrol Hub

RV6. Sparsely wooded area

RV4. Eliminate PLA overlook position

RV5. Destroy generator

Ambush diversion Saber 3

Malkovo

Metres
0   250   500

04

PRIMARY MISSION OBJECTIVES

Insertion

This is a stealth mission. The goal is to move silently and remain unseen as you complete your objective of disabling the fuel depot. The mission takes place at night, and you will be equipped with suppressed weapons that make very little sound, enabling you to kill an enemy without the sound of the weapon to alert any PLA nearby. The PLA here won't be expecting you, so they will all be off-guard and not scanning the area vigilantly for any sign of an approaching enemy. This will make it easier for you to move around. With the PLA off-guard and under cover of night, you can easily get within 100 meters of the enemy without them spotting you. If a PLA soldier has his back to you, you can ease forward in a crouch for nearly 20 meters without being spotted.

At the start of the mission, your men are tactically on Return Fire, which means they will not fire their weapon unless they are fired upon. There are several places in this mission where you will actually want your men to be set to Fire On My Lead, as their supporting gunfire will make sure your target goes down. However, once they fire for the first time, they will switch to Weapons Free and fire on any potential threat they see, so you'll want to immediately switch your men back to Fire On My Lead if you do shoot and kill an enemy, but want to remain in stealth mode **[Screen 01]**.

If you stay in stealth mode and avoid raising the alarm up to a certain point (RV4), Saber 3 will create a diversion to the east that will attract several of the PLA forces inside the fueling compound. When they have gone, you will experience less resistance once you enter the compound. If you raise the alarm before Saber 3 creates the diversion, Saber 3 will withdraw, and you will be on your own against a very aggressive PLA force.

The alarm will be raised if you are spotted at any time during the mission. This will cause the PLA to become aggressive and actively seek your position. In addition, an eight-man PLA Spec Ops Team will enter the fray from the northwest to track you down. This mission will get considerably more difficult if the alarm is raised. To complete it more easily, it is best to remain quiet and remain in stealth mode avoiding raising an alarm for as long as possible. As it is dark, the use of Night Vision can help you see much more clearly directly ahead, although it does narrow your field of vision.

Since the basic idea of this mission is to remain in stealth mode the whole time, we will show you the best approach to your objectives first. However, since it is possible to 'Go Loud' and boldly attack the PLA with guns blazing, we'll cover that scenario and its consequences at the end of this section (see Going Loud later in this section).

1 When you are ready, move from the insertion point and head southeast toward RV1. Before moving out, you may want to have your men form a tight spread and change them to Fire on Your Lead. When you reach RV1, you'll see a PLA soldier talking to the driver of a vehicle. Immediately stop and watch them. The soldier will walk away to the east after a minute or so, and the vehicle will drive off. The vehicle eventually makes its way down to the front of the fueling compound and parks where the driver will take up a patrol position around the vehicle. Once the PLA soldier walks off and the vehicle has gone, move forward to the checkpoint that has opened up, and trigger it to save your progress **[Screen 01]**.

With the vehicle gone, you can quickly follow up behind the solider and take him out if you want. This is by no means necessary, and you could run the risk of raising the alarm if you aren't quick and don't use stealth. However, even if you manage to kill the PLA soldier here, it will place the rest of the PLA on a low level alert, which could prove problematic later on. Oddly enough, there is one small bonus with this approach, but it is only small; the alerted PLA at RV3 will move away from the position they are guarding (see RV3 later in this section). If you don't kill the PLA soldier here at RV1, he will go and take up position at a lookout post to the east near RV2.

2 From RV1, head north to RV2. Stick to the trees and don't get too close to the lookout post ahead. When you reach RV2, you'll be on top of a small hill in an exposed position. Look to the east and you'll see a PLA soldier with his back to you as he monitors the fueling compound down below. If you did kill the PLA soldier at RV1 (and the alarm was not raised), this soldier will be looking in your direction instead of toward the north. Killing the PLA soldier at RV1 will alert this PLA soldier, so he will now be aware that someone might sneak up on him. However, you can get within 100 meters without being seen in the low light conditions. If you want to take him out, get close, crouch, and fire a well aimed round to his head to dispatch instantly him before he can raise the alarm. If you are not quick enough, he will quickly raise the alarm and blow your cover.

If you choose to kill this guard, but did not dispatch the PLA at RV1, you can opt to take him out now. He is often positioned to the right of the outpost

or directly in front of it. If he is in front, sneak round the right side to take him out quickly. However, his patrol route around the lookout post will rarely take him right up to the top where he will discover dead comrade, so you can safely walk off and leave him alive if you want. Ultimately there is little reason to kill either of these soldiers if you are using stealth.

PRO TIP!

Use your binoculars and look north to do some recon while at RV2!

While you are on this hill at RV2, take some time out to do some recon. Equip your binoculars and scan the compound below. Take note of the two guards

at sandbag emplacements guarding the northern entrance, as well as the driver who has now parked his vehicle and has taken up a position at a sandbag emplacement just west of the northern entrance. Of particular interest are two patrol teams; the first is a couple of PLA patrolling the perimeter of the compound in a clockwise and counterclockwise direction.

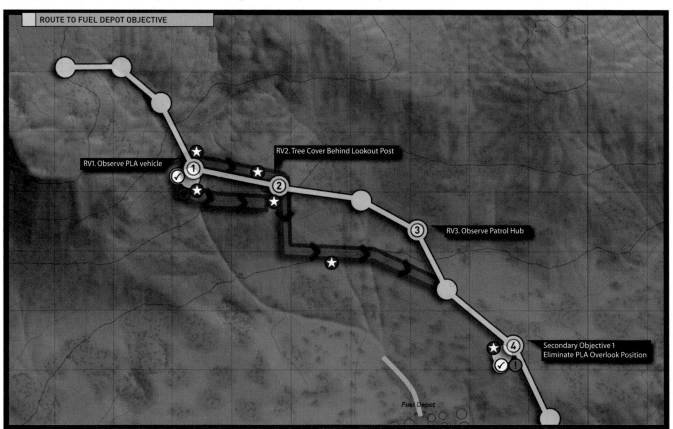

ROUTE TO FUEL DEPOT OBJECTIVE

RV1. Observe PLA vehicle

RV2. Tree Cover Behind Lookout Post

RV3. Observe Patrol Hub

Secondary Objective 1
Eliminate PLA Overlook Position

Fuel Depot

04

More important is the three-man PLA team patrolling the western grounds **[Screen 02]**. Look to the west and you will see three PLA soldiers running toward the woods and, if you wait, you'll see them return to the western gate of the compound; this is their patrol route. Remember this three-man patrol, as they will become of critical importance later in this mission.

Finally, take a look at the eastern entrance of the compound and you'll see an off-road vehicle and four PLA soldiers there. The eastern entrance is where you'll want to enter the compound, so that team is rather troublesome. Fortunately, if you use stealth and allow Saber 3 to create a diversion, all four PLA will board the vehicle and drive off to face Saber 3; a huge advantage and a good reason to remain in stealth mode.

PRO TIP!   (i)

This is a great opportunity if you're looking to kill a PLA soldier with your knife. Crouch down and get within 50 meters of the PLA at the sandbag emplacement, then lie down and crawl all the way up to the PLA while he has his back to you. Now stand up with the knife equipped and aim for his neck. One cut and it's over.

(3) From RV2, head southeast to RV3. Once you get close, you'll see a tall radio antenna with two PLA soldiers under it; they have their backs to you, and there is a checkpoint there. To trigger that checkpoint, you'll have to go to the antenna, which means alerting the PLA soldiers. If you sneak up behind the soldiers to within 50 meters or so, you can easily fire a head shot at one of the soldiers, but the other will quickly return fire and will soon raise the alarm. Taking both of these soldiers out before either can raise the alarm will be pretty tricky **[Screen 03]**. In addition, there is another checkpoint at RV4, making this checkpoint at RV3 rather pointless if you use stealth and sneak over to RV4 and trigger the checkpoint there.

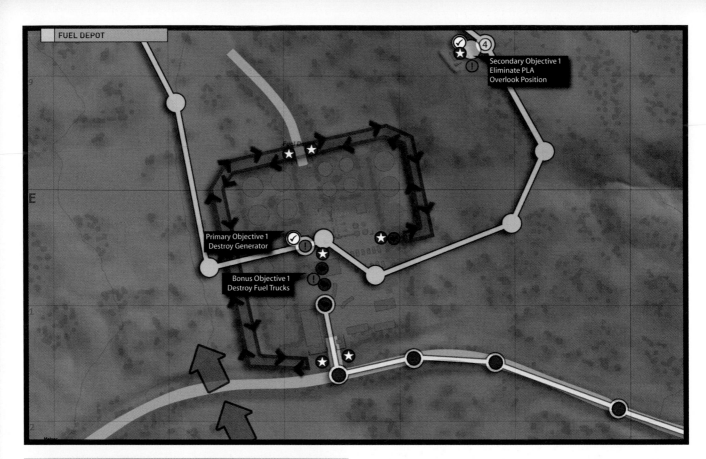

FUEL DEPOT

Secondary Objective 1
Eliminate PLA
Overlook Position

Primary Objective 1
Destroy Generator

Bonus Objective 1
Destroy Fuel Trucks

01

By far the best method here is to give these two soldiers a wide berth and head due east to the tree line. Move in a wide clockwise circle away from RV3, stick to the tree line, and make your way to RV4 and the checkpoint there. If you do this, you can easily make it to one of the most critical checkpoints in this mission without raising the alarm.

Interestingly enough, if you did kill the PLA soldier at RV1, these soldiers will move off 100 meters or so to the west and take up a position out in the open. This allows you to crouch down and sneak up to the radio antenna and trigger the checkpoint there without having to fight the two PLA soldiers. This makes killing the PLA at RV1 somewhat worthwhile, but again, this means all the PLA will be on a low level of alert, and will be searching for you more aggressively. This low level of alert becomes rather problematic once you get near and inside the fueling compound, so again, your best approach is to leave all the PLA alive and remain in stealth mode to make your way to RV4 and the checkpoint there.

Get into Position for a Diversionary Strike
Once you reach RV4, make sure to trigger the checkpoint here and make sure to switch your men to Fire on Your Lead if you haven't done so already. Crouch down and head southwest toward the small hut ahead. There

is a PLA sentry there with his back to you. In a crouch, you can advance to within roughly 30 meters and he will not be alerted to your presence. Sight the PLA and aim for his head. Squeeze off one well placed round, and this sentry is done for **[Screen 01]**. If your shot does not kill, your men will also quickly open fire (if they have been told to fire on your lead), to ensure that this PLA goes down without raising the alarm.

Once the PLA is down, enter the small hut and you'll be told that Saber 3 are getting ready to create their diversion. Now you have to wait until the diversion starts; do not enter the compound at this time! Instead, ease to the left of the small hut and equip the binoculars. Now scan the compound below as you wait for Saber 3 to make a move. You should look southwest between the tall central towers of the compound where you will see a PLA soldier crouched down and ready in position just west of the fuel generator. **[Screen 02]**. It is important to know about this PLA, as you will soon be confronting him.

PRO TIP! ⓘ
Once you have killed the PLA at RV4, hold tight and wait. Saber 3 will soon radio you once it has created the diversion, meaning you can then enter the compound below; just wait patiently and allow Saber 3 some time.

Also, keep an eye out for the two-man patrol that circles the compound perimeter. You'll need to know where they are before you make your move and enter the compound. Hold your position here until Saber 3 makes its move, and you can then proceed.

⑤ Destroy Fuel Depot Generator
Once Saber 3 creates the diversion, a checkpoint will automatically trigger, and you must now enter the compound. Make sure you know where the two-man perimeter patrol team is located. If one of them is coming toward you, wait until they pass by and are heading north, then slip in behind them and follow them up to the eastern entrance of the compound. You can take the patrol sentry out of you like, but it's just as easy to sneak behind him and then slip into the compound.

Once you enter from the east, head due west and you'll see a PLA soldier crouched in a combat position. He won't see you until you get fairly close, so continue in and toward him with your weapon at the ready. When you are close, go for a head shot to take him down quickly **[Screen 03]**. As you do this, make sure your men are set to Fire on Your Lead, which will ensure this PLA is out of your way. Once he is down, equip the C4 charges and run directly to the fuel generator. Quickly lay a charge on the generator, and you are ready to make your escape.

Immediately head out of the western gate and run due west. As you do, the PLA guard that drove the vehicle in at the start of the mission will generally come running to confront you. Quickly order your men to engage him as you continue moving west. However, if you did your recon at RV2 earlier, you'll know there is also a three-man PLA team running a patrol on this western side, not to mention the two-man perimeter patrol. Things can get sticky here, which means you need to move very quickly, so once you have

gone a few meters west out of the compound, turn hard right and head north to the trees ahead. As you do so, detonate the C4.

When the generator blows, a checkpoint will fire and the PLA will be alerted to your presence. You must now make your way quickly to the north where the Extraction Chopper will meet you. Run hard north to RV6 and, if you are being attacked, go full auto and lay down some suppressing fire on your aggressors to buy you some time to keep running north.

Note: leaving via the west gate and proceeding due north will often be a difficult task due to the western patrol, the perimeter patrol, the PLA at the vehicle and the Spec Ops teams entering from the northwest once the alarm is raised. The ensuing firefight could be fierce and risky; if you run into difficulties, consider the alternative escape route as detailed in the Going Loud strategies listed later in this section.

04

BONUS OBJECTIVE AT RV5: DESTROY ALL THE PLA FUEL TRUCKS

Once you have placed the C4 charge on the fuel generator, you have the option of tackling the Bonus Objective for this mission. Check your map and you will see there are two large fuel trucks marked on it; these are your Bonus Objective. You may or may not have raised the alarm yet, and this will be easier if the alarm has not been raised. Quickly run to the trucks and place a C4 charge on each one **[Screen 01]**. You can do this by pressing the Aim Weapon button (LT on the Xbox 360 Controller / L2 button on the PS3 controller). Doing this will switch you from the C4 detonator and place another C4 charge in your hand. Pressing the Fire Weapon button now will allow you to place another charge.

Repeat this process for each truck until you have placed a charge on each. Now quickly leave via the western gate, and then detonate the C4 charges when you are clear. When you trigger the detonator, all three charges will immediately go off, which means simultaneously clearing both your Primary and Bonus Objectives.

6 Continue north through the trees and go through RV6. There is a checkpoint here, so make your way to it and trigger it. If you did your recon at RV2, then you'll remember there is a PLA Spec Ops team that will enter from the northwest, which means they are ahead of you. Try to skirt around them by moving slightly northeast as you proceed to the extraction point, but keep look out for them. If you encounter them, use the trees for cover and take them out quickly. Move fast, try to avoid the Spec Ops team and get to the extraction point in double quick time!

7 **Rendezvous with Team at Extraction Point**
Once you are in the area of RV7, survey the ruins and you'll spot four PLA soldiers here. You'll need to take them out to extract safely. The best way is to approach RV7 from the west, and then come in and attack the PLA. They are often watching the south, so attacking from the west will allow you to flank them and catch them off guard. Have your men attack the PLA here as you adopt a crouching position and move in and attack with them. Be fast, going for a head shot whenever possible, and take out the four PLA here **[Screen 02]**.

As you are dealing with the PLA at the extraction site, be aware of being flanked at your rear. The Spec Ops or other PLA from the compound may have pursued you here, so keep an eye on your map to make sure you are not ambushed. Once the extraction chopper gets near, it will employ its guns and enter the firefight and help you eliminate any remaining PLA. When it lands, order your men to enter the chopper quickly and then follow them on board **[Screen 03]**. If there are PLA running toward your position, but they are still 50 or more meters away, ignore them and dash to the chopper. The chopper will take off the moment you are in, and this mission is over.

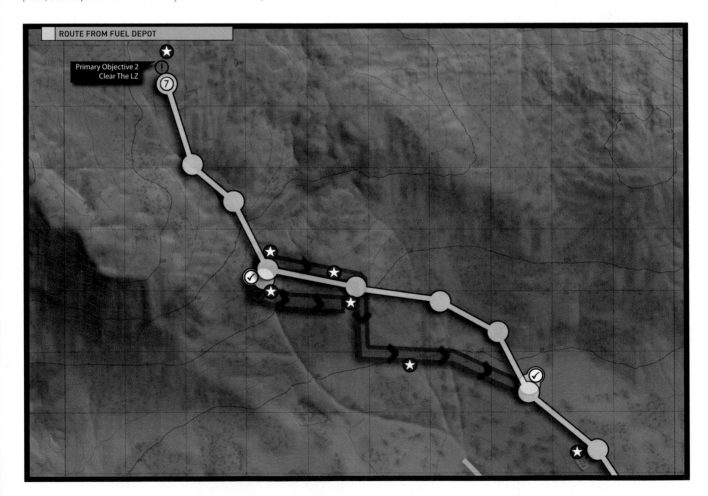

ROUTE FROM FUEL DEPOT

Primary Objective 2
Clear The LZ

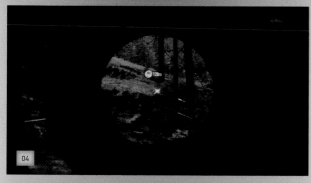

Going Loud

If you'd rather discard the cloak-and-dagger pose and abandon stealth, you have the option of 'Going Loud', which means you will boldly assault the PLA and let them raise the alarm. If you use this approach, Saber 3 will leave immediately and you will not be able to count on their help, and will have to make your own way into the compound. This also means that you will immediately fail the Secondary Objective.

Interestingly enough, this approach can be somewhat easier, depending on your approach to the next firefights. Start by going to RV1 and quickly assaulting and killing both the soldier and the driver here. As you do this, make sure to have your men set to Fire on Your Lead. However, don't kill the driver too quickly; you want him to raise the alarm before he dies! Now that you have attacked the PLA, your men will have reverted to Free Fire and will fire on an any incoming enemies, which is exactly what you want now.

Once both the PLA at RV1 are down, get ready for some guests! Find a good position amongst the trees that allows you a good view of the south and east. Now that the alarm has been raised, the PLA will come to you. The best method of attack is to simply hold your ground and take them out as they come storming in.

The first PLA you are likely to face are the ones from RV2 and RV3. They will quickly move in from the east, so watch out for them, stick to the trees for cover and take them out. The four PLA at the northeastern corner of the complex will soon board the vehicle and come in with the two guards from the southern gate. They will enter your area from the south, so be ready and take them out when they arrive. Using a grenade on the vehicle is a good idea if you're close and clear. You can also lay down some smoke grenades just before the PLA arrive, and then flank them from the east and west, catching them in your crossfire. To do this, simply order your men to move to a western position as you take up a position to the east. Watch the south and, when the PLA come in, order your men to attack and then follow suit **[Screen 04]**.

Keep an eye on your map as you are doing this to monitor any approaching PLA. Once you have dealt with the immediate PLA attacking you, board one of the vehicles here. You don't want to stay in this area longer than necessary, since the PLA Spec Ops Team will soon arrive!

Now you are in the vehicle, drive over to RV3 to trigger the checkpoint there, and then go to RV4 as usual where you should take out the PLA in the small hut. The PLA in the hut will be alert and will be looking out for you, so you'll have to be quick as you come over the hill to take your shot. He will be facing you, but if you're fast, he'll go down easily. Now go right of the hut and equip your binoculars to recon the area. Look to the northwest in particular, as you will soon see something rather disturbing: a large PLA Spec-Ops force will be running toward your position **[Screen 05]**.

The Spec-Ops Team is a good distance away, so there is no use waiting for them. Instead, take your men and enter the compound from the east as normal. This will cause the Spec Ops Team to enter the fueling compound via the northern entrance, so you don't have much time now.

From the eastern entrance, move forward and kill the PLA near the generator, and hastily plant your C4 charge. If you want the Bonus Objective, plant charges on the two trucks as well. Now quickly run back the way you came, and then exit via the eastern gate, detonating the charges as you do so. Continue due east into the trees, which will offer you some valuable cover, and then head north back to RV4 and get back into your vehicle.

Now drive your vehicle to RV7, the extraction point. The Spec Ops Team and any other PLA in the area will be present in the fuel depot slowly trying to turn round and follow you, so you are now in a good position. As you get to RV7, you'll want to approach it from the western side and then go past it so that you can enter the area from the south. Once you are south of RV7, disembark, and make your way on foot into the evac area. Kill the four PLA here, and wait for the chopper to arrive. Once it lands, waste no time in boarding it to end the mission.

BLEEDING EDGE
MISSION 07

The overriding objective of Bleeding Edge is to secure the fuel depot that is occupied by the PLA. To achieve this you will have to punch a hole through the PLA's defensive lines. You will be supported by three LAV25's. It is critical that these LAV25s support the final assault on the fuel depot, without them the mission will be aborted.

Equipment and Vehicles

There are only 2 ammo crates in this mission, so not much ammo at all. Near the first crate is where you'll take out the AT gunner and nab his Queen Bee, so more often than not, you'll want nothing more than the equipment from the first crate. There are a lot of PLA to take out in this mission. Most will be dealt with from a distance using your M16A4 Marksman that you start with. Depending on your accuracy, it is very possible to run out of ammo for that weapon as you are assaulting the fuel depot. Luckily, the second ammo crate near the fuel depot has a PLA Marksman and Assault rifle that you can pillage and use to finish the mission off.

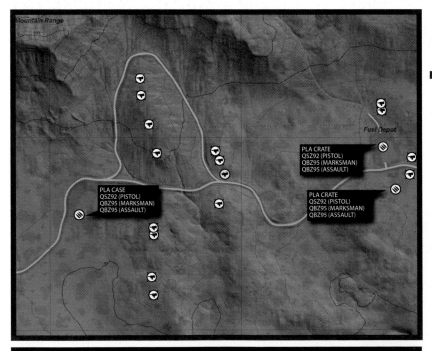

MISSION WEAPONS AND VEHICLES

Item	US
Weapons	US Knife
	MEU (SOC) Pistol
	MP5A4 Sub-Machine Gun
	M16A4 Assault Rifle
	M16A4 Assault Rifle (Marksman)
	M16A4 Assault Rifle (Assault)
	M249 Light Machine Gun
	M21 Sniper Rifle
	US Fragmentation Grenade
	US Smoke Grenade
	US Coloured Smoke Grenade Red
	US Anti Personnel Mine
	IR Stobe
	SMAW Rocket Launcher
Vehicles	LAV25
	MH-60S

Item	PLA
Weapons	PLA Knife
	QSZ92 Pistol
	QBZ95 Assault Rifle
	QBZ95 Assault Rifle (Marksman)
	QBZ95 Assault Rifle (Assault)
	QBB95 Light Machine Gun
	Type 67-II Medium Machine Gun
	QBU88 Sniper Rifle
	PLA Fragmentation Grenade
	PLA Smoke Grenade
	PLA Coloured Smoke Grenade Red
	PLA Claymore Mine
	PLA Anti Personnel Mine
	Field Dressing PLA
	PF98 Queen Bee Rocket Launcher
	QW-2 SAM Anti Aircraft Homing Missile
Vehicles	BJS2022 with HMG
Emplacements	QJC 88 Heavy Machine Gun *
	LG-3 Auto Grenade Launcher *

* Tall mount

Primary Objectives	Secondary Objectives	Bonus Objectives
Eliminate AT teams covering the road	Eliminate MG nest	Eliminate the remaining troops on the second line with one mortar barrage
Locate and eliminate PLA spotter team	Locate and eliminate PLA AA team	
Destroy key defenses around the fuel depot		

OBJECTIVE OVERVIEW

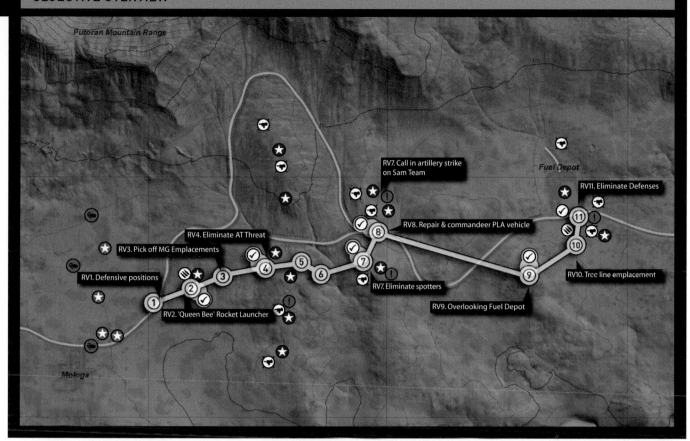

Putoran Mountain Range

RV7. Call in artillery strike on Sam Team

Fuel Depot

RV11. Eliminate Defenses

RV8. Repair & commandeer PLA vehicle

RV4. Eliminate AT Threat

RV3. Pick off MG Emplacements

RV1. Defensive positions

RV10. Tree line emplacement

RV7. Eliminate spotters

RV2. 'Queen Bee' Rocket Launcher

RV9. Overlooking Fuel Depot

Mologa

04

MISSION OBJECTIVES

1 In this mission you're tasked with capturing the fuel depot, and it won't be easy. Along the way there are many PLA, including 2 heavy lines of well dug-in soldiers. The USMC will be sending in LAV25 armored vehicles to capture and hold the fuel depot, but the PLA along the way have AT teams that can destroy the LAV25s. It's your job to run ahead and take out the AT teams before they can destroy your tanks. When you're ready to begin, head northeast to RV2. Note that there is an LAV25 at RV1 that you could takeover and drive yourself, but that defeats the purpose of the mission. It's best to just leave the LAV25 to the team that already commands it **[Screen 01]**.

2 There is a bonus objective to this mission in which you are tasked with eliminating all of the anti-tank infantry in the area. Gunners are scattered about at all the various RV points, so achieving this objective isn't as simple as going to just one point and killing someone. Instead, you should seek out and find every living PLA in the area and take them out. By killing every PLA in this mission, you're sure to get all of the AT gunners and achieve this Bonus Objective.

Run forward to a small concrete structure and then head right (due east) to a wrecked car on the side of the road. Take cover behind the car and face the tree line where three PLA are dug-in. Have your men flank right and then use your M16A4 Marksman to pick off the PLA from your cover point. If you're having problems making your shots, have your men lay down suppressing fire on the PLA at the tree line. This will allow you to advance forward to another wrecked car further ahead in the field. From that position, taking out the PLA is a bit easier. Once all three of the PLA are down, make sure to check the fallen AT gunner and scavenge his Queen Bee. It will come in handy later **[Screen 02]**. Just past the tree line you'll find a checkpoint. Trigger it to save your progress.

01

02

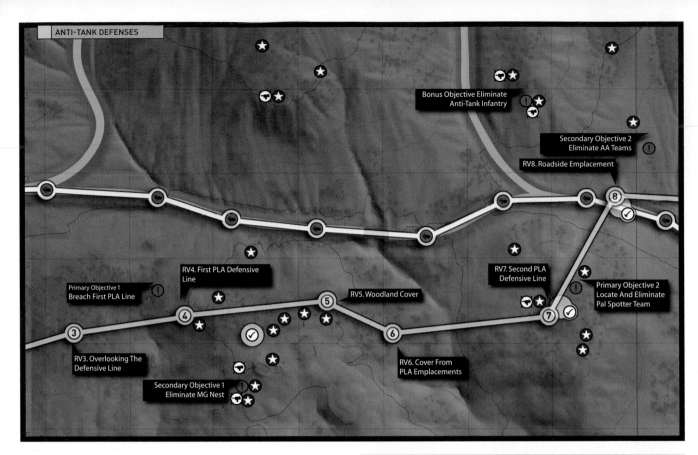

ANTI-TANK DEFENSES

Bonus Objective Eliminate
Anti-Tank Infantry

Secondary Objective 2
Eliminate AA Teams

RV8. Roadside Emplacement

RV4. First PLA Defensive
Line

RV7. Second PLA
Defensive Line

Primary Objective 1
Breach First PLA Line

RV5. Woodland Cover

Primary Objective 2
Locate And Eliminate
Pal Spotter Team

RV3. Overlooking The
Defensive Line

RV6. Cover From
PLA Emplacements

Secondary Objective 1
Eliminate MG Nest

It should be noted that the AT gunner here will often fire off a round, but if you kill him before he is able to, his Queen Bee will have 3 full rounds in it. A Queen Bee with 3 rounds is ideal for later in this mission at the fuel depot. If you get to the AT gunner and his Queen Bee has less than 3 rounds, then strongly consider starting over at the last checkpoint or even restarting the mission. Taking a Queen Bee from that gunner with 3 rounds will definitely make your life a lot easier at the fuel depot later in this mission.

PRO TIP! ⓘ

Make sure to take the Queen Bee from the fallen AT gunner – but save the rounds for the end of the mission at the fuel depot.

③ Eliminate MG nest

Head east to reach RV3. Off to your left you'll see a pair of emplaced MGs. As you near RV3, you'll see a sandbag position. Just before you reach that, there is a small clear spot of raised ground. Stop there and go prone. Now target the two emplaced MG gunners off to your left. They are nearly 400 meters out, but with a steady aim you should be able to take them both out easily **[Screen 01]**. Just make sure you set your rifle to single round fire mode for better accuracy. Once both of them are down, you'll have completed your first secondary objective. It's time to move forward to the first line of the PLA further to the east.

As you are taking out the MG gunners in the distance, it's often a good idea to open your map before you start and have your men flank right on the PLA line ahead (RV4). It takes your men quite some time to move into flanking position, and there's not much they can do to help you with the emplaced MG gunners. So it's best to multi-task and use your time wisely. Have your men move on to flank the PLA line at RV4 while you deal with the MG gunners. Then you can move on as well.

④ Eliminate AT teams covering the road

Head east toward the next line. Ahead and to your right you'll find a low wall you can take cover behind. Have your men assault the first line ahead as you move to take cover behind the wall. Form your cover position, use long-range fire to support your men and take out the PLA.

As you are assaulting the first line, you'll receive a radio communication that the LAV25s are about to start moving in. This part of the mission is now timed. You have roughly 3 minutes to take out the AT gunner ahead, or they will begin destroying the LAV25s. If two of them are destroyed, then this mission is over. Quickly take out the PLA due east from your position behind the wall, then have your men assault the northern portion of the PLA line ahead **[Screen 02]**.

04

Run due east as your men are moving in and this will allow you to flank the AT gunner on their left side. Once you reach the line, turn left and head north. The first AT gunner is dug-in behind a small brick structure. There are actually two small brick structures here, and the AT gunner is behind the most northern one from your position. Approach these structures in a crouch from the south, and you can easily get close. Once you are near, step out and around the structures with your weapon ready. Be fast, and pump a few rounds into the PLA behind the northern-most structure. At this close range, they will fall fast.

When those two are down, look further ahead and slightly to the northeast. You'll see the second AT gunner positioned behind some sandbags with camouflage netting draped over it **[Screen 03]**. Most often, he will not see you, making it very easy to take him out from where you are located. If he does fire, order your men to use suppressing fire on him while you use the small brick structure and the low wall for cover. Time your attack right, and pop out from cover for a killing shot when the AT gunner is reloading or taking cover from your men's suppressing fire. Once he is down, your first Primary Objective is complete.

If you need an alternate strategy to this approach, then have the Medic stick with you and then order your other two men in to assault the PLA line. As before, move wide to the south as you come up on the PLA line. Often, you can target the AT gunners from the cover of some boulders. You'll find these at the tree line as you make your way to the low wall which is further ahead to the northeast **[Screen 04]**. Once you find those boulders, have your Medic suppress the PLA due east as you take out the AT gunners a little over to the left behind the brick structures. As you are doing this, your other two men will be assaulting the line meaning most of the PLA will be focused on them. This will make sniping a bit easier.

(7) **Locate and eliminate PLA spotter team**
With the AT threat eliminated, you now need to press on further east to the second PLA line. This one is even more fortified than the first, so you'll need to be cautious. As you press further east, look for the checkpoint ahead and trigger it to save your progress. Also, be on the lookout for PLA soldiers in the trees ahead. Very often PLA soldiers from the first line will have abandoned their posts and ducked into the trees. You can easily walk right up on one before you know it. Keep alert as you move forward.

Once you reach the checkpoint, you'll see some tents off to your right. Head southeast between them to a small brick structure ahead. Go around the right side of those structures and then head east into the trees ahead where RV6 is located. At RV6 you'll find a small brick structure. Take up a position behind it and have your men flank right on the PLA line ahead. Now go prone and ease out past the right side of the structure and target the PLA ahead. Your first target should be the MG gunner and his comrade **[Screen 05]**. After that, snipe the PLA to the left of those two. You'll find him behind some sandbags.

Once those three are down, scan the tree line for any other PLA that may be about. Once you're sure there aren't any other PLA, stand up and step forward in a crouch. Just past where the MG gunner was located, you can often spy the upper torso of another PLA behind some sandbags under a camouflage net. Target him with your long-range fire, and take him out. As you are assaulting this line, you will receive a radio communication about PLA AA teams in the area. You'll want to take them out as well.

Run due east toward the tree line ahead. As you do so, call your men to you (Follow Me) to ensure they don't head north and attack the PLA over there. Make your way to the first set of sandbags you come to and get ready to assault the first AA team in the woods ahead **[Screen 06]**. Have your men engage them as you ease forward in a crouch. Make sure to keep the trees between you and the PLA ahead so that you are covered, and take them both out. Once both are dead, the first of the AA teams is down. Taking this first AA team out now will make achieving your next secondary objective at RV8 much easier, so take a little time to kill that AA team now.

PRO TIP!

While you're in this position, take out the first of the three AA teams that is just above you on the hill hiding amongst the trees.

At this point, you'll receive communication that the PLA line is breached and you'll be granted an Air Strike. The purpose of this is to take out the spotter teams to the north. Head north across the hill and equip your binoculars. Look north and you'll see four PLA soldiers. Two of them are behind a sandbag emplacement, one is just ahead of them in the trees, and the

fourth is further west at an emplaced gun. Call in your Air Strike and aim for the middle ground between all four of the PLA **[Screen 01]**. Use your Air Strike with a Barrage spread, and all four will be eliminated. This will not only take out the final spotter team thus saving your LAV25s, but it will also unlock an Achievement/Trophy.

8 Locate and eliminate PLA AA team

Head north to RV8 and the checkpoint there. The idea is to use the PLA vehicle (BJS2022) that you find there for transportation to your overwatch position at RV9. However, before you do so, there are two PLA AA teams in the area that you should take out first. If you eliminate all of the PLA AA teams in this mission, a transport chopper will come in and deliver another fire team to the Fuel Depot. Those reinforcements will make that assault much easier, so it is worth your while to dispatch the AA teams now.

From RV8, check your map and you'll see the first AA team is off to the right to the northeast. Have your men assault them as you follow up with long-range fire. The AA team is using the trees for cover, but you can easily pick them off from the road with your scoped M16A4.

Once that team is down, check the map once more, and you'll see the next team located in the trees to the northwest. Head toward the trees to the northeast (where you just eliminated the other AA team) and then move north to flank the AA team in the woods to the northwest. Once you get close, crouch and target the PLA and take them out. If you also took out the AA team at RV7 earlier, then all AA teams are now dead and you'll receive a radio communication informing you that reinforcements are inbound. Good news indeed!

Head back to the PLA vehicle at RV8 and you'll find it is damaged. Repair it to make it road worthy, then climb onboard and head over to RV9 **[Screen 02]**.

9 Destroy key defenses around the fuel depot

There is a checkpoint here between two small emplacements. Trigger it and get out of your vehicle. There is a sizeable PLA force northeast of your location that you must now deal with. If you grabbed the Queen Bee earlier in this mission and still have it, equip it now! As you are getting ready to assault the PLA, you'll notice that the reinforcements you were awarded for taking out the three AA teams has arrived just south of your location. Check your map to see them offload from the chopper and bring up your rear – or just turn around and watch them land **[Screen 03]**!

Equip the Queen Been and ease down the hill toward the PLA. Look for soldiers that are bunched up so that you can take out more than one at a time. These will be long-range shots, so you'll need to aim a little high to hit the PLA. Using the first horizontal line below dead center on your crosshairs is usually enough. Use all of your Queen Bee ammo on the PLA below. Make emplaced gunners your primary targets, as well as any group of two or more soldiers. If you have all three rounds from earlier, this will make the mission a bit easier.

Your best targets for the Queen Bee are the AT gunner and his comrade at the sandbag in front of the northern-most building, the northern building itself (just behind the AT gunner at the sandbags), and the emplace gunner due north of your position. The building has two or more PLA inside, so taking it out is a great call. If you have only one Queen Bee, then by far your best and most important target is the AT gunner at the sandbags **[Screen 04]**. If you don't take him out, and fast, he'll destroy the LAV25s as they move down the road to the depot.

Once the Queen Bee is empty, or if you didn't have it at all, then you'll have to move down the hill in a crouch and get close enough to snipe the AT gunner. This is a risky move, but you'll need to do it to ensure the safety of your LAV25s. Once the AT gunner is down, run back up to the hill where your men should be waiting.

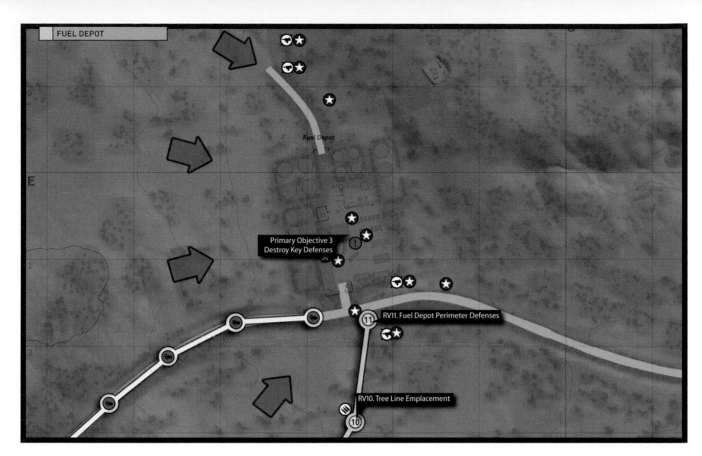

FUEL DEPOT

Primary Objective 3
Destroy Key Defenses

RV11. Fuel Depot Perimeter Defenses

RV10. Tree Line Emplacement

Now, have your men follow you northeast through the trees ahead. Stick to the far eastern edge of the trees to avoid the PLA. You'll soon come to a small emplacement and a burnt-out tank. There is an ammo crate here you can pilfer for a PLA Marksman or Assault rifle if you need it. Take cover behind the tank and have your men flank right on the PLA positioned near the fuel depot. The PLA will concentrate on your men moving in on them allowing you to snipe at them from your position. Take out all of the PLA at the perimeter of the fuel depot, and you'll receive a message that the first line of defense is down, and the rest is located to the north.

Have your men regroup on you, and then head north giving the fuel depot a wide birth. Keep moving northeast to a small building on a hilltop over look-

ing the last bit of PLA defense. You'll remember this small building as it was RV4 in Mission 6 **[Screen 05]**. Once you make it to this hilltop perch, have your men assault the PLA down below, and support them with long-range fire as you snipe at them from above. Once they are all down, head back into the fuel depot and pick off any remaining PLA there. At this point, the PLA's moral will crumble, and they will retreat to the east signaling your capture of the fuel depot and the end of this mission.

ACHIEVEMENT / TROPHY

Resource Management – By securing the Fuel Depot, you will unlock this Achievement for the 360 or a Trophy for the PS3.

LOOKING FOR LOIS
MISSION 08

A US Marine team has been captured by the PLA. The PLA is moving the prisoners from the frontline where they were captured deeper into enemy territory. The PLA obviously plan to use the POWs as bargaining chips in this war. There is no way you can let that happen. It's up to you and your team to infiltrate the area, rescue the POWs, and then make it safely to the evac site. You'll be deep behind enemy lines, where stealth as well as good combat skills will be called into play. This won't be easy; but failure is not an option!

Equipment and Vehicles

You'll see your standard fare of weapons in the ammo crates of this mission. However, there is one shining gem, and that is the QBU88 sniper rifle. You can nab one of these from both the sniper and the crate at RV1, and you can grab another (to re-stock your ammo) at RV7. The QBU88 and Mk16 you start with are by far the superior weapons in this Mission and all that you'll need. You'll notice there is an ammo crate at the PLA Radio Station, but going there is not part of this mission. Nor is it advisable since there is a very heavy PLA force there including armored vehicles. It is a certain deathtrap should you get curious and venture that way.

MISSION WEAPONS AND VEHICLES

Item	US
Weapons	US Knife
	MEU (SOC) Pistol
	MP5A4 Sub-Machine Gun
	Mk17 Mod 0 Assault Rifle (Marksman)
	Mk16 Mod 0 Assault Rifle (Assault)
	Mk48 Mod 0 Medium Machine Gun
	M21 Sniper Rifle
	M107 Anti Material Rifle
	US Fragmentation Grenade
	US Smoke Grenade
	US Coloured Smoke Grenade Red
	US Claymore
	US Anti Tank Mine
	US Demolition Charge
	IR Stobe
Vehicles	AH-1Z Ground Attack
	MH-60S

Item	PLA
Weapons	PLA Knife
	QSZ92 Pistol
	QCW05 Sub-Machine Gun
	QBZ95 Assault Rifle
	QBZ95 Assault Rifle (Marksman)
	QBZ95 Assault Rifle (Assault)
	Type 81-1 Assault Rifle (Marksman)
	Type 81-1 Assault Rifle (Assault)
	QBB95 Light Machine Gun
	Type 67-II Medium Machine Gun
	QBU88 Sniper Rifle
	M99 Anti Material Rifle
	PLA Fragmentation Grenade
	PLA Smoke Grenade
	PLA Coloured Smoke Grenade Red
	PLA Claymore Mine
	PLA Anti Personnel Mine
	PLA Anti Tank Mine
	Field Dressing PLA
	PF98 Queen Bee Rocket Launcher
Vehicles	Type 99 Tank
	Type 97 Infantry Fighting Vehicle
	Type 92 WZ551A APC
	Type 95 Anti-Aircraft Artillery
	BJS2022
	BJS2022 with HMG
	SX2190 Cargo Truck
	Z-10 Attack
	Mi-171 Transport
Emplacements	QJC 88 Heavy Machine Gun *

* Tall mount

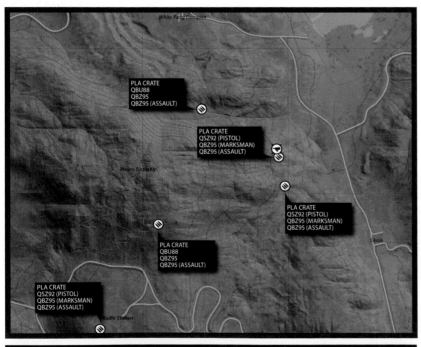

Primary Objectives	Secondary Objectives		Bonus Objectives
Rendezvous with POWs	Remain undetected until the end of the valley		Ensure all POWs
Extract POWs	Clear the landing zone before further reinforcements arrive		survive

OBJECTIVE OVERVIEW

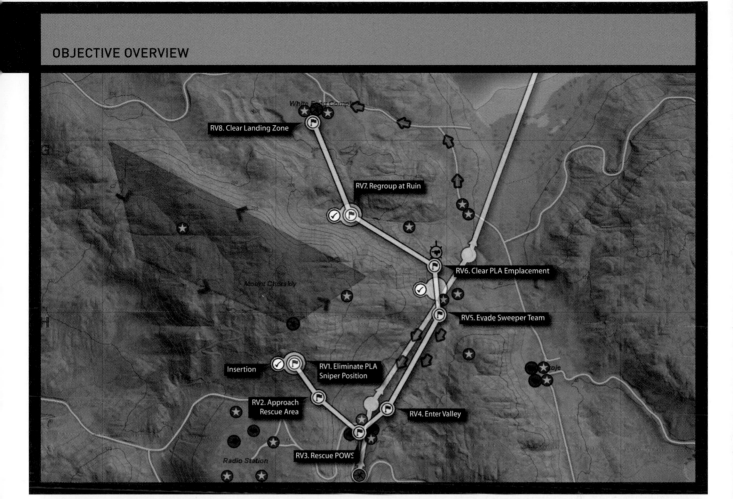

RV8. Clear Landing Zone

RV7. Regroup at Ruin

RV6. Clear PLA Emplacement

RV5. Evade Sweeper Team

Insertion

RV1. Eliminate PLA Sniper Position

RV2. Approach Rescue Area

RV4. Enter Valley

RV3. Rescue POWs

White Face Camp

Mount Cherokly

Radio Station

04

MISSION OBJECTIVES

01

Insertion Point

At the start of the mission you'll be told about the POWS and that they are being moved by a PLA convoy. A UAV (Unmanned Aerial Vehicle) code-named Castle 4 is tracking the convoy. Using the UAV's recon, a USMC attack chopper, call sign Trident, will soon attack the lead convoy vehicle to disable it and stop the convoy. Once this happens, you'll need to move in and rendezvous with the convoy.

1. Start by having your men fire on your lead. This will keep them from getting trigger happy once you get to RV1. Head southwest toward RV1,

and as you do, change your ammo to use the under-slung grenade launcher with an HE round. Once you see the small hut at RV1, you'll learn there are two snipers inside watching over the road below where the PLA convoy will soon be passing. You need to take these snipers out.

The easiest thing to do is circle around to the western side of the hut, and then fire a single HE grenade through the door so that it lands between the snipers **[Screen 01]**. This will take them both out in one go. Now enter the hut and scavenge the QBU88 Sniper rifle off the bodies as it will come in handy later in the mission.

It should be noted that there is an ammo crate in this small hut. If you use the HE grenade to kill the two snipers, you'll also destroy the ammo crate. The crate contains a QBU88 sniper rifle. Since you can lift one from the dead PLA, you may just want to go ahead and use the grenade to kill the PLA and blow the ammo crate. However, you can get three additional clips from the crate if you leave it intact. So the sniper rifle you take from the PLA will have seven clips, and you can get three more from the crates for a total of 10. If you want the extra ammo, then take the PLA out with regular gunfire. You can easily get a headshot on one through the open roof, and then circle round to the door and catch the second PLA before he gets out.

Once the snipers are down move towards RV2, and you'll receive radio communication that the Trident has stopped the convoy, but there seems to be a firefight going on where the convoy stopped. After you kill the snipers, watch the southeastern sky and you can actually see the USMC Chopper come in and attack. You now need to get to the convoy site to rendezvous with the POWs. Before going too far past the Sniper area, take out your binoculars and

recon the area. If you look to the southwest, you'll see a PLA radio station and a lot of PLA **[Screen 01]**. That station doesn't figure in your mission, so definitely stay away from it. The PLA forces in there are considerable. There is a checkpoint at RV1, so make sure you trigger it. When you are ready, make your way down the hill to the southeast toward RV2 and then to RV3.

③ Rendezvous with POWs

Once you reach RV3 you'll find that the POWs have armed themselves and are in a firefight with their former captors. You can use the PLA sniper rifle you lifted from the sniper at RV1 to take out some of the PLA from the hill you are on. However, the PLA below are so fixated on the POWs, that it's more expedient to stick with your Mk16 and move down into the fray. You can

easily come up behind the PLA and flank their rear. Have your men assault the PLA here, while you do the same. If you like, switch to HE grenades and lob a few at the enemy. Once all of the PLA are down, the POWS will join your team.

When you come down to join the firefight here, don't run to the POWs as this will allow the PLA to concentrate their fire on you as well. Also, don't get too close to the PLAs as you flank them or you could get caught in friendly cross-fire from the Marine POWs. Just get close enough to target the PLA, and then attack **[Screen 02]**.

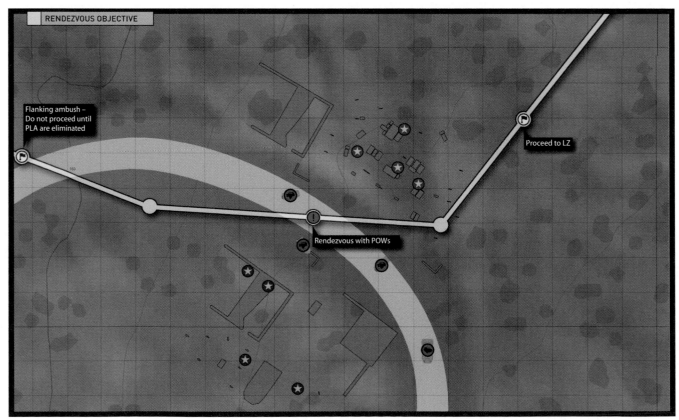

RENDEZVOUS OBJECTIVE

Flanking ambush –
Do not proceed until
PLA are eliminated

Proceed to LZ

Rendezvous with POWs

Now that the POWs have joined you, you have to get them to the evac site. You'll see a PLA vehicle here that seems to be intact, but the PLA obviously took the keys with them. You can not use this vehicle – so don't waste your time. You'll be hoofing it for the rest of the mission.

There are four Marine POWs in all. As part of your team, the Marine POWs will follow your orders just like your men. You'll basically control all of them as if they were a 5th man on your team. You can lose two POWs in this mission, but if three or more die, then you will fail the mission. Once the POWs are with you, a checkpoint will fire to save your progress and you're ready to move on.

From here on out, you'll see PLA transport choppers about the area. These choppers are searching for you, and will often drop Spec Ops teams off to come after you. Never engage one of these choppers as it will immediately

alert the PLA to your position thus drawing down a Spec Ops team onto your location.

4   When you're ready to move out, have all of your men adopt a tight spread and make sure they only fire on your lead. As you move forward now, you face a secondary objective of getting through the valley ahead unseen by enemy forces. With your men in a tight spread, you're less likely to be spotted, and if they only fire on your lead, they won't give away your location inadvertently by attacking any PLA that you are trying to sneak away from.

Due to the strong PLA presence in this area, your evac LZ (Landing Zone) is 2 kilometers north of your present location meaning a long trek through enemy territory. Head toward RV4 and you'll soon see a PLA chopper come in with a Spec Ops team **[Screen 03]**. You'll need to avoid them and not be spotted if you wish to clear your Secondary Objective.

As you get close to RV4 you'll see a small farming post. The PLA chopper will drop off the Spec Ops team to the east of the farming post, so don't hang around there long! Once you are close to the farming post, immediately turn to the north and back away from the area where the Spec Ops team has landed. Stay in a tight formation with everyone set to fire on your lead, and run North. You'll soon come to the ruins of a building that you can rest at. When you're ready, continue forward to RV5 which is just over 500 meters to the north. While you have avoided the Spec Ops team, they will track you, so you'll need to stay constantly on the move lest they catch up with you.

If, on the other hand you don't care about the Secondary Objective, feel free to equip your sniper rifle and pick off the Spec Ops team from a distance.

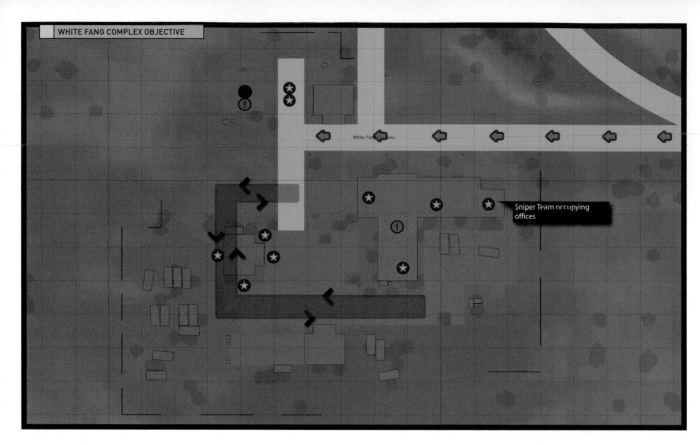

Sniper Team occupying offices

Order the Marine POWs to lay down suppressing fire and then order your men to assault the Spec Ops teams. You can easily pick them off from distance, especially with the POWs offering suppressing fire. Over all, there is no real reason to engage the Spec Ops teams, especially since it will blow your chance at the Secondary Objective. Further, failing the Secondary Objective will alert all PLA in the area to your presence. This will cause them to leave their posts or patrols and actively move towards your location which will greatly increase the difficulty of the mission.

⑤ Remain undetected until the end of the valley

Here you'll be at the bottom of a tall hill. On top of the hill is a small guard outpost with two PLA soldiers inside. They are looking to the northeast and will not see your approach from the south. Move to the very edge of the tree line at RV5, and then switch to the PLA sniper rifle. Target the PLA on the left, and take him down [Screen 01]. One shot should do it if you aim carefully. The second PLA soldier will immediately turn and attack you. Your men will often take him down, but if not, another sniper round is all it takes.

Once they are both dead, move up to the outpost and then go north past it to the checkpoint. Trigger the checkpoint to save your progress and then continue on to RV6. If you remain undetected up to RV5, then you will clear your first Secondary Objective.

⑥ At RV6 you'll come across a small house. You'll come in from the south,

and there are two PLA soldiers guarding the northern side of the house. They will be facing north, so it's easy to sneak up on them. One option is to use the door on the southern side of the house to go inside and then shoot the PLA through the windows. However, this means you'll only be able to take out one at a time giving the second PLA time to ready himself and fire on you. If you go this route, be fast and take out the second PLA before he can do the same to you.

A much better approach to this is to equip the under-slung grenade launcher with an HE grenade. Now, get into position on the western side of the house. When you're ready, step out and you'll see the two PLAs at a sandbag emplacement. Fire your grenade at their feet, and both of them will be history. This is by far the fastest and safest approach to this encounter. Alternatively, consider staying on the southern side of the house and tossing a grenade over the roof so that it lands amongst the unsuspecting PLA [Screen 02]!

Once the PLA are down, you can enter the house to find an ammo crate. However, the only weapons in that crate are a PLA Marksman and Assault rifle, and your weaponry will be superior, especially if you took the sniper rifle back at RV1.

When you're ready, head north to a small road, and you'll soon encounter a Spec Ops team. Try to stay at a distance and snipe at them with your sniper rifle. Your men and the Marine POWs will often do a good job of taking out the PLA. If you're having a problem here, order the Marines to use suppressing fire, have your men engage the PLA, and then you rely on your sniper rifle to pick them off. Once they are all down, make haste down the road towards RV7. The other Spec Ops team you avoided back at RV4 is actively tracking you, and if you sit still too long, they can often catch you.

An alternative approach to taking out the Spec Ops team is to stay at the house behind the sandbags. Have your Medic operate the emplaced gun there while you equip the sniper rifle. Use the sandbags for cover, and order the Marines inside the house. Now snipe the Spec Ops teams as they approach your position. As you do this, order your other two men to assault the Spec Ops team. Once the PLA are dead, have everyone regroup on you and head north down the road.

Continue down the road to reach RV7 and a checkpoint. There is also an ammo crate at RV7 with a QBU88 sniper rifle, so make sure to top up your ammo for that weapon before moving on. Once you have triggered the checkpoint and restocked your sniper rifle ammo, head north through the hills to reach RV8 and the White Fang Complex where your evac chopper will meet you.

⑧ Clear the landing zone before further reinforcements arrive / Extract POWs / Ensure all POWs survive

Once you get close to RV8, you'll learn that the PLA have fortified the complex with their troops. Before going to RV8, climb up the hill to the south of the airport and use your binoculars to recon the area below. When you're ready, make sure everyone is set to fire on your lead and then send your men to the southwestern corner of the complex (near RV8). Next, take the Marine POWS to the southeastern corner with you. Once everyone is in position, use your sniper rifle and begin taking out the PLA. This will trigger the Marines to begin picking off targets and firing. Once the firefight begins, quickly use the map to have your men assault the PLA near their location.

04

01

02

finish off the last of the PLA making sure to use the buildings for cover, and then your evac chopper will land. If you did this before PLA reinforcements arrived (which isn't very hard to do), then you will have achieved your second Secondary Objective. Now, have everyone follow you over to the evac chopper, and then get on board. Command them to board as well, and this mission is over. If all four of the Marine POWs made it, then you will have achieved your Bonus Objective.

Alternate Strategies for RV8

If you are having problems with RV8, or simply want to make doubly sure all of the Marines make it out alive, have the Marines move to a safe location and leave them there. Now take your men to RV8 and enter the complex via the southwestern entrance there. Use the buildings for cover, and take out the PLA as they come for you. Watch your map, and have your men engage anyone that gets near. It's a good idea to equip your grenade launcher here to take out two or more PLA at once since they tend to group together.

Once you have taken out the PLA in the immediate area, spread out and have your men assault the buildings ahead where they can sweep the halls and kill any snipers that are about. You should head to the southeastern gate as they do this and take out any PLA you come across. As before, you want to do this quickly before reinforcements arrive. Once you have eliminated most of the PLA, go ahead and order the Marines to come in and help you dispatch any stragglers. Otherwise, finish the PLA with just your own men, and then call the Marines in once the evac chopper arrives.

An even safer route is to stay on the hill to the south of the complex. You'll be a good 400 meters out, and can easily use your sniper rifle to pick off the PLA in relative safety.

ACHIEVEMENT / TROPHY

Heroic Rescue – Rescuing at least three of the hostages will award you this Achievement for the 360 or a Trophy for the PS3.

ACHIEVEMENT / TROPHY

Perfect Rescue – Rescuing all four of the hostages will award you this Achievement for the 360 or a Trophy for the PS3.

As the firefight is going on, make your way around to the eastern gate of the complex and move inside. Move carefully, making sure to equip your Mk16, and take out the PLA. If there are PLA near you, have the Marines assault them. There is a building near the eastern gate where snipers are typically hiding. Enter the building and sweep its hallways looking for any PLA. Once in the building, use the map to coordinate your men and the Marines in the firefight outside. Watch the windows and try to take out any PLA you see.

Make your way to the northern exit of the building and aid your men in mopping up any of the PLA that are left. The evac chopper is more than likely in a holding pattern at this point waiting for you to kill the PLA in the complex. You need to hurry, or more PLA will show up via a convoy. Quickly

TRUMPETS SOUND
MISSION 09

The mission progress can be split into two halves. The first half involves clearing the way forward for the tank group Gridiron to ensure it doesn't sustain too many casualties. Once this is complete, you will have to make your way across a valley with mortar fire raining down on you to take out the four Spotter teams at the top of the mountain.

Equipment and Vehicles

Looking at the equipment map, you will be struck by a staggering array of ammo crates. There is a mind-numbing amount of firepower available, which is also the first indication of a nightmarish amount of PLA forces to deal with. Long range weapons will be your friends in this mission, so at RV1 simply do yourself a favor and grab the M4A1. Use it judiciously and accurately, and it will last you for the whole mission. Should you run out of ammo, pilfer one of the myriad of crates for a QBZ95 Marksman. If you plan to go for the Secondary Objective in this mission (recommended), then you'll want to raid one of the crates around RV21 for a Queen Bee. There are three to choose from, with the one on the road just south of RV21 being the easiest of them all to pilfer. Apart from that, you can rob the many AT gunners along the way to RV21 to acquire a Queen Bee.

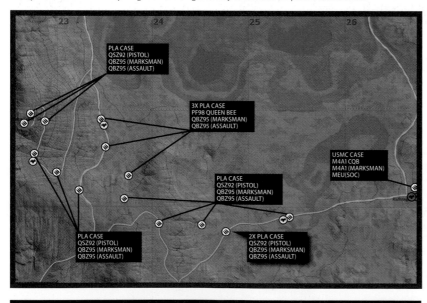

PLA CASE
QSZ92 (PISTOL)
QBZ95 (MARKSMAN)
QBZ95 (ASSAULT)

3X PLA CASE
PF98 QUEEN BEE
QBZ95 (MARKSMAN)
QBZ95 (ASSAULT)

USMC CASE
M4A1 CQB
M4A1 (MARKSMAN)
MEU(SOC)

PLA CASE
QSZ92 (PISTOL)
QBZ95 (MARKSMAN)
QBZ95 (ASSAULT)

PLA CASE
QSZ92 (PISTOL)
QBZ95 (MARKSMAN)
QBZ95 (ASSAULT)

2X PLA CASE
QSZ92 (PISTOL)
QBZ95 (MARKSMAN)
QBZ95 (ASSAULT)

MISSION WEAPONS AND VEHICLES

Item	US
Weapons	US Knife
	MEU (SOC) Pistol
	MP5A4 Sub-Machine Gun
	M16A4 Assault Rifle
	M16A4 Assault Rifle (Marksman)
	M16A4 Assault Rifle (Assault)
	M4A1 Assault Rifle (CQB)
	M4A1 Assault Rifle (Marksman)
	US Fragmentation Grenade
	US Smoke Grenade
	US Coloured Smoke Grenade Red
	US Anti Personnel Mine
	IR Stobe
Vehicles	M1A2 Abrams
	AAVP7A1
	M1025 HMMWV with Machinegun
	AH-1Z Ground Attack

Item	PLA
Weapons	PLA Knife
	QSZ92 Pistol
	QBZ95 Assault Rifle
	QBZ95 Assault Rifle (Marksman)
	QBZ95 Assault Rifle (Assault)
	Type 81-1 Assault Rifle (Marksman)
	QBB95 Light Machine Gun
	35 x 32mm HE Grenade
	35 x 32mm HEDP Grenade
	PLA Fragmentation Grenade
	PLA Smoke Grenade
	PLA Coloured Smoke Grenade Red
	PLA Claymore Mine
	PLA Anti Personnel Mine
	Field Dressing PLA
	PF98 Queen Bee Rocket Launcher
Vehicles	Type 89A Tank Destroyer
	Type 95 Anti-Aircraft Artillery
	BJS2022
	BJS2022 with HMG

Primary Objectives	Secondary Objectives	Bonus Objectives
Ensure M1A2s clear the first checkpoint Destroy PLA AT defenses Eliminate PLA Mortar Site	Destroy AAA vehicles for CAS mission	Ensure there are no casualties to the M1A2s

OBJECTIVE OVERVIEW

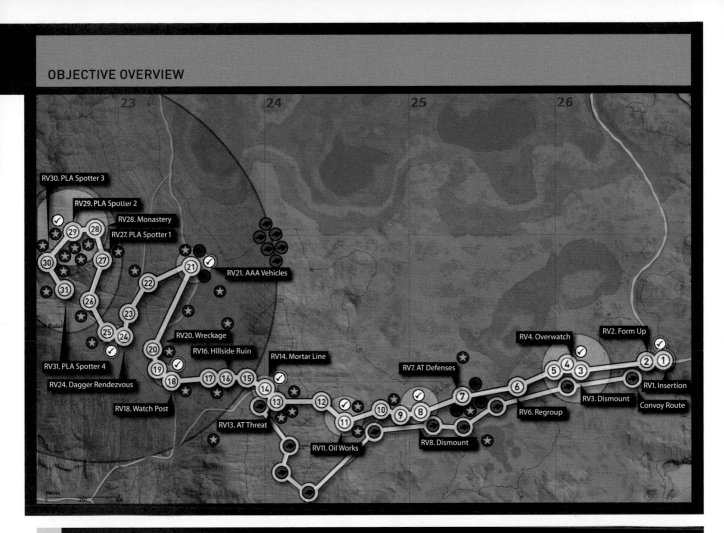

MISSION OBJECTIVES

① As you look at the overview map for this mission, it is soon obvious that you're in for a long, hard fight. Not only is there a vast amount of ground to cover, but large numbers of PLA will be guarding it. You'll need to work closely with your men and the rest of the friendly fire-teams to pull this one off. Perseverance, determination and teamwork will get you through this one with flying colors.

At the start of the mission, go straight to the ammo crate and grab the M4A1 Marksman and ammo. It is imperative that you grab this weapon, as it will make life much easier. The M16A4 Assault Rifle you start with has no scope and uses iron sights. While this doesn't make it a bad weapon, particularly as it has an under-slung grenade launcher, it does make it harder to aim, especially at a distance.

Once you have stocked up on weaponry, board the HMMWV vehicle nearby and have your men follow suit. Now drive west to RV4 and trigger the checkpoint there. As you are driving, you will notice two other vehicles fall in with you. These are two more Dagger fire-teams that will support you through this mission. It pays to stay close to these guys in a firefight, as their extra artillery will help you take out the PLA. The longer these guys live, the further they will accompany you on the mission, so watch out for them wherever possible [Screen 01].

Keep moving forward, but don't drive to RV5, as there are Type 89A Tank Destroyers ahead that will shoot you. Instead, park at RV4 and leave your men in the vehicle. Now crouch down and go over to RV5 and take cover behind the pile of logs you'll find there.

Ensure M1A2s clear the first checkpoint

⑤ Directly ahead in the field below you'll see two PLA Type 89A Tank Destroyers that will open fire on you the moment they spot you. Make sure to use the logs for cover to avoid being killed here. The objective is now to call in Mortar Strikes to destroy three PLA AT teams. There is one to the south on your left, one just left of the two Tank Destroyers, and a final team to the north on your right. Finally, there is a third Type 89A to the right of the two that are directly ahead. Ease to your right and look through the bushes to see it.

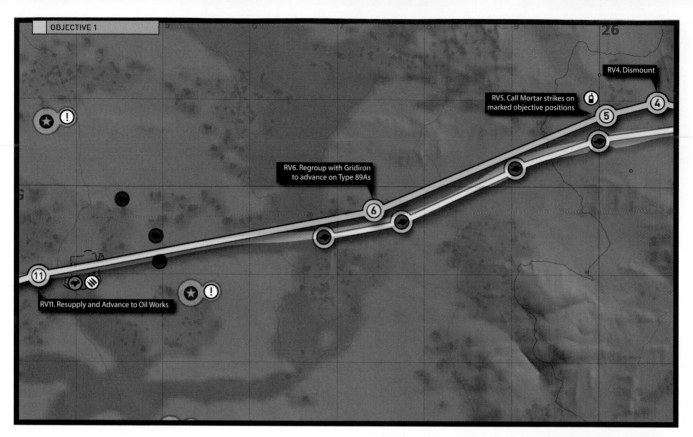

OBJECTIVE 1

RV4. Dismount

RV5. Call Mortar strikes on marked objective positions

RV6. Regroup with Gridiron to advance on Type 89As

RV11. Resupply and Advance to Oil Works

Equip your binoculars and prepare to call in the Mortar Strikes. You have nine strikes available during this part of the mission which you can't take with you, so once this is over, the strikes are gone for ever, so go for broke here! Also, once you have killed the three AT teams, the objective will be accomplished, and the strikes will be taken away from you. This means killing the Type 89As is not part of the objective.

You can, however, kill the Type 89As with the Mortar Strikes if you like, but you must do so before you kill all three AT teams. It will therefore be best to start by calling a Mortar Strike with a Barrage spread on the two Type 89As directly ahead. Aim between the two of them, and the barrage should take them both out. Now, ease to your right and take out the third Type 89A **[Screen 01]**.

Once you have called the strikes, it takes a few seconds for them to start, but you do not have to wait. Instead, keep moving and keep calling strike after strike until you have ordered strikes on all the Type 89As and all three AT teams. Just remember to hit the Type 89As first. Once the three AT teams are eliminated, your first Primary Objective will be complete, you will lose the Mortar Strikes and it will be time to move on.

If you do not take out the Type 89As with the Mortar Strikes, then Gridiron (your team of Abram tanks) will attack them. While this is just fine, you have to be aware that Type 89As may fire off a round or two and destroy one of your Abrams, in which case, you will fail your Bonus Objective. It is far better, as you have nine Mortar Strikes available, to take the Type 89As out yourself rather then risk damage to Gridiron.

Once you have cleared the Primary Objective here, get back into your vehicle and drive west through RV6 and RV7 as you make your way west to RV8.

(8) There is a checkpoint here, so make sure you trigger it. As you approach RV8, head left and off the road towards the trees. You will see a PLA team on the road up ahead that you will need to engage, but it's best to get off the road and take cover behind the trees before doing so. As you make your way to the trees, the PLA team ahead may be able to disable your vehicle. If this happens, immediately disembark and make a dash to the trees ahead.

Once you are in the cover of the trees, advance to the west and look for the PLA team guarding the gate to the Oil Works. There is a sandbag emplacement here where they will generally be stationed, unless they came running

toward you when you approached in your vehicle. Once you sight them, take them out with the M4A1 Marksman you picked up at RV1 at the start of the mission. The scope on that weapon makes it fairly easy to pick off the PLA through the trees you are using for cover **[Screen 02]**.

Alternatively, you can use the under-slung grenade launcher on your M16A4 to take out two more of the PLA at once. The M16A4 doesn't have a scope, so you'll have to aim with the iron sights, which can be a slightly tricky. Further-

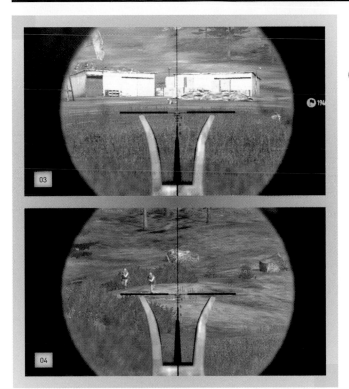

OIL WORKS

SP. Advance with Dagger teams in support

RV10. Assault entrance and hold for regroup

RV11. Oil works Regroup and resupply

SP. Use trucks as cover to engage PLA AT Team

RV9. Dismount in clearing

SP. Vantage point to take out PLA troops in woods to north west

SP. Use trucks for cover to clear area

SP. Use buildings as cover to advance

04

on the scene. If you happen to kill the PLA before they arrive, it's advisable to wait for the Dagger teams to catch up to you as the next confrontation may be a little hairy.

11 When you're ready, enter the oil field ahead via the gates. You should keep to the left side of the area as you push forward, and the other two Dagger teams will arrive and split up, with one team going to the right and the other to the left. Three PLA fire-teams up ahead will be advancing from the west. Two of the teams will be on the left side with you, and will often make a bee-line for your position. The first of the two teams is fairly close, so use the silos and equipment on this side for cover as you engage the PLA. Again, the M4A1 is the weapon of choice here, as it allows you to easily pick off the PLA at a distance.

The second of the two PLA teams will come from a small emplacement a few hundred meters further west. Look ahead, and you'll see them running towards you. If you are quick in dispatching the first PLA team, it will be fairly easy to deal with the second at a distance [**Screen 03**]. The first PLA will frequently break off and attack the Dagger teams, which will give you a small amount of time as you look to engage the second team ahead.

If you get into trouble here, duck into a building or behind a silo and order your men to flank left to distract the PLA team. You can then flank them to the right to make combat easier. However, remember that there is another PLA team to the right which the other Dagger teams will be engaging. If the PLA on that side see you, they could launch an attack.

The PLA teams on the left side may sometimes take cover behind large fuel barrels: a big mistake! If you see them hiding behind the barrels, waste no time in opening fire on the barrels to detonate them for an easy kill. Once you have destroyed all the PLA in the area, it's time to push further west.

12 At RV12 you'll be facing a small gulley that leads up a hill. Your next firefight with three AT teams will be waiting for you at the top of the hill. As you move up the gulley, you'll often be attacked by three-man PLA teams, but the teams may have already moved down to engage the other Dagger teams while you were in the Oil Works. Either way, make sure to remain vigilant as you head up the gulley. If the PLA try to storm you, take them out from a distance [**Screen 04**].

03

04

more, the grenade launcher fires following an arc trajectory, which means you'll have to aim a little high to ensure the grenade reaches its target. This is a very effective technique if you're fast and skilled at using the grenade launcher. However, the PLA aren't likely to sit still as you line up your shots, so you may want to stick with the more reliable M4A1.

While you are confronting the PLA at the gate, the other two Dagger teams will arrive to reinforce you; the PLA are sure to be finished once they arrive

If you don't see any PLA running towards you, you should make your way to the top of the hill asap. Open your map and look to the road ahead at the top of the hill. Have your men flank left and then head to the right and up the hill. The aim is for you to reach the road at the top to be positioned slightly northeast of RV13 while your men come in from the southeast. This tactic will enable you to catch the AT teams up ahead in your crossfire, as you can also use the trees on the hill to cover your advance.

(13) Destroy PLA AT defenses

Once you reach RV13, you should be northeast of the PLA AT teams and your men should be flanking from the left. You should immediately see the PLA moving around in the road ahead as they engage your men. From the trees, and using your M4A1, target the PLA and lend your men support in taking them out **[Screen 01]**. There are two teams in the immediate vicinity, so clear them out as quickly as possible. If PLA fire gets too dangerous at your position in the trees, run forward, cross the road and use the small outpost building there for cover.

Once the first two AT teams are down, check your map and you'll see the third and final team in a copse of trees near the road ahead. If you made it to the small outpost building, then look down the road to the east and the third team will generally be on the right side of the road in the trees there. Have your men attack the area as you again use your M4A1 to pick the PLA off at a distance from your current position.

When all the PLA here are dead, feel free to scavenge their bodies for weapons. They are all AT gunners, which means plenty of Queen Bees if you want them! However, if you opt for a Queen Bee, you are strongly advised to keep the M4A1 Marksman and drop the M16A4 in favor of the Queen Bee. The long range and superior scope of the M4A1 will make all future encounters much easier than the iron sights and shorter range of the M16A4. When you are ready, head west up the road a little way to trigger the checkpoint there and save your progress.

(16) Ensure there are no casualties to the M1A2s

Keep heading west from RV13. As you cross through RV14, you'll see some abandoned Abram tanks off to the right. Stay away from these! They are soon to be targeted by PLA mortar fire, so there's no way you can commandeer them for your own use **[Screen 02]**.

If you protect all your M1A2 Abrams up to this point (RV14), then you will have succeeded in the Bonus Objective!

ACHIEVEMENT / TROPHY

Keep 'em Rolling: Make sure all the Abrams in Gridiron arrive at the RV14 rendezvous point, and you'll earn this Achievement for the 360 or a Trophy for the PS3.

Keep going west and go down the hill ahead to RV16. On your way, look to the north and you'll see a small PLA camp in the distance; you can head to RV16 to avoid the camp.

Once you cross through RV15 and to reach RV16, you will have entered the PLA Mortar Zone. While you are in this zone, PLA forces on top of the mountain at the monastery will bombard you with mortar fire. They won't be very accurate at first, but the longer you are in the zone, the more accurate their aim will become. If you stay in the same position or remain in the zone for too long, the PLA will zero in on you with mortar fire. For this reason, you should always stay on the move to make yourself a harder target, and proceed through the Mortar Zone as quickly as possible.

Once you reach the inside perimeter of the Mortar Zone near the monastery (see the overview map), you'll be too close for the mortars to target you and therefore from that threat. You should stay on the move constantly while you are in the zone. Your men will often comment on how close the mortars are coming, which will give you an idea of how precise the PLA aim is, so never remain in one position for too long. Speed is your best ally in the zone, which of course means that firefights should be won as quickly as possible, since prolonged battles with PLA on the ground will mean that the PLA spotters at the monastery have more time to zero in on you.

One thing to consider is that the PLA at the monastery will never fire on a PLA position. So once you face and destroy a PLA team at a location, you will

AAA OBJECTIVE

RV21. Clear remaining PLA forces in village and resupply

SP. Use ruins for cover on village approach

(22)

RV22. Continue assault up to monastery

SP. Assault PLA watchpoint and use vantage point to destroy AAA

SP. Eliminate PLA in village and equip Queen Bee

SP. Break off road for natural cover on approach

be safe in the immediate area the PLA had been occupying. The PLA spotters will never fire mortars at their own camps, so, once the PLA there are dead, so you can use these locations to take a short rest.

As you get near RV16, you'll see a small, dilapidated building with three PLA around it; they will soon notice you and attack. Have your men flank left as you rely on your M4A1 to pick off the PLA at range. The PLA will often use the fallen logs near the building for cover, so be patient and pick your shots carefully. There is no rush here, so let your men flank left while you snipe the PLA from your position. Once your men are close, they will often finish off the PLA, or at least push the PLA out into the open to enable you to take aim and shoot more easily. Once all the PLA here are dead, you can always look through the ammo crates in the building, and then continue through RV17 and proceed to RV18.

(18) As you approach the road at RV18, you'll see more PLA at a small checkpoint [**Screen 03**]. They will frequently take cover behind the small building and the log piles, and will often climb up the hill to the west. As soon as you are close enough to see them, have your men assault the PLA or flank left (although flanking left takes a lot longer to be effective). As your men are following your orders, use the M4A1 to pick off the PLA from a distance.

There are only three PLA here and, if you remain in a crouch and use the ridge you are occupying for cover, you can easily dispatch the PLA here. Once the PLA are down, move to RV18, and then head north to RV19 where you'll find a checkpoint you should trigger to save your progress. Continue up the road to RV20 from there.

(20) Here, you'll encounter more PLA near the burning remains of a wrecked vehicle. Once they spot you, they will scatter and get off the road (often up the hill on your left) to seek cover. There are four PLA here and, once they reach cover, it will become a little harder to take them out. Your best bet is to quickly run forward and storm RV20 in an attempt to catch them off guard.

Before you reach RV20, use your map to have your men launch an assault on the area, and then sprint ahead. If you are quick, you can easily reach RV20 while the PLA are still on the road and exposed. While they are firing on you, they will spend more time trying to find cover, which provides the perfect opportunity to use your M4A1 to take them out. If they reach cover, have your men engage them head-on while you hold your ground and continue sniping them [**Screen 04**]. If the firefight gets too hot, duck off the road to the right and use the ridge there for cover.

Once you have killed the PLA here, you are faced with a decision: you can either follow the RV chain north to RV21 and the Secondary Objective, or you can head west toward the monastery and RV24. If you go west to RV24, you'll fail the Secondary Objective and actually make the mission a bit harder for yourself.

The Secondary Objective at RV21 has you destroying two AAA vehicles. Once these are destroyed, US Attack Choppers will be free to fly into the area and offer some support. The choppers will attack and destroy a considerable number of the PLA lying in wait for you further up the mountain. It is in your best interest to tackle the Secondary Objective to make the firefights near the monastery slightly easier to tackle. If you skip the Secondary Objective, the choppers will not be able to fly in, and you'll have to deal with the PLA near the monastery. If you want the challenge of a great deal more combat up top, then skip the Secondary Objective. If, however, you want to even out the odds a little, then complete the Secondary Objective to allow the choppers to come in and raze the PLA above.

(21) **Destroy AAA vehicles for CAS mission**

Your Secondary Objective lies at RV21 and you will need a Queen Bee and at least two rockets to complete it. If you don't have a Queen Bee now, you'll have to acquire one along the way. From RV20, head northeast, and you'll soon come to a small village. There are PLA here that will effectively use the buildings in the village for cover, making them dangerous and hard targets.

Have your men flank the village to the left as you move and enter the village from the southeastern corner. Copy the PLA and use the buildings for cover. Take your time, and watch your map closely. Have your men engage the PLA one at a time as you lend support by picking the PLA off when they move out into the open to fire on you. There are four here to pick off, so be patient and accurate with your aim. Once they are dead, raid the ammo crates here for a Queen Bee [**Screen 05**].

Now that you have the valuable rocket launcher, you must proceed to RV21. You can head northeast to another small encampment where you'll face more PLA, or you can take a less risky approach by heading northwest and avoid the PLA village to the northeast. We suggest you head northwest, as the encounter to the northeast won't gain you much of an advantage.

Head northwest from the village towards RV21; it will be best to get nearly due west of RV21, and then enter the area from that location. Move due east into RV21 to be better prepared to deal with the two PLA soldiers stationed here. The PLA will be near some buildings and will spot you quickly; they

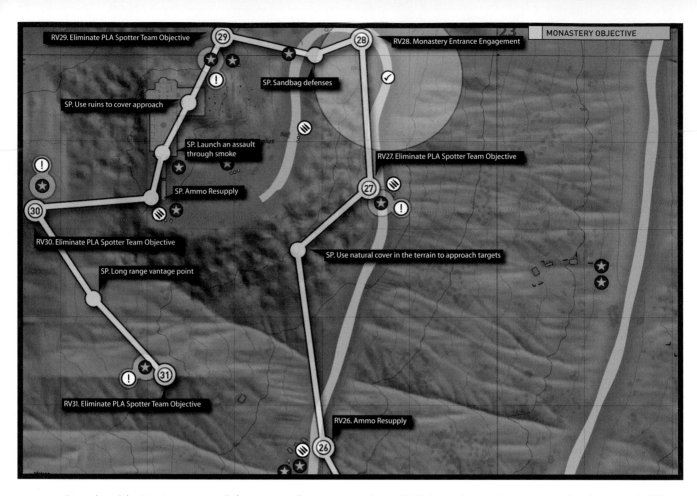

RV29. Eliminate PLA Spotter Team Objective

RV28. Monastery Entrance Engagement

SP. Sandbag defenses

SP. Use ruins to cover approach

SP. Launch an assault through smoke

RV27. Eliminate PLA Spotter Team Objective

SP. Ammo Resupply

RV30. Eliminate PLA Spotter Team Objective

SP. Use natural cover in the terrain to approach targets

SP. Long range vantage point

RV31. Eliminate PLA Spotter Team Objective

RV26. Ammo Resupply

are aggressive, and won't hesitate to pursue you. Before you actually enter RV21 and are spotted, have your men flank the area to the right. Now press on toward RV21 until you can just see the PLA and engage them from range with your M4A1. As you do so, order your men to directly engage the PLA, and they will soon fall to your superior might.

Once those two are dead, you will be free to take out the AAA vehicles. Equip the Queen Bee, and blow them both up from a safe distance [Screen 01]. Once they have been destroyed, you will receive radio confirmation that the choppers will now provide some backup. Great news!

Make sure to trigger the checkpoint here, and then find the abandoned vehicle in this area. Board the vehicle and then follow the new RV point to RV22. If you get back on the road too near RV22, you'll have to face a couple of PLA, so it is best to stay off road and drive through the field parallel to the

[Screen 02]. Continue this cautious process of easing forward for a shot and then moving back for cover, and you'll soon eliminate the first Spotter team. That's one down and three to go! Now continue up to RV28 at the curve in the road where a checkpoint is sited. Trigger the save and then start your final assault.

(29) Most of the action will take place here, especially if most of the other Dagger teams are alive. The wide curve in the road and the hill behind it offers great cover, even more than at RV27. Ease forward and around the curve to spot the PLA. Order your men to attack or engage, or simply let

road until you are close to RV23. Once you reach RV23, get back on the road and head to RV24 and the checkpoint in that area.

(24) This location is the rendezvous point for your team and the remainder of the other two Dagger teams you started the mission with. Depending on how they coped, they may be here or may all be dead. Check your map and look for them. If you don't see them in the vicinity, it means you are on your own. If the rest of the Dagger team is here, then they will have probably taken out the PLA stationed near RV25 (or be in the process of doing so when you arrive).

If neither of the other Dagger teams made it, then you'll have to engage the PLA at RV25 yourself. The terrain at RV25 is very open with little more than the lay of the land to offer you cover, so you'll want to take the PLA out quickly, preferably from a distance. Once they are dead, continue up the road.

(26) Here you'll be confronted by more PLA. If you took out the AAA vehicles earlier, their numbers will be considerably reduced. The PLA will use the buildings and sandbags for cover as you approach. You, on the other hand, have very little cover, as you are marching up the road towards them.

As you near RV26, it's best to go east (to your right) and go off-road to use the ridge line there for cover. Get as close as you can to RV26, have your men flank right or left, then begin picking off the PLA with your Marksman Rifle. At this point, you may be running low on ammo for your original M4A1, so you may have to scrounge from PLA Marksman.

Once you have killed all the PLA here at RV26, raid the ammo crates here for a PLA Marksman if your M4A1 has less than two full clips. Don't discard your M4A1 unless it is empty, as every round is valuable. Ideally, you'll have at least two full clips in your inventory with a third clip in the rifle, as well as a Queen Bee as your secondary weapon. When you are ready, it's time to begin the last leg of this long and arduous mission: the assault on the Monastery.

(27) Continue up the road to RV27. Walk slowly, as you don't want to suddenly pop up in front of the PLA and be shot. Ease forward and, when you can see them, use the natural rise of the land for cover. Ease forward a little so you can see the PLA, take your shot, and then move back for cover. As you do this, order your men to engage or attack the PLA

them fire with you. Flanking at this point will be too slow, so keep your men with you, or order active engagements or attacks.

Ease forward and sight the PLA with your long range weapons. Pick them off one at a time, and make sure to monitor the hilltops up ahead [Screen 03]. If the firefight becomes too fierce, move back down the road where the hill will cover you. Keep up this cautious forward and backward approach, and take out all the PLA in the immediate vicinity. Just don't run too far forward and you'll be safe.

As you are doing so, PLA from further off will run toward you, making it easy to take out two Spotter groups right here. So hold your ground, use the natural cover, and take out all the PLA.

(30) **Eliminate PLA Mortar Site / Ensure there are no casualties to the M1A2s**
Once they are all dead, move toward the monastery and circle around it clockwise and to the east. You'll soon come over small rise and see another Spotter team. If you have the Queen Bee, use it for an easy kill [Screen 04]. Otherwise you could rely on long range fire and have your men engage the PLA.

Depending on how the fight progressed at the start, you may have already killed the Spotter team at RV31 as they tend to come running toward RV29 during the firefight. When you have killed all the PLA at RV30, you may receive a message from command that it is over. Check the screen in the lower left-hand corner to see how many of the Spotter teams you have eliminated. If it is 4/4, then you're done and you can simply stay put until the mission ends. If it is only 3/4, then move on to RV31 to take out the final team, and you have completed this mission.

ACHIEVEMENT / TROPHY

Uphill Struggle: Kill all the PLA Spotters at the monastery, and you'll disable the PLA Mortar Site, thus earning you this Achievement for the 360 or a Trophy for the PS3.

DECAPITATION
MISSION 10

Your Primary Objective in this mission is to move inland from your beach insertion point and destroy a radio tower located in the center of Skira. By taking this tower out, you will effectively cut off all PLA communications. As you move in to take out the radio antenna, you will be alerted that a PLA VIP is entering the area via a PLA chopper. You'll need to recon this VIP to discern his identity, and possibly take him out if so ordered.

Equipment and Vehicles

This mission comes with the standard fare of PLA Marksman and Assault rifles. The easiest of the crates to get to are at RV2 and RV8. The other two crates are in undesirable locations that you'll never want to approach! One set of crates can be found at the start of the mission down in the FARP area, and you won't want to go down there, as it is heavily guarded with PLA. The other is in the radio station compound, which is another area you are advised to stay away from. Also, by the time you get to RV8 and the crate there, you really don't need weapons any more, but instead need good driving skills. Since this mission is primarily a stealth mission, the weaponry you start with is more than enough and is superior to what you could scavenge from the crates anyway.

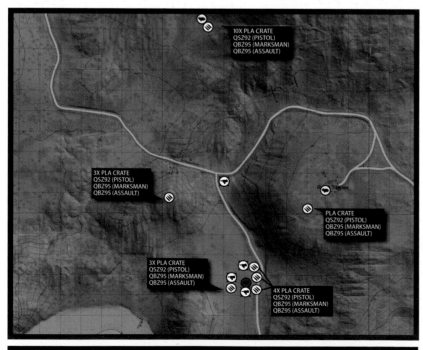

10X PLA CRATE
QSZ92 (PISTOL)
QBZ95 (MARKSMAN)
QBZ95 (ASSAULT)

3X PLA CRATE
QSZ92 (PISTOL)
QBZ95 (MARKSMAN)
QBZ95 (ASSAULT)

PLA CRATE
QSZ92 (PISTOL)
QBZ95 (MARKSMAN)
QBZ95 (ASSAULT)

3X PLA CRATE
QSZ92 (PISTOL)
QBZ95 (MARKSMAN)
QBZ95 (ASSAULT)

4X PLA CRATE
QSZ92 (PISTOL)
QBZ95 (MARKSMAN)
QBZ95 (ASSAULT)

MISSION WEAPONS AND VEHICLES

Item	US
Weapons	US Knife
	MEU (SOC) Pistol
	MP5A4 Sub-Machine Gun
	M16A4 Assault Rifle (Assault)
	M16A4 Assault Rifle (Stealth)
	Mk17 Mod 0 Assault Rifle (Marksman)
	M249 Light Machine Gun
	M21 Sniper Rifle
	M107 Anti Material Rifle
	US Fragmentation Grenade
	US Smoke Grenade
	US Claymore
	US Anti Personnel Mine
	US Demolition Charge
	IR Stobe
Vehicles	SURC Boat

Item	PLA
Weapons	PLA Knife
	QSZ92 Pistol
	QCW05 Sub-Machine Gun
	QBZ95 Assault Rifle
	QBZ95 Assault Rifle (Marksman)
	QBZ95 Assault Rifle (Assault)
	QBB95 Light Machine Gun
	QBU88 Sniper Rifle
	35 x 32mm HE Grenade
	35 x 32mm HEDP Grenade
	PLA Fragmentation Grenade
	PLA Smoke Grenade
	PLA Coloured Smoke Grenade Red
	PLA Claymore Mine
	PLA Anti Personnel Mine
	Field Dressing PLA
Vehicles	Type 92 WZ551A APC
	BJS2022
	SX2190 Cargo Truck
	Z-10 Attack
	Mi-171 Transport
	Mi-171V5 Ground Attack
Emplacements	QJC 88 Heavy Machine Gun *

* Tall mount

Primary Objectives	Secondary Objectives	Bonus Objectives
Neutralize the radio station by any means	Observe General Han's movements	Kill Han and neutralize the radio station with 1 JDAM air strike.
Eliminate General Han		
Rendezvous with team at extraction point		

OBJECTIVE OVERVIEW

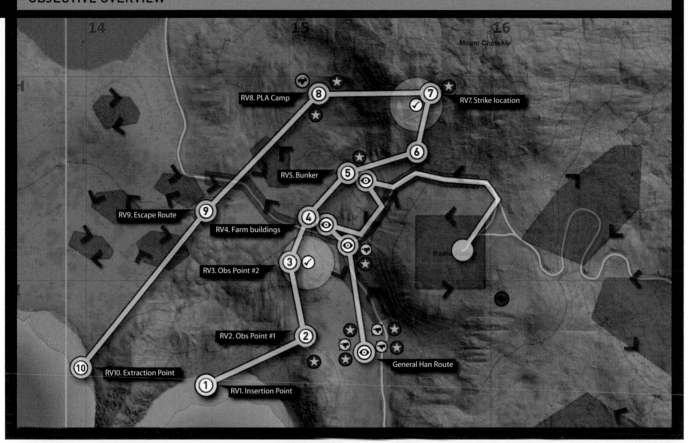

MISSION OBJECTIVES

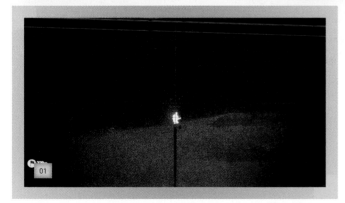

From the insertion point, move inland toward RV2, and you'll soon become alerted to a sniper on the hilltop a long distance ahead. He's a good 300 meters away but you can take him out with your 82A1 Sniper rifle. This weapon has thermal vision and a good scope, putting this long-range shot well within your means. At 300 meters out, you'll have to aim a little high, due to bullet drop, in order to actually hit him [**Screen 01**].

When you peer through the scope, notice the horizontal lines just below dead center on your crosshairs. You'll need to use the second line down as your targeting sight. Align this second line with the distant sniper's neck and take your shot. Do this correctly, and the sniper will never even know what hit him. If you miss, realign your shot and try again. The sniper here is the only PLA in the area, so making a little noise at this point will not get you into difficulties. Once the sniper is down, move to his position and you'll find RV2.

(1) You'll be dropped off at the beach by ship, and from there you'll need to move inland. It's night-time, and you are equipped with suppressed weapons, all of which should clue you in that this mission is all about stealth. When you first start the mission, the PLA do not know you're here, nor do they expect you, so they are at ease. Should they spot you and you raise the alarm, the PLA (and there are many in the area) will begin actively searching for you, making this a particularly difficult mission.

Always make sure your men follow you in a tight spread and that they are set to fire on your lead only. To be doubly sure, you could even set your men to cease fire or, better yet, to return fire. This means they will only fire if fired upon.

(2) As you are moving to RV2 you'll receive a radio communication that a PLA VIP has entered the area. Command believes the VIP to be General Han, the second-in-command of the PLA forces, but they need you to do some recon to be sure of his identity. Make your way to RV2 and take up a position on the flat area near the destroyed building there. Wait a bit, and Han's chopper will land.

After the chopper has landed, General Han will exit with his bodyguards and soon head west to talk to another PLA soldier. While this is happening, you need to equip your binoculars and watch Han carefully. You don't need to move any closer – just hold your position and keep HAN in view with your binoculars until you get a radio communication.

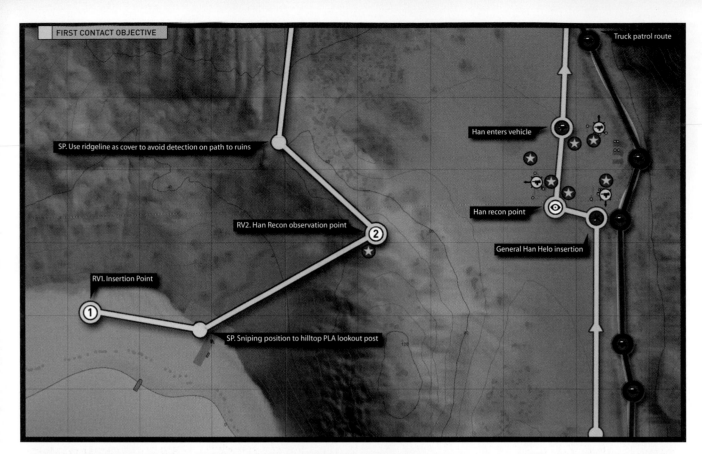

FIRST CONTACT OBJECTIVE

Truck patrol route

SP. Use ridgeline as cover to avoid detection on path to ruins

Han enters vehicle

RV2. Han Recon observation point

Han recon point

RV1. Insertion Point

General Han Helo insertion

SP. Sniping position to hilltop PLA lookout post

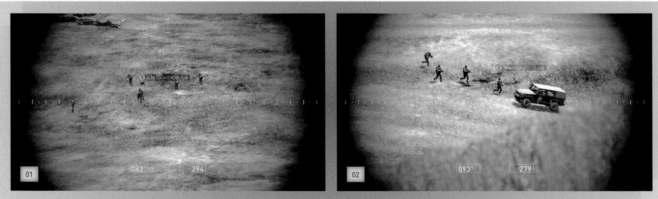

Once you have identified the VIP as definitely being Han (by simply observing him with your binoculars as he talks to the other PLA soldier), command will tell you to hold your fire and not to try and kill him. Instead, they want you to follow him for some more recon to discern what exactly he is doing in the area. Now begins your Secondary Objective, which is to 'Observe General Han's movements'.

To complete this Secondary Objective, you'll need to be stealthy and not raise the alarm. If you raise the alarm, then this objective will fail. To successfully recon Han, you'll need to follow him and observe him with your binoculars at various locations (General Han's route is detailed on the overview map). You'll be able to recon him from your normal RV points, so stick to the RV route and you'll get your opportunities for the recon.

To successfully recon Han, you just need to observe him with your binoculars for five full seconds [Screen 01]. Han will stop at three other points later in this mission, and will remain at each point for five minutes. You must get into position before the five minutes expires, if you wish to succeed. Once you have performed the recon, Han will immediately leave and go to his next position. This means you can trigger his early departure, thus speeding

up the mission slightly, since you won't have to wait the full five minutes Han would normally spend at a single location.

If you miss one of the recon points, then you will fail the Secondary Objective. Further, if you ever kill Han before the Secondary Objective has been completed, you will fail it and the alarm will be raised.

There is a big plus to completing the Secondary Objective. If you succeed, you will be awarded a JDAM (Joint Directed Attack Munitions) Air Strike, which you can use later and make finishing this mission a whole lot easier. It is in your best interest to remain stealthy and avoid raising the alarm. You will then recon Han successfully, complete the Secondary Objective and earn that JDAM strike.

Once you have successfully identified Han and triggered your Secondary Objective, Han will drive off in a vehicle to his new location. Now, make haste and head over to RV3 where your next recon point awaits. Since you'll be doing recon and trying to avoid a firefight, you can leave your binoculars equipped as you move on to RV3.

(3) Head due north down the hill from RV2 and through the trees ahead. You'll soon come to a tall hill you'll need to climb. At the top of the hill you'll find the ruins of a building. Amongst the ruins are ammo crates that you can pilfer if you wish, but your current inventory is far superior to what is in the crates – especially when you consider this is primarily a stealth mission with little call for a firefight.

From the ruins of the building, head north-east down the hill to the edge of the trees so that you can see Han. Keep your binoculars trained on him and watch him enter the vehicle and drive off **[Screen 02]**. When this happens, command will ask if Han was in that vehicle, to which you will reply in the affirmative.

Han will now drive a short distance away to a farmhouse. You'll need to move a little to your left to a position on the northern side of the hill you are on. Ease down the hill to the edge of the tree line and again use your binoculars to observe Han, and then watch him enter his vehicle. Again, you'll be asked if Han is in the vehicle that's leaving the area, to which you will reply in the affirmative.

You'll now need to head to RV5, where the next recon point will be available to Han. Start by heading down the northern slope of the hill to RV4, then turn east and head to RV5. Be aware that a PLA patrol will cross the road ahead of you. The patrol is between you and RV4 and will cross near the small fence ahead that you need to go through. In order to successfully cross the road over to RV4 and remain undetected, keep an eye out and spot the patrol (your men will usually spot it for you) and wait for it to move out of the area before you cross over to RV4 **[Screen 03]**.

(5) **Observe General Han's movements**
Head east and stay on the left-hand side of the road near the line of trees. You'll be heading for a concrete bunker on a hill a short distance ahead. The bad news is that there are PLA soldiers on the northern side of that bunker, so you'll need to be very careful. In fact, in order to successfully recon Han here, you should not enter the RV point yet!

Instead, head east to a small hill across from the bunker. You need to find a spot amongst the trees from where you can watch Han move up to the bunker. All you need to do at this point is spot Han and radio back to command that you can see the VIP **[Screen 04]**. Once command comes back with 'Copy', you are free to move on. There is no need to hang around or watch Han get in his vehicle, but you can if you like. At this point, you are done with your recon of Han. Your Secondary Objective will automatically complete once

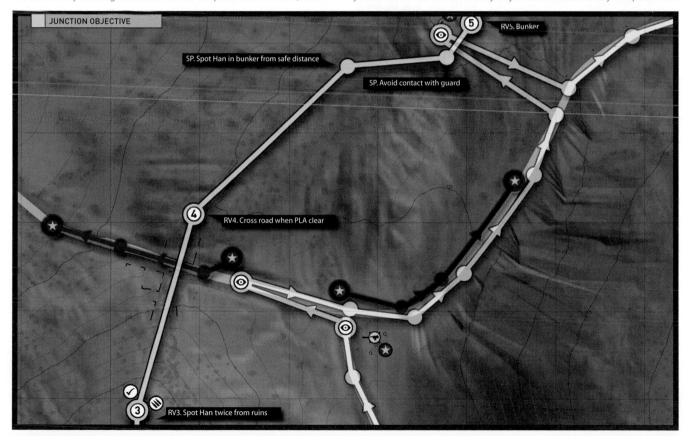

JUNCTION OBJECTIVE

SP. Spot Han in bunker from safe distance

(5) RV5. Bunker

SP. Avoid contact with guard

(4) RV4. Cross road when PLA clear

(3) RV3. Spot Han twice from ruins

Han reaches the radio station. Han will now board his vehicle and move to the radio station, so there really isn't much else to do here.

Considering that there are PLA on the northern side of the bunker at RV5, and RV5 gets very close to it, it's best to stay away from RV5 all together. Instead, follow the little trail at the base of the hill the bunker sits on. Stay low and head north-east along the trail and RV6 will soon become visible. Make your way to RV6, and then on to RV7. When Han finally reaches the radio station, you'll engage in a radio conversation with command about Han. You'll then have completed the Secondary Objective and will be granted the JDAM air strike. This will also open a second Primary Objective of killing Han.

If you blow the Secondary Objective at any time, then this mission gets a bit harder. Whilst you can kill Han at any time during the observation portion of the mission, it will cause the Secondary Objective to fail and raise the alarm, but it will complete your second Primary Objective of killing Han. That's not so bad, except for the alarm being raised.

The really bad part is your first Primary Objective of disabling the radio station. The compound there is overrun with PLA, and you really don't want to enter it and attempt to disable the station manually. Your best friend by far is the JDAM strike and so you should try to achieve your Secondary Objective at all costs in order to earn it. If, however, you find yourself failing to obtain the JDAM, then you will have to breach the radio station compound and plant a C4 charge on the antenna. See the 'Blitzkrieg' tactics found at the end of this section for details on how to do that successfully.

⑦ Neutralize the radio station by any means / Kill General Han

There is a house at RV7, so approach it from the south. You'll be moving due north, and the idea is to head directly for the house, using it as cover. There are two PLA snipers on the northern and eastern sides of the house, and if you stay due south, they will not be able to see you.

Keep a close eye on the house as you move forward, as the snipers will sometimes come round and might spot you. Make sure your men are set to fire on your lead, and it's a good idea to activate your Night Vision so that you can see more clearly. When you are close to the house, ease around to the right (east) and look for the snipers. Take them out as quickly as possible so they don't raise the alarm. Once they are down, trigger the checkpoint here.

Now continue north behind the house up the tall hill you'll see there. On reaching the top, turn and look south. Equip your binoculars and make sure you have Night Vision on. Find the radio station far away to the south and locate the radio antenna there. It's now time to use that JDAM air strike [Screen 01].

It should be noted that, if Han still hasn't reached the radio station at this point, you'll need to wait until he does. Once he has reached it, you'll receive the JDAM strike (if you successfully did the recon). Target the central antenna with your air strike. Han is near the antenna, so if you target it, you'll be able to kill Han and disable the radio station all in one go. Once the strike is over and both Han and the radio station are down, you'll have completed both Primary Objectives, and the alarm will have been raised. The PLA are now very angry and actively searching for you, so it's time to beat a hasty exit from this area and get to the evac location on the beach at RV10.

8 Rendezvous with team at extraction point

Head west from RV7 toward RV8. Check your map and you'll see a large truck at that location. The truck is your goal and you'll use it to make your escape. Progress west along the hill, and you'll soon spot two snipers down below you to the south. Make sure your men are set to fire on your lead, and then equip your Sniper rifle. Use the thermal scope to scan the area and find the snipers. If you don't seem them below you to the south, then they are more than likely guarding the truck at RV8 **[Screen 02]**. Fire on one, making sure you get a one-hit kill, and then quickly sight the other. Your men will open fire as well, often killing or at least suppressing the second sniper long enough for you to make the kill. Once both snipers are dead, continue on to the truck and trigger the checkpoint there.

Now, you need to drive the truck out of the area and reach RV10. If you go straight ahead from RV8 to RV9, you will cross the path of a PLA patrol, so it's best to steer slightly west of the patrol's perimeter and then swing back east to cross the road and avoid the multiple patrols to the west (see the overview map for patrol locations and perimeters). There are many patrols in the area

looking for you, and you'll more than likely get the message that you have been spotted, but don't worry about it. Just stay west of the patrol route directly ahead of RV8 and then swing back east to cross the road and miss direct contact with the patrols to the west, and you'll be fine.

The truck you're driving is large and a bit unstable, so you'll need to watch your speed, as it is very easy to tip this monster over. Try not to make any sudden turns to the right or left. If things begin to feel shaky, start tapping the brake to slow down, and make sure not to run over any large stones.

If you are attacked by PLA on the way to the beach and the truck is disabled, get out and engage the attacking PLA. When they are down, repair your truck and move on. If the truck flips over, there is nothing you can do, and you'll have to go on foot. If that happens, it's a good idea to reload at the last checkpoint, since that puts you right back at RV8.

Avoid the patrols and drive on to the beach, where you'll meet up with Saber 3 at the extraction point. Make sure you don't run Saber 3 over – they are on your side **[Screen 0309]**! Dismount from the truck once you are there, approach Saber 3 and this mission is over.

Blitzkrieg

If you want a really quick and surprisingly easy end to this mission, and don't care about the Secondary Objective, or if you failed the Secondary Objective and need a new plan, here is something to try. At RV1, when Han first shows up on the scene, equip your Sniper rifle and take him out immediately. With him dead, you'll fail the Secondary Objective but will immediately complete the second Primary Objective of killing Han.

Now head north to RV3. Once there, turn due east toward the radio station and make your way there. You'll need to make sure your men are in a tight spread and set to fire on your lead. Head down the mountain and cross the road ahead. You should cross directly in between the FARP to the south

(your right) and the small checkpoint to the north. Once across the road, head up the next mountain in front you.

At the top of the mountain you'll see the large radio antenna in the distance. Head directly for it and you'll come to a large building surrounded by chain fencing. Go to the right of it (south) and then around to where you'll find an open gate. Run in quickly and plant a C4 charge on the antenna and then immediately backtrack the way you came. Once you are a safe distance away, blow the antenna and you'll complete your first Primary Objective and open the extraction point.

Now return the way you came, all the way back to RV3. You shouldn't be spotted as you do this, if you follow the same route that got you here. Once at RV3, make your way back to your insertion point and then simply follow the coast all the way around to the extraction point **[Screen 0410]**. If you do this, you can kill Han, destroy the antenna, and never encounter another PLA soldier. Granted that this is a rather boring approach, but it is effective. It involves a lot of walking and mountain-climbing, but it is possible if you choose to do it and don't care about failing the Secondary Objective.

DRAGON FURY
MISSION 11

Dragon Fury consists of two battles. The first is the battle to take Skoje village and the second is the final big battle to take the Naval base, the final PLA stronghold. You and your men will work along the left flank towards the Skoje battle, while also helping the right-flank battle (by picking off soldiers and vehicles) due to the higher vantage points. Finally, you'll be tasked with strengthening the final US push into the Naval base and securing it.

Equipment and Vehicles

You've a lot of ground to cover, but not many ammo crates. Only four for the whole mission, and all of those appear well before you reach the Naval base. In fact, the last one is in Skoje Village, so once you board the choppers and fly to the next location there are no more ammo crates. This means you definitely need to hit the crates in Skoje village before moving on, if you plan on restocking your arsenal. At the start of the mission you may want to grab a Queen Bee from the crate around RV3, or you can just pilfer one from a fallen AT gunner. But, since you won't need that Queen Bee until Skoje Village, you can wait till then to grab the much needed rocket launcher. Before you leave Skoje on the choppers, strongly consider grabbing the Sniper Rifle from the northern most crate in the village as it comes in handy for long-range shots later in the mission.

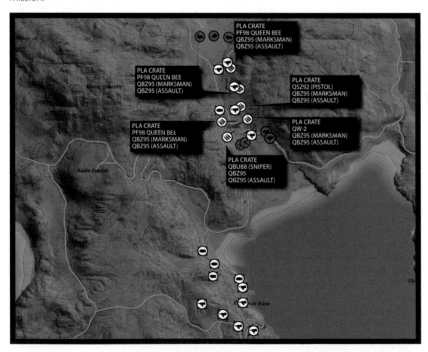

PLA CRATE
PF98 QUEEN BEE
QBZ95 (MARKSMAN)
QBZ95 (ASSAULT)

PLA CRATE
PF98 QUEEN BEE
QBZ95 (MARKSMAN)
QBZ95 (ASSAULT)

PLA CRATE
QSZ92 (PISTOL)
QBZ95 (MARKSMAN)
QBZ95 (ASSAULT)

PLA CRATE
PF98 QUEEN BEE
QBZ95 (MARKSMAN)
QBZ95 (ASSAULT)

PLA CRATE
QW-2
QBZ95 (MARKSMAN)
QBZ95 (ASSAULT)

PLA CRATE
QBU88 (SNIPER)
QBZ95
QBZ95 (ASSAULT)

MISSION WEAPONS AND VEHICLES

Item	US
Weapons	US Knife
	MEU (SOC) Pistol
	MP5A4 Sub-Machine Gun
	M16A4 Assault Rifle
	M16A4 Assault Rifle (CQB)
	M16A4 Assault Rifle (Marksman)
	M16A4 Assault Rifle (Assault)
	M16A4 Assault Rifle (Night Ops)
	M4A1 Assault Rifle
	M249 Light Machine Gun
	US Fragmentation Grenade
	US Smoke Grenade
	US Coloured Smoke Grenade Red
	US Claymore
	US Anti Personnel Mine
	US Anti Tank Mine
	US Demolition Charge
	IR Stobe
	FGM-148 Javelin Guided Anti-Tank Missile
	SMAW Rocket Launcher
Vehicles	M1A2 Abrams
	LAV25
	M1025 HMMWV with Grenade Launcher
	MH-60S

Item	PLA
Weapons	PLA Knife
	QSZ92 Pistol
	QCW05 Sub-Machine Gun
	QBZ95 Assault Rifle
	QBZ95 Assault Rifle (Marksman)
	QBZ95 Assault Rifle (Assault)
	QBB95 Light Machine Gun
	Type 67-II Medium Machine Gun
	QBU88 Sniper Rifle
	M99 Anti Material Rifle
	PLA Fragmentation Grenade
	PLA Smoke Grenade
	PLA Coloured Smoke Grenade Red
	PLA Claymore Mine
	PLA Anti Personnel Mine
	PLA Anti Tank Mine
	Field Dressing PLA
	PF98 Queen Bee Rocket Launcher
	QW-2 SAM Anti Aircraft Homing Missile
	QBZ95NO Assault Rifle
Vehicles	Type 99 Tank
	Type 89A Tank Destroyer
	Type 92 WZ551A APC
	Type 95 Anti-Aircraft Artillery
Emplacements	QJC 88 Heavy Machine Gun *
	LG-3 Auto Grenade Launcher *

* Tall mount

Primary Objectives	Secondary Objectives	Bonus Objectives
Eliminate PLA Armor in valley	Eliminate PLA defensive position	Fly MH-60S Helicopter
Capture Skoje Village	Capture General Zheng alive	from Skoje Village to the
Eliminate PLA resistance at Naval base		landing zone.

OBJECTIVE OVERVIEW

RV1. Mission Start

RV4. Primary objective 1 Clearing armor in the valley

RV6. Repel PLA counter attack

RV5. Secondary Objective 1 Clear MG emplacement

RV9. Primary Objective 2 Destroy both AAA in Skoje

RV11. Hitch a ride in Helo to Naval base

Mount Cherskiy

Radio Station

PLA Stronghold surrounding Naval base Helo no-fly zone

RV17. Helo Landing site

RV20. Begin assault on Naval base defensive line

RV19. Assault bunker

Kozhanov Base

RV23. Final assault on Naval base

Skiri Lighthouse

MISSION OBJECTIVES

(3) Eliminate PLA Armor in valley

You'll be moving up the left flank of the PLA forces ahead, while your armored vehicles (two LAV25s and one Abram) push up the right flank. Ahead is your first Primary Objective, a PLA tank that you'll have to take out. Start by heading south toward RV2. If you check your map, you'll see there are several PLA scattered around the area ahead of you. You'll also see the welcome sight of four other USMC fire-teams pushing ahead. Two of those teams are on the left flank with you, and they do a good job of taking out the PLA ahead as they move forward.

This part of the mission is timed. In four minutes, one of your armored vehicles will move forward toward the PLA APC and tank. If you have not taken the tank out, your armored vehicle will be destroyed. One minute after that (five minutes into the mission) a second vehicle will move forward and could also be destroyed. If two of the three armored vehicles are destroyed at any time before you reach RV8, the mission will fail. So you'll need to move quickly to take out that tank.

Push on to RV2 and then to RV3. As you approach RV3, you'll come to a road. As soon as you reach it, stop and drop to a crouch. Now peer through your M16A4's scope. This scope is thermal and will show you PLA and USMC friendlies ahead [Screen 01]. You should see some PLA directly ahead to the southeast. There is an AT Gunner in the crowd ahead, so take some time here to snipe him from a distance, as well as any other PLA ahead.

Remember that there are friendly USMC fire-teams ahead too, so check your fire. Once you have killed the PLA directly across the road, turn to your right and you'll

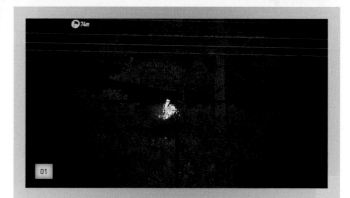

see a small house with an emplaced MG Gunner. Target him from your position and eliminate him with long-range shots. When he is dead, you have a choice.

The next thing you need to do is take out the PLA tank further to the south. However, there is also a PLA APC just north of the tank. You've only got one Javelin, and that should be used on the tank. You can use the Javelin from the road where you are (just before RV3) to destroy the tank from this distance, but as soon as the tank is down, the LAV25s will move forward toward the APC. It's possible the APC could take out two or more of the LAV25s, thus failing the mission.

For a fast and sure win, go across the road and find one of the AT gunners you've just killed and take the Queen Bee from him. This will swap your Jav-

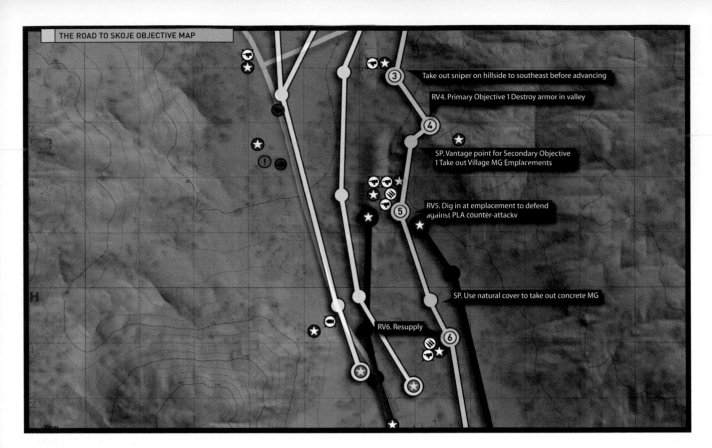

Take out sniper on hillside to southeast before advancing

RV4. Primary Objective 1 Destroy armor in valley

SP. Vantage point for Secondary Objective 1 Take out Village MG Emplacements

RV5. Dig in at emplacement to defend against PLA counter-attackv

SP. Use natural cover to take out concrete MG

RV6. Resupply

elin for the Queen Bee, so before you move off, memorize where this fallen soldier is as you'll want to come back for the Javelin. A nice trick is to use the Move command to move your men to the fallen PLA's position. Then you can just look for the on-screen Move marker to find your way back to the PLA and grab your Javelin. Alternatively, drop an IR Strobe grenade on top of the body, and then you can use your Night Vision to find the flashing light and the PLA who has your Javelin.

If you can't scrounge a Queen Bee from a fallen PLA, then make your way up to RV3, where you'll find a small hut. This is the same spot that had the emplaced MG gunner you took out earlier. Inside the hut is an ammo crate with a Queen Bee.

Now that you have a Queen Bee, make sure it is equipped with HEAT rockets. When you're ready, find the APC just south of your location. Aim at it with the Queen Bee. You'll be over 300 meters out, so you'll need to use the second horizontal line down from the cross-hairs to target the APC from this distance. If you are 350 or more meters out, then use the third horizontal line down for targeting. Once you have secured your target, fire the Queen Bee and destroy the APC [Screen 01].

More than likely the AT gunner you nabbed the Queen Bee from never got to use it, which means you should have one more HEAT rocket. If so, you can use it to take out the PLA tank to the south – be aware that an HE round will not do the job. Reload a HEAT round and move south a bit so you can see the tank. Now target the tank and use the second horizontal line down from

the center of your crosshairs for aiming. Take your shot, and if your aim is true, the tank will be done for and you still have a Javelin!

If you miss with the Queen Bee or don't have another HEAT rocket, then go get your Javelin and target the tank from the road for an easy kill. The range of the Javelin is incredible, so all you need do is sight the tank, wait for the display to indicate a lock, then fire. That's it: the tank is toast. Destroying the tank will complete your first Primary Objective **[Screen 02]**.

If you fail to find a Queen Bee in the area of RV3, or just don't like this approach, then you'll need to move on to RV4 and use the Javelin there on the tank. If you have to do it this way, there is a possibility that you will lose one of the LAV25s before the other US troops take out the APC. Sometimes they get the APC first with no casualties, but more often than not, one of the LAV25s will be destroyed. If this happens, don't worry just yet, as you can still succeed with the mission. Just make sure a second LAV25 isn't destroyed before you reach RV8. This means always looking ahead and spotting the AT gunners before they can set up and take a shot. There are lots of AT gunners ahead, so you will need to be vigilant, because they will not hesitate to fire on the LAV25s if they get within range.

4   Eliminate PLA defensive position

When you reach RV4, look southeast up the mountain and you'll see a sniper. Take him out before he notices you and your team. If you didn't take out the tank at RV3, head forward and slightly to the east, so that you can see the PLA tank off in the distance. Use your Javelin to destroy it and hope the LAV25s and USMC fire-teams with them can handle the APC without being destroyed. With the tank down, it's time to move on towards RV5 and hope for the best.

If things go badly here and the APC is destroying two LAV25s and causing you to fail the mission, you may need to restart from the last checkpoint and try an alternate strategy. Alternatively, you may first want to run to the hut behind the emplaced gunner to raid the ammo crate for a Queen Bee and try to take out the APC after the tank is down. Be warned that taking out the APC after the tank is down is a hit or miss endeavor. If the APC is on its mark and aiming accurately, it will destroy the LAV25s before you have time to get a Queen Bee, prep it, shoulder it, find a position, aim and then fire. At other times, the APC may be off-target, so you'll have time to squeeze off a shot and destroy it. And beyond that, the USMCs on the field may just take care of the APC all by themselves. It's random. If you get a bad roll here, consider restarting the mission and trying some of the alternate strategies we have set out.

Once the tank and APC are done for and you get close to RV5, you'll be notified of a PLA defense line ahead, which consists of two emplaced MG gunners. Shortly after that, you'll learn that US choppers are going to enter the area in 10 minutes. So once again the mission is timed. When you are alerted to the choppers coming in, you have 10 minutes to make it to Skoje and destroy the two AAA units there or they will take out your choppers. If both choppers get destroyed, you'll fail this mission.

Move forward, but at an eastern angle so that you climb the mountain to your left. The idea is to get to some high ground before you come upon the two emplaced MG gunners ahead **[Screen 03]**. As you get near, you'll see low walls in the area you can use for cover. Don't get too close, but instead use your thermal scope to spot the MG gunners ahead and take them out. When they are both dead, you will have completed your first Secondary Objective. But don't celebrate yet. The clock is ticking and you must get to Skoje village and take out those AAA vehicles.

5

As you near RV5, stop when you are still 30 meters out and peer through your thermal scope. Scan the area ahead, and you'll see three PLA running in from the left. Crouch down to steady your aim and take them out. When all three are dead, continue to scan the area for any other PLA you can spot and take them out as well. After you have killed all the PLA you can see from 30 meters out, continue on to RV5 **[Screen 04]**.

If you run into RV5 without stopping early to take out the encroaching PLA, you will be caught in a PLA pincer movement and pinned by crossfire. Finding yourself in this scenario can be a tight and deadly situation, so it's best to stop 30 meters or so short of RV5 and take out the PLA at range.

Once the encroaching PLA are out of the picture, continue forward to a small bunker where there is an emplaced gunner. When you can see it clearly, stop and scan the area ahead with your thermal scope. Take out all of the PLA you can see, including the emplaced gunner, and then move through RV6 and RV7 to the checkpoint. Make sure you trigger the checkpoint to save your progress.

8   Capture Skoje Village / Fly MH-60S Helicopter from Skoje Village to the landing zone.

You'll now be entering Skoje village via its northern perimeter. There are several PLA milling about the village, so you'll need to be careful and rely heavily on the buildings for cover. As you enter the village, you'll see directly ahead a building with a tractor near its door. There is often a PLA soldier to the left (east), near the building, so look for him as you move forward and take him out.

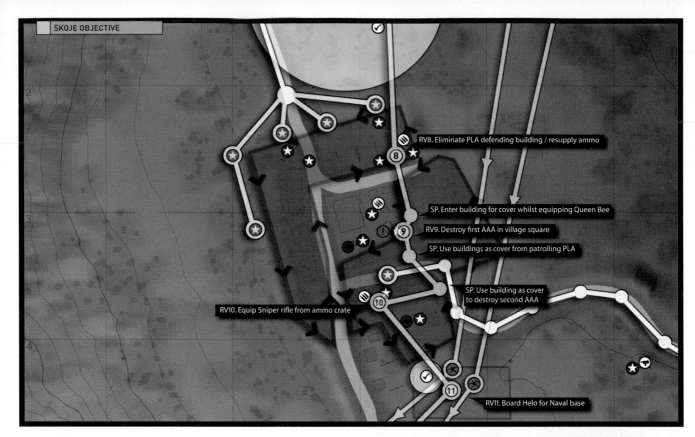

RV8. Eliminate PLA defending building / resupply ammo

SP. Enter building for cover whilst equipping Queen Bee

RV9. Destroy first AAA in village square

SP. Use buildings as cover from patrolling PLA

SP. Use building as cover to destroy second AAA

RV10. Equip Sniper rifle from ammo crate

RV11. Board Helo for Naval base

When you reach the building, you'll want to go in. Before you enter, turn on Night Vision and then push the door open. There are two PLA soldiers inside. They will usually have their backs to you as they monitor the southern windows **[Screen 01]** Quickly shoot them in the back if this is the case. If they are not directly ahead, then have your men attack the building and flush out the PLA. To be certain they have their backs to you, check your map. If they are looking in your direction, then you'll want to give this building a miss for now and get your men to attack it instead. You can come back in safely, once they've cleared it.

Once the PLA threat in the building is eliminated enter the building and find the ammo crate inside. The crate contains a Queen Bee. You'll need one with HEAT rounds in order to take out the two AAA vehicles here. Once you have the Queen Bee, exit the building and head south through the village. Keep an eye on your map and look for PLA. Take cover frequently and kill all the PLA you encounter.

Near the center of the village is the first AAA vehicle. Equip the Queen Bee with a HEAT rocket and destroy the AAA vehicle. If you only have one HEAT round and two HE rounds, then use the HE rounds on the first vehicle at the center of the village, but make sure you hit it in the rear where it is more vulnerable.

Now load another HEAT round and head south to the edge of the village, where you'll see the next AAA vehicle. Be careful here, and don't run blindly south. Also, don't stay in the center of the village, as it is often pounded by AAA vehicle mortar fire that can kill you in an instant.

Stick to the edge of the village (preferably the eastern perimeter) and head south. Watch ahead of you and check the map frequently for any PLA that may be hiding there. When you can sight the AAA vehicle, hit it with a HEAT rocket to destroy it **[Screen 02]**. There is usually a PLA AT gunner near the last AAA vehicle, so take him out and then scan the rest of the village for any remaining PLA. Once all the PLA are dead in the village, you will have secured the village and completed your second Primary Objective.

If you were able to eliminate the AAA vehicles before the choppers were destroyed, then two choppers will soon arrive just south of the second AAA vehicle you destroyed. Check your map to see them en route. While

you are waiting for them, head back to the building just north of the second AAA vehicle. This is the building where a PLA soldier was hiding (see map). Enter that building and raid the ammo crate for a QBU88 Sniper Rifle, as it will come in handy later. When you have the sniper rifle and the choppers are on the scene, board one of the choppers and get your men to follow suit.

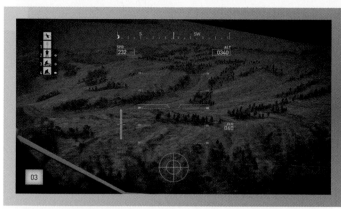

PRO TIP! ⓘ

Grab the QBU88 Sniper Rifle from the southern crate before leaving the village!

Once on board, you can either ride as a passenger to the landing site or pilot the chopper yourself. If you want to get the Bonus Objective, then you need to pilot it yourself **[Screen 03]**. As the pilot, fly southwest until you see a purple smoke grenade indicating the landing area. If you're having a problem finding the landing area, look for the checkpoint marker on the map. That checkpoint is in the landing area.

⑰ This is the helicopter landing sight. On landing, disembark with your men and go southeast toward the next RV point. While you may be very tempted to pilot the helicopter to the Naval base, that is a futile endeavor doomed to ultimate failure. There is heavy AAA fire protecting the base, and if you get too close in the chopper you will be shot down immediately. Instead, you'll need to leg it across country. Head southeast, following the RV markers on-screen, and along the way you will come over a small rise to confront a lone AT gunner at a sandbag emplacement. Take him out and move to the sandbag emplacement.

When you reach the sandbag emplacement, turn left toward the next RV marker. A PLA is manning a sandbag emplacement nearly 400 meters out on a distant hill **[Screen 04]**. Go prone and lie on the ground, then pick the

Land in the designated area and you'll complete the Bonus Objective and be ready to carry on with the mission. If both choppers survive, two new USMC fire-teams will board the second one and fly to the landing zone, offering you much needed reinforcements in the upcoming battle.

If only one chopper makes it, you should take it to the landing zone, but you won't have the benefit of the other two fire-teams as reinforcements, which will make the imminent battles a bit tougher. If none of the choppers make it you will fail the mission, so at least one has to survive.

ACHIEVEMENT / TROPHY 🏆

Vertical Envelopment -- Fly the MH-60S chopper yourself (you must be the pilot) from Skoje Village to the landing zone and you'll unlock this Achievement for the 360 or a Trophy for the PS3.

PLA off with the Sniper rifle from the QBU88 you grabbed at Skoje Village. This shot is also possible with your M16A4; just adjust your aim a little more upwards.

As you are picking the PLA off, more PLA will come over the rise from time to time. Take them out as well, but they will often move out of the area and head north to confront the friendly fire-teams reinforcing you (assuming you saved the second chopper and got the bonus of the extra fire-teams).

As soon as the PLA are down, head to the emplacement on the far hill. When you reach it, a new RV marker will open to the southeast. Follow it over to the edge of the hill, then look down with your thermal scope and you'll see a PLA about 350 meters out. Go prone on the hill and snipe this PLA.

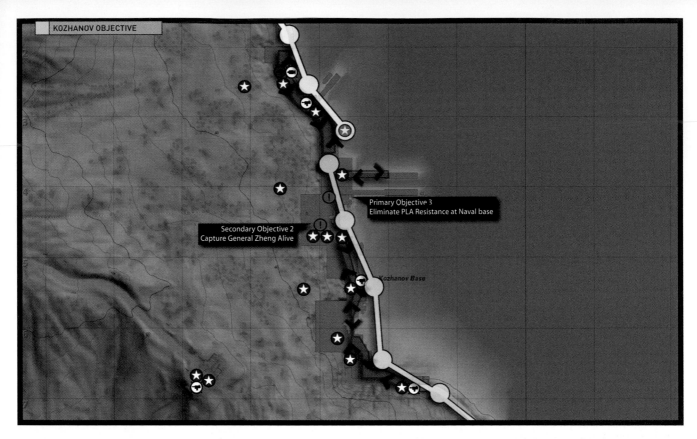

Secondary Objective 2
Capture General Zheng Alive

Primary Objective 3
Eliminate PLA Resistance at Naval base

Kozhanov Base

There is another PLA soldier further ahead in a bunker, but that is over 500 meters away, so give him a miss for now. Instead, head southeast toward the place where you killed the other PLA. When you reach the emplacement where the first PLA was, target the next PLA in the bunker ahead. While you are dealing with the PLA in the bunker, you'll soon get a radio message that you have a fire mission available.

23 Keep going southeast from the small emplacement to the next RV marker, which is on a hill. Climb up the hill to the top, but move slowly over the crest. Just the other side, down in the road, is a PLA soldier at an MG emplacement that can cut you down in seconds **[Screen 01]** Make sure you approach the hill crest in the crouch position, and only go far enough over the rise for you to see the PLA ahead. Take him out quickly. You could use your fire mission here, but it's a bit of a waste. Far better saved for later. Then again, technically speaking, nothing in this mission really requires the fire mission, so feel free to use it at your leisure – it won't make much of a difference when or where, if you even use it at all.

PRO TIP! (i)

Save the fire mission you gain in this area for the Naval base, where you'll get more PLA bangs for your buck.

After you have dealt with the emplaced gunner, move down the hill and then head east over the hill behind where he was stationed. You'll soon come to the far side of the hill and you'll be looking down on a checkpoint in the road. There are two PLA soldiers there, so take them out at range from your position on the hill. Now move down to the road where there is a game checkpoint that you can trigger to save your progress. You are now ready to launch the final assault on the Naval base.

23 **Eliminate PLA resistance at Naval base /
Capture General Zheng alive**
Either follow the road around to the Naval base, or head northwest over the hill to reach it. Once at the base, you might be tempted to stay up in the hills and snipe the PLA below, but that isn't a wise move. When you first enter the base, there are 12 PLA to deal with. Each time you kill one, a new one will respawn and join the fight. The PLA will continue to respawn until you

reach the bridges at the center of the base. Up to 20 PLA can respawn, which means that, if you just hang back, you'll have to kill an additional 20 PLA. So it's actually a bit easier and less ammo-intensive to just enter the base and engage the PLA while you move to the checkpoint at the center.

When you're ready, run into the base and make your way to the two bridges at the center of the ASAP. Rely heavily on your thermal scope for seeing the PLA as you move forward. Use the buildings for cover, but stay away from the explosive barrels. If the PLA make the mistake of ducking near a barrel, then shoot it to make it explode and kill the soldier.

Push steadily forward through RV21 and make your way to RV22 where there is a checkpoint. A good approach to take from the start is, as soon as you enter the Base, move due west to the first buildings you find. Immediately go behind those buildings and you'll see several PLA waiting back there to surprise you **[Screen 02]**. Act fast and take them all out quickly so that you are the one surprising them. You'll encounter at least five PLA back there, so be ready for a fast and furious fight. If you get into trouble, duck into the alley on the right between the two buildings. Keep moving north behind these buildings and you'll soon be far enough into the base to stop the PLA from respawning.

When you reach the checkpoint near the center of the Naval base, you are practically at the end. Your Secondary Objective of capturing Zheng is just ahead and to the left. Zheng is hiding in a small room in the building to your left. You don't have to do anything about him though. As long as he is still alive once you complete the mission, then you'll achieve the Secondary Objective. So make sure you don't kill him **[Screen 03]**

It's advisable to move your men further ahead and north of the checkpoint. As they are moving, more PLA will come forward, so help your men take them out. Occasionally, General Zheng will come out and attack, but that's bad news, as your men will kill him. If Zheng comes out, you'll have to tell your men to cease firing, then have them move fast to the north. This is a bad situation since you'll be the only one capable of firing, and you'll be concentrating on not hitting Zheng. If other PLA are in the area as well, you're in for some pain.

Get past Zheng as quickly as possible, and run after your men to the heart of the Naval base and push forward. Since you are at a checkpoint, you can

reload as often as it takes if you are having problems getting past Zheng. He doesn't always come out and attack, but he will do it fairly often, which will really complicate things.

Reach the heart of the base, and you're nearly through, with only a few more PLA left. These last few remnants of the PLA army will often come running to you in a mad rush, so hold your ground and take them out. If they don't come running, you can see them on your map. If you still have your fire mission, go ahead and use it now to take them out. There is a PLA tank a long distance to the north, but you don't have to take it out. Your only requirement is to kill the last of the PLA to the north (and they typically run to you in a kamikaze charge), and then your work here is done. When the last of the PLA are down, you'll get a message that the base is secure. If Zheng is still alive, the message will also inform you that Capone will move in to capture Zheng alive. You're mission is complete.

Congratulations, you have beaten the game!

Alternate Strategies

While you're in the Naval base, you can actually jump into the water, if you wish. If you do, there is no easy way of getting back out (and your men will not follow you). However, you are able to swim and, if you follow the perimeter of the piers and docks to the far north, you can trigger the end of the mission from the safety of the water, without having to fight **[Screen 04]**. Not terribly exciting, but it is possible.

ACHIEVEMENT / TROPHY

Ship It – Finish the mission (and thus the assault on the Naval base) and you'll unlock this Achievement for the 360 or a Trophy for the PS3.

ONLINE ENGAGEMENTS
CHAPTER 05

Operation Flashpoint: Dragon Rising features both full Co-operative play through its main campaign, and dedicated online Multiplayer modes. In this chapter we'll provide everything needed to take full advantage of these modes. This includes a full Co-op campaign walkthrough and detailed analysis of each of the four unique multiplayer maps, with easy-to-reference force summaries for selecting the right soldier for the job.

ABOUT THIS CHAPTER

Here we will cover the strategic and tactical options available when playing in Co-op and in the Multiplayer modes Annihilation and Infiltration. For Co-operative play, the focus is on tactics that Co-op players can use which would not be as effective if attempted in single player mode. Even a single extra player taking control of a member of the fire team can open new tactical possibilities, or allow for different approaches to engagements.

Co-op Mission Briefing

The full details of the campaign mode can be found in the Campaign Mission Briefing chapter. Instead of going back over the scenarios and events of each mission, we will simply provide additional tactics or alternate routes here, to take advantage of the additional players. The information is provided in the following format:

FORCE SUMMARY

This will explain what your most valuable assets and equipment are for the mission ahead, and which fire team member will be most beneficial for players to take control of when not using a full four-player team.

Squad Name

This is the currently designated fire team name. You will be addressed using this name in all communications with the officers in command of that particular mission. The squad name also gives a quick indication of the squad's intended role for the mission.

Squad Member Details

This gives the number, name and rank of the individual squad member. You'll also see the soldier's class icon by his name, indication what his primary role is. See the Specialized Training chapter for a full rundown of the various types of classes available.

SPEC OPS SQUAD: ENGINEER TEAM SABER TWO

2ND LIEUTENANT. MULHOLLAND (SF LEADER)

Initial Loadout		
	Primary Weapon	Mk16 Mod 0 (Assault)
	Primary Weapon Ammunition	9x30 FMJ round magazines, 9xHE projected grenades, 3xHEDP projected grenades
	Secondary Weapon	–
	Secondary Weapon Ammunition	–
	Additional Equipment	2x M67 Grenades, 2xM18 Smoke Grenade, 3xIR Strobes, 4xC4 Demo Charges, 1xNVG

Initial Loadout

The squad member's primary and secondary weapons are listed here, along with any additional equipment. This list does not include equipment that all soldiers have by default, such as the combat knife, pistol, binoculars and field dressing.

Engagement Point Maps

Each key point in a mission will be shown on a map like this one, which we will use to show suggested routes through specific areas, along with the positions of any type of flanking maneuvers described in the text. The legend for these maps is exactly the same as the legend used in the main Mission Briefing chapter.

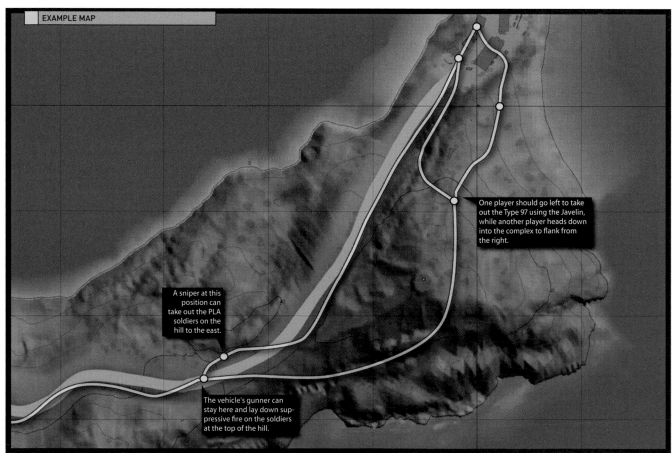

EXAMPLE MAP

One player should go left to take out the Type 97 using the Javelin, while another player heads down into the complex to flank from the right.

A sniper at this position can take out the PLA soldiers on the hill to the east.

The vehicle's gunner can stay here and lay down suppressive fire on the soldiers at the top of the hill.

MULTIPLAYER BASICS
CHAPTER 05

Outside of the Co-op campaign, there are also two additional Multiplayer modes in Operation Flashpoint: Dragon Rising; the team deathmatch-style Annihilation, and a Search & Destroy mode called Infiltration. In this section of the chapter we'll go over the basics of starting a game, and the rules and options available to players across these modes.

GETTING STARTED

Like many online games there are a few steps that players must go through in order to either join or start a multiplayer game. Once you're inside the online or system link menus, you are given the option to either browse the available servers and look for a specific game type or map, create a match to your own specifications, or look at your overall multiplayer statistics.

Browse Servers

The Browse Servers menu lets players search for any available games. You can also alter the search criteria to look for a specific type of game. **[Screen 01]** By moving the highlighted section either left or right, you can select one of the three filters that are available by pressing the Action Button. The filters themselves are fairly self explanatory: The Game Mode filter will let players select the exact type of game they wish to join, and the Map filter lets them search for a game on a particular map. To the right of that there is a column headed by a grayed-out character silhouette, which can be used to filter the amount of participating players within a Game Mode that the player is looking for.

Once a game has been found you will be able to highlight the Session by moving down onto it. You will then be provided with some more information about the specific rules which the host has set up, such as difficulty and time limit; if you are happy with the rules you can then press the Action Button again to join that host's server and be taken to the Multiplayer Lobby. If there are no games currently active that meet your search criteria, you can press the Reload Button to refresh the page and see if any new games have started up or become available.

Multiplayer Lobby

The Multiplayer Lobby is where players will gather while they wait for everyone to be ready and for the host to start the game. **[Screen 02]** This screen is dominated by the large table on the left-hand side, which lists all of the players currently in the lobby. In the list you can see the player's name, Ready status, which team they are playing on, and the strength of their connection. When an individual player is highlighted you will get a small summary displayed in the box at the bottom right of the screen. In here you will be able to see the player's rank, along with some of their statistics.

To indicate your Ready status you need to press the Start Button, which will then turn the grayed-out circle to the left of the player's name bright yellow and place a check mark in it, so it's clear who is ready and who is not. When all players have set their Ready status the host can then press the Start Button to begin a 10-second countdown until the match begins. Once the countdown has begun only the host has the power to stop it. Even if a player changes their status, the count will continue, unless the host notices it and decides to stop and wait.

Before the match starts players will also have the option to change which team they are playing on (USMC or PLA). By default, as players join they will be assigned to alternating teams as the game tries to balance both sides, but by pressing the Reload Button you can bypass this and switch to a different side.

Create Match

Selecting Create Match from the main online menu will bring you to the server creation screen, which gives you all of the options you need to set up any game mode to your exact specifications. **[Screen 03]** When selecting Co-operative Single Mission, Annihilation or Infiltration you will be able to bring up the Map List by pressing the Combat Support Button. From here, you will be able to select the exact map that you wish to create a game on. Note that this option is not possible with Cooperative Campaign mode, as that uses the player's saved progress through the game to start a game. By pressing the Reload Button you are able to bring up a list of Advanced Options, which can be used to customize the rule set of your game.

ADVANCED OPTIONS

Option	Possible Values	Description
Min players to start (Infiltration and Annihilation)	2-8 players	Amount of players needed to start the game
Min players to start (Campaign)	2-4	Amount of players needed to start the game
Game Time (Annihilation)	5-60 minutes	Total time for the game selectable in five-minute increments
Game Time (Infiltration)	15-60 minutes	Total time for the game selectable in five-minute increments
Spawn Time	20-60 seconds	Time it takes for a player to respawn after dying
Respawn Type	Unrestricted, Restricted, No Respawn	Respawn rules for players after they die
Friendly Fire	Yes/No	Select whether or not friendly fire is allowed
Team Kill Kick	Yes/No	Select whether or not players will be removed from the server for a friendly kill.
Team Kill Kick Count	1-25	How many team kills are allowed before a player is removed
Score Limit (Annihilation)	1-500 kills	Total kill count that needs to be reached by one team to win
Number of private slots	0-7	The amount of slots which you wish to reserve for invited players only

Respawning

Respawning in either Annihilation or Infiltration is handled a bit differently than in the Co-op Campaign. When creating a match in one of these game modes the host is able to select one of three respawn types, which will determine what happens when a player dies.

1) Unrestricted: This is the default setting for both Annihilation and Infiltration, and will allow the players to respawn as the same character as many times as they like.

2) Restricted: As the name implies, this setting limits the amount of potential respawns to the number of AI characters that are currently alive in the game. This means that every time a player dies the character which they were using is considered dead and is gone for good. The player must then choose to respawn as one of the other AI controlled characters. Each subsequent death by the player or their team-mates will slowly reduce the number of potential AI characters available, and when they have all been used you will no longer be able to respawn.

3) No Respawn: With this option selected players will not even be able to come back as one of the AI characters, so as soon as they are killed they are out of the game for good.

Ranking up

As the player kills opponents and wins matches in Annihilation and Infiltration they will earn Experience Points (XP). These points are used to track the player's progress and skill level, which is reflected by the different ranks that are obtained at fixed XP intervals. The ranks follow the traditional military

MULTIPLAYER RANKS

Rank Insignia	Rank Name	XP Needed
	Private	0
	Private First Class	50
	Lance Corporal	150
	Corporal	300
	Sergeant	550
	Staff Sergeant	950
	Gunnery Sergeant	1,500
	1st Sergeant	2,300
	Master Sergeant	3,350
	Master Gunnery Sergeant	4,700
	Sergeant Major	6,400
	Warrant Officer	8,500
	2nd Lieutenant	11,000
	1st Lieutenant	14,000
	Captain	17,500
	Major	21,600
	Lieutenant Colonel	26,350
	Colonel	31,850
	Brigadier General	38,150

hierarchy, with players starting out as a lowly Private, from which they have to work hard and play well in order to reach the highest rank of Brigadier General.

Scoring

Scoring in Dragon Rising's Multiplayer modes is relatively simple. Killing an enemy soldier (either player- or AI-controlled) awards the player with 1 point. Destroying a vehicle won't give any extra points, but it will award a point for each player inside the vehicle. You will also be awarded 10 bonus points at the end of a match if you are on the winning team. Players on the losing team simply get XP for the total number of kills they managed to get during the match.

CO-OP BASICS

Playing co-operatively with other players puts the focus on communication and teamwork. Co-op mode is designed to make players stick together and help each other, and to punish the whole team for each player's mistakes. This makes it a highly rewarding experience, but there are some important rules to take note of, and some subtle differences for players used to the single player campaign.

The Tether Zone

The tether zone and how it works is explained in the Basic Training chapter. Here we'll briefly take a look at how it affects your options in Co-op play. The tether zone is there to encourage players to act as a single unit, much like a real military unit would. Going off too far on your own without any support from your team-mates will very likely result in a quick demise, and make tackling objectives more difficult for the rest of the team. **[Screen 01]**

Having the tether zone displayed on the screen at all times (on Normal difficulty) means that you are always aware of where your team-mates are in relation to you without having to check the map. This allows you to be able to tell at a glance if a player is heading towards a group of enemies that you can see from an elevated position, but which they can't, as they are at the bottom of a hill.

Co-op Respawning

When a player is killed in Co-op play they will be taken out of the action and must watch the remaining players as they progress through the mission. In this state you can choose which remaining player to 'follow', using the Quick Command button. You will be able to respawn and rejoin the action after a countdown has expired, providing your team's pool of available respawns isn't empty. These work as 'lives', and are shared between all members of the team. On Normal mode you'll start out with six available respawns, and can gain an additional two every time your team reaches a checkpoint.

Experienced mode gives you only two respawns to start with and on Hardcore there are none at all, so once a player dies they are out of the mission for good. While you are dead and are watching your team-mates you will see a timer at the top of the screen. The timer starts at 50 seconds and counts down to zero. This is how long you have to wait before you can respawn. **[Screen 02]**

For respawning to happen the area has to be clear of enemies, so try and give your team some advance warning that your countdown has finished, so that they make sure they are in a safe location. During this waiting period you can still be valuable to the other players, because the third-person view that you are watching from gives you a much better view of the area surrounding a player. You will often be able to inform them of a threat from behind that they are unable to see.

Checkpoints

When playing in a Co-op campaign, checkpoints do not serve as mid-mission save points as in the single player game. Instead, they will add two additional respawns to your team's total respawn count. While losing the save function may seem like a heavy blow to your team, the fact that they have less importance in co-op actually increases your ability to improvise and tackle missions in any way you choose. Now, you only have to grab a checkpoint if a mission is going badly and you really need a couple of extra respawns.

Formations

Much like the single player game, having your team adopt certain formations during a Co-op game will often be extremely advantageous. Unlike the single player game, however, you have a much larger range of choices available to you. For players just starting in Co-op it might be wise first to try

and get your team to use the formation conventions set in the single player game. This means that when you say you should adopt a V formation, for example, everyone knows roughly where they should be. **[Screen 03]**

Once the team is used to moving like this, rather than everyone being bunched up and disorganized, then you can start getting more creative by coming up with your own formations that work well for certain situations, or even just variations on the existing ones. The only limits here are your imagination and the willingness of your group to experiment.

STRATEGIC CO-OPERATION

Here we'll cover the Co-operative play in detail, in the form of a complete walkthrough of the Campaign mode. This walkthrough is focused entirely on the strategies that co-op teams can use that would either be very difficult and time-consuming, or altogether impossible in the single player Campaign. Because of the primary focus on engagement strategies, a lot of the general details for movements and objectives are not covered here, so players looking for that information should refer to the Mission Briefing chapter.

DRAGON RISING
MISSION 01

	Primary Objectives	Secondary Objectives	Bonus Objectives
01	Destroy Early Warning Radar	Destroy Surface-to-Air Missiles	Skirinka Island Tour
02	Secure Landing Zone	Destroy Sunburn anti-ship system	
03	Extract by Helicopter	Destroy Surface-to-Air Missiles	

Combat Support: 1x Howitzer Artillery awarded when the Primary Objective to destroy the Early Warning Radar is complete.

FORCE SUMMARY

As you can see from the loadouts, Corporal Winters has by far the greatest amount of useful equipment for you to use. So if you are playing the mission with only two players, then he should be the first choice for the second player. The other two members of the squad are roughly equally valuable to a player; it just depends on their own preferred playing style. If you want to be operating at around middle distance from the enemy groups and engaging them with heavy amounts of suppressing fire, then you should take Knox. For a more of a long-range sniper, take Morales.

SPEC OPS SQUAD: ENGINEER TEAM SABER TWO

2ND LIEUTENANT. MULHOLLAND (SF LEADER)

Initial Loadout	Primary Weapon	Mk16 Mod 0 (Assault)
	Primary Weapon Ammunition	9x30 FMJ round magazines, 9xHE projected grenades, 3xHEDP projected grenades
	Secondary Weapon	–
	Secondary Weapon Ammunition	–
	Additional Equipment	2x M67 Grenades, 2xM18 Smoke Grenade, 3xIR Strobes, 4xC4 Demo Charges, 1xNVG

CORPORAL. KNOX (SF MACHINEGUNNER)

Initial Loadout	Primary Weapon	M249 SAW
	Primary Weapon Ammunition	5x200 FMJ round ammo boxes
	Secondary Weapon	–
	Secondary Weapon Ammunition	–
	Additional Equipment	1xM67 Grenades, 1xM18 Smoke Grenade, 1xNVG

CORPORAL. MORALES (SF MEDIC)

Initial Loadout	Primary Weapon	Mk17 Mod 0 (Marksman)
	Primary Weapon Ammunition	9x20 FMJ round magazines
	Secondary Weapon	–
	Secondary Weapon Ammunition	–
	Additional Equipment	2xM67 Grenades, 2xM18 Smoke Grenade, 1xMedical Kit, 1xNVG

CORPORAL WINTERS (SF ENGINEER)

Initial Loadout	Primary Weapon	Mk17 Mod 0 (Marksman)
	Primary Weapon Ammunition	9x20 FMJ round magazines
	Secondary Weapon	SMAW
	Secondary Weapon Ammunition	3xHEAT Rockets
	Additional Equipment	4xM67 Grenades, 2xM18 Smoke Grenades, 3xC4 Demo Charges, 5xM14 AP Mine, 2xM21 AT Mine, 1xNVG

Forward Thinking

Right at the start of the mission, if you have a player in control of Winters, you can set up a nice little trap that will make things much easier for you later on. Instead of heading down to the hilltop, turn around and start running up the road towards the lighthouse. After running up the straight section of road for a short time you will come to a shallow left-hand turn. This is where you will want to set your trap.

Winters should equip his AT mines and then lay them out so that they are spread evenly across the road. You might even want to lay down a couple of the AP mines as well **[Screen 01]**. Now, when you are heading to the LZ after clearing the village, the two PLA vehicles that come down the road will trigger the AT mines and, with any luck, both should be blown up. The AP mines you planted can take out any soldiers that survive. Once you've done this and are heading back towards the hilltop, don't forget to have someone grab the Marksman rifle from the ammo crates near the start of the mission.

01

Taking the hilltop

As you easily outman and outgun the two PLA soldiers at the top of the hill, this is a relatively easy encounter, but the surrounding area does allow for some flanking maneuvers that will speed you up even further. One or two members of your squad should take up positions by the broken wall and start laying down some suppressing fire. While they are keeping the enemies busy other members of your squad can either:

(A) Flank round to the left, using the burnt-out vehicle for cover, and then come up the hill on the other side and take out the soldiers, or

(B) Flank round to the right using the clump of trees on this side for cover while you move round until you can see the soldiers hiding behind the sandbags.

You could also have one player go round either side for a pincer maneuver; just make sure that they watch their lines of sight and don't get caught in any friendly fire.

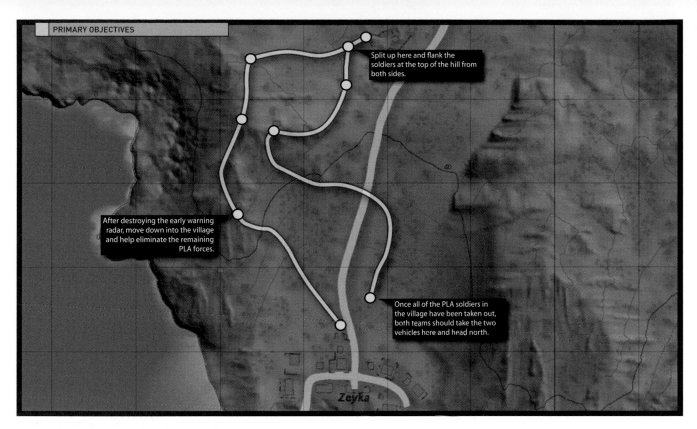

PRIMARY OBJECTIVES

Split up here and flank the soldiers at the top of the hill from both sides.

After destroying the early warning radar, move down into the village and help eliminate the remaining PLA forces.

Once all of the PLA soldiers in the village have been taken out, both teams should take the two vehicles here and head north.

Zeyka

Assaulting the Radar Site

Use the crest of the hill for cover while the whole team engages the enemy group behind the sandbags. If there are any enemies around the wooden shack, the Fire Team Leader should fire off a round from his underslung grenade launcher at the barrel next to it to take the building out. If the soldiers behind the sandbags are proving difficult to hit then you should send one or two players down the hillside to the right, so that they can come round and flank them from the side. **[Screen 02]**

Capturing the Village

From the hilltop, have one player stay with the Fire Team Leader while he takes care of blowing the radar site with a demo charge and then calls in the Artillery on the village below. While they are taking care of that, the other players should move round to the east until they get into a good position to start taking out some of the PLA guards around the outskirts of the village, especially the two in the guard posts.

Once the Artillery strike is over, the Fire Team Leader and the player with him should move straight into the village and use the trees for cover while they take out any remaining PLA soldiers. The other players who were in the sniping positions should then start to move into the village from there, specifically looking to engage the PLA forces in the line of trees to the south-east. The other Saber teams should be moving in on the other side of those men, so they will provide you with some extra support. When the area is clear, have each team of two men get into one of the PLA vehicles in the area and then both vehicles should start heading up to the LZ.

Securing the LZ

If you prepped the road with mines at the start of the mission there should be very little left of the two enemy vehicles for you to deal with. If there are just one or two PLA soldiers left on foot you should easily be able to take them out with your mounted guns. If one of the vehicles survives (or you decided not to mine the road in the first place and are dealing with both enemy vehicles), your two vehicle gunners should try and immobilize them from as far back up the road as they can, and then pick the PLA soldiers off from distance when they get out.

If you are finding it difficult to nail the PLA vehicles with your mounted guns then you may want to make the player using Winters get out and use his SMAW to take out one or both of the vehicles **[Screen 03]**. If you choose to do this then the broken wall along the left-hand side of the road makes a perfect staging area. Once they are both taken out you will have the option to either head straight to the extraction point and end the mission, or continue on and clear all of the Secondary Objectives, starting with the SAM site on the west of the island.

02

03

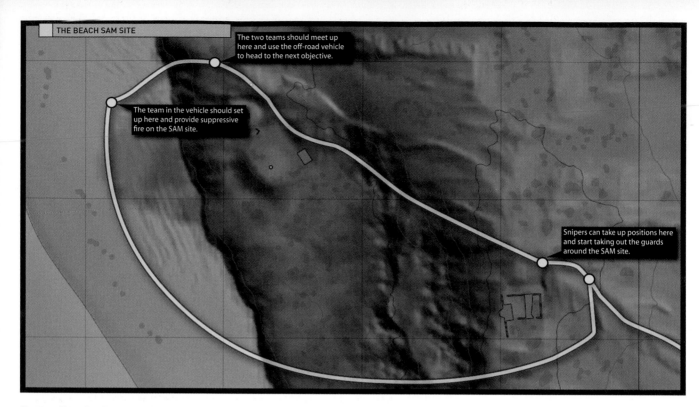

THE BEACH SAM SITE

The two teams should meet up here and use the off-road vehicle to head to the next objective.

The team in the vehicle should set up here and provide suppressive fire on the SAM site.

Snipers can take up positions here and start taking out the guards around the SAM site.

Destroying the Beach SAM site

Continue up the main road in the vehicles until you come to a sharp right-hand turn around 450 meters or so away from the SAM site. This is your cue to start heading off-road towards the objective. Keep going straight up the hill in your vehicle and park up by the ruins at the top. Within the ruins you will find a set of ammo boxes with a couple of Marksman rifles and a deadly Sniper rifle, so make sure you fit your team out evenly with these so that every player ends up with a scoped weapon to make the upcoming engagements easier.

Once everyone is fully equipped, two players should move north-west towards the objective and take up positions at the crest of the hill overlooking it. Meanwhile, the other two can get back into one of the vehicles and head back to the south slightly, before turning west and driving down onto the beach. Once the vehicle is on the beach it should start heading towards the SAM site and begin laying down suppressing fire on any enemies in sight. [Screen 01]

While the vehicle gets into position, the Sniper team up at the top of the hill should scan the area looking for the PLA group on patrol in the area. They should open fire on any spotted enemies straight away. If they can't see the patrol group then they can use the distraction caused by the vehicle to easily pick off the confused PLA soldiers defending the SAM site. Once the vehicle has started engaging the group that are defending the site, the patrol group will often move in to aid them, so this is usually the best way to flush them out if you can't see them directly. Once the area's clear, move in and destroy the SAM launcher with a demo charge.

Taking out the Sunburn Launcher

With the SAM site taken care of, it's time to head over to the eastern side of the island to take out the Sunburn Launcher, so get everyone back in their vehicles and start driving east towards the next objective. As you move across the island you should see a clearing in the trees on the other side of the road, which is precisely where you should be heading. Continue driving up the hill until you come to a large rocky outcrop near the top and stop there. [Screen 02]

As with the previous location, there are two groups of PLA soldiers in this area, one defending the site itself and another on patrol in the area. As the patrol group could be anywhere along their route when you arrive in the area, you need to be extremely cautious when moving into this position. If you come into contact with them then take up positions behind the rocks and

the vehicle and take them out. If you don't see them upon your arrival then you should just carry on attacking the objective and engage them along the way.

Two players should head south-east into the trees to perform a flanking maneuver on the defending PLA, and then the other players should head directly north to the crest of the hill overlooking the area. Once there they can begin engaging the targets from long range, while the other players come around and flank them at close range.

If neither team has encountered the PLA patrol group at this time, then one

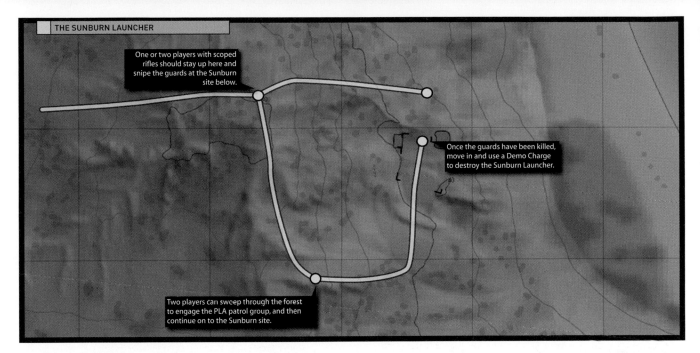

THE SUNBURN LAUNCHER

One or two players with scoped rifles should stay up here and snipe the guards at the Sunburn site below.

Once the guards have been killed, move in and use a Demo Charge to destroy the Sunburn Launcher.

Two players can sweep through the forest to engage the PLA patrol group, and then continue on to the Sunburn site.

member of the Sniper team should keep an eye on the slope of the hill to the north-east, as they may be coming up there, in which case both of them should turn and engage them.

Once both groups of PLA have been killed, move in and blow the Sunburn Launcher and then get back in the vehicles and start heading for the final SAM site at the lighthouse.

Road to the Lighthouse

When you get to around 500 meters away from the objective, you should start to see a large hill to the north-east with some ruins at the top. As soon as one of your vehicle gunners has a clear shot on the sandbagged area, park the vehicle ands have him start laying down suppressing fire. Whichever player grabbed the Sniper rifle earlier on should then exit the vehicle

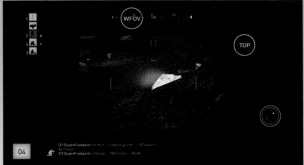

and take up a position on top of the small hill to the north and start picking off some of the enemies at the top. **[Screen 03]**

While those two players are keeping the enemies pinned down at long range, the other two should also exit the vehicle and then start making their way up the large hill towards the enemies. While moving in they should stick to the right-hand side of the hill, so that they can use the ridgeline for cover. When they are near the top they can then cut across and flank the enemies behind the sandbags and finish them off easily.

The two-man team up on the hill needs to beware of the PLA unit patrolling the ridgeline on the other side of this area heading down to the lighthouse, so they should make sure they stick close to the ruins for cover until they are sure it's clear. While they are in the ruins, both of them should grab a Marksman rifle from the ammo boxes and one of them also needs to take the Javelin. To find the PLA patrol, one player should move down to the north-east on the right-hand side of the ridgeline, using it for cover while trying to spot the patrol down at the base of the hill. The other player should move down the ridgeline, just in case the patrol is starting to make its way up from the bottom. Whoever finds them first should receive immediate backup from the other person.

Assault on the Lighthouse

Once the patrol has been dealt with, the player with the Javelin should move to the north-west side of the hill and continue moving along the side of it, with the Javelin equipped, until they get line of sight on the Type 97 at the bottom. **[Screen 04]** Meanwhile, the other player on the hill can continue north-east as far as the bottom, and hold position there until the Type 97 is destroyed, unless they come into contact with an enemy.

The sniper at the top of the road and the vehicle gunner should make their way down the road on foot, holding a position around the corner from the tank until it has been destroyed. They should then continue to move towards the lighthouse (using the hill as cover) and look to taking out any PLA they can see. The player with the Javelin will have the best view of the area, so they can pass on any information about enemy movements to the team while trying to take out any enemies they come across with their rifle.

With a lot of firepower now coming in from one side, the player to the north-east should have quite a distraction going for them. This should allow the player to start moving into the area, specifically looking to clear buildings. As the main force on the other side clears out some of the enemies, they should be continuously moving up towards the main area and then help with any building clearance that's needed. When it's all clear, place the charge, blow the SAM site and then head back to the vehicles. Next, either go to the LZ and complete the mission, or complete the bonus objective first and then leave.

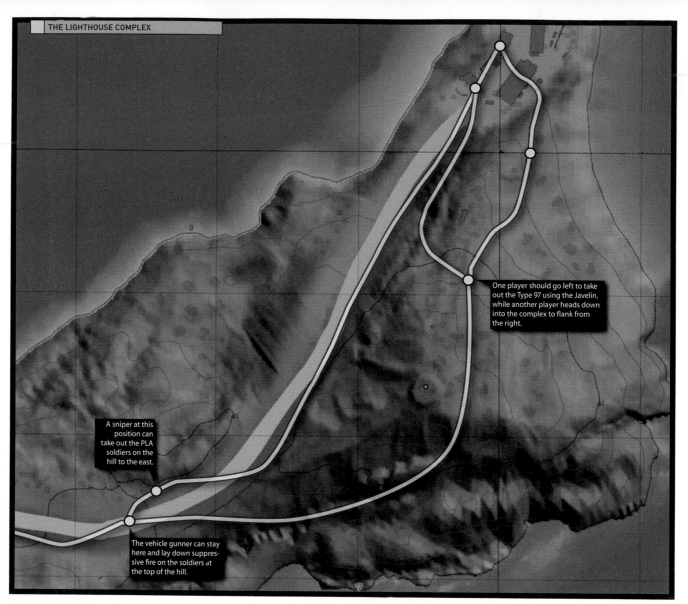

One player should go left to take out the Type 97 using the Javelin, while another player heads down into the complex to flank from the right.

A sniper at this position can take out the PLA soldiers on the hill to the east.

The vehicle gunner can stay here and lay down suppressive fire on the soldiers at the top of the hill.

BLINDING THE DRAGON
MISSION 02

	Primary Objectives	Secondary Objectives	Bonus Objectives
01	Destroy Sunburn Site	Remain Undetected by PLA forces	Eliminate the PLA Commander without raising the alarm
02	Disable Air Defenses	Complete flanking maneuver with Saber Three	
03	Proceed to Overwatch		

Combat Support: 1xHowitzer Artillery awarded when the Primary Objective of destroying the Sunburn site is complete.

FORCE SUMMARY

Much like in the first mission, Winters should once again be the first choice for a second player-controlled character, as the Sniper rifle he carries will be extremely useful in picking off targets at long range without the enemies getting a chance to return fire. Morales should be next in line, as the thermal scope on his Night Ops rifle will come in very handy for picking out targets amongst the bushes.

As Knox comes initially armed with an LMG, and this is primarily a stealth mission, his role is somewhat less significant than that of the other members, but he can come in very handy if your team is discovered. To give him a more active role, you should make sure this player takes one of the Marksman-type rifles from the ammo boxes at the start of the mission to help in long-range combat.

SPEC OPS SQUAD: ENGINEER SCOUT TEAM SABER TWO

2ND LIEUTENANT. MULHOLLAND (SF LEADER)

Initial Loadout	Primary Weapon	Mk17 Mod 0 (Night Ops)
	Primary Weapon Ammunition	9x20 FMJ round magazines
	Secondary Weapon	–
	Secondary Weapon Ammunition	–
	Additional Equipment	2xM67 Grenades, 2xM18 Smoke Grenades, 3x IR Strobes, 6xC4 Demo Charges, 1xNVG

CORPORAL KNOX (SF MACHINEGUNNER)

Initial Loadout	Primary Weapon	MK48 Mod 0
	Primary Weapon Ammunition	5x100 FMJ round ammo boxes
	Secondary Weapon	–
	Secondary Weapon Ammunition	–
	Additional Equipment	1xM67 Grenade, 1xM18 Smoke Grenade, 1xNVG

CORPORAL MORALES (SF MEDIC)

Initial Loadout	Primary Weapon	Mk17 Mod 0 (Night Ops)
	Primary Weapon Ammunition	9x20 FMJ round magazines
	Secondary Weapon	–
	Secondary Weapon Ammunition	–
	Additional Equipment	2xM67 Grenades, 2xM18 Smoke Grenade, 1xMedical Kit, 1xNVG

CORPORAL. WINTERS (SF SNIPER)

Initial Loadout	Primary Weapon	MP5A4
	Primary Weapon Ammunition	5x30 FMJ round magazines
	Secondary Weapon	M21
	Secondary Weapon Ammunition	12x20 FMJ round magazines
	Additional Equipment	2xM67 Grenades, 2xM18 Smoke Grenades, 2xM18A1 Claymore Mines, 1xNVG

Guard post at the end of the gully

If you wish to kill the guards here you should get a number of your squad members to line up their shots. You can then use a combination of the Night Vision Goggles and the weapon's IR beams to see who is targeting whom, and then all open fire on them when in position. For a stealthy approach you should get to about 50 meters away from the guards and then head due south up the other side of the gully. If you take quite a wide-flanking angle from their position you should be able to navigate around them safely without alerting them, and then simply continue on to the Sunburn flanking position. **[Screen 01]**.

The Sunburn site

After reaching the building at the flanking position, if you are aiming to take out the PLA soldiers guarding it, one player should take up position at the second-floor window, while another stays at the side of the small outhouse. These two players will be providing the long-range support for the other two, who should move up using the hay bales as cover and then look to engage the guards from much closer range. As before, with the benefit of the IR beams you will be able to avoid doubling up on targets to really maximize the effectiveness of the group. When all of the visible guards have been killed, the forward team should move around the Sunburn Launcher just to make sure the area is clear, and then proceed to place the demo charges.

For a lower-key stealth approach you can simply wait for the other Saber team to get into position and start their assault. This should draw the guards away from the Sunburn Launcher, which will allow one member of the team to run up and place the demo charge unhindered. Whichever route you decide to take, speed will be extremely important; as soon as you either kill one of the guards or blow the Sunburn Launcher, the PLA attack helicopter will be alerted and be called into the area, along with one of the nearby patrol groups. You can hide amongst the trees until they move on, or you can hide up in the house at the flanking position until the coast is clear, and then move on.

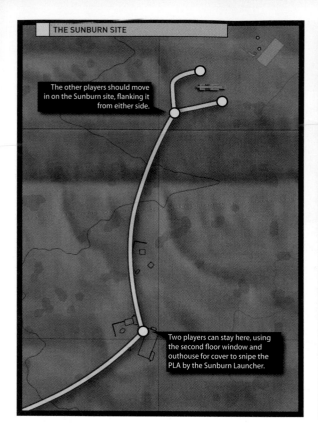

THE SUNBURN SITE

The other players should move in on the Sunburn site, flanking it from either side.

Two players can stay here, using the second floor window and outhouse for cover to snipe the PLA by the Sunburn Launcher.

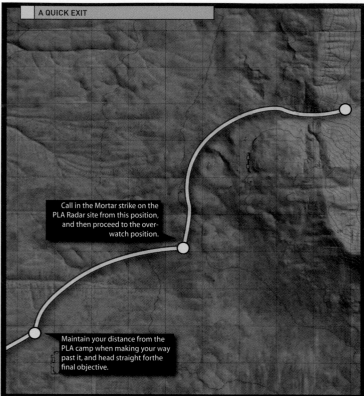

A QUICK EXIT

Call in the Mortar strike on the PLA Radar site from this position, and then proceed to the overwatch position.

Maintain your distance from the PLA camp when making your way past it, and head straight for the final objective.

A quick exit

At this point, if you wish, you can actually skip a couple of major engagements and head straight to your next Primary Objective. All you need to do is head directly due north-east, always remembering to stay crouched down and to keep at least 100m or so between you and the PLA base, so that you don't alert the guards. Use the natural lie of the land for cover until you reach the line of trees and then continue up through it until you are well clear of the village. Keep heading towards the target through the trees until you get about 180m away.

This is the perfect position from which to target the objective area with your Artillery. Even though you can't see the radar array directly, you can see the tall support structure right next to it, so target that and call in your strike **[Screen 01]**. The Artillery strike will easily take out the radar for you and complete the objective, as well as taking out most of the PLA guards up there. If you choose, you can head up and clear the area of any that are left, or you can choose to run around the hill and head to the north before cutting across and heading to the overwatch position.

Outskirts of the PLA Base

From the flanking position you should head pretty much due east along the raised ground through the trees and follow it round when it starts to head north-east. When you are about 150m away you should be able to have a player with a scoped weapon get a clear shot on a guard to the far east of the base **[Screen 02]**. If you just wound this enemy you should be able to lure the other guard, who is out of sight, into the open, allowing you to take him out with ease. Once they are both down you should head north until you are in line with the large house, and then move up and use it for cover.

Clearing the Base

Once you are in position near the building, have one player move up the outside stairs and take up a position by one of the second-floor openings, looking down onto the entrance to the main central area. The rest of the group should move up to the corner of the building and then move out and engage any PLA soldiers out in the open. When it's clear, two players should move up into the central area, with support from the player in the building, and clear out any PLA they come across. The remaining player should continue heading north past the entrance, and then come around the side

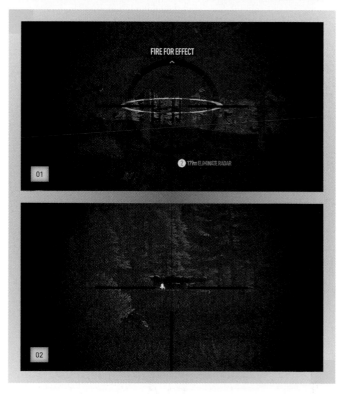

FIRE FOR EFFECT

179m ELIMINATE RADAR

01

02

of the next building, engaging any guards in this area.

Once the player on the second floor of the farmhouse has run out of potential targets, they should head down the stairs and then exit into the central areas, helping to take out any hostiles left on the southern side of the village. One of the players already in the central area should then continue heading east to clear out any remaining targets on this side, while the other player goes north to join up with the player flanking around the outside. Once the area is clear of troops, resupply at the ammo crates before continuing.

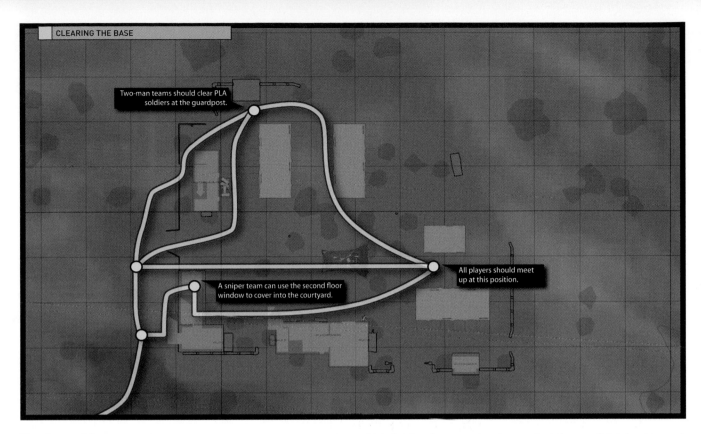

CLEARING THE BASE

Two-man teams should clear PLA soldiers at the guardpost.

All players should meet up at this position.

A sniper team can use the second floor window to cover into the courtyard.

05

The downed trees

As soon as the PLA base is clear you should continue north-east until you reach an area with a large number of downed trees. Once there, your team should take up positions behind these to fire on the large group of PLA soldiers on top of the hill 250m ahead of you. **[Screen 03]** Alternatively, you could use your Artillery strike now if you didn't use it on the base; simply target the SAM launcher on top of the hill and then let the big guns clear the area for you. Whichever method you decide to use, you should move up to the top of the hill and make sure it's clear, as this makes for the perfect location to start dealing with the final objective.

The PLA Radar

If you haven't used your Artillery strike, you should call it in now from the top of the hill. This will take out the radar and greatly reduce the number of PLA soldiers guarding it, leaving your team to pick off the remainder from long range. This is also your best option if you are not using the Artillery strike, as your team's superior weaponry gives you a significant advantage at long range.

Once all visible targets have been taken out, the team should move up to secure the objective. You may want to have two members continue north

a bit before heading up, so that they can flank the area slightly, just in case there are some PLA forces still alive around the radar. If the area is secure, then all that is left to do is place the C4 and then take out the radar array, before continuing north-east to reach the overwatch position and complete the mission.

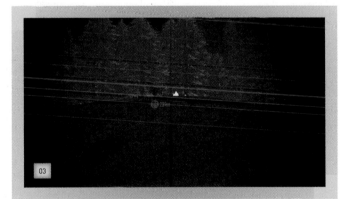

03

UNITED WE STAND
MISSION 03

	Primary Objectives	Secondary Objectives	Bonus Objective
01	Secure Beachhead	Protect AAVP from AT Teams	Destroy PLA Armor
02	Eliminate PLA Spotter Team		
03	Eliminate PLA Anti-air Teams		

Combat Support: No Combat Support is available during this mission

FORCE SUMMARY

For the sheer amount of defensive tactical options Briggs offers when it comes to defending the village, he should ideally be the first choice for a second player in a two-player Co-op game. Alternatively, the LMG that Jedburgh comes with can really help with the opening sections of the mission, so if you are having trouble there you may want to control him. He should also be the third spot in a three-player game. Apart from the always fairly useful Medical Kit, Avery doesn't bring many extra tactical options to the party, so any player using him in the fourth spot should look to supplement their loadout with some of the PLA weaponry as soon as possible.

RIFLE SQUAD: HEAVY ASSAULT TEAM DAGGER ONE BRAVO

SERGEANT. HUNTER (FIRE TEAM LEADER)

Initial Loadout	Primary Weapon	M16A4 (CQB)
	Primary Weapon Ammunition	12x30 FMJ round magazines
	Secondary Weapon	–
	Secondary Weapon Ammunition	–
	Additional Equipment	6xM67 Grenades, 2xM18 Smoke Grenade, 4xM18A1 Claymore Mines

LANCE CORPORAL. BRIGGS (GRENADIER)

Initial Loadout	Primary Weapon	M16A4 (Assault)
	Primary Weapon Ammunition	7x30 FMJ round magazines, 9xHE projected grenades, 3xHEDP projected grenades
	Secondary Weapon	–
	Secondary Weapon Ammunition	–
	Additional Equipment	2xM67 Grenades, 1xM18 Smoke Grenades, 6xM14 AP Mines

PRIVATE FIRST CLASS. AVERY (MEDIC)

Initial Loadout	Primary Weapon	M16A4
	Primary Weapon Ammunition	7x30 FMJ round magazines
	Secondary Weapon	–
	Secondary Weapon Ammunition	–
	Additional Equipment	1xMedical Kit

PRIVATE FIRST CLASS. JEDBURGH (MACHINEGUNNER)

Initial Loadout	Primary Weapon	M249 SAW
	Primary Weapon Ammunition	4x200 FMJ round ammo boxes
	Secondary Weapon	–
	Secondary Weapon Ammunition	–
	Additional Equipment	4xM67 Grenade

The first AT team

Move up the beach into the trees until you come across the pile of downed logs; use these for cover while you take out the first two-man AT team. When engaging them you should either try to get a couple of players to take up positions at either end of the trees to fire on them, or have the Briggs switch to his underslung grenade launcher and fire off a couple of rounds to kill them both.

Pushing ahead

After you've taken out the first AT team, split your squad up into two groups and have one of them head to the right to engage the PLA group by the MG position, just outside the line of trees. The other group should continue on through the trees to take out the second AT team, who are usually found near the ruined walls along the roadside. Both groups of players should be able to get plenty of cover from the trees, so taking out the targets will be relatively easy.

With so many enemy AT gunners in the area, try and have each member of your team pick up one of their rocket launchers. **[Screen 01]**. One from each team, along with the one from the ammo boxes by the farmhouse later on, should give you one for each player. If you do this you should remember the positions of the AT gunners you kill and loot the bodies as quickly as you can, since finding them later on in the thick grass may be difficult.

Assaulting the farmhouse

Once the team tackling the MG nest has finished, they should move up to the ruined wall and start laying down some suppressing fire on the other MG group to the right of the large farmhouse in the distance. If one of these players is in control of Briggs, then a few rounds from his underslung grenade launcher can really work wonders here. **[Screen 02]**. This should distract them enough to enable your other team to move up along the wall to the rocks on the left and take out the last AT team. They must be sure to check and clear the other side of the burnt-out tank on the road, as there can sometimes be a couple of PLA soldiers hiding here for an ambush.

If either group of players spots and can get a clear shot on the PLA APC on the road just behind the farmhouse, then they should take the shot as quickly as they can with one of the Queen Bees they picked up along the way. You will need to be quick off the mark, however, or else the friendly forces rolling in behind you will take out the armor, and you won't complete the bonus objective for an Achievement. When the PLA AT team has been killed, both groups of players should move up to the farmhouse and help finish off the last few PLA around the MG area from close range.

Resupplying at the farmhouse

The ammo box near the farmhouse contains both a Queen Bee Rocket Launcher and handy PLA Marksman rifle, and you should try and make sure that one player has both of these weapons on them (preferably one of the players not about to get into the APC). As you start to move south towards the next RV point, you'll see friendly APCs moving along in the same direction. Shortly after they start to move, the lead vehicle is taken out by PLA mortars, called in by the Spotter team on top of the hill by the radio tower. Before you start heading up there to deal with the Spotter team, two players should get into one of the APCs to the rear. **[Screen 03]**

PLA spotters

The players in control of the APC should move it into a position where they can start laying down some heavy suppressing fire on the Spotter team's location at the top of the hill. The two players on foot should start by heading towards the destroyed van and then head left up the hill towards a group of trees that can be used for cover. They should keep following the RV points up the hill until they reach the top, and then turn to the right and move slowly forward, until they can get a shot on a few members of the Spotter team.

Coming in from this flanking position will give them both the element of surprise and positional advantage, so they should be able to take out all of the enemies quickly and easily. The final member of the Spotter team can be found just to the West of the main group's position near a small building. This guy will more than likely have his back to the flanking players, as he is more concerned with the fire coming in from the APC below, so taking him out will be very easy. The spotter teams are armed with handy Marksman-type rifles, which one player should pick up.

The village outskirts

Have both players on top of the hill move south-west of the Spotter team's locations to an overwatch position above the village. One of them should equip their Queen Bee and fire off a couple of rockets at the group of PLA soldiers around the sandbagged area at the village entrance, while the other player here tries to take out single targets with their rifle. There are a few AT

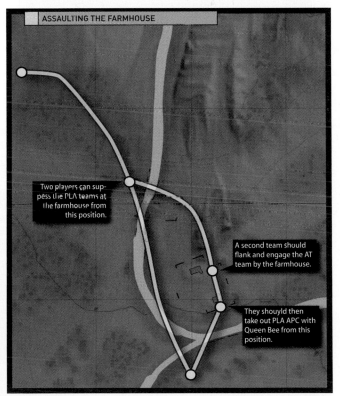

ASSAULTING THE FARMHOUSE

Two players can suppress the PLA teams at the farmhouse from this position.

A second team should flank and engage the AT team by the farmhouse.

They should then take out PLA APC with Queen Bee from this position.

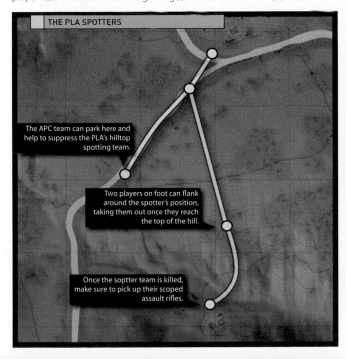

THE PLA SPOTTERS

The APC team can park here and help to suppress the PLA's hilltop spotting team.

Two players on foot can flank around the spotter's position, taking them out once they reach the top of the hill.

Once the soptter team is killed, make sure to pick up their scoped assault rifles.

gunners in this area, so taking them out quickly like this is essential if you are to bring your APC in safely.

Once the team on the hill has taken out those first AT gunners, the APC should roll in fully and start looking for targets to take out. There are still some other AT gunners and support gunners within the village, so make sure you take out any targets quickly. For now, the APC should continue to scan the village entrance looking for enemies to kill, using target information they get from players on foot, as these will often have a better view of the area.

Sniping from the overwatch position

Once the player with the Queen Bee up on the hill has used all of their rockets, they should switch to the PLA Marksman rifle and continue picking off targets from here, as it's an excellent sniping position. It will add an extra layer of covering fire while the other player starts to move down the hill towards the RV point, and the first of the AA teams. If the village is looking relatively clear from the overwatch position, the sniper might want to move to the left slightly, so that he can assist the player moving in on the AA teams with some more direct long-range support at that location. **[Screen 01]**.

AA team by the barn

The player moving in on the first AA team should use the wall for cover while they get into position to take out both targets. If the sniper up at the overwatch position is providing covering fire this should be easy, and they may even be able to move along the entire length of the wall and flank the AA team from the side. By this time this is done, the sniper, in conjunction with the APC, should have taken out most of the easily visible targets from the position up on the hill. They should then run down and join up with the other player by the barn where the first AA team was.

Sniping from the barn

When both players are in position behind the barn, they should move forward slightly and start to engage the PLA forces to the south-west, including the second AA team. The barn itself should provide more than enough cover from incoming fire and, if ammo is getting low, there should be AA team bodies to loot. If there are still some PLA soldiers left alive, more to the west of this location in the center of the village, one of the snipers should move round to the opposite corner of the barn to get a better firing angle on that area. It's also a good idea to have the players in the APC move deeper into the village to help clear the enemies on that side. **[Screen 02]**

Final push into the village

Once it's clear, both players by the barn should move towards the next RV point, which is leading them to the last AA team locate to the south-west of the village. You'll be moving across a lot of fairly open ground, so try to use the hay bales for cover and move quickly to minimize the chances of being ambushed by a hidden PLA soldier. When they are finally in the village, there is plenty of available cover from all of the buildings, but this is also true for any remaining PLA soldiers, so always be extremely careful when moving round corners or past windows until you are sure it is clear.

The players in the APC should also start to move up along the main road to offer some heavy fire support for the players on foot, while they continue to advance on the final AA team. When the APC is coming up the main road it is quite possible that the players can get a chance to fire on the AA team, so they should always keep an eye on the objective marker to see if they can get some shots in to make things easier for the team. Now all that's left is to clear up any remaining PLA in the village. If you get the all-clear from control then you know the village is free of any PLA forces, so you won't need to go seeking them out.

Positioning the APC

Fending off the PLA counter-attack is the time when the players in the APC can shine, as they will be far more effective at using its deadly arsenal than the AI-controlled friendly forces. The ideal position for them to take up is at the main crossroads on the western edge of the village. From here they will be able to fire on a large number of the PLA counter-attack waves without having to move around very much, but they should give priority to the PLA vehicle as soon as it arrives (or any AT/support gunners that they spot).

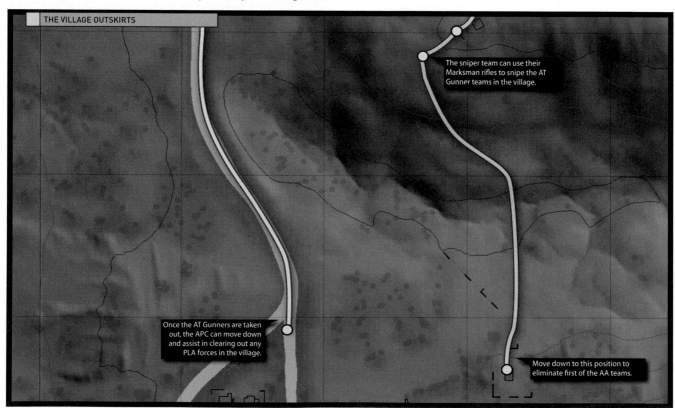

THE VILLAGE OUTSKIRTS

The sniper team can use their Marksman rifles to snipe the AT Gunner teams in the village.

Once the AT Gunners are taken out, the APC can move down and assist in clearing out any PLA forces in the village.

Move down to this position to eliminate first of the AA teams.

If anyone on the team is already familiar with the mission and knows the timing of the PLA attack waves, they should pass on the information to the players in control of the APC. This will help them to maneuver around the area, ensuring they are in a good position when a group of enemies shows up. If the player in control of Briggs is in the APC, they should swap him out for someone else, as he will be far more useful on foot when defending the village.

Defending on foot

The player in control of Briggs has within his equipment a large amount of mines that can be extremely useful here. The AT mines should be deployed to the far east of the village, a short distance past the MG position, just in case the vehicle from this side happens to make it this far down. The second AT mine should then be placed on the road going south, where the other vehicle comes from, as back up for your APC.

The remaining player on foot should move up to the second floor of the building near the assigned defend point, as the openings up here provide an excellent sniping position. If they are running low on ammo, or need a Marksman rifle, these can be found in the ammo box just outside this building. Once up there, the player in control of Briggs should lay their AP mines 20m away around the Eastern side of the building just in case any PLA make it through the trees.

When all the mines are in position, that player can then head up to the second floor of the building and join the other player in sniping the PLA forces as they come in. Alternatively, they can act as a more mobile unit and move between the east and west of the Village as needed (being careful not to trip the AP mines). If they choose to go down this route, then using the MG emplacements on either side of the village can prove very effective **[Screen 03]**. Once you have killed off sufficient waves of the PLA counter-attack the remainder of their forces will withdraw and you will have completed the mission.

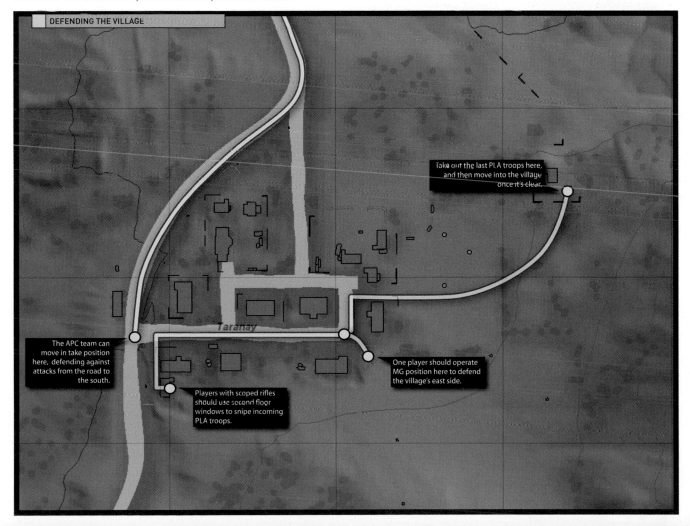

DEFENDING THE VILLAGE

Take out the last PLA troops here, and then move into the village once it's clear.

Taranay

The APC team can move in take position here, defending against attacks from the road to the south.

Players with scoped rifles should use second floor windows to snipe incoming PLA troops.

One player should operate MG position here to defend the village's east side.

EAGLE OFFENSE
MISSION 04

	Primary Objectives	Secondary Objectives	Bonus Objective
01	Destroy or incapacitate two PLA Type 97s	Fire Mortars on PLA Position in the ruins	Destroy or incapacitate the PLA transport helicopter
02	Take control of the Control Tower	Fire CAS on incoming PLA re-enforcement vehicles	
03	Hold the Control Tower against oncoming PLA reinforcements	Destroy or incapacitate the PLA attack helicopter	

Combat Support: 1xMedium Mortar Artillery awarded for successful recon of PLA forces in the houses to the south..

FORCE SUMMARY

Briggs once again should be the first choice for a second player, as the SMAW he comes with will be extremely useful over the entire course of this mission for dealing with the large amount of PLA armor. Jedburgh's LMG will be very useful for clearing PLA soldiers from the airfield during your assault on the control tower, so he should take up the third position. As this mission takes place mainly at close quarters, the lack of any scope on Avery's rifle should not affect the player very much, but his lack of any standout weaponry or equipment still means that this is the last spot that should be filled.

RIFLE SQUAD: ANTI-TANK TEAM DAGGER ONE BRAVO

SERGEANT. HUNTER (FIRE TEAM LEADER)

Initial Loadout		
	Primary Weapon	M4A1 (Marksman)
	Primary Weapon Ammunition	9x30 FMJ round magazines
	Secondary Weapon	SMAW
	Secondary Weapon Ammunition	2xHEAT Rockets, 2xHEF Rockets
	Additional Equipment	4xM67 Grenades, 1xM18 Smoke Grenade, 3xIR Strobe, 3xM14 AP Mine

PRIVATE FIRST CLASS. JEDBURGH (MACHINEGUNNER)

Initial Loadout		
	Primary Weapon	Mk48 Mod 0
	Primary Weapon Ammunition	9x100 FMJ round ammo boxes
	Secondary Weapon	–
	Secondary Weapon Ammunition	–
	Additional Equipment	2xM67 Grenades

PRIVATE FIRST CLASS. AVERY (MEDIC)

Initial Loadout		
	Primary Weapon	M16A4
	Primary Weapon Ammunition	10x30 FMJ round magazines
	Secondary Weapon	–
	Secondary Weapon Ammunition	–
	Additional Equipment	1xMedical Kit

LANCE CORPORAL BRIGGS (ANTI-TANK SPECIALIST)

Initial Loadout		
	Primary Weapon	M16A4
	Primary Weapon Ammunition	9x30 FMJ round magazines
	Secondary Weapon	SMAW
	Secondary Weapon Ammunition	2xHEF Rockets, 2xHEAT Rockets
	Additional Equipment	1xM67 Grenade

Taking out the MG threat

Start off by having the Fire Team Leader run straight to the corner of the small concrete bunker, while the rest of the players move alongside it, so that they don't get fired upon by the PLA soldier manning the MG to the southeast. The Fire Team Leader should then move out to the right slowly, while in aim mode, with their Marksman rifle until they have a shot on the solider manning the emplaced MG. **[Screen 01]**. As soon as he is dead, the whole group should move out and start running east towards the RV point by the hill a couple of hundred meters ahead of you.

Destroying the PLA armor

Both players with SMAWs should equip them at the bottom of the hill, where they are safe. They should then move up to the crest of the hill and fire on each of the PLA tanks as soon as they come into view. To avoid any ammo wastage it's a good idea to assign targets first before moving up the hill, ensuring that both players do not fire on the same tank. When both tanks are destroyed, everyone should regroup and then head south-east towards the next objective.

Clearing the road

When you reach the RV point, take up position behind the sandbags to give yourself some cover from the incoming fire from the PLA to the south. Your task now is to recon those forces, so that you can then vector in a mortar strike **[Screen 02]**. While one player on your team is taking care of calling in the mortar strike, two others should be keeping an eye out in the skies for the PLA transport helicopter that is also doing some recon of the area.

Once they've spotted it, one player should hop onto the nearby emplaced grenade launcher and start firing, while the other player does the same with their rifle. If they manage to shoot this down, they will have completed the bonus objective for this mission. The final member of your team should be watching the hill to the south-east, as there will often be one or two PLA soldiers coming over the top to engage you that will need to be taken care of quickly before they can fire on the rest of the team.

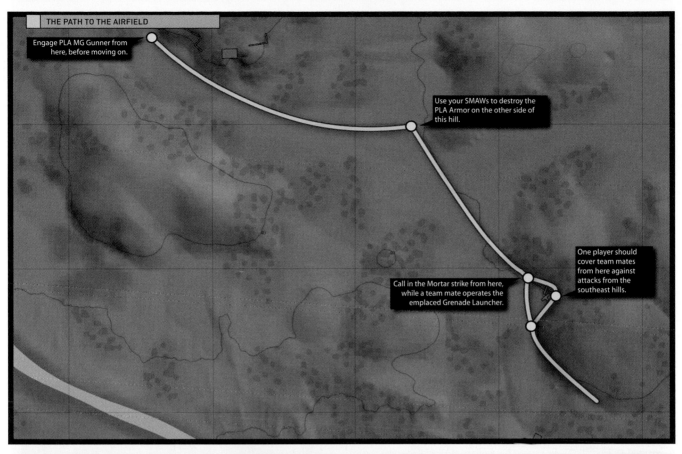

THE PATH TO THE AIRFIELD

Engage PLA MG Gunner from here, before moving on.

Use your SMAWs to destroy the PLA Armor on the other side of this hill.

One player should cover team mates from here against attacks from the southeast hills.

Call in the Mortar strike from here, while a team mate operates the emplaced Grenade Launcher.

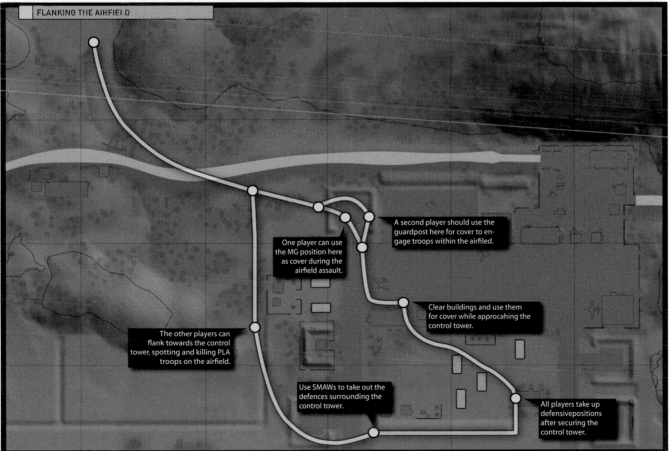

FLANKING THE AIRFIELD

A second player should use the guardpost here for cover to engage troops within the airfiled.

One player can use the MG position here as cover during the airfield assault.

Clear buildings and use them for cover while approacahing the control tower.

The other players can flank towards the control tower, spotting and killing PLA troops on the airfield.

Use SMAWs to take out the defences surrounding the control tower.

All players take up defensivepositions after securing the control tower.

The path to the airfield

As soon as the mortar strike hits, the convoy will continue rolling into the airfield and you will be told to advance to that position as quickly as you can, so start running. The convoy should finish off any PLA remaining in the houses to the south, so you shouldn't have to worry about them too much. If there are any that get in your sights as you make your way down there you should take them out quickly and move on. Next, it's your job to clear the tower before they zero in on the convoy's location and take it out with mortars.

Outskirts of the airfield

When you are about 300m away from the control tower you should split up your team in order to secure the airfield faster. Two players should continue along the RV points and take up position behind the small concrete PLA guard post, as it will provide them excellent cover from the bulk of the forces within the airfield.

There will be plenty of targets for them to take out from this position, but they should focus on the large amount of infantry around the buildings to the south and south-east, and the two off-road vehicles to the east. It may help to have one player move forward past the guard post and go prone near the small dirt mound in front of it, as this will stop the PLA fire from being concentrated on one position, and also give a better place from which to fire on the vehicles.

Flanking the airfield

Meanwhile, the other two players should turn to the south-west and head to the other side of the airfield, past all of the fenced-off areas, making sure they stay on the western side of the buildings to avoid any PLA fire. This flanking position provides an excellent place for the start of an assault on the defenses in and around the building on the outskirts of the airfield, while they are distracted by the main battle on the other side.

These players will also have a clear run straight down towards the control tower itself, so once they have cleared out a few of the initial enemies they should move closer to the control tower, using the small dirt mounds for cover while they start to take out the forces surrounding it. Using a SMAW here can be very effective in clearing out the large group of enemies by the sandbags, but you need to make sure you don't hit, and so destroy, the control tower, as that will cost you some very convenient cover. **[Screen 01]**.

When the airfield starts to look relatively clear, the two players at the guard post should move up and clear the buildings to the south-east to make sure there are no PLA left there, before using them for cover while helping to assault the forces surrounding the control tower.

Clearing the control tower

When the surrounding area is clear, both groups of players should join up and then enter and clear the control tower. Be especially careful when moving up the stairs to the second floor, as there will usually be at least one PLA soldier up here, so don't let him get the drop on you.

With the tower under your control you must now fend off the PLA counterattack. Only one man is really required as a spotter to call in the air strikes, and should take a position by one of the windows up on the second floor. A player with a SMAW should then head out onto the second floor walkway so that they can act as a last line of defense against any incoming PLA armor.

The rest of the team should take up defensive positions around the tower to provide some extra support and deal with any PLA soldiers who happen to make it to the airfield on foot.

Holding off the PLA

The player on the second floor who is calling in the CAS on the PLA armor units should try and time the strike so that it hits the units just as they are coming to a stop, in order to offload the troops within. This will greatly minimize the chances of one of the strikes missing its target. If you do miss with one of the air strikes, it will be up to the player on the walkway to take out the vehicle with their SMAW. Once they run out of ammo for that they should quickly head back down and grab the Queen Bee from the ammo boxes just outside the control tower, and then head back up to the walkway.

As soon as you get word that the PLA attack helicopter is inbound, one of the players on the ground floor defending the control tower should grab the SAM launcher from the ammo boxes inside the tower. They should then move up to the second floor walkway facing north-east and attempt to use it to get a lock-on as soon as they can so that they can take out the helicopter before it gets anywhere near the airfield **[Screen 02]**. Shooting the enemy helicopter down will trigger the friendly helicopter to be called in a lot sooner than it otherwise would, which means you will have to take out fewer of the PLA armor units to obtain victory.

Continue taking out the tanks and any advancing troops until the friendly chopper gets here. You then only need to hold out for a little while longer until the PLA decide to call it a day and you will have secured the airfield and achieved your final objective.

POWDER TRAIL
MISSION 05

	Primary Objectives	Secondary Objectives	Bonus Objective
01	Search for downed crew	Support recon team Dagger One Echo	Destroy PLA Armor near Mologa
02	Rescue helicopter crew	Search last known position of helicopter	
03	Safely extract helicopter crew	Destroy AA site	

Combat Support: 1xHowitzer Artillery awarded for successful completion of the Secondary Objective: to search the last known position of the helicopter.

FORCE SUMMARY

As you will be attacking a large number of well-established PLA positions in this mission, the underslung grenade launcher on Briggs's weapon will be an invaluable tool, so his should be the first position filled. Also, since this is a very long mission, you might want to have your third player take the role of Avery, as you may well need a quicker response when asking for healing than the AI can provide. Jedburgh, as usual, comes with his trusty LMG, which always comes in handy for suppressing fire and is probably of equal value to Avery in this mission, so it will just come down to player preference.

RIFLE SQUAD: ANTI-TANK TEAM DAGGER ONE BRAVO

SERGEANT. HUNTER (FIRE TEAM LEADER)

Initial Loadout		
	Primary Weapon	M4A1 (CQB)
	Primary Weapon Ammunition	8x30 FMJ round magazines
	Secondary Weapon	SMAW
	Secondary Weapon Ammunition	2xHEAT Rockets, 2xHEF Rockets
	Additional Equipment	2xM67 Grenades, 1xM18 Smoke Grenade, 3xIR Strobe

LANCE CORPORAL BRIGGS (GRENADIER)

Initial Loadout		
	Primary Weapon	M16A4 (Assault)
	Primary Weapon Ammunition	7x30 FMJ round magazines, 9xHE projected grenades, 3xHEDP projected grenades
	Secondary Weapon	–
	Secondary Weapon Ammunition	–
	Additional Equipment	2xM67 Grenades, 1xM18 Smoke Grenade, 3xM14 AP Mine

PRIVATE FIRST CLASS AVERY (MEDIC)

Initial Loadout		
	Primary Weapon	M16A4
	Primary Weapon Ammunition	7x30 FMJ round magazine
	Secondary Weapon	–
	Secondary Weapon Ammunition	–
	Additional Equipment	1xMedical Kit

PRIVATE FIRST CLASS JEDBURGH (MACHINEGUNNER)

Initial Loadout		
	Primary Weapon	Mk48 Mod 0
	Primary Weapon Ammunition	3x200 FMJ round ammo boxes
	Secondary Weapon	–
	Secondary Weapon Ammunition	–
	Additional Equipment	1xM67 Grenade

Supporting Echo Squad

As soon as the mission begins the team should start running north-east towards Echo Squad. When you are about 100m away from them, start to head more towards the north, veering away from Echo slightly. This will allow you to get your sights on the PLA soldiers emerging from the tree line on the other side of the road much sooner.

Two players should move up into the trees to use them for cover while they clear out the remaining PLA around them. Meanwhile, the other two should follow the road round to the east, while shooting some suppressing fire into the trees and then, when they are past the trees, they should begin firing on the PLA soldiers just ahead of them on the other side of the road. When all of the PLA in the area have been killed, all the players should re-group at Echo Squad's location

Joining up with Echo

Make sure one member of your team loots the ammo box near the vehicle's location for the Marksman rifle. Others should grab some ammo from it, along with the extra SMAW. **[Screen 03]**. Once you are all stocked up, everyone should get into the vehicle and start to head north towards the next objective. Instead of following the road round when it turns down the hill, you should take the vehicle off-road and keep heading directly north to the target, as this is the most efficient route, and you will also bypass a couple of PLA soldiers guarding the road.

The PLA checkpoint

Once you start heading off-road you should check your map for a small cluster of buildings along the road, directly between you and your objective. This is a PLA checkpoint. Use the map or the RV markers to gauge your distance, and when you are around 280m away from it have two players exit the vehicle. The vehicle should then move off to the north-east into the trees for cover, and the player who is manning the mounted gun should be laying down suppressing fire on one of the MG positions at the checkpoint. The driver of the vehicle should try to remain mobile, to avoid taking too much direct fire from the MG.

While the PLA soldiers at the checkpoint are preoccupied with the vehicle's diversion, the other two players should move to the top of the nearby hill to the north-west on foot and get into the prone position. This will give them some extra accuracy and make it harder for the PLA to hit them while they try to kill the PLA soldiers manning the MGs.

PLA road patrol

There is another small group of PLA soldiers on the road to the north-east, including an AT gunner. The players in the vehicle should stay where they are, as they will be too easy a target for him. The players on foot should

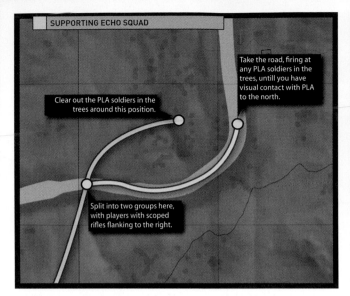

SUPPORTING ECHO SQUAD

Clear out the PLA soldiers in the trees around this position.

Take the road, firing at any PLA soldiers in the trees, untill you have visual contact with PLA to the north.

Split into two groups here, with players with scoped rifles flanking to the right.

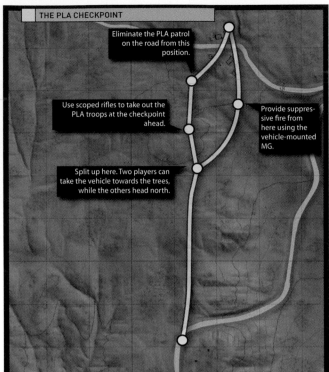

THE PLA CHECKPOINT

Eliminate the PLA patrol on the road from this position.

Use scoped rifles to take out the PLA troops at the checkpoint ahead.

Provide suppressive fire from here using the vehicle-mounted MG.

Split up here. Two players can take the vehicle towards the trees, while the others head north.

move to the top of the hill in front of the one they are on. From here they should have a perfect vantage point from which to take out all three members of the enemy group. **[Screen 01]**.

When they have been taken out, the players in the vehicle should drive up until they are about 80m shy of the checkpoint, so that they can still cover the area, and then have the two players on foot move in and make sure it is totally clear. Once the location has been secured, bring the vehicle straight up and meet up with the two players on foot. Everyone should now get back in the vehicle and the whole group should continue on up the small dirt road on the opposite side of the checkpoint towards the objective.

Clearing the AA site

Just before you reach the small group of buildings by the last known position of the downed crew, a couple of players should once again exit the vehicle. There are a few PLA soldiers on emplaced weapons, as well as some AT and support gunners, looking down on this location from the other side of the buildings. The two players on foot should take up positions either side of the main building, and start taking out some of the enemies with their rifles (starting with the ones operating the MGs and the AT gunners), while the vehicle moves to a flanking position on the other side of the trees to the north-west, before engaging the enemies. The player driving the vehicle should also disembark and start helping the team to kill some of the PLA.

Once the main threats at the first line of defense have been taken out, you should get the all-clear to call in an Artillery strike, which one of the players should use straight away on the AA vehicle that you can see on top of the hill in the distance. If you're lucky this should also take out some of the PLA guarding the area up there. Once the strike is over, the two players by the building should start to head north-east towards the large white building, and the players with the vehicle should head east, so that the gunner can get a better angle in order to lay some suppressing fire down on the hill by the AA vehicles. **[Screen 02]**

All of the players on foot should use the area around this white building for cover while they take out any PLA that survived the Artillery strike. Once all visible targets have been killed, the vehicle should drive round to the north-east on the other side of the white building, before starting to move up the hill slowly, while the players on foot do the same from their position. Both group of players should now continue up the hill until they are at the AA site, and then make sure the area is clear of PLA soldiers before moving on.

Hillside combat

From the AA site your team should make their way down the hill to the east towards the next RV marker, stopping as soon as you receive a message from Saber Two. This message triggers a small group of four PLA soldiers to start making their way to your position from across the road below. Luckily, the height of your current position will give you a significant tactical advantage when taking them out.

Three players on the team should start engaging the incoming PLA as soon as they come into view, while using the bushes and rocks around the hillside for cover. While they are doing that, the Fire Team Leader should move to the south away from them slightly, into a position looking straight up the road below. Shortly, a PLA Transport Truck carrying some additional troops will begin to move into the area along this road, and it will be this player's job to take it out using their SMAW. One direct hit will be enough to take out the vehicle and all of its occupants. The best time to hit it is while it's still in motion, traveling straight along the road **[Screen 03]**. Taking it out like this is much simpler than having to engage another group of PLA soldiers amongst the trees.

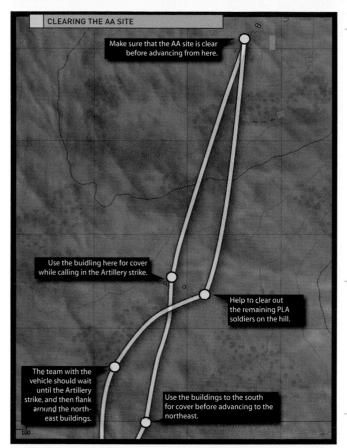

CLEARING THE AA SITE

Make sure that the AA site is clear before advancing from here.

Use the buidling here for cover while calling in the Artillery strike.

Help to clear out the remaining PLA soldiers on the hill.

The team with the vehicle should wait until the Artillery strike, and then flank around the north-east buildings.

Use the buildings to the south for cover before advancing to the northeast.

Assaulting the crash site

As you move towards the downed helicopter you should split your team into two, with one group heading straight for the helicopter so that they can use it for cover. The other group should move across onto the road and advance using the burnt-out APC for cover. In the distance, on the other side of the helicopter, you should be able to see a white building in which a PLA soldier is operating a MG placement. This is the main threat to the team from the helicopter, so they should look to taking out the MG operator from as far away as they can with their rifles.

The other team, meanwhile, have their own troubles to contend with, in the form of another MG operator behind some sandbags on the other side of the line of trees. You can use the APC for cover to help take him out, but you may find it easier to have one player stay there and lay down some suppressing fire, while the other moves up into the trees to get a clearer shot on him. Once the MG threats have been taken out, there are still some PLA units in the area that must be dealt with. So you will need to have both groups of players move up, using the trees for cover while they sweep the area and kill the last couple of PLA soldiers.

The road to the village

When you are moving towards the village where the downed crew is located, don't head straight for the objective marker. Instead, you should keep moving east along the main road. As you get closer to the village, PLA forces at the top will come out to engage your group. As soon as they do, all of the players should head straight into the trees to use them as cover while they take out the hostiles. **[Screen 04]** Keep going along the road, taking out any PLA you come across until you reach a small dirt trail on the right-hand side; follow this down until you come to the outskirts of the village.

Village outskirts

Shortly after you reach the edge of the village, a PLA transport helicopter will fly into the area to drop off some additional ground forces. You could just let

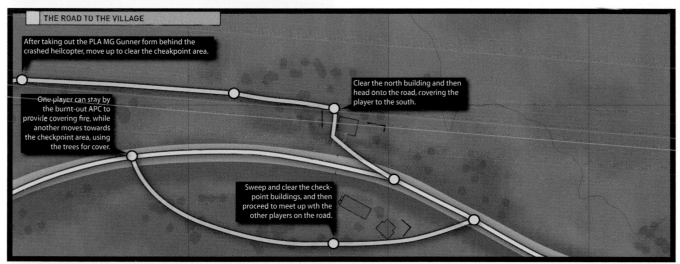

THE ROAD TO THE VILLAGE

After taking out the PLA MG Gunner form behind the crashed heilcopter, move up to clear the cheakpoint area.

One player can stay by the burnt-out APC to provide covering fire, while another moves towards the checkpoint area, using the trees for cover.

Clear the north building and then head onto the road, covering the player to the south.

Sweep and clear the check-point buildings, and then proceed to meet up wth the other players on the road.

03

04

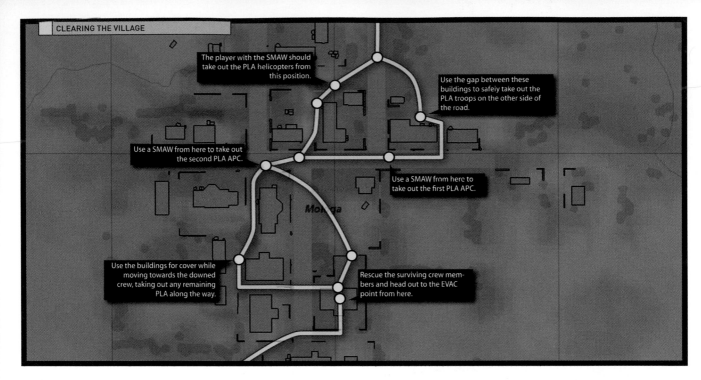

CLEARING THE VILLAGE

The player with the SMAW should take out the PLA helicopters from this position.

Use the gap between these buildings to safely take out the PLA troops on the other side of the road.

Use a SMAW from here to take out the second PLA APC.

Use a SMAW from here to take out the first PLA APC.

Use the buildings for cover while moving towards the downed crew, taking out any remaining PLA along the way.

Rescue the surviving crew members and head out to the EVAC point from here.

Molnga

it land in the distance, but this will make things harder for you in the long run, so the best option is to shoot it down. This responsibility once again falls to the Fire Team Leader, although another player should accompany him as backup. This pair of players should move west along the outskirts of the village, following the Helicopter's movements, and the team leader should equip their SMAW as soon as they can. You should wait until the helicopter approaches its landing, as it will be moving very slowly at this time and will be a much easier target for you.

While the Fire Team Leader is taking care of the helicopter, the player with him should turn his sights south into the village, where he should start picking off some of the PLA soldiers already stationed there.

Clearing the village

The majority of PLA forces in the village are stationed on the eastern side, and that is where the other pair of players will be heading. From the dirt trail they should head east, using the large building for cover as they make their way to the small gap between buildings. Both players should try to get an angle from this location so that they can take out the small group of PLA forces on the other side from a position of safety. [Screen 01].

Two PLA APCs will very soon be making their way down the road to the outskirts of the village, so both groups of players need to clear their initial areas as quickly as possible and move to the other side of the buildings for cover. There is also another PLA transport helicopter inbound around the same time, which will land in the same area. So if you have enough rockets left in the SMAW you should take it out now before the APCs can get into position.

Destroying the PLA APCs

Now it's time to start taking out those APCs. The first one parks on the small dirt track you used to enter the village. The Fire Team Leader should head back towards the east of the village, using the buildings for cover until they are near the dirt track. With the SMAW equipped, edge out slightly until you have a clear shot and destroy the first APC. While the leader is doing that, the player that was with him should hold position and look to engage the PLA soldiers, who should be entering the village from the west after getting dropped off by the PLA transport helicopter (if it didn't get shot down).

Taking out this APC first clears the way for the two players that were clearing the eastern side to join up with the rest of the group. With cover from the other players, the Fire Team Leader should start to head over to the second APC, which is parked over on the western outskirts of the village. The best

way to approach it is to move west through the village, along the central dirt road, sticking to the right-hand side so that the buildings provide cover. As you get near the final two buildings on the right-hand side of this road, pull up the SMAW and then move out to the left slightly, while using its scope, until the APC is in sight and an easy shot. [Screen 02]

Rescue and evac

With the area now totally clear of any PLA presence, the whole group of players should head down to the building that the downed crew is holding up in. As soon as they join up with your team you should start heading south-west to the extraction point as quickly as you can, as there shouldn't be any other hostiles along the way to slow you down.

01

02

HIP SHOT
MISSION 06

	Primary Objectives	Secondary Objectives	Bonus Objective
01	Destroy fuel depot generator	Get into position for the diversionary strike	Destroy all of the PLA fuel trucks
02	Clear the landing zone		

Combat Support: No Combat Support is available during this mission.

FORCE SUMMARY

There is not much to separate any of the team members during this mission, as they all carry almost identical weapons and equipment. The only choice is whether or not the second player joining wants to provide support with Morales's Medical Kit, or help with laying the demo charges the other two team members have with them.

SPEC OPS SQUAD: SO STEALTH OPS TEAM SABER TWO

2ND LIEUTENANT. MULHOLLAND (SF FIRE TEAM LEADER)

Initial Loadout	Primary Weapon	Mk16 Mod 0 (Stealth)
	Primary Weapon Ammunition	9x30 subsonic rounds magazines
	Secondary Weapon	–
	Secondary Weapon Ammunition	–
	Additional Equipment	2xM67 Grenades, 2xM18 Smoke Grenades, 3xIR Strobes, 4xC4 Demo Charges, 1xNVG

CORPORAL. WINTERS (SF RIFLEMAN)

Initial Loadout	Primary Weapon	M16A4 (Stealth)
	Primary Weapon Ammunition	9x30 subsonic round magazines
	Secondary Weapon	–
	Secondary Weapon Ammunition	–
	Additional Equipment	1xM67 Grenade, 1xM18 Smoke Grenade, 3xC4 Demo Charges, 1xNVG

CORPORAL. KNOX (SF RIFLEMAN)

Initial Loadout	Primary Weapon	M4A1 (Stealth)
	Primary Weapon Ammunition	9x30 subsonic round magazines
	Secondary Weapon	–
	Secondary Weapon Ammunition	–
	Additional Equipment	1xM67 Grenade, 1xM18 Smoke Grenade, 3xC4 Demo Charges, 1xNVG

CORPORAL. MORALES (SF MEDIC)

Initial Loadout	Primary Weapon	M16A4 (Stealth)
	Primary Weapon Ammunition	9x30 subsonic round magazines
	Secondary Weapon	–
	Secondary Weapon Ammunition	–
	Additional Equipment	2xM67 Grenades, 2xM18 Smoke Grenades, 1xMedical Kit, 1xNVG

Encounter by the vehicle

Once the mission begins, all of the players should start running south-east, following the RV markers until they come over the crest of a small hill and can see the PLA vehicle with a PLA soldier standing alongside it. After they finish their short conversation the vehicle will drive off and the soldier will begin to head into the trees. As soon as the vehicle has gone, one or two players should take out the PLA soldier before he gets too far away. Using the weapon's IR beams will make lining up your shots here, and throughout the mission, much easier, so you should activate them beforehand [**Screen 03**].

03

If you are going for a more stealthy approach to the mission, you can opt to let the soldier continue on his way without killing him, but doing so will deny you the chance of snagging the Marksman rifle from his body, which may prove useful later on. Whichever choice you make, you will need to head east out of this area into the trees and continue on to the next location.

PLA guard platform

When your team exits the tree line and comes over the crest of the hill they should be able to see a PLA soldier standing on a platform to the south. If you killed the soldier back at the start this one will be on his own, and should be very easy for your team to take out. If, however, you didn't kill the first soldier, then he will usually take up a position to the side of the front of this platform, and you'll need to be careful when moving around the area. This soldier also has a Marksman rifle, so if you do kill him make sure a different player grabs his weapon.

As before, you can choose a stealthy option here as well, by simply continuing along the hillside to the south-east towards the next marker, while making sure you keep as much distance between your team and the platform as you can. Staying crouched down while moving around this area will also help you a great deal to remain undetected.

The radio tower

If you are going to engage the two guards by the radio tower you should assign two players to each enemy to make sure that they will take them out quickly and quietly.

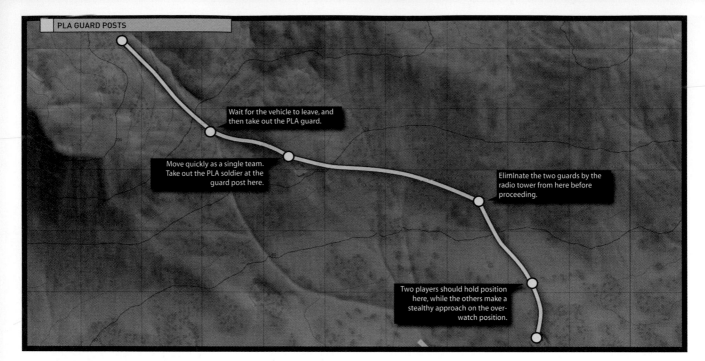

PLA GUARD POSTS

Wait for the vehicle to leave, and then take out the PLA guard.

Move quickly as a single team. Take out the PLA soldier at the guard post here.

Eliminate the two guards by the radio tower from here before proceeding.

Two players should hold position here, while the others make a stealthy approach on the over-watch position.

To get the best shot the team should crouch down and move towards the tower slowly until they are about 200m away from the main objective in the distance. **[Screen 01]** Once everyone is in position one player should give some kind of audible countdown to make sure that both groups of players fire at the same time, so as not to allow one of the enemies to sound the alert.

This position is also very easy to bypass completely if you want to avoid the encounter. All you need to do is get your team to give the tower a wide berth to the east while they move past it, and neither soldier will have a hope of spotting you.

Securing the overwatch position

There is only one PLA guard stationed in the ruined building here, but he is very alert and your team needs to be very careful to avoid being spotted. To make things easier you may want to have most of the players hang back just outside the trees while one player moves towards the building very slowly while crouching.

To get the best shooting angle, this player should head along a south-west-erly path towards the right-hand side of the building. When they get close to the tree there they should move out to the west until they can get a clear shot on the PLA soldier through the opening in the building. **[Screen 02]** At this point they will only be around 25m away from the enemy, so they will need to watch their noise levels and take the shot as soon as they can. Once he's down, the rest of the team can move up to the building and wait for the diversionary strike to finish.

Approaching the fuel depot

After the diversion the whole team should head south-east along the tree line until they are parallel with the middle of the eastern edge of the depot, and wait there in bushes for the patrolling guard, who should be about to come into view. To make the shot easier, wait for him to move a bit closer before taking him out, but don't wait too long as you don't want him to spot your team.

Inside the Depot

As the team moves into the depot they should use the large fuel tanks to mask their approach from the PLA soldier, who is crouched on the other side of the tanks to the west. To take this guy out two players should line up and take a shot at him from between the left-hand set of fuel tanks. They need to be sure not to miss, or the alarm will certainly be raised **[Screen 03]**.

Placing the charges

Once the guard has been killed, the whole team should move up slowly and quietly, trying to stay as close to the center of the depot as they can and out of the lights so that the guards to the north and south do not spot them. One player with some C4 should head towards the raised platform by the refueling area and place one or two charges by the fuel trucks. Another player with C4 should head over to the generator area and place a charge there, but neither player should detonate them just yet.

While the charges are being placed, the remaining two players should

01

02

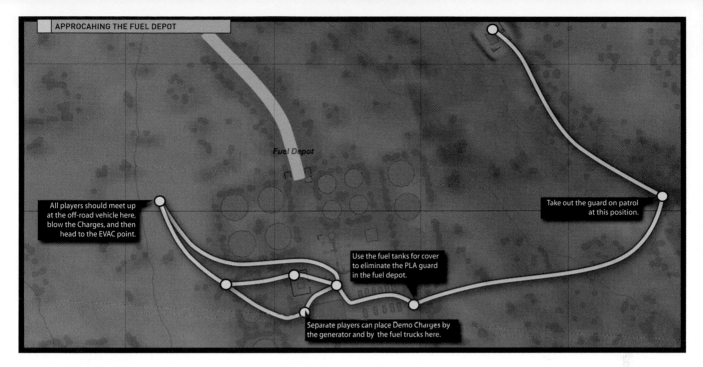

APPROCAHING THE FUEL DEPOT

Fuel Depot

All players should meet up at the off-road vehicle here, blow the Charges, and then head to the EVAC point.

Take out the guard on patrol at this position.

Use the fuel tanks for cover to eliminate the PLA guard in the fuel depot.

Separate players can place Demo Charges by the generator and by the fuel trucks here.

05

continue on through the depot to the western edge, where there may be another PLA patrol. If there is a single guard, and he is either close or moving towards your position, the players should kill him quickly. If, however, he's moving away, then they should hold fire. If there is a group of PLA soldiers, the players should hide behind the large fuel silos and let them pass by.

Blowing the generator

The two players on the Western edge of the depot should now begin to move to the north-west towards the parked PLA off-road vehicle, and when they are close enough they should proceed to kill the occupants. The other two players who were placing the charges should also be starting to head out of the depot along the same path that the first team took, and then meet up with them at the vehicle. There are also some ammo boxes near here that contain some useful weapons and ammo. Once in position, they should now blow the demo charges to destroy the generator and the two fuel trucks, and then immediately get into the vehicle and start driving towards the evac point.

If things go wrong

If at any point during the attack on the depot the alarm gets sounded, all of the nearby PLA soldiers will be called into the area that you are in. This means you will need to find cover as soon as you can. Try and stay well clear of any fuel containers to avoid getting killed, should a stray bullet blow them up, and the same goes for the barrels in the area. The concrete barriers running around most of the fuel silos and the perimeter of the depot provide the most likely cover while fighting the PLA. **[Screen 04]** Things are also made worse by the arrival of a PLA Spec Ops team, who get dropped off by

helicopter to the north-west and then start hunting you down.

If your team is still on the eastern side of the depot, they may find it useful to retreat to the house at the overwatch position, as it offers good cover and a clear view of the entire area. If you choose to make a stand here, though, you will need to be careful that the vehicle that was sent off during the diversion does not flank you from the south. With there being such a large number of enemies to deal with, should you trigger the alarm, it is clearly much better to try and get through the depot as stealthily as you can.

Heading to the extraction point

While making your escape, you should try and avoid as many enemies as you can in order to reach the LZ quickly. If you take a slightly more scenic route to the north-west you should be able to avoid some of the PLA soldiers on the hill. There is a PLA patrol group situated extremely close to the LZ, but if you take too long to get there they will begin to move away from the area to search for you.

When your team is getting close to the LZ they should keep an eye out for movement on the hill nearby. Once an enemy is spotted, everyone should exit the vehicle immediately and begin firing on them. You won't want to take any chances with this group, as it has a couple of support gunners who can easily destroy your vehicle. If you were quick enough getting to the LZ, the PLA group should still be at the top of the hill, in which case you should exit the vehicle and use the walls for cover. With so many cover options available in this small area it would be best if a couple of players used them to flank around to the side of the enemies. Once all of the enemies are dead, the chopper should land and, when your whole team is on board, the mission will be complete.

03

04

	Primary Objectives	Secondary Objectives	Bonus Objective
01	Eliminate AT teams covering the road	Eliminate MG nest	Eliminate the remaining troops on the second line with one Mortar Barrage
02	Locate and eliminate PLA Spotter team	Locate and eliminate PLA AA team	
03	Destroy key defenses around the fuel depot		

Combat Support: 1x Howitzer Artillery awarded for clearing the southern spotters on the second defensive line (northern spotters need to be alive for Combat Support to be granted)

FORCE SUMMARY

Both Briggs and Jedburgh will be extremely useful when dealing with the large amount of PLA soldiers behind sandbags in this mission. A player in control of Jedburgh should be looking to play a more supportive role by putting down large amounts of suppressing fire on the enemy locations, which will allow their allies to flank the locations easily. Briggs, on the other hand, is more suited to a player who likes a more direct assault role, thanks to his handy underslung grenade launcher. As there are a lot of intense firefights during this mission, you may have more need for a Med Kit than usual, so if you only have three players in your group you might want to try and get one of them to pick Avery.

ASSAULT SQUAD: ASSAULT TEAM DAGGER ONE BRAVO

SERGEANT. HUNTER (FIRE TEAM LEADER)

Initial Loadout	Primary Weapon	M16A4 (Marksman)
	Primary Weapon Ammunition	7x30 FMJ round magazines
	Secondary Weapon	–
	Secondary Weapon Ammunition	–
	Additional Equipment	2xM67 Grenades, 1xM18 Smoke Grenade, 3xIR Strobes

LANCE CORPORAL. BRIGGS (GRENADIER)

Initial Loadout	Primary Weapon	M16A4 (Assault)
	Primary Weapon Ammunition	7x30 FMJ round magazines, 9xHE projected grenades, 3xHEDP projected grenades
	Secondary Weapon	–
	Secondary Weapon Ammunition	–
	Additional Equipment	2xM67 Grenades, 1xM18 Smoke Grenade, 3xM14 AP Mine

PRIVATE FIRST CLASS. AVERY (MEDIC)

Initial Loadout	Primary Weapon	M16A4
	Primary Weapon Ammunition	7x30 FMJ round magazines
	Secondary Weapon	–
	Secondary Weapon Ammunition	–
	Additional Equipment	1xMedical Kit

PRIVATE FIRST CLASS. JEDBURGH (MACHINEGUNNER)

Initial Loadout	Primary Weapon	M249 SAW
	Primary Weapon Ammunition	3x200 FMJ round ammo boxes
	Secondary Weapon	–
	Secondary Weapon Ammunition	–
	Additional Equipment	1xM67 Grenade

Tree line assault

Have the team start running down the road until they come to a couple of wrecked cars about 150m away from the PLA soldiers, just outside the trees. From here, two players should use the cars for cover and begin laying down suppressing fire, while the other two players head slightly north so that the barn sits between them and the enemies. This should provide them with all they cover they need to run straight up to the barn and take up positions on either side of it to help eliminate any remaining PLA. **[Screen 01]**

Make sure you check that the immediate area within the trees is also clear of any enemies, as there will often be a couple of PLA soldiers in that area. After they have all been killed, the team should re-group and one player should grab the Chinese Marksman rifle from the ammo crate by the sandbags before they start making their way through the woods.

The First defensive line

After running through the woods for a short time, you should see a small wooden outpost with some sandbags nearby, and you might also start to come under fire from the PLA forces up on the hill ahead of this area. Both players with Marksman rifles should use the sandbags for cover and then go prone and continue crawling up past them until they have a clear view over the area. It will be very difficult for the PLA soldiers to hit them at this distance, while they are prone, so they should be able to line up their shots easily. The first priority for them should be the MG on the hill to the east and then, once he is killed, they should start picking off enemies from the main group to the north-east.

The other two players should head north into the woods until they come across a burnt-out vehicle to use for cover. From here they should be able to get a clear shot on the first AT team by the sandbags to the east, who can be easily taken out if one of the players is controlling Briggs, using his underslung grenade launcher. If they don't have that option, then there is plenty of cover around to allow you to get even closer.

Taking the hill

During your assault on the defensive line you'll receive a message informing you that the friendly armor units have started rolling into the area. Once you

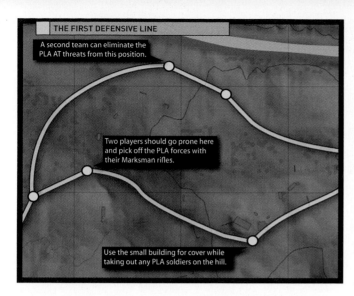

THE FIRST DEFENSIVE LINE

A second team can eliminate the PLA AT threats from this position.

Two players should go prone here and pick off the PLA forces with their Marksman rifles.

Use the small building for cover while taking out any PLA soldiers on the hill.

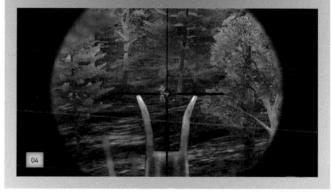

get this, you need to move as quickly as possible to eliminate the AT threats. The second AT team is usually situated by the sandbags near the top of the hill to the south of the first one, so the two players who took them out should move up and deal with the second team.

By now the players back by the wooden outpost, sniping the area, should be running low on enemies left to kill, so they should start moving east towards the enemy positions until they come to a small concrete building. This is another great spot from which to pick off another couple of enemies, if any are visible, before finally heading up the hill. **[Screen 02]** This group of players, combined with the other two that were on AT threat detail, should try and time their movements so that they end up attacking the hill at the same time and trap the enemy in a pincer maneuver. When all of the enemies have been taken out, the team should start heading east quickly through the woods, while keeping an eye out for any PLA soldiers in the area who fled from the first defensive line.

The second defensive line

If you continue heading east through the woods, you'll come upon a small concrete building at the foot of the hill being used by the PLA to form a second defensive line. Tackling this area can be approached very much like the first defensive line. Two players with Marksman rifles should take up positions next to the building and begin taking out enemies. The two other players should again head north on a flanking maneuver, this time towards the nearby bridge, using the walls and rocks for cover as they move until they reach the dried-up river bed. After a while they will come to the bridge, which they should then pass under. **[Screen 03]** From here they should make a quick dash east to reach the trees, which they can then use for cover while they engage the enemy positions.

Send the player using Briggs on the flanking group so that they can again use their grenade launcher. This will make it much easier to take out some of the entrenched enemies. Taking out the three spotter teams should be both groups' primary target, so try and identify them among the other PLA soldiers and kill them first to stop the mortar strikes.

An alternate route

The terrain here also offers another good flanking opportunity in the form of the gully to the south-east of the concrete building. Rather than going north to the bridge, the two players could instead use this gully to go unnoticed right round the side of the PLA defenses, and then come up just behind their defensive line for some quick kills.

This can be quite risky, as the players who use this approach will end up very close to the enemy, so there should always be at least two people in this group. For an even more advanced approach, you can combine both flanking maneuvers by keeping only one player at the concrete building, while two others use the gully and the final player heads north to the bridge for a triple-pronged attack.

Clearing the area

More so than at the first defensive line, there are a lot more PLA soldiers in the trees. Getting a shot at these troops can be awkward from back at the concrete building, so the players there may need to move in while there are still a few enemies in the area. There's plenty of cover around, so this shouldn't be too much of a problem, especially if the others players that flanked to either the north or south are closing in at the same time to provide support.

Around this time you will also be granted an Artillery strike, which you can use to take out the PLA Spotter teams in the woods to the north. Just make sure that any players who were over on that side are well clear of the area before you call it in. Once the woods at the top of the hill have been cleared, all players should regroup and begin heading north-east towards the main road.

Eliminating the AA teams

As the team comes over the crest of the hill they should be able to see the first PLA AA team in the woods on the other side of the road. Any players with Marksman rifles should adopt a prone position, while still high on the hill, to give them a perfect firing angle on the enemy soldiers. **[Screen 04]** A total of three teams need to be killed, so watch for where the next one appears as you kill each previous one. Taking care of these enemies will grant you some additional friendly forces to assist your imminent assault on the fuel depot. Once they have all been killed, everyone should continue down the hill, where they will find a handy PLA off-road vehicle that can be used to reach the overwatch position quickly.

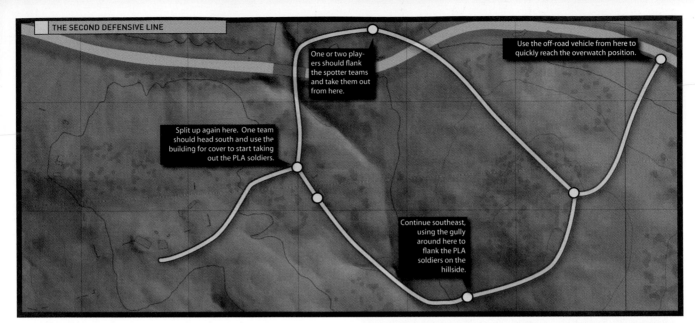

THE SECOND DEFENSIVE LINE

One or two players should flank the spotter teams and take them out from here.

Use the off-road vehicle from here to quickly reach the overwatch position.

Split up again here. One team should head south and use the building for cover to start taking out the PLA soldiers.

Continue southeast, using the gully around here to flank the PLA soldiers on the hillside.

Fuel depot Assault

When the vehicle reaches the overwatch position, two players should remain inside it while two others continue north-east on foot into the trees below. The two players on foot should ideally be carrying Marksmen-type rifles, as it will be their job to take out some of the initial AT threats. This will pave the way for the players in the vehicle to roll in and help clear up the remaining PLA forces with the mounted Heavy Machine Gun. After running through the woods for a short while, they should come across a burnt-out APC, which will provide them with excellent cover from which to start tackling those AT threats.

There are lots of PLA soldiers in the area, but it is quite easy to identify the AT gunner, thanks to the large rocket launcher on his back, so killing him off first should not be too difficult. As soon as he is dead, the team with the vehicle should start moving in, while the Sniper team starts to focus on taking out the emplaced MG operators. Once the MG positions have been taken out and the vehicle is in the area, it should be very easy to clean up the remaining PLA forces on this side of the depot. If the Sniper team needs to get a better view of the area, they should move up to the nearby sandbag area, from where they can continue picking off enemies. **[Screen 01]**

Capturing the fuel depot

After the southern side of the depot has been cleared, all that remains is to take out the remaining PLA defenses on the northern edge. This is best accomplished by using a pincer maneuver in which the players in control of the vehicle head around the western edge of the depot, while the players on foot come around from the east. The main focus of both groups at this time is to take out the specifically identified PLA soldiers, who count as a defensive position, before they cause too many casualties to the incoming friendly forces. There is one AT gunner in this area, so whichever team sees him first should take him out as quickly as possible.

There should only be a handful of PLA soldiers on this side of the depot, so taking them out may sound pretty straightforward, but there are still some PLA forces within the depot itself who will be firing on both teams as well. The concrete barriers around the outside of the depot provide perfect cover for the players on foot from the PLA soldiers both inside and outside the depot, but the players in the vehicle will have to rely more on their mobility. The best way of handling this situation is to take down the enemies on the outside first, since, if you entered the depot while all of the forces on the northern side were still intact, you would risk causing too much collateral damage from all the incoming fire. Once all of the enemies on the northern edge have been killed, all players should move into the depot on foot and clear out the last few soldiers in order to successfully capture the depot.

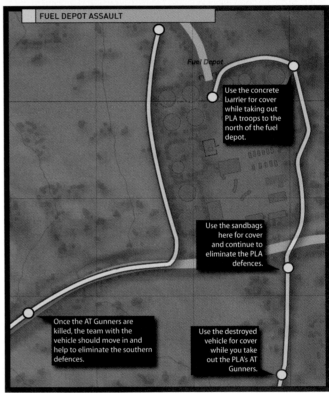

FUEL DEPOT ASSAULT

Fuel Depot

Use the concrete barrier for cover while taking out PLA troops to the north of the fuel depot.

Use the sandbags here for cover and continue to eliminate the PLA defences.

Once the AT Gunners are killed, the team with the vehicle should move in and help to eliminate the southern defences.

Use the destroyed vehicle for cover while you take out the PLA's AT Gunners.

01

LOOKING FOR LOIS
MISSION 08

	Primary Objectives	Secondary Objectives	Bonus Objective
01	Rendezvous with POWs	Remain undetected until the end of the valley	Ensure all POWs survive
02	Extract POWs	Clear the Landing Zone before further reinforcements arrive	

Combat Support: No Combat Support is available for this mission

FORCE SUMMARY

Morales or Winters are the best strategic choices for a second and third player on this mission, since you'll want to be doing a lot of your fighting at long range to keep the POWs safe, and this is where their scoped weapons excel. The LMG that Knox comes equipped with is not without its own merits, though, as you will find that having some suppressing fire at the start and end of the mission is very useful. If you choose to have the player in control of Knox pick up the Sniper rifle near the start of the mission, they will suddenly become quite the powerhouse at both long and mid ranges.

SPEC OPS SQUAD: SO RESCUE TEAM SABER TWO

2ND LIEUTENANT. MULHOLLAND (SF LEADER)

Initial Loadout	Primary Weapon	Mk16 Mod 0 (Assault)
	Primary Weapon Ammunition	9x30 FMJ round magazines, 9xHE projected grenades, 3xHEDP projected grenades
	Secondary Weapon	–
	Secondary Weapon Ammunition	–
	Additional Equipment	2xM67 Grenades, 2xM18 Smoke Grenades, 3x IR Strobes, 2xM21 AT Mines, 1xNVG

CORPORAL. KNOX (SF MACHINEGUNNER)

Initial Loadout	Primary Weapon	Mk48 Mod 0
	Primary Weapon Ammunition	5x100 FMJ round ammo boxes
	Secondary Weapon	–
	Secondary Weapon Ammunition	–
	Additional Equipment	1xM67 Grenade, 1xM18 Smoke Grenade, 1xNVG

CORPORAL. MORALES (SF MEDIC)

Initial Loadout	Primary Weapon	Mk17 Mod 0 (Marksman)
	Primary Weapon Ammunition	9x20 FMJ round magazines
	Secondary Weapon	–
	Secondary Weapon Ammunition	–
	Additional Equipment	2xM67 Grenades, 2xM18 Smoke Grenades, 1xMedical Kit, 1xNVG

CORPORAL. WINTERS (SF SNIPER)

Initial Loadout	Primary Weapon	MP5A4
	Primary Weapon Ammunition	5x30 FMJ round magazines
	Secondary Weapon	M21
	Secondary Weapon Ammunition	12x20 FMJ round magazines
	Additional Equipment	2xM67 Grenades, 2xM18 Smoke Grenades, 2xM18A1 Claymore Mines, 1xNVG

PLA sniper position

From the start of the mission, the team should head south-west for about 60m until they come to a large group of rocks overlooking a partially destroyed building down the mountainside to the south. From here, players with either a Marksman or Sniper rifle should be able to get a clear shot on the two PLA soldiers stationed inside. **[Screen 02]**

The two remaining players should move down towards the house and come around to the front of it from the left-hand flank. From here they can finish off the soldiers in case the Marksman team's bullets didn't quite get the job done. Or, if one of them missed entirely, and the enemies were alerted, having players on the right of the house will often mean they will be at the enemy's back, as they nearly always move to the left when they go to investigate the noise.

Moving down the mountain

Make sure before you head out that one player grabs one of the QBU-88s from the downed PLA sniper and another player picks up the one from the ammo crates in the house. Ideally, these two players should be the ones in control of Mulholland and Knox, as they lack any kind of scoped weapon in their starting loadout. Once the team is fully geared up, everyone should continue on down the mountain, heading south-east towards the large ruins. Directly east, below these ruins, is a smaller derelict building with a

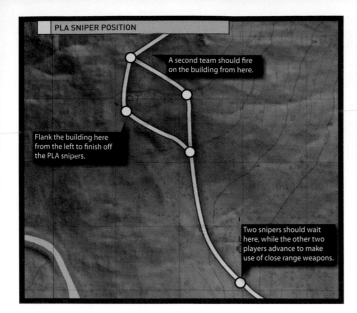

PLA SNIPER POSITION

A second team should fire on the building from here.

Flank the building here from the left to finish off the PLA snipers.

Two snipers should wait here, while the other two players advance to make use of close range weapons.

01

02

03

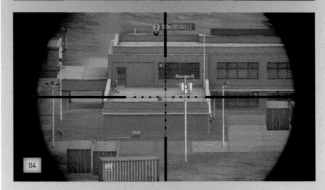

04

nice clear area of ground just to the south of it: an excellent place to set up a sniper position. **[Screen 03]**.

The players using Morales and Winters should take up a prone position at this location and begin immediately engaging the PLA forces who have the POWs pinned down at the bottom of the mountain. This then leaves Mulholland and Knox, who should advance down the mountain and use their superior close-range weapons from within the tree line to take out any PLA soldiers who are still alive.

Rendezvous with the POWs

Once the area is clear of PLA soldiers, all of the players should move down to the base of the mountain and regroup with the POWs. From this point on, the safety of the POWs should be the number one priority of the team, and the correct spacing and formation will go a long way to ensuring this. Two players should ideally take point, around 10-20m ahead of the Fire Team Leader, who should order the POWs to follow him. The final player should bring up the rear at about the same distance behind him to watch for attacks from behind.

This spacing should allow the leader and the POW group to move either forward or backward out of any engagement, and still have players there to provide support. Once everyone in is position, they should start moving northeast towards an overwatch position near an abandoned house just above a valley. Taking this route around the hill is a much safer option than going straight over the top, where you will undoubtedly place the POWs at risk.

Traversing the Valley

As you approach the house you will see a PLA transport helicopter carrying a Spec Ops team, which will land in the distance to the north-east. To complete a Secondary Objective you will need to evade this enemy group until you reach the end of the valley. As their first stop will be to head back to where you rescued the POWs, you will be able to get a good lead on them if you stick to the left-hand side of the valley, so that they don't see you as you move past them. Speed will be your greatest ally in making it through the valley, so everyone should move as quickly as possible, while avoiding any unnecessary firefights.

As it is just a Secondary Objective and not mission-critical, you could also choose to take out the Spec Ops team as soon as they land from the overwatch position. This is an excellent place from which a couple of players can use their Sniper rifles to take out the PLA troops at a safe distance.

Guard post at the end of the valley

Near the end of the valley there is a large, flat clearing from which you can clearly see two PLA soldiers near a guard post to the north-east. **[Screen 01]** The two players on point should use their Sniper rifles to eliminate both of the

guards as soon as they reach this position. This will ensure the POWs don't take any stray incoming fire. Once both guards have been killed, the group should continue moving north towards a large building just outside the trees.

Assaulting the PLA farm building

This large abandoned farm building has been requisitioned for use by the PLA, and they have set up an MG position on the northern side to cover the area. Luckily, the player's team will be approaching from the south, and will not have to worry about the MG emplacement, but there are still the two PLA guards to deal with.

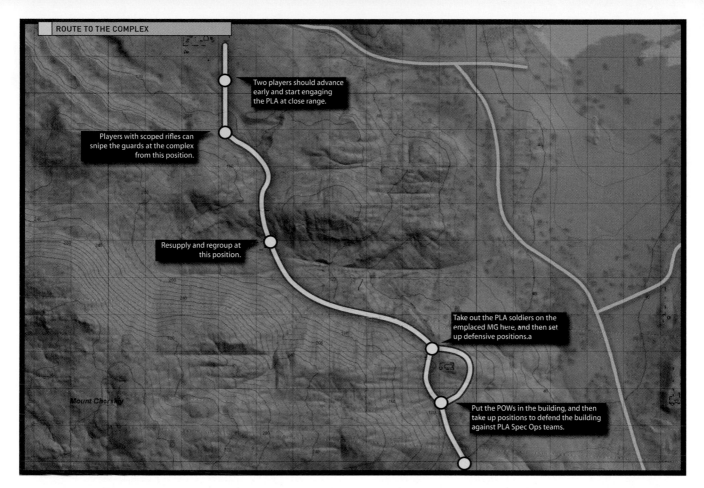

ROUTE TO THE COMPLEX

Two players should advance early and start engaging the PLA at close range.

Players with scoped rifles can snipe the guards at the complex from this position.

Resupply and regroup at this position.

Take out the PLA soldiers on the emplaced MG here, and then set up defensive positions.a

Put the POWs in the building, and then take up positions to defend the building against PLA Spec Ops teams.

Mount Chorsley

05

The two players leading the group should split up once they get close to the building, and one of them should flank around it to either side. As they will be approaching from behind, it should be no problem getting the drop on the two unsuspecting PLA guards and taking them out easily.

PLA counter-attack

As soon as the two guards at the farmhouse have been killed, the nearby PLA Spec Ops patrols will be alerted and ordered to counter-attack the position straight away. Depending on whether, or how, any PLA patrols were encountered when moving through the valley, this could mean either an attack from just the north or from the south as well. To be safe, it's most advisable to set up defenses to cover both sides of the building, so that you are not caught by surprise. To start with, the player in control of Winters should head back slightly to the South and set up his Claymore Mines around the tree line for some extra defense.**[Screen 02]** Once the mines have been laid, that player, together with one other, should head into the house and take up firing positions by the windows looking south.

A good idea at this point would be to bring the POWs into the house to provide them some extra cover until the position is clear. The two remaining players should head around to the north of the building, where one of them should man the MG, while the other sets up with their Sniper rifle to cover the area down to the north-west. Once the PLA group to the north-west have been killed by the players at the front of the house, the whole group should leave the building quickly and head north-west, rather than waiting around for any potential PLA reinforcements from the south..

Regroup position

After leaving the farmhouse, continue heading around the side of the mountain until some ruins below to the north-west come into view, and then move down to this location. This whole area should be clear of any PLA

forces. Since there is no real need for caution, you should move as quickly as possible, while keeping the POWs close by.

Within the ruins is a set of ammo crates containing yet another QBU-88, which one player should grab to get additional ammo. The player with the other QBU-88 from the start should pick up the ammo from this crate. Once everyone has got what they need, the whole group, including POWs, should head up the hill to the next set of ruins to the north. From here you can see the extraction point in the distance, along with a PLA transport helicopter dropping off some additional troops to defend the area. These ruins do not offer an ideal shooting position, however, so the players should continue north-west over the hill until the LZ is directly north of them, around 400m away. **[Screen 03]**

Securing White Fang Complex

This overwatch position on the side of the mountain gives the players an excellent view over the entire complex, a perfect position from which to start sniping some of the PLA guards. To start with, every player should go prone and start taking out some of the easily visible guards, especially the ones on the roof of the main building. **[Screen 04]** Once the number of guards has been thinned out somewhat, two players should switch to their close-range weapons and begin making their way down to the complex. The other two should hold their position with the POWs and continue taking out the guards.

The buildings on the outskirts of the complex will provide excellent cover for the close-assault group of players while they look for and engage any PLA soldiers, staying out of the line of sight of the snipers up on the hill. If there are no visible targets at all for the snipers, or none get flushed out by the close-assault group, then they should break cover and start heading towards the complex with the POWs. Once all of the guards have been killed and one of the players is close enough to the LZ, the evac helicopter will cease its holding pattern and land, at which time everyone, including the POWs, should get aboard and make their escape before reinforcements arrive.

TRUMPET'S SOUND
MISSION 09

	Primary Objectives	Secondary Objectives	Bonus Objective
01	Ensure M1A2s clear the first checkpoint	Eliminate AAA vehicles in the valley	Ensure that no M1A2s are destroyed
02	Destroy PLA AT defenses		
03	Eliminate PLA Mortar Site		

Combat Support: 9xHeavy Mortar Artillery awarded when you reach the overwatch position at the first objective. Note that, once the three AT teams have been taken out, Combat Support will be lost.

FORCE SUMMARY

Both Briggs and Jedburgh would be excellent choices for a second player on this mission, as they offer very good, but very different, tactical options to the team. Briggs brings with him the extra firepower of another underslung grenade launcher, which will come in very hand for taking out the large numbers of entrenched PLA soldiers on this mission. Jedburgh, on the other hand, starting with his M16A4, allows the Fire Team Leader to pick up the Marksman rifle at the start of the mission, giving the team access to a long-range sniping duo.

While either of those team members would also work equally well as a third player, it might be wise to consider getting them to pick Avery instead. Crossing the large open valley in this mission, while being under constant bombardment from the PLA mortar teams, means you are quite likely to be taking some indirect damage from the blasts, so you may have frequent need of Avery's Medical Kit.

RIFLE SQUAD: HEAVY ASSAULT TEAM DAGGER ONE BRAVO

SERGEANT. HUNTER (FIRE TEAM LEADER)

Initial Loadout	Primary Weapon	M16A4 (Assault)
	Primary Weapon Ammunition	7x30 FMJ round magazines, 7xHE projected grenades, 2xHEDP projected grenades
	Secondary Weapon	–
	Secondary Weapon Ammunition	–
	Additional Equipment	2xM67 Grenades, 1xM18 Smoke Grenade, 3xIR Strobes, 3xM14 AP Mines, 1xNVG

LANCE CORPORAL. BRIGGS (GRENADIER)

Initial Loadout	Primary Weapon	M16A4 (Assault)
	Primary Weapon Ammunition	7x30 FMJ round magazines, 9xHE projected grenades, 3xHEDP projected grenades
	Secondary Weapon	–
	Secondary Weapon Ammunition	–
	Additional Equipment	2xM67 Grenades, 1xM18 Smoke Grenade, 3xM14 AP Mines

PRIVATE FIRST CLASS. AVERY (MEDIC)

Initial Loadout	Primary Weapon	M16A4
	Primary Weapon Ammunition	7x30 FMJ round magazines
	Secondary Weapon	–
	Secondary Weapon Ammunition	–
	Additional Equipment	1xMedical Kit

PRIVATE FIRST CLASS. JEDBURGH (RIFLEMAN)

Initial Loadout	Primary Weapon	M16A4 (Marksman)
	Primary Weapon Ammunition	7x30 FMJ round magazines
	Secondary Weapon	–
	Secondary Weapon Ammunition	–
	Additional Equipment	2xM67 Grenades, 1xM18 Smoke Grenade

Rally point

Before getting into the HMMWV and heading out with the other teams in the area, one of the players should make sure they grab the Marksman rifle from the ammo crates near the sandbags. Ideally, this player shouldn't be the one in control of Jedburgh, as he already starts with one. Having two players armed with a Marksman will open up your combat options significantly from the outset. Once everyone is armed, they should get into the HMMWV and head down the road, past all of the friendly tanks, to the overwatch position.

The driver of the vehicle should make sure he keeps to the right of the road and stops well back from the large pile of logs at the overwatch position, so as to avoid taking fire from the PLA tank killers in the valley below. The Fire Team Leader should then get out of the vehicle and move up to the logs and start calling in the Artillery bombardments. Targeting all of the tank killers first is the best way to go. When they are destroyed, call in strikes on the AT teams. **[Screen 01]** There isn't much for the other players to do until the area has been cleared, so they should hold position in the HMMWV for now..

Assaulting the oil works perimeter

After all of the Artillery has been called in, the spotter should get back into the HMMWV with the rest of the players and they should all start driving straight down the road. After a few hundred meters there is an abandoned PLA guard post that you can simply drive through without any worries, and after another couple of hundred meters the oil works in the distance should come into view. As soon as it does, the driver should take the HMMWV off-road, heading to the west, so that a small ridge and trees block the line of fire from the PLA guards stationed outside the oil works.

This group of guards consists of AT and support gunners, so they will make short work of the vehicle if they get a clear shot. To take them out, two players with the Marksman rifles should exit the vehicle and then move up to the tree line to get a clear shot on them.

Clearing the oil works

Once the main threat to the HMMWV has been taken out, the players inside

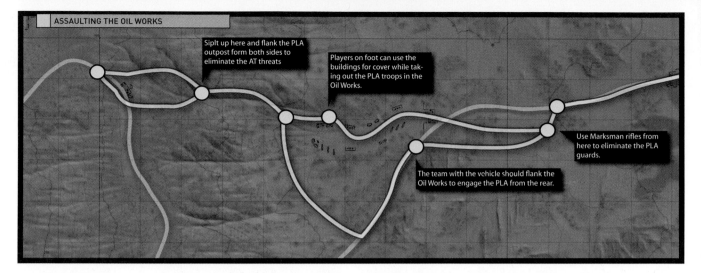

ASSAULTING THE OIL WORKS

Siplt up here and flank the PLA outpost form both sides to eliminate the AT threats

Players on foot can use the buildings for cover while taking out the PLA troops in the Oil Works.

Use Marksman rifles from here to eliminate the PLA guards.

The team with the vehicle should flank the Oil Works to engage the PLA from the rear.

it should get back onto the road and advance on the entrance to the oil works supported by some suppressing fire from the vehicle gunner. Once the vehicle gets close to the exit, the driver should position it behind one of the buildings so that both occupants can get out and grab one of the PLA Marksman rifles from the nearby ammo crates. As soon as they have them, they should get back into the HMMWV and continue down the round to the south-west. While they are driving along the road the gunner can continue to fire on the PLA forces at the back of the oil works, or they can choose to hold fire until the driver reaches a good flanking position.

While the vehicle is causing a distraction, the two players on foot should move up to the small buildings at the entrance to the oil works and use them for cover while they start taking out the PLA soldiers around the buildings in the middle of the area. **[Screen 02]** As soon as they have been taken out, the Marksman team should move up, using the oil pumps on the left-hand side for cover so that they can get into a better position to start taking out the soldiers at the back of the area.

Heading up the dried riverbed

After all of the PLA forces in the immediate area have been killed, the two players on foot should start running through the oil works, while the HM-MWV moves in from the side so that all of the players can regroup. There is another set of ammo crates here, so any player who needs to can restock on ammo. If there are any AT gunner bodies about, you should also loot them to get the Queen Bee Rocket Launcher. Around this time, a four man PLA patrol will begin moving into the area down the dried riverbed to the north-west. If the vehicle gunner can get a clear shot on them he should be able to take the whole group out very quickly. The other players can take up positions beside the vehicle and fire on the patrol with their rifles.

Once the enemy group has been killed, all players should start to head up the riverbed, as there are large numbers of AT gunners in the upcoming areas, and the vehicle is an easy target for them. When the group is climbing the riverbed they should try and keep to the right-hand side in the trees, as

another PLA patrol will come over the top of the hill to the south-west when you are about halfway along it. With the trees for cover and all of the players equipped with Marksman rifles, it should be very easy to take out this small patrol.

Taking out the AT threat

After you've taken out the PLA troops on the south-west of the riverbed, two players should run across it, heading south-west, while the other two players continue straight up the hill to the west, moving directly towards the AT threat. The PLA outpost at the top of the riverbed contains a large number of enemy soldiers backing up the AT gunners, so when either group of players gets near the top of the riverbed they should crouch down and always try to remain in cover. The players coming up from the west should begin engaging the PLA troops near the sandbags as soon as they come into view, using either their Marksman rifles or underslung grenade launchers.

Meanwhile, the other two players should continue flanking up the hill to the south-west until they reach a group of rocks, which they can take cover behind and start engaging the PLA soldiers. **[Screen 03]** After the first group of visible enemies have been killed, the flanking team should head west towards the road, as there will often be a couple of PLA troops left on the other side of it in the trees. The other two players should then head north-west, using the trees for cover and firing on any PLA forces they see along the way, until they reach the road, whereupon they should look south into the guard post and finish off any PLA soldiers still left alive. After all of the enemies have been killed, make sure you search the bodies for any additional Queen Bees, so that as many players as possible have one.

Traversing the hillside

After clearing the PLA outpost, the players should head north-west alongside the friendly forces until two burnt-out tanks come into view. Stay well clear of these tanks, as they will soon be fired upon by the PLA mortar teams up near the monastery, and this strike will easily kill any player caught by

02

03

it. Once the strike is over, continue running west along the side of the hill until you reach a partially destroyed building where there are more ammo crates, in case anyone is running low). There are numerous buildings like this around the valley, and they offer a safe haven from the mortar fire, since the PLA patrols use them for resupplying, and the Spotter teams don't want to risk any friendly-fire incidents.

The group should then continue heading west, past the first house, until they near the ridge of a small hill, at which time they should crouch and then continue to move forward slowly. On the other side of this hill is another house, but this one is occupied by a PLA patrol group, so, as soon as they come into view, all players should begin taking them out with their Marksman rifles. This needs to be done quickly, as the group is out in the open and in danger of being hit with a mortar strike. As soon as everyone in the patrol has been killed, all of the players should run quickly to the house where it is safe.

Clearing the road

From their position at the house, the players should follow the road round to the north-west until they come to a small grouping of wooden huts with some ammo crates nearby. A short distance further on down the road there is another PLA patrol by another house. The wooden hut provides an excellent place from which to fire on them. Two players should take up positions on either side of the hut, and then proceed to take out the patrol with their Marksman rifles.

When all of the enemies are dead (and anyone that needs ammo has got some from the ammo crate), the players should continue on down the road for around 200m, until it takes a sharp right-hand turn. From here, the group of wooden houses to the north-east should be clearly visible, along with the PLA soldiers occupying them. Two players should seek cover by the embankment on the right-hand side of the road and begin firing on the enemy soldiers below. **[Screen 01]** The other two players should run across the road and enter the trees further down the road and slightly to the north-west, and then move into a flanking position, using the trees for cover while they engage the soldiers around the house. When the area is clear, all players should regroup at the houses, where there is also another ammo crate with a Queen Bee for anyone that still needs one.

Crippling the PLA AA vehicles

From these houses the players should head north-east into the trees towards a group of stone buildings in a clearing on the other side, which they can use for cover. The AA vehicles are clearly visible from this position to the north-west, along with a few PLA soldiers who are guarding them. Two players should move up to the most northerly of the buildings with Queen Bees equipped, and then proceed to use them for cover while they use the rocket launchers to take out the AA vehicles.

One of the other players should use the broken wall on the western edge of the area to provide cover for the rocket launcher-wielding players, by firing on the PLA soldiers guarding the AA vehicles. The remaining player should head to the broken wall to the north-east and begin taking out the PLA patrol a couple of hundred meters ahead of this position. As the players are out in the open here, this all needs to be done as quickly as possible, so that the PLA spotters do not home in your position with their mortar strikes. As soon as both of the AA vehicles have been destroyed and the guards killed, everyone should move up as quickly as they can to the houses to the north-west, where the enemy was stationed. Parked up next the road here is a PLA off-road vehicle next to some ammo crates, so everyone should re-supply and then get in the vehicle.

The long road to the Monastery

Rather than following the road directly from where the vehicle was parked, the driver should turn south-west and take the vehicle off-road to cut across the hillside and pick up the road again on the other side, which will save a lot of time. While it is technically possible to continue up the hillside and bypass the next section of road, the severe incline of the hill and rocky terrain make it ill-advised to do so. A much better option from here on is simply to follow the road as quickly as possible. While traveling along the road the vehicle gunner should turn his sights to the north-west and try to take out any PLA soldiers on the sections of road above them before the vehicle gets too close to them.

After a sharp, right-hand turn there is another set of wooden buildings and some ammo crates. About 250m north of this location is the first of four PLA Spotter teams in the area that need to be eliminated. These teams often contain an AT gunner, so keep an eye out for them and make them your first priority. As the player's team approaches the crest of the hill, just before the Spotter team, two of them should get out of the vehicle and move to the left of the road near the side of the mountain. They should then continue forward on foot until they reach a position from which to fire on the Spotter team. **[Screen 02]** When the players on foot are nearing their position, the driver should bring it along the road, so that the gunner can start laying down suppressing fire on the enemy soldiers. This will then allow the players on foot to take them out pretty easily with their Marksman rifles.

Breaching the Monastery's defenses

When the first Spotter team has been eliminated, all players should regroup at the vehicle and then carry on along the road until they see a sharp left turn. At this point everyone should disembark form the vehicle. Although you have support from friendly helicopters (thanks to having destroyed the PLA AA vehicles earlier in the mission) the Monastery will no doubt still have a large contingent of PLA soldiers guarding it, so it pays to be cautious when advancing, even if the clock is ticking.

Two players should continue along the road and then use the natural embankment on the left for cover, while they start engaging the second Spotter team to the west. The other two players should head west straight

away up the hill and then use the large rocks at the top for cover, while they start taking out the PLA defenses on the road to the south-west. Once the Spotter team has been dispatched, the two players by the embankment should move up along the road and use the sandbags on the right-hand side for cover, while they help mop up the enemies further up the road to the south.

Finishing off the Spotter teams

As you only have to take out the four Spotter teams, clearing out the Monastery shouldn't be the team's primary focus. Since this only requires two players, as soon as the road area is mostly clear the two players by the sandbags should head straight up the hill to the west. Move fast, and aim to stay out of the line of sight of most of the PLA guards. The ruins of the Monastery will provide more than enough cover to carry on moving round the base of the hill largely unhindered, until the third Spotter team comes into view about 200m away to the south-west. There is plenty of natural cover around this hillside, which, when coupled with the distance the players are from the spotters, makes them fairly easy to kill with Marksman rifles.

Once the players have wiped out the third Spotter team, they should start heading away from the Monastery, directly towards their location, until they

02

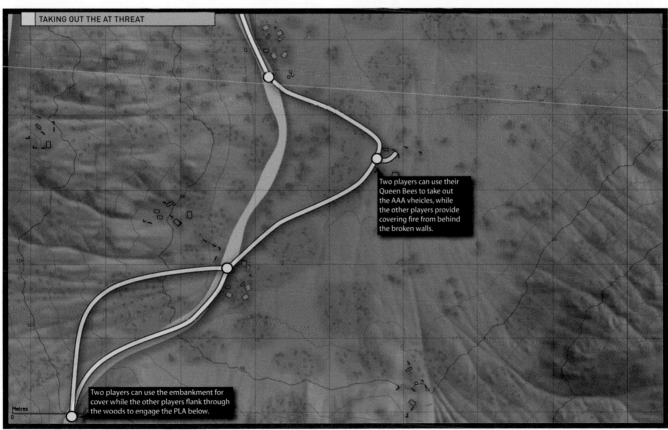

TAKING OUT THE AT THREAT

Two players can use their Queen Bees to take out the AAA vheicles, while the other players provide covering fire from behind the broken walls.

Two players can use the embankment for cover while the other players flank through the woods to engage the PLA below.

Metres
0

05

reach the top of a small hill about 60m shy of it. From here the players should be able to get a good view of the final Spotter team to the south, which will be easy to take out with some crouched Marksman shots. **[Screen 01]**

To make sure the players who have been tasked with taking out the Spotter teams have the time to take out their targets, the other two players by the rocks should try to clear as many of the PLA soldiers from around the Monastery as they can, and create as big a diversion as possible. When all the targets visible from their position by the rocks have been killed, they should run up and cross the road, so that they can use the small, ruined wall for cover. This wall follows the road up to the Monastery for nearly its entire length and provides excellent cover for the players, as they make their way along it taking out any enemies they come across. Engaging the PLA forces aggressively from this side of the Monastery will mean that the players on the other side should not have to fire on anything other than the Spotter teams. Once they have been annihilated, the mission is complete.

01

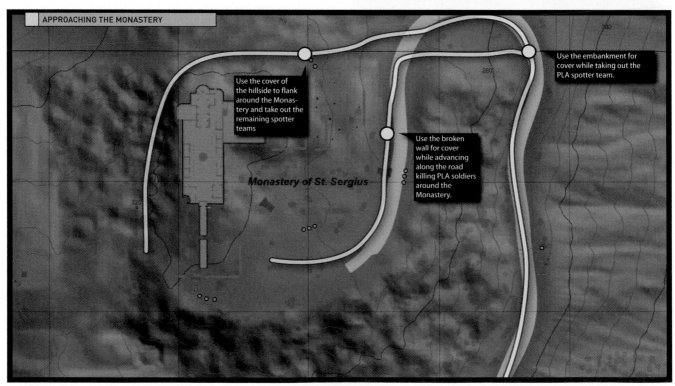

APPROACHING THE MONASTERY

Use the cover of the hillside to flank around the Monastery and take out the remaining spotter teams

Use the embankment for cover while taking out the PLA spotter team.

Use the broken wall for cover while advancing along the road killing PLA soldiers around the Monastery.

Monastery of St. Sergius

DECAPITATION
MISSION 10

	Primary Objectives	Secondary Objectives	Bonus Objective
01	Neutralize the radio station by any means	Observe General Han's Movements	Kill General Han and destroy the radio station at the same time with the same JDAM strike
02	Eliminate General Han		
03	Rendezvous with team at extraction point		

Combat Support: 1x JDAM air strike awarded for completing the Secondary Objective: to observe General Han's movements

FORCE SUMMARY

Stealth is highly important during this mission, and this priority should be reflected in the choice of character, with the first positions filled by team members who come with weapons with silencers. This, unfortunately, means that a player with Knox may not have much of an offensive role to play in this mission, unless the team gets detected. To counteract this, you may want to have that player take on a large percentage of the recon duties, as this will allow the rest of the team to cover the area and engage hostiles with their stealth weapons when needed.

Mulholland and Winters also bring with them incredibly powerful Sniper rifles, and while they may have silencers, you will be able to kill enemies from so far away that sound will not be a factor. They will still need to pick their targets carefully, however, as any dead bodies found by a PLA patrol will alert them to your presence and make the mission much tougher.

SPEC OPS SQUAD: SO STEALTH SNIPER TEAM SABER TWO

2ND LIEUTENANT. MULHOLLAND (SF LEADER)

Initial Loadout	Primary Weapon	M16A4 (Stealth)
	Primary Weapon Ammunition	5x30 subsonic round magazines
	Secondary Weapon	Model 82A1 (Night Ops)
	Secondary Weapon Ammunition	9x10 FMJ round magazines
	Additional Equipment	2xM67 Grenades, 2xM18 Smoke Grenades, 3xIR Strobes, 3xC4 Demo Charges, 1xNVG

CORPORAL. KNOX (SF RIFLEMAN)

Initial Loadout	Primary Weapon	Mk17 Mod 0 (Marksman)
	Primary Weapon Ammunition	12x20 FMJ round magazines
	Secondary Weapon	–
	Secondary Weapon Ammunition	–
	Additional Equipment	4xM67 Grenades, 2xM18 Smoke Grenades, 3xIR Strobes, 1xNVG

CORPORAL. MORALES (SF MEDIC)

Initial Loadout	Primary Weapon	M16A4 (Stealth)
	Primary Weapon Ammunition	9x30 subsonic round magazines
	Secondary Weapon	–
	Secondary Weapon Ammunition	–
	Additional Equipment	2xM67 Grenades, 2xM18 Smoke Grenades, 1xMedical Kit, 1xNVG

CORPORAL. WINTERS (SF SNIPER)

Initial Loadout	Primary Weapon	M16A4 (Stealth)
	Primary Weapon Ammunition	5x30 subsonic round magazines
	Secondary Weapon	Model 82A1 (Night Ops)
	Secondary Weapon Ammunition	9x10 FMJ round magazines
	Additional Equipment	1xM67 Grenades, 1xM18 Smoke Grenades, 2xM18A1 Claymore Mine, 1xNVG

Eyes on the FARP

This mission requires the players to use stealth even more than in previous missions and, as such, there are few places where they will actually engage enemies, let alone have room for complex flanking maneuvers. Because of this, even when playing this mission in Co-op, players are advised to follow the mission outline found in the Single Player Campaign chapter, all the way up to the concrete bunker, which is the final location from which you have to recon General Han's position.

Snipers at the overwatch position

From the concrete bunker, the players should follow the dirt trail round the hill below it and up to the north-east. This area is totally clear of enemies, so just run up the trail as quickly as possible. When the trail starts to head directly north, you should be able to see a house at the top of the hill some 300m in the distance; around the house are two PLA snipers, which need to be taken out. Once the group gets to approximately 200m from the house, they should split up for a pincer maneuver, attacking with snipers from both sides.

Two players should head north-east up the slope and approach the house from the right-hand side, while the other two players (ideally at least one with a Sniper rifle) should head north-west to the top of the hill opposite the

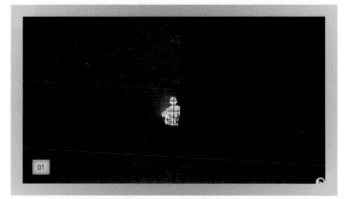
01

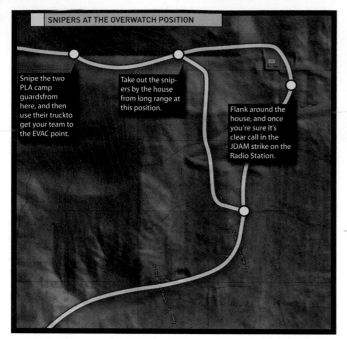

SNIPERS AT THE OVERWATCH POSITION

Snipe the two PLA camp guards from here, and then use their truck to get your team to the EVAC point.

Take out the snipers by the house from long range at this position.

Flank around the house, and once you're sure it's clear call in the JDAM strike on the Radio Station.

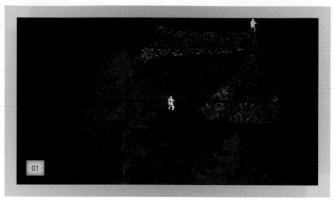

01

house. From here the Sniper team should be able to get a clear shot on one of the snipers. **[Screen 01]** They should take him out as soon as he comes into view.

The two players heading north-east to the other side need to be careful as they advance, as the other PLA sniper often likes to wander down this side of the hill, so they should be ready to engage him at close range if needed. Once they are both down, all of the players should move up to the overwatch position and proceed to call in the JDAM strike on the radio station to destroy it and kill General Han.

Proceed to the evac location

As soon as General Han and the radio station have been taken out, the players need to start moving, as the PLA forces have been alerted and are homing in on their position. While heading directly south-west may seem like the best and quickest option, this will in fact lead you straight into a large number of enemy forces; instead, players should head north-west from the overwatch position towards a small PLA camp. Here two PLA soldiers are guarding a large ammo supply and a Transport Truck. Taking the guards down is best done at long range from the top of the hill, so that both players with Sniper rifles can get a good firing angle on them. **[Screen 01]**

Once the guards are dead the players should head down to the camp as quickly as they can, and then gather some supplies before getting into the truck. There are a lot of PLA patrols between this location and the extraction point, but with a bit of careful driving it is possible to avoid all of them. From the camp, the driver of the truck should head due west until they come to a road, at which point they should turn and head southwest, straight for the extraction point. If at any time the players do come into contact with a PLA patrol they should exit the truck immediately and use it for cover while they take out the enemies. Then they can repair the truck if needed and carry on towards the extraction point.

DRAGON FURY
MISSION 11

	Primary Objectives	Secondary Objectives	Bonus Objective:
01	Eliminate PLA armor in the valley	Eliminate PLA defensive position	Pilot the helicopter safely from Skoje village to the landing zone near the naval base
02	Capture Skoje Village	Capture General Zheng alive	
03	Eliminate PLA resistance at the Naval Base		

Combat Support: 1xMedium Mortar Artillery awarded for clearing RV21 and entering the area with the two PLA MG nests

FORCE SUMMARY

Your squad for the final mission is very evenly equipped, with no character having any major advantage over the others. The CQB rifle that Jedburgh starts with will allow you pick off targets slightly easier than with the traditional iron sights that Avery and Briggs come with, and this can come in quite handy early in the mission. Although a couple of characters start this mission with mines, there aren't many opportunities to put them to good use, so they shouldn't factor much in your selection. The one exception to this is the C4 that Briggs has. With a bit of co-ordination from your teammates, these can be used to take out the AA vehicles in Skoje village, which means you can use your rockets elsewhere.

RIFLE SQUAD: CQB ASSAULT TEAM DAGGER ONE BRAVO

SERGEANT. HUNTER (FIRE TEAM LEADER)

Initial Loadout		
	Primary Weapon	M16A4 (Night Ops)
	Primary Weapon Ammunition	7x30 FMJ round magazines
	Secondary Weapon	FGM-148 Javelin
	Secondary Weapon Ammunition	1xTandem HEAT Guided Missile Reload
	Additional Equipment	2xM67 Grenades, 1xM18 Smoke Grenade, 3xIR Strobe, 1xNVG

PRIVATE FIRST CLASS. JEDBURGH (RIFLEMAN)

Initial Loadout		
	Primary Weapon	M4A1 (CQB)
	Primary Weapon Ammunition	7x30 FMJ round magazines
	Secondary Weapon	–
	Secondary Weapon Ammunition	–
	Additional Equipment	2xM67 Grenades, 1xM18 Smoke Grenade, 2xM18A1 Claymore Mines, 1xNVG

PRIVATE FIRST CLASS. AVERY (MEDIC)

Initial Loadout	Primary Weapon	M16A4
	Primary Weapon Ammunition	7x30 FMJ round magazines
	Secondary Weapon	–
	Secondary Weapon Ammunition	–
	Additional Equipment	1xMedical Kit, 1xNVG

LANCE CORPORAL. BRIGGS (COMBAT ENGINEER)

Initial Loadout	Primary Weapon	M16A4
	Primary Weapon Ammunition	8x30 FMJ round magazines
	Secondary Weapon	–
	Secondary Weapon Ammunition	–
	Additional Equipment	2xM67 Grenades, 2xM18 Smoke Grenades, 2xC4 Demo Charges, 2xM21 AT Mine, 5xM14 AP Mines, 1xNVG

Clearing the first MG nest

From the starting position, the players should run quickly to the south for around 500m until they reach a road. At this time, the PLA soldier on the emplaced MG, together with a couple of other PLA soldiers around him at the house ahead of this position, should become viewable. Thankfully, though, they are preoccupied with the other advancing friendly forces. This allows the players to move up to the other side of the road safely into the trees and use them for cover while they take out the MG operator and surrounding enemies, if the other friendlies haven't taken care of them already.

Destroying the PLA armor

Once the area around the house has been cleared, the Fire Team Leader should move south-west, back towards the road. There is a nice clear view from this position to the PLA tank, which they should then proceed to take out with their Javelin. One other player should move to this position with them, as there will often be a few PLA soldiers further along the road that they can take out with their rifle.

The two other players should move up to the house and raid the ammo crate inside it for the Queen Bee and Marksman rifle. Then, once the tank is destroyed and the new objective to take out the MG emplacement on the left flank appears, they should move south-east from the house up the hill towards the objective. About halfway up the hill they should be able to get a good view of the two soldiers in the MG nest to the south. This is an excellent position from which to take them out from, as there is plenty of cover available. [Screen 02]

PLA counter-attack

All players should now regroup at the house near the second MG position, which has just been cleared. There is another ammo crate in this house, (containing a Queen Bee and Marksman rifle) so make sure that these are

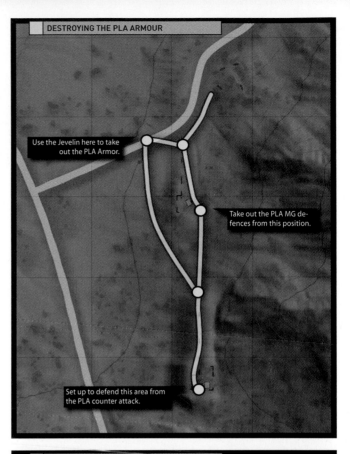

DESTROYING THE PLA ARMOUR

Use the Jevelin here to take out the PLA Armor.

Take out the PLA MG defences from this position.

Set up to defend this area from the PLA counter attack.

05

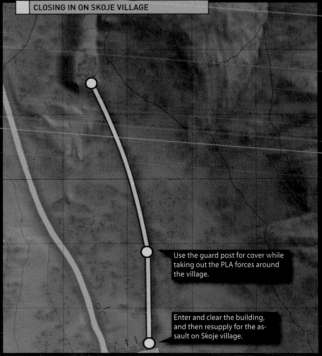

CLOSING IN ON SKOJE VILLAGE

Use the guard post for cover while taking out the PLA forces around the village.

Enter and clear the building, and then resupply for the assault on Skoje village.

distributed evenly. There will be a small PLA counter-attack on this location shortly, so even though the clock is ticking, it's advisable to stay up here and deal with it before continuing.

The counter-attack consists of five PLA soldiers in total, three approaching from the left and two from the right in a pincer maneuver. One player should get set up on the MG facing Skoje village and aim the sights to the left, while another player should crouch behind the sandbags on the left-hand side to provide backup. The two other players should take up positions behind the sandbags on the right of the MG and wait for soldiers to make their approach; once they are in range, both groups of players should take out the targets on their respective sides.

Closing in on Skoje Village

When the counter-attack has been successfully fended off, all players should start moving south again towards Skoje village. The outskirts of the village are fairly well guarded, so make sure you stick close to the trees for cover when moving in. The first threat that needs to be handled is a small PLA guard post positioned just on the inner edge of the trees, which has another emplaced MG. As there is only one soldier at this position, it should be easy to clear with a couple of players using their Marksman shots, while the others continue to advance.

This guard post is also a great place from which to clear out a lot of the PLA soldiers in the surrounding area. Two players should take up a position on the left-hand side and look to clear out the forces at the first line of houses in the village; the other two players should head to the right-hand side and help out the friendly forces on the right-hand flank to the south-west. **[Screen 01]**

Skoje staging area

You don't have the luxury of spending too much time at the guard post, picking off targets, as the friendly helicopters will be entering the airspace soon, and the AAA vehicles must be destroyed. After enough soldiers have been killed to allow the players to move up safely, they should head direct south from the guard post towards the large building on the eastern side of the village. There will usually be two PLA guards in this building, so if they

haven't been killed already make sure you check the windows before entering, and then take them out.

Inside the building are some ammo crates that players can use to resupply themselves and get organized before continuing with the final assault on Skoje. At this point, two players should equip their Queen Bees so that they are ready to fire as soon as they get into position. The other two players will be taking point with their rifles and clearing the area, so that the rocket launcher team can take out the AAA vehicles.

Clearing the skies

The two lead players should exit the house first via one of the doors to the south, and then move west along the main road towards the large central building. While moving along the road, they should constantly have their sights trained on the alleyways between the buildings to the south, as there will often be PLA soldiers hiding in these areas. As they get close to the small building, just east of the central one, they should slow their advance down, because there will definitely be a minimum of two PLA soldiers in the alley. Both players should ease out slowly and take them out immediately, then one of them should run across and take up a position next to the central building. With one player now on either side of the alley, they should start

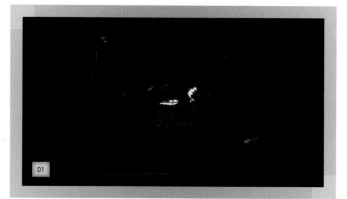

01

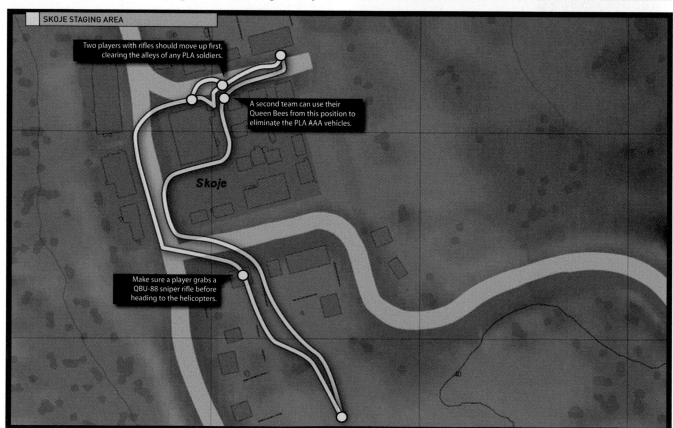

SKOJE STAGING AREA

Two players with rifles should move up first, clearing the alleys of any PLA soldiers.

A second team can use their Queen Bees from this position to eliminate the PLA AAA vehicles.

Skoje

Make sure a player grabs a QBU-88 sniper rifle before heading to the helicopters.

clearing out any PLA soldiers guarding the AAA vehicle at the southern edge of the village.**[Screen 02]**

Once the path has been cleared by the lead team, the two players on AAA detail should move up with their rocket launchers ready to fire. When they reach the alley where the lead team is positioned, they should be able to get a perfect firing angle on the AAA vehicle station on the southern edge of the village; one rocket from each player should get the job done. **[Screen 03]** As soon as that AAA threat has been nullified the players should reload their Queen Bees and then move forward until they get a clear shot on the AAA vehicle just the other side of the central building.

Gaining control of Skoje

When both AAA vehicles have been destroyed, the path will be clear for Trident to land safely just south of the village, and some additional reinforcements will also enter the village to help clear up the last few PLA soldiers. The players with their Queen Bees out should switch to Assault rifles, and then all players should continue west along the road until it joins up with the main road heading south. Moving down the road on this side of the village is a much safer option, as it cuts down on the possible firing angles the enemies have on the players. It also offers much better firing angles for players to engage the PLA forces.

Two players should stick close to the inside of the road, while the other two players head to the outside edge to cover further down into the village. Continue to move down the road clearing enemies until you reach another road leading east back across the village. The second house on the southern side of this road has some ammo crates containing a QBU-88 Sniper rifle, so make sure one of the players picks this up. This house is often guarded by

a couple of PLA soldiers, so make sure you check the windows for enemies before entering. Once the weapon has been secured and the PLA forces killed, everyone should continue south to the helicopters and then take the flight to the landing area near the Naval Base.

Sweeping the hills

From the LZ, the players should start heading south until they come to a road, at which point they should turn south-east and head through the trees along this side of the hill. A few hundred meters along the hillside there is a PLA guard post, just after the crest of a small hill. As soon as this comes into view, one of the players should take out the lone soldier inside. When he is dead, all of the players should move up to the guard post and take up prone sniping positions. A quick scan of the ridge line north and north-east of this position will reveal a large number of PLA soldiers, including one on an emplaced MG. It is a much better option to take them out at long range from here than to move up and engage them at close quarters. **[Screen 04]**

05

There may also be additional PLA soldiers hidden behind trees, or on the other side of the ridge, so it's a good idea to try and wound, rather than kill, the enemies that are initially fired upon, so that others in the area come running out to their aid. This can end up drawing out a considerable number of enemies, contributing greatly to the task of clearing the enemies around the base, so it's really worthwhile spending some time here doing this, especially since there are no time restrictions in place.

Assaulting the ruins

Once the ridgeline to the north is looks clear, the players should get back up and start running towards the MG nest that was just cleared on top of the hill to the north-east. When they have reached that position, two of them should move up to the broken walls to the south-east and use them for cover while they take out the small cluster of PLA soldiers at the next set of ruins about 300m to the south-east.

While they are taking out the PLA soldiers at a distance, the other two players should head to the east and move slightly down the hill, as there are often one or two PLA soldiers they would otherwise be unable to see making their way up from the ruins. There isn't much cover in this area, so the enemies will need to be taken out quickly as soon as they come into view. As soon as the ruins to the south-east are clear, all of the players should head down to them and regroup, at which time there should also be a message from command letting you know that there is combat support available.

Taking down the last MG nests

Upon reaching this set of ruins, one player should target and take out the PLA soldiers by the guard post on the other side of the road to the south-east, while the rest of the players carry on running down this side of the road towards the top of the hill, around 170m south-east of the ruins. By the roadside on the other side of the hill there is another PLA soldier on an emplaced MG, and although you could use your mortar strike here, it is generally better saved for later. Instead, have one player move down onto the road and then move up to act as a decoy by drawing enemy fire. The other two players should then come up over the crest of the hill and take him out. While the bulk of the team is dealing with the MG threat, the sniper at the ruins should move up and rejoin the group. **[Screen 01]**

Once the MG nest is clear, the players should move up and head east over the hill past the guard post, stopping just before coming over the crest of it. On the road below this hill is an MG nest on one side of the road, backed up by a heavily-armed support gunner on the other side. This is an excellent location from which to use your mortar strike, as all you have to do is target the centre of the road with a barrage, which should easily take care of both enemies. To make lining up the strike easier it can pay to have one or two players move down the road to draw the fire of the PLA soldiers, allowing the Fire Team Leader to call the strike in in relative safety. **[Screen 02]**

Coming around to the south side of the Naval Base before launching an assault may seem like the long way round, but tactically it's a much sounder option. Coming in from the middle would mean getting caught in crossfire and make establishing a defendable position much harder. What's more, to the north is a fearsome PLA Type-99 tank.

Entering the Naval Base

From the MG nest, the player with the QBU-88 should head direct north across the hill until just short of the cliff overlooking the entrance to the Naval Base. The remaining players should follow the road around the hill, making sure they keep to the left-hand side for maximum cover. Once near the entrance, they should move out slightly to catch the attention of the PLA soldier on the emplaced MG, and then head back into cover. This then allows the player up on the hilltop to move forward and take an easy shot on the enemy from above.

As soon as this enemy is dead the sniper on the hill should get into a prone position, facing north-west into the base, and start taking out the PLA forces inside the base, while also passing on information about enemy positions to the other players. The players at the entrance should then move up quickly into the base, sticking to the left-hand side near the cliff, until they have passed the containers and are alongside the first main building. The small, extruding part of this building will give the players plenty of cover while

they clear out a few of the nearby enemies; it's also worth shooting out the barrels to the north to both increase visibility and eliminate a potential threat. **[Screen 03]**

Securing the Naval Base

After the barrels have been destroyed, one player should move up to the small concrete wall just north of the building, with covering fire from the two players by the building. Once there, they should crouch down and start laying down some suppressing fire so that the two players by the building can move up to the sandbags north-west of the building. From this position it's worth taking out as many barrels and fuel tanks as you can see, as there

will often be PLA soldiers nearby who will get killed in the blast, and it will eliminate any possibility of friendly players getting caught in an explosion caused by a stray bullet.

Once the area has been partially cleared, the two players by the sandbags should move across the bridge and position themselves next to the containers. **[Screen 04]** From here they can provide covering fire as the player by the wall crosses the bridge. This player should then follow the wall northwards and use the destroyed fuel tanks as cover to allow them to continue up to the back of the building near the waterfront. There should be plenty of dead PLA soldiers scattered about, so any player starting to run low on ammo should grab some from one of the bodies.

The north side of the Base should be relatively clear now, thanks to the efforts of the sniper back on the hill, so, with a bit of covering fire from the player by the waterside building, the two players by the containers should be able to move up safely to the building General Zheng is hiding in. One player should then crouch by the sandbags and defend the area, while the other goes in and gets a positive ID on the General. Once that's done, all that's left is for a couple of players to cross the second bridge to the north, and then use the large building near the side of the cliff for cover, while they take out the last couple of PLA soldiers.

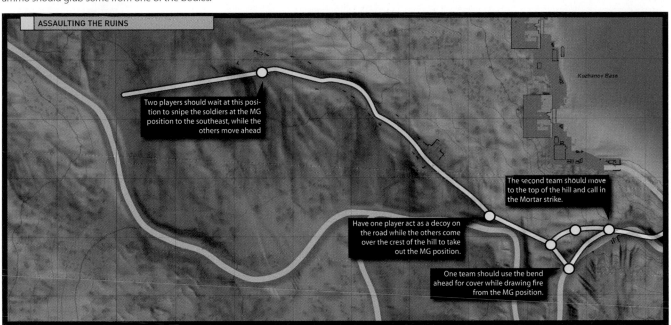

ASSAULTING THE RUINS

Two players should wait at this position to snipe the soldiers at the MG position to the southeast, while the others move ahead

The second team should move to the top of the hill and call in the Mortar strike.

Have one player act as a decoy on the road while the others come over the crest of the hill to take out the MG position.

One team should use the bend ahead for cover while drawing fire from the MG position.

Kozhanov Base

05

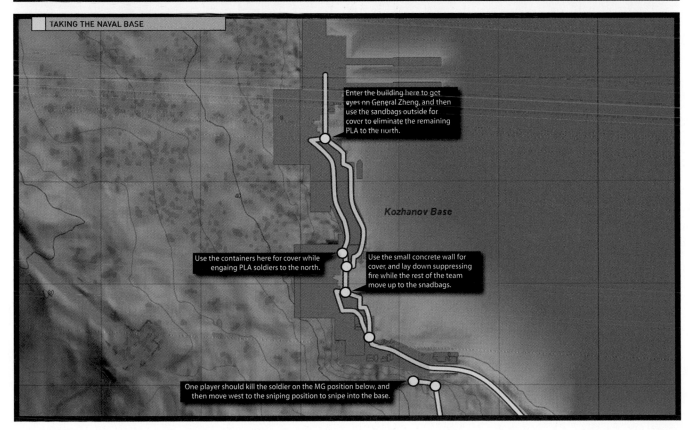

TAKING THE NAVAL BASE

Enter the building here to get eyes on General Zheng, and then use the sandbags outside for cover to eliminate the remaining PLA to the north.

Kozhanov Base

Use the containers here for cover while engaing PLA soldiers to the north.

Use the small concrete wall for cover, and lay down suppressing fire while the rest of the team move up to the snadbags.

One player should kill the soldier on the MG position below, and then move west to the sniping position to snipe into the base.

ANNIHILATION
CHAPTER 05

This is a classic team deathmatch-style game mode. In this mode players form two teams, with the simple objective of defeating and destroying the opposing team. Players have access to AI units and all of the equipment generally available in the single-player. Players select their own equipment based upon the Fire Team they choose to be in. The teams begin at opposite ends of a host-selected map and advance to contact. Once engaged, the two teams must wage war until either the time expires or the score limit is reached. Whichever team has the highest score when the time runs out, or reaches the score limit first, will be victorious. If both teams have the same score when the time ends, the match will be considered a draw.

CHOKEPOINT
MAP 01

This Annihilation map is fought around Aynskoye Village and Lake Taimyr. The buildings on either side of the bridge (which forms the natural chokepoint from which the mission gets its name) give both teams a good amount of cover to fire from, while they try to protect their side of the tactically crucial bridge. Whichever side loses control of their side of the bridge and allows the enemy to get a foothold in their territory will certainly find it much harder to achieve victory. Both teams have access to air, land and amphibious vehicles, so there are plenty of tactical options to consider when deciding where, and how, to engage the enemy.

USMC FORCE SUMMARY

AVAILABLE INFANTRY

Team	Class Icon	Team Member
Engineer Team		Combat Engineer
		Anti-Tank Specialist
		Anti-Tank Specialist
		Rifleman

Team	Class Icon	Team Member
Medium MG Team		Machinegunner
		Rifleman
		Machinegunner
		Medic

Team	Class Icon	Team Member
Sniper Team		Sniper
		Sniper
		Medic
		Machinegunner

Team	Class Icon	Team Member
Helicopter Transport Crew		Machinegunner
		Rifleman
		Medic
		Machinegunner

AVAILABLE VEHICLES

Vehicle Type	Number of Vehicles
M1025 (equipped with M2HB Heavy MG)	2
M1025 (equipped with Mk19 Grenade Launcher)	1
MH-60S	2
SURC PT	1

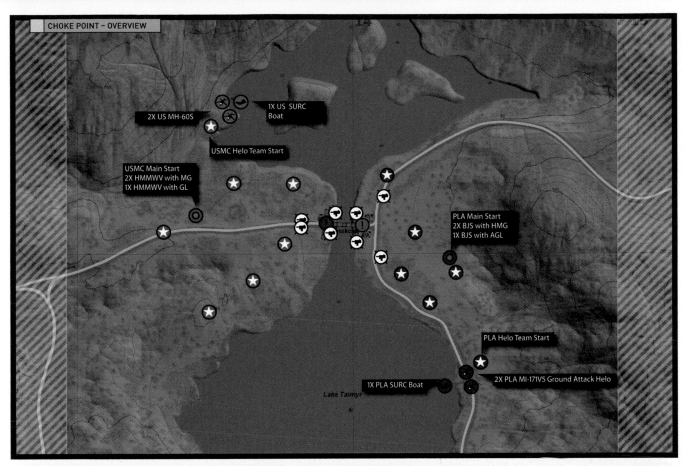

CHOKE POINT – OVERVIEW

211

2X US MH-60S

1X US SURC Boat

USMC Helo Team Start

USMC Main Start
2X HMMWV with MG
1X HMMWV with GL

PLA Main Start
2X BJS with HMG
1X BJS with AGL

PLA Helo Team Start

1X PLA SURC Boat

2X PLA MI-171V5 Ground Attack Helo

Lake Taimyr

05

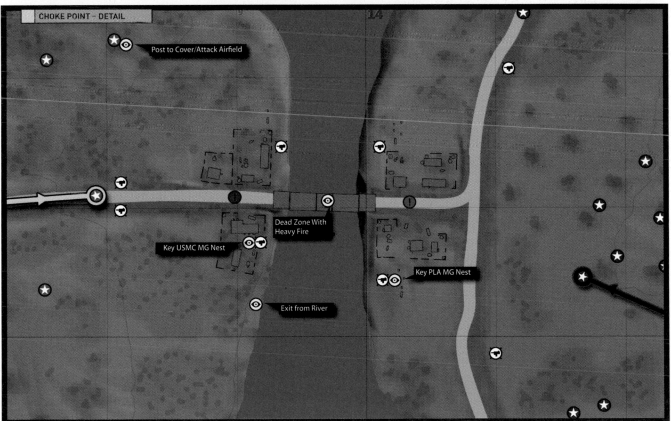

CHOKE POINT – DETAIL

Post to Cover/Attack Airfield

Dead Zone With Heavy Fire

Key USMC MG Nest

Exit from River

Key PLA MG Nest

USMC INFANTRY TACTICS

Engineer Team

At the start of the map the primary goal of the Engineer Team should be to get down to the bridge from the starting point as fast as they can in one of the M1025s. The Combat Engineers should then attempt to lay down some of their Mines as far across the bridge as is safe to do so. The main bulk of their available AP and AT Mines should be used on the main road section of the bridge, while one or two AP Mines are used to cover the small walkway to the side.

To assist them in their task, the other members of this team should try and lay down some covering fire, with the AT gunners in particular looking to take out any enemy vehicles that are closing in on the bridge. The Rifleman should either stay on the gun that was mounted to the M1025 they took, or leave the vehicle and use one of the MG positions to the side of the bridge for some heavy suppressing fire. The Engineer Team's primary role from that point on should be to try to maintain the security of the bridge. This will mean a lot of moving between the houses, so the enemies do not pin down their location, while laying down as much suppressive fire as possible across the bridge. **[Screen 01]**

Medium MG Team

The MG Team is a somewhat workman-like team on this map, as they are able to provide a lot of assistance to the other teams, no matter where they go on the map. With two Machinegunners in the team, they will be able to provide some excellent backup to the Engineer Team while they try to secure the bridge. They can also serve very well as a second vehicle team by getting into the second helicopter and joining up with the Helicopter Team for some double strafing runs on the PLA side of the bridge.

As this team packs a lot of firepower, they can also be very effective by going on long flanking maneuvers around the lake in one of the M1025s, coming up from behind the enemy for a surprise attack.

Sniper Team

The buildings around the bridge can be quite effective positions for snipers for a short time, but it is a little bit close to the action, and is also the first place the enemy will expect them to be. The islands in the middle of the lake to the north also make excellent positions for a sniper to fire into the PLA side of the village. As well as being out of the way, they facilitate small changes of location to help avoid detection.

If either of the snipers are heading to one of the islands, they should make sure they take one of the M1025s from the starting position to the shore of the lake to get them there faster. **[Screen 02]** This also holds true if they are heading to one of the other good sniping positions in the line of trees along the southwest bank of the lake. Players using either the medic or machinegunner on this team should support them by helping to spot targets and provide short-range backup if an enemy gets too close.

Helicopter Transport Crew

As the name suggests, this team's primary role is the operation of the MH-60S Helicopters. Thankfully, their spawn point is right next to the helicopters, which means they start out over 500 meters away from the other US Fire Teams. Since they start on their own, away from any other friendly forces, they will need to rely on the vehicles nearby to get anything done. This is not just limited to the Helicopters, however, as the nearby SURC is also an extremely effective vehicle. It's advisable to split the team into two to allow a combination of vehicles to mount an assault on the PLA.

USMC VEHICLE TACTICS

The MH-60S Helicopters that the USMC forces have available to them on this map come equipped with two side-mounted miniguns, which means that pilots need to pay special attention to the angles they take when approaching a target, so that the gunner can get a clear shot. If both guns are manned, an extremely effective maneuver is to fly directly over the PLA side of the village and then hover above the location. This will allow the gunners to fire on both sides of the shore where the PLA are, completely decimating any enemies in the area. This may make the Helicopter a relatively easy target for any PLA soldiers with rocket launchers or other heavy weapons, so it shouldn't be attempted for long, or without plenty of cover from friendly forces on the ground. **[Screen 03]**

When engaging the PLA helicopter in air-to-air combat, USMC pilots need to remember that the enemy's weapon systems are forward-firing, so they

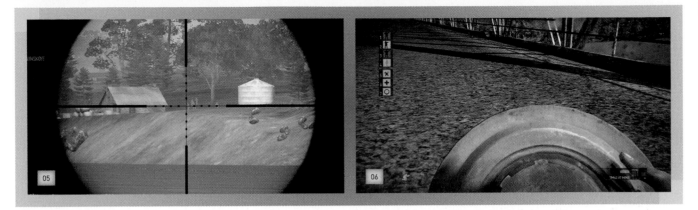

should always attempt to get round to the side of the PLA helicopter, where it's safe. When using the SURC in the northern half of the lake, USMC players should remember to make good use of the islands, as they provide an excellent source of cover which the southern half doesn't have. This permits the driver of the boat to just ease out backwards from behind an island, allowing the rear gunner to fire off volleys of grenades onto the PLA side of the village.

PLA FORCE SUMMARY

AVAILABLE INFANTRY

Team	Class Icon	Team Member
 Grenadier Team		Grenadier
		Medic
		Rifleman
		Combat Engineer

Team	Class Icon	Team Member
 Helicopter Transport Crew		Grenadier
		Rifleman
		Machinegunner
		Medic

Team	Class Icon	Team Member
 Sniper Team		Sniper
		Medic
		Machinegunner
		Sniper

Team	Class Icon	Team Member
 Anti-Tank Team		Anti-Tank Specialist
		Machinegunner
		Anti-Tank Specialist
		Combat Engineer

PLA INFANTRY TACTICS

Grenadier Team

The Grenadier Team primary aim should be to attempt to secure the PLA side of the bridge. As it is not quite as straightforward for PLA forces to reach the bridge as it is for the USMC, this will often be an uphill battle from the start. The underslung Grenade Launcher on the Grenadier's weapon can be a great equalizer, however, as the grenades can be fired very effectively while still a large distance away from the enemy. **[Screen 04]** This, coupled with their large damage and blast radius, can make them extremely deadly to any USMC forces trying to secure the bridge at the start of a round.

While the Grenadier is firing off volleys of grenades to keep the enemy busy, the other members of the team should move up into the village and try to take up positions as close to the bridge as they can. The small, corrugated hut can be a great position to fire from, but any players here need to be careful, because any USMC player with a Rocket Launcher can easily take this building down, and the player along with it; make sure you are constantly on the lookout and take down any AT gunners quickly.

Sniper Team

The PLA side of the village is somewhat sprawling, which makes it more difficult to defend the USMC side, especially with the lack of effective MG positions. PLA snipers should therefore consider staying a bit closer to base than their USMC counterparts in order to help defend the area. Thankfully, the line of trees a short distance away from the spawn area offers plenty of good positions from which to fire across the lake. As this group of trees is to the side of the village, it is often possible to get a good angle and catch USMC players attempting to hide behind the buildings on the opposite side. An alternate, and equally effective, position is the second-floor window of the northern building in the village. This position is far enough away from the action for the sniper to be effective, and the small window makes it very hard for enemies to get a clean shot on them.

If the other teams are handling village defenses well enough on their own, it can also be very effective if the PLA Sniper Team takes up a position on the islands to the north of the lake. From there, PLA snipers will be able to keep watch over the area from where the USMC Helicopter Crew originates and along the main road used by USMC forces to get to the village. Good PLA snipers can totally demoralize the opposition from this location, but they will need to rely on the other members of their team to make sure they don't get flanked from behind. **[Screen 05]**

Anti-Tank Team

This is the PLA's heavy weapons specialist team, and their main role will be to take down any USMC vehicles or fortified positions. To maximize their destructive potential it is advisable for this team to secure the BJ2022 with the LG3 equipped. This will allow the gunner to fire off long volleys of deadly grenades onto the USMC side of the lake to distract them, while the AT gunners line up their shots from close by.

At the start of the round, the USMC M1025s will often move straight along the road directly towards the village so, to catch them, PLA AT gunners will need to head straight for the shore of the lake from the spawn area and try to get a clean shot on any incoming vehicles on the other side. Whenever there is a lull in the action, or the bridge area is looking slightly clear, the player using the Combat Engineer should try to lay down some mines on the bridge for extra security. **[Screen 06]**

Helicopter Transport Crew

The helicopters on this map are one of the PLA's strongest weapons and at least one, preferably two, needs to be launched into action as soon as possible. This is made a great deal easier by the fact that only one player is need to fly and operate weapons in the PLA helicopter, whereas a USMC helicopter needs three players to be fully armed. With two players each operating a helicopter there are still two available players free in this group to take control of the PTBR and offer ground support for the pilots.

Because of the forward-facing weaponry on the PLA Helicopter, the pilots will frequently need to take a very direct, and thus dangerous, flight path towards the USMC side of the lake. To lower the risk of being shot down, they should approach as low to the ground as they can and then come up over the trees to fire and then fly off quickly.

PLA VEHICLE TACTICS

AVAILABLE VEHICLES

Vehicle Type	Amount of Vehicles
BJ2022 (equipped with QJC-88 HMG)	2
BJ2022 (equipped with LG3 Grenade Launcher)	1
Mi-171V5	2
PT Boat	1

Don't head straight to the village from the starting point, as the USMC will often be looking in that direction at the beginning. Instead, head to the southwest corner of the lake and then fly direct north until you reach the village, before firing off volleys of rockets at targets below. From the village the helicopter should fly northwest towards the area where the USMC Helicopter Crew spawns to see if there are any enemies of vehicles left in the area. If so, take them out with another volley of rockets.

The openness of the southern half of the lake does not lend itself to the stealthy grenade barrages from the PTBR that are possible from behind the cover of the islands in the north. PLA boat operators should instead rely on quick strafing runs along the shore of the lake, making full use of the side-mounted MGs. When approaching the bridge, the boat driver should make a shallow turn well in advance to give the gunners the maximum time possible to fire on their targets. Then, as the boat heads back to the friendly side of the lake, the rear gunner can provide covering fire to try to deter any USMC AT gunners from taking a shot.

BATTLE FOR MOLOGA RIDGE
MAP 02

This map centers on the conflict over control of Mologa village, which is to be found northwest of the large mountain ridge from which it takes its name. The USMC forces start northeast of the village on a road that leads directly to it. This gives them a small but significant speed advantage in getting to the village. PLA forces start from the south, just behind the ridge, which provides them with some excellent cover from which to launch assaults on the village. On this map, both teams have access to their forces' strongest armored units, so there will be plenty of shells flying from both sides. Victory is all but ensured for the team that gets a foothold in the village first.

USMC FORCE SUMMARY

AVAILABLE INFANTRY

Team	Class Icon	Team Member
Engineer Team		Combat Engineer
		Combat Engineer
		Anti-Tank Specialist
		Rifleman

Team	Class Icon	Team Member
Medium MG Team		Machinegunner
		Rifleman
		Machinegunner
		Rifleman

Team	Class Icon	Team Member
Sniper Team		Sniper
		Sniper
		Rifleman
		Machinegunner

Team	Class Icon	Team Member
Medic Team		Medic
		Rifleman
		Machinegunner
		Medic

AVAILABLE VEHICLES

Vehicle Type	Amount of Vehicles
DPV	2
LAV-25	2
M1A2	2
AH-6J	1

BATTLE FOR MOLOGA RIDGE – OVERVIEW

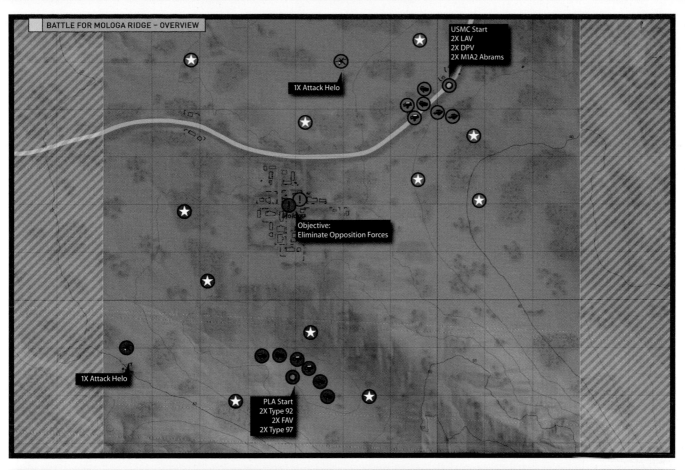

USMC Start
2X LAV
2X DPV
2X M1A2 Abrams

1X Attack Helo

Objective:
Eliminate Opposition Forces

1X Attack Helo

PLA Start
2X Type 92
2X FAV
2X Type 97

BATTLE FOR MOLOGA RIDGE – DETAIL

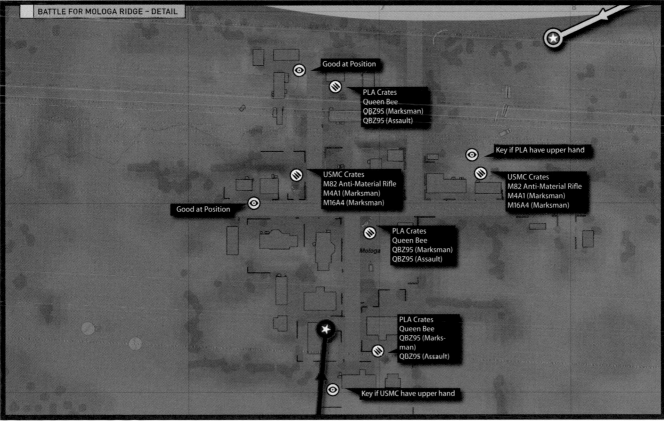

Good at Position

PLA Crates
Queen Bee
QBZ95 (Marksman)
QBZ95 (Assault)

Key if PLA have upper hand

USMC Crates
M82 Anti-Material Rifle
M4A1 (Marksman)
M16A4 (Marksman)

USMC Crates
M82 Anti-Material Rifle
M4A1 (Marksman)
M16A4 (Marksman)

Good at Position

PLA Crates
Queen Bee
QBZ95 (Marksman)
QBZ95 (Assault)

PLA Crates
Queen Bee
QBZ95 (Marks-
man)
QBZ95 (Assault)

Key if USMC have upper hand

05

USMC INFANTRY TACTICS

Engineer Team

The sheer number of mines available to this team, thanks to the two Combat Engineers, can be used to deadly effect in the small, narrow dirt lanes that enemies are forced to use when moving around the village. Placing mines in front of access points into buildings can also be very effective in denying the enemy the opportunity to get into a good shooting position without your having to actually watch the location. This allows the engineers to move off to a different building and rig it with a C4 charge, before retreating to a safe location. From there they can switch to their main weapon and try to 'guide' enemy players towards where the explosive has been placed, at which point they can switch to the trigger device and detonate the charge, taking the enemy out.

Although the AT gunner starts with only a couple of rockets, there are numerous Queen Bees to be found in the ammo crates around the village. To make sure they remain an effective AT threat, players should try and stay relatively close to one of these ammo sources, but not too close so that the crates get taken out in an explosion. The houses around the north of the village are excellent for this, as they are close to the ammo crates and offer a good line of sight down to the PLA side. **[Screen 01]**

Medium MG Team

The MG Team is best suited to handling enemy infantry and, as such, they should primarily try and operate in and around the outskirts of the village. The interior of the village offers a large selection of excellent positions from which the team can start laying down some suppressing fire. This can involve anything, from firing through a window from inside a building to firing over a broken wall; the most important thing for players to remember is to always watch the spacing between them.

To avoid having the whole team wiped out by a single shell, players should always try not to occupy the same building, or to get too close to each other in other positions. To help them with their infantry killing, this team is also perfectly suited to using the LAV-25s. The speed and strength of the vehicle will allow the team to get right into the thick of the action, at which time the two machinegunners can exit and add their own significant firepower to that of the vehicle and take down large groups of enemy soldiers.

Sniper Team

As there is so much potential heavy weapons' fire on this map, getting to, and changing, locations quickly is highly important to the Sniper Team. To help them do this, they should take over one of the DPVs from the start area. These extremely fast vehicles will let the snipers move about much quicker, while also giving them extra firepower if they get into trouble.

There are a number of good sniping positions within the village, where second-floor windows or the sides of buildings can be used for cover, but things can often get quite intense. Sometimes it is better for the Sniper Team to back off a little to get a better view of the area and select their targets more easily. **[Screen 02]** The group of trees just south of the small group of houses that lie northwest of the village is an excellent position, with a direct line of sight straight past the village to the PLA start area. The two snipers should ideally operate together, away from the other two members of this team, who should stick close to the village and relay information back about enemy locations.

Medic Team

Establishing a strong foothold as quickly as possible is the most important factor in this mission, and so the Medic Team should focus on that rather than on support, since there will usually not be much call for medical assistance at the start of a round. Taking control of one of the M1A2s is a good option for them at the start of a round, as it will help the other teams a great deal. Once the tank has established a good shooting position around the outskirts of the village, a couple of team members should leave the vehicle and try to gather some extra weapons from the ammo crates. Depending on which crates are used, the players will be able to help with either taking down enemy armor with the Queen Bee or taking out enemy AT gunners with the M82A1. **[Screen 03]**

While the players outside the tank are inside the village they should try and assist any friendly soldiers who need medical assistance, as there are likely to be a lot of players taking moderate damage from explosive shell-splash damage, or from being in close proximity to a building that's being destroyed.

USMC VEHICLE TACTICS

The M1A2s are best utilized along the road on which the USMC start out. This fairly straight open area lets the tanks move around as needed to find their targets, while still using the buildings for cover. Support from infantry around the village will be absolutely necessary for the slow tanks to be effective and remain safe, especially against an enemy helicopter. This is best done by having one or two players within the village spotting for the tank and passing on target information and threat assessments.

The LAV-25s have good off-road mobility and can be used very effectively for flanking maneuvers by having them head south from the starting area some distance away to the east of the village, and then heading west across the top of the ridge to fire on the PLA forces from behind. This must be done with caution, however, as the PLA may have spotters on the ridge line, so drivers need to make sure the area is clear and they are not heading into a trap. The most deadly force on the map, however, may well be the AH-6J, with its extremely powerful weapons and high maneuverability. It is capable of taking down anything the enemy has to offer. Strafing runs along the centre of the village with the miniguns can cut down large groups of enemy troops in no time and, while rockets can also be very effective in this situation, they are best saved for either enemy armor or a specific building that is a known enemy stronghold.

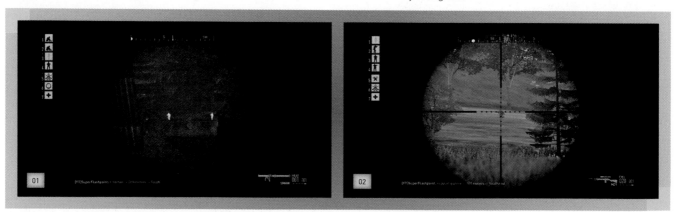

PLA FORCE SUMMARY

AVAILABLE INFANTRY

Team	Class Icon	Team Member
Grenadier Team		Grenadier
		Rifleman
		Rifleman
		Combat Engineer

Team	Class Icon	Team Member
Medic Team		Medic
		Machinegunner
		Rifleman
		Medic

Team	Class Icon	Team Member
Sniper Team		Sniper
		Machinegunner
		Sniper
		Rifleman

Team	Class Icon	Team Member
Anti-Tank Team		Anti-Tank Specialist
		Machinegunner
		Anti-Tank Specialist
		Combat Engineer

AVAILABLE VEHICLES

Vehicle Type	Amount of Vehicles
FAV	2
Type 92 WZ551A	2
ZBD97	2
AH-6J	1

PLA INFANTRY TACTICS

This team should aim to establish a position on the ridge line with one Type 92 and one Type 99, if possible. Having a strong armored presence up on the ridge can prove devastating for the USMC forces along the road to the north. The Grenadiers can also be extremely effective from the ridge with their underslung Grenade Launcher, which can reach the USMC forces easily when fired with a slight arc. **[Screen 04]** If there is a break in the action, the Combat Engineers on this team should try and head down into the village to set up some traps with their mines.

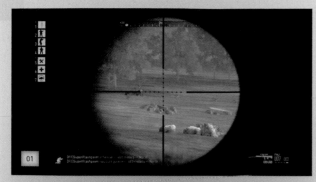

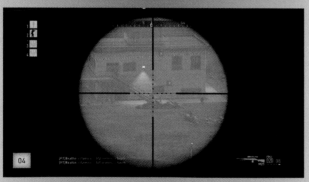

Medic Team

Similar to the USMC Medic Team, their PLA counterpart is best used in an offensive capacity at the start of the round by operating one of the Type 99 Tanks. An excellent place for them to position the tank is the area around the large silos to the west of the village. From here the tank will be able to fire on enemy armor along the road, and also on infantry positions within the village, with the added cover of the silos for protection. As the village is only a short distance away from the silos, the medics will also be able to run to the aid of any wounded allies in the area.

If the players are looking to fill a more supportive role then they should head to the ridge, where a large number of friendly forces will be stationed. A second tank can still be quite effective and, at the same time, will allow the medics to help wounded soldiers in the area. If they choose to come up here and keep most of the PLA armor in a single position, they will need to keep a keen eye out in the skies above for the enemy helicopter. Shooting the helicopter down as soon as it appears will be vital, as it has the power to wipe out a large group of vehicles in a single pass.

Sniper Team

The ridge east of the PLA starting point can be reached very quickly by snipers using the FAVs, and there are a couple of sandbagged areas along the way that are excellent places for sniping USMC forces as they move towards the village. **[Screen 01]** There will be little call to leave the ridge, as there are not many other positions that offer as good a view of the area as that one, but the snipers up there will still need to change positions so that USMC armor does not get a fix on their location. With such a good view of the area it is very unlikely that any enemies will be able to get close to the snipers; the main threat will come from the enemy AH-6J.

If there is no assistance up on the ridge from other teams it will be up to the other members of this team to deal with the helicopter. To accomplish this they should head down into the village in one of the FAVs and try to get a Queen Bee Rocket Launcher. **[Screen 02]** They can then either head back up to the sniping position and defend the area from there, or help out in the village and only use the Queen Bee if one of the snipers asks for assistance. Alternatively, the snipers can attempt to take out the pilot of the helicopter with their rifles; this can be done but is also very difficult due to the high speed of the helicopter.

Anti-Tank Team

The interior of the village is where this team is best put to use. The myriad houses offer great vantage points for the AT gunners where they can try and line up shots on enemy armor along the road, while receiving cover fire from the machinegunner. With some heavy cover fire from the other members of this team and the teams on the ridge, the Combat Engineers should try to lay their AT mines along the road to the north of the village to prevent its use by enemy vehicles. They can then head back into the village and use their AP mines around some of the ammo crates to take out enemy soldiers trying to resupply.

Once the road has been mined or the enemy vehicles have been destroyed, the members of this team should split up, head into different buildings and take on the enemy soldiers from the windows with their rifles. The AT gunners, however, should always make sure they have some ammo for their rocket launcher, just in case they need to take out an enemy-held building.

PLA VEHICLE TACTICS

The USMC are likely to be using their AH-6J a great deal to try and destroy the PLA forces along the ridge, and the best means of taking down that vehicle is another AH-6J. Players in control of the helicopter can also make use of the ridge by making it hover out of sight behind it. Then, when they get the word from the troops at the top that the enemy helicopter is approaching, they can fly up and take them by surprise.

Also, as the USMC starting area is out in the open along a road, it can make them easy targets for the helicopter's miniguns, which can reach them even when fired from above the ridge. **[Screen 03]** A strong armored presence on the ridge will certainly make things easier for the PLA soldiers in the village, as it offers an unparalleled view of the area, allowing them to bombard the enemy constantly with shells.

INFILTRATION
CHAPTER 05

In Infiltration, players will get to choose to be either a part of a small and highly specialized US Spec Ops squad, or a member of a larger PLA squad. The Spec Ops Team is tasked with infiltrating the enemy position and taking out a designated target, while superior in number PLA forces have to defend the area. Victory is achieved when either the Spec Ops Team destroys the target, or the PLA forces manage to defend until the time expires. This mode allows players to focus more on

tactics and preparation than annihilation, and will reward the teams that come up with the superior strategies. The PLA forces always start closer to the objective, so they will have the chance to try and set up an impenetrable defensive wall. The Spec Ops Team on the other hand will need to rely on stealth and probing attack to try and ascertain a weak point before moving in to strike.

HIGH POINT
MAP 01

High Point is set in and around Raskova Airfield, which contains the radio tower objective point. This airfield should be immediately familiar to players who have been through the Campaign mode, although a lot of tweaks have been introduced so that the same strategies will not be as useful. Knowing

the lie of the land will still be extremely useful for players, however, as a lot of the cover points still remain the same. US forces must move in and gain control of the airfield for long enough to give them time to plant and detonate a C4 charge somewhere in the radio tower to achieve victory.

USMC FORCE SUMMARY

AVAILABLE INFANTRY

Team	Class Icon	Team Member
SO Night Ops Team		SF Leader
		SF Medic
		SF Rifleman
		SF Rifleman

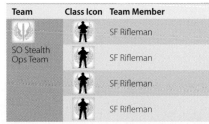

Team	Class Icon	Team Member
SO Stealth Ops Team		SF Rifleman
		SF Rifleman
		SF Rifleman
		SF Rifleman

Team	Class Icon	Team Member
SO Stealth Sniper Team		SF Sniper
		SF Sniper

AVAILABLE VEHICLES

Vehicles Type	Amount of Vehicles
DPV	4

USMC STRATEGY

The US starts on a beach about 1.5km northwest of the radio tower with four Desert Patrol Vehicles in front of them, each seating three people each (one driver and two gunners). These provide enough transport for the entire squad to move around the map. There are also small ammo crates under camouflage nets next to this starting position with more demo charges in them. Make sure all human players are equipped with these. The Fire Team Leaders in the US team also have access to three smoke mortar strikes between them, which can be called in at any time. It is normally best for the US team to split up their attacking force, as the superior numbers of the PLA will probably overwhelm them if they are spotted.

The Stealth Sniper Team have a few good positions open to them, most notably the cliff overlooking the airbase to the north. If the US Team take this area, they will be able to snipe into the base easily, as they have superior scopes to those on the PLA's weaponry. This spot also has an emplaced MG and some sandbags for cover, which will be necessary in order to keep control of the area, especially as the PLA can mount a formidable counter-attack from the east. **[Screen 04]**

Due to the relative proximity to the PLA spawning area, they may have taken it before the US Teams arrive, so any players heading to this location should be ready for a fight. Two other notable sniping positions are from along the runway into the base, and also from the temporary defenses to the south of the runway, facing the radio tower. The US may wish to give the area a wide berth with their vehicles, if they want to remain undetected.

The other two US Teams, Night Ops and Stealth Ops, have a number of different approach vectors. Coming in from the north, down the cliff or along

the road, may seem like the quickest way into the base, but it is also the most hazardous. The PLA have a lot of cover around here and may be able to take down players from distance as they approach. They also have an MG nest in the northwest that has a wide field of view, if they have got it manned, so make sure you keep an eye on this position when moving towards the airfield. **[Screen 05]**

On the road leading to the airfield is a small, abandoned village, which can be used for cover to mask approaching players and also offer them cover when engaging the enemy from a distance. South of the village area is a small hillock which can be used for cover, but past this point are only a few trees to protect approaches to the runway. **[Screen 06]**

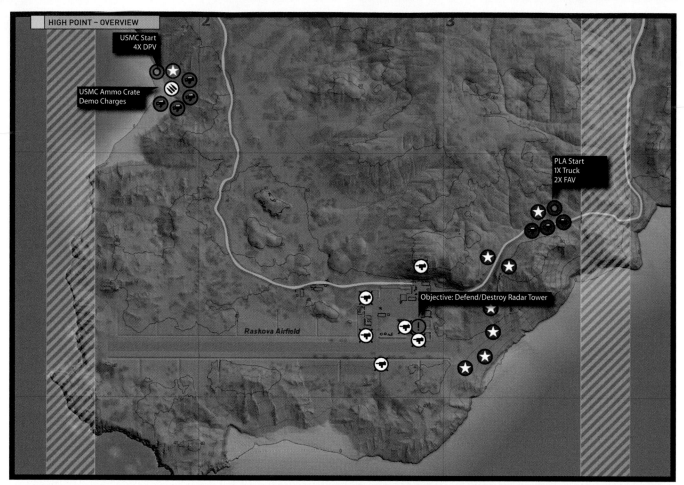

HIGH POINT – OVERVIEW

USMC Start
4X DPV

USMC Ammo Crate
Demo Charges

PLA Start
1X Truck
2X FAV

Objective: Defend/Destroy Radar Tower

Raskova Airfield

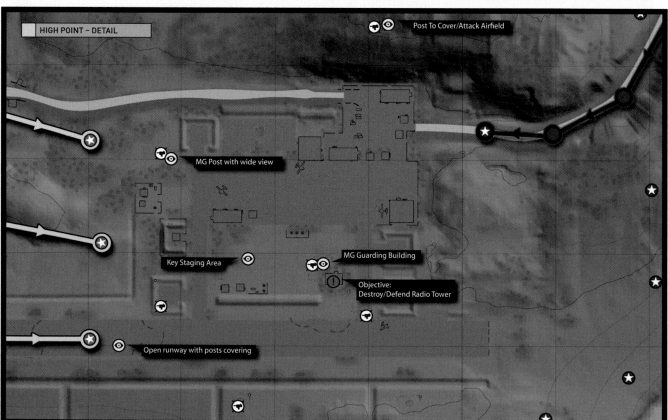

HIGH POINT – DETAIL

Post To Cover/Attack Airfield

MG Post with wide view

Key Staging Area

MG Guarding Building

Objective:
Destroy/Defend Radio Tower

Open runway with posts covering

When approaching the western side of the airfield, there are plenty of buildings and trees to cover an approach. Once inside the perimeter of the airfield, the building in the southwest corner of the plane parking bay is an excellent place to hole up before a final assault on the tower. Unfortunately, there is a machinegun nest the PLA can use that points directly towards this building, so take the MG gunner out as quickly as possible and lay down suppressing fire so that it can't be used. Watch out for riflemen in the upper levels of the tower itself, as the building offers an excellent vantage point and good cover, so is a likely enemy position.

Another approach to the base for the US team is along the runway itself, or just to the south of it. The runway has practically no cover at all, but the ditches that run north and south of it can provide just enough cover for players to sneak along. Near the radio tower is a collection of temporary

observation posts, some of which are equipped with MGs: specifically, one facing west and one south, right next to the radio tower. Once the US Teams manage to get past the first MG post, they can either keep to the south of the runway and launch an attack from the temporary huts, or move to the north side and use the long ridge and small buildings along from the tower.

On the US forces' final approach to the radio tower, it is recommended that they use the smoke mortars to cover players as they move in, as there is no substantial hard cover in any direction. At the moment the smoke hits, the best plan is for most US players to rush the tower and create panic among the PLA forces. This should provide just enough time for one player to plant the charge and detonate it for victory.

PLA FORCE SUMMARY

AVAILABLE INFANTRY

Team	Class Icon	Team Member
Squad Command Team		Fire Team Leader
		Rifleman
		Rifleman
		Rifleman
		Medic

Team	Class Icon	Team Member
Engineer Team		Combat Engineer
		Combat Engineer
		Combat Engineer
		Rifleman

Team	Class Icon	Team Member
Medic Team		Medic
		Medic
		Rifleman
		Rifleman

Team	Class Icon	Team Member
Light MG Team		Machinegunner
		Machinergunner
		Rifleman
		Rifleman
		Machinegunner

Team	Class Icon	Team Member
Support Team		Fire Team Leader
		Rifleman
		Medic
		Rifleman

AVAILABLE VEHICLES

Vehicle Type	Amount of Vehicles
FAV	2
SX2190	1

PLA STRATEGY

The PLA troops start off around 500m to the northeast along the road from the airfield. Most of the troops start in the PLA truck, while the PLA Support Team starts on foot by two PLA FAVs. The PLA Fire Team Leaders have access to one Mortar strike and three Medium air strikes between them, which can be called in at any time. At the start of the round, the PLA's primary concern should be to get the bulk of their forces to the objective as quickly as possible, so that the US team cannot catch them unawares.

The objective is to stop the US from destroying the radio tower, so it makes good sense to have a lot of PLA forces directly around it. There are two emplaced MGs around the tower, one facing south and one facing northwest. The northwest gun is the more useful of the two, as it overlooks a group of trees and buildings that the US forces often use to mask their approach. **[Screen 01]** The many sandbags around the tower, as well as those inside of the building, provide excellent cover, especially for soldiers with rifle weaponry. From the first floor and roof you can easily cover most approaches, including having a good line of sight to the MG nest on the cliff to the north.

A small contingent of PLA forces may want to head to the cliff camp so that the US Team can't use it as a sniping position. It also gives the PLA good spotting positions if they get their binoculars out. The MG can be used on the immediate area below the camp, but is better for scaring the US teams rather than eliminating them efficiently.

If the PLA successfully engage and eliminate US players at close range, it is highly advisable to make sure their superior weapons are scavenged.

These weapons have under-slung grenade launchers and thermal scopes, which make defending the area much easier, so if a US Spec Ops weapon is acquired, it is recommended that the soldier falls back to a good defensive position to make the most of it. Two recommended areas would be the hangar to the east, as it has a good view of the north side of the base, or the control tower itself. If a player manages to get their hands on a thermal scope, they will have the best visibility on the PLA side, so they should try to call out targets for the rest of the PLA forces.

It is most likely that the US team will attack somewhere along the west flank, but in case they manage to maneuver around this flank successfully, it is best to keep most of the PLA within a short distance of the tower itself. A good tactic is to send out single soldiers to specific key points, where they can act as an early warning signal for the rest of the squad if engaged by the enemy. It may also be beneficial to get human players to mount the two MG emplacements to the west to ensure that the most direct route is also covered properly. **[Screen 01]**

It is important to bear in mind that the FAVs (as well as the DPVs, if they are commandeered from the US team) can be parked in good defensive positions to add extra support, due to the fact that they each have two MGs mounted on them. This may help defend the objective from more angles that the emplaced MGs allow. **[Screen 02]**

The two key US approaches are along the runway and through the buildings on the western side of the airfield. Keep them at bay for as long as possible, concentrating on one Fire Team at a time, so they have less chance to heal each other and spawn back together. If the US Teams appear to be staying in one place, call in a small air strike on whatever they are using for cover, or, if they are spread out over a large area, use a scattered mortar strike. Remember that both weapons have a delay after they are called, especially in the case of the air strike, which takes around 20 seconds to deploy, so make sure you use it well.

If the US Team gets close to the radio tower, or they fire smoke rounds, all players should concentrate fire on defending the base at all costs, using explosives or firing machine guns into the smoke to take out as many US soldiers as possible. Keep your eyes peeled for any US soldiers who are not firing their weapons. These will be the Fire Team Leaders who will be preparing their C4 charges, so make sure you kill them as quickly as possible.

ON HOME SOIL
MAP 02

Combat on this map will be predominantly confined to the narrow alleys of Madlenka Village and the open valley surrounding it. US Spec Ops forces have to make their way across the expansive area with only minimal cover, as they try to destroy the Sunburn Launcher in the courtyard to the south of the village. PLA forces will need to make full use of the houses within the village to set up kill zones for the approaching enemies. With so many possible approach vectors for the US Team, the only thing limiting them is their lack of vehicles. PLA forces must use this to their advantage and use the superior speed offered by their vehicles to track down their slow, but stealthy, enemies.

USMC FORCE SUMMARY

AVAILABLE INFANTRY

Team	Class Icon	Team Member
SO Night Ops Team		SF Leader
		SF Medic
		SF Rifleman
		SF Rifleman

Team	Class Icon	Team Member
SO Stealth Ops Team		SF Rifleman
		SF Rifleman
		SF Rifleman
		SF Rifleman

Team	Class Icon	Team Member
SO Stealth Sniper Team		SF Sniper
		SF Sniper

AVAILABLE VEHICLES

No vehicles are available to the USMC forces on this map

USMC STRATEGY

The US team starts up the beach about 1km north of the radio tower without any extra transport; they must make their way across the map on foot. There are also small ammo crates under camouflage nets next to this starting position with more demo charges in them, so make sure all human players take these. The Fire Team Leaders of the US teams also have access to three smoke mortar strikes between them that can be called at any time.

It is advisable for the US team to start moving as quickly as possible towards Madlenka but, as the PLA will always arrive a long time before them, they should not be afraid to allow more time to get into advantageous positions, such as flanking or encircling the area.

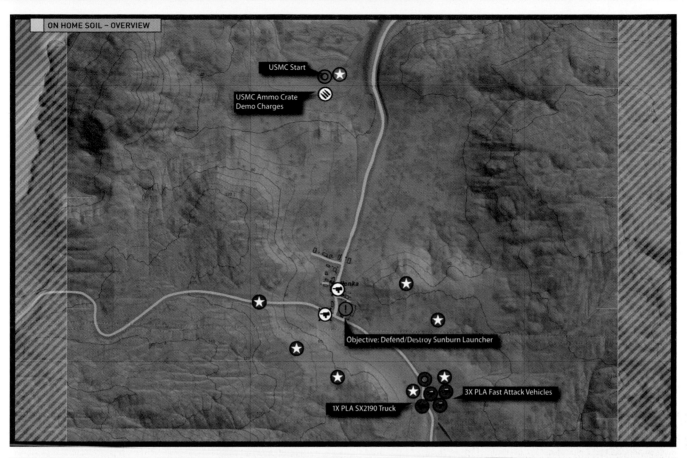

ON HOME SOIL – OVERVIEW

USMC Start

USMC Ammo Crate
Demo Charges

Objective: Defend/Destroy Sunburn Launcher

3X PLA Fast Attack Vehicles

1X PLA SX2190 Truck

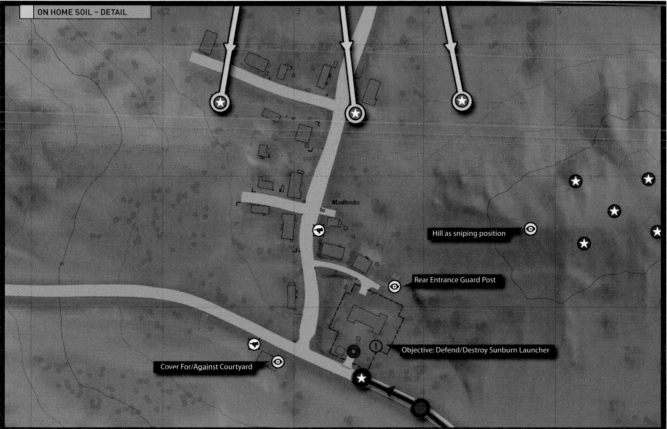

ON HOME SOIL – DETAIL

Madlenka

Hill as sniping position

Rear Entrance Guard Post

Objective: Defend/Destroy Sunburn Launcher

Cover For/Against Courtyard

05

The most beneficial sniping position is from the hill to the northeast of the courtyard building, but the PLA may also have knowledge of this and a Recon Team may be waiting here. **[Screen 01]** If players can take this position, the view into the courtyard with the US thermal scopes will make it easy to take out much of the defending force. From here players can then launch their assault down towards the rear entrance. The whole of the courtyard, however, has many physical barriers around it, so it's easy to defend. If there are enough C4 available, players can use some to destroy the east wall and surprise the enemy; why not time this with some cover from the smoke mortars to maximize the effect?

To avoid detection, the US Team can approach through the buildings on the west side of the main road, which provides more cover. **[Screen 02]** It is advisable to go between or behind the buildings rather than on the road, because there is an emplaced MG facing down the road. Flanking this position from the west should be fairly simple if there is an enemy on the MG. Once the US Team have advanced to near the back entrance to the courtyard, a good tactic might be to enter the building to use it as cover, since it's dark inside, and whittle down the PLA defenses before making a charge for the back gate.

Another tactic for this area is to attack the front entrance on the south side by flanking a long way round to the west and then to the south of the village, and to snipe into the courtyard from here. Watch out for respawning PLA coming from the southeast, however. At the courtyard, the USMC should do all they can to get inside the area and be as aggressive as possible, since the PLA's superior numbers enable them to get reinforcements quite quickly. The moment players have entered the courtyard they need to act as quickly as possible and create confusion for the Fire Team Leader while they lay the charges.

PLA FORCE SUMMARY

AVAILABLE INFANTRY

Team	Class Icon	Team Member
Squad Command Team		Fire Team Leader
		Rifleman
		Rifleman
		Rifleman
		Medic

Team	Class Icon	Team Member
Engineer Team		Combat Engineer
		Combat Engineer
		Combat Engineer
		Rifleman

Team	Class Icon	Team Member
Medic Team		Medic
		Medic
		Rifleman
		Rifleman

Team	Class Icon	Team Member
Light MG Team		Machinegunner
		Machinergunner
		Rifleman
		Rifleman
		Machinegunner

Team	Class Icon	Team Member
Support Team		Fire Team Leader
		Rifleman
		Medic
		Rifleman

AVAILABLE VEHICLES

Vehicle Type	Amount of Vehicles
FAV	3
SX2190	1

PLA STRATEGY

The PLA troops start off around 500m to the southeast along the road from the village. Most of the troops start in the PLA truck, and the PLA Support Team start on foot by three PLA Fast Attack Vehicles, each seating three people (one driver and two gunners). The PLA Fire Team Leaders have access to one mortar strike and three small air strikes between them, which can be called in at any time.

At the start of the round, the PLA's primary concern should be to get the bulk of their forces to the objective as quickly as possible, so that the USMC can't catch them unawares. One of the most effective attack vectors for the US team is from the hill to the northeast of the village. The best option for the PLA is to block this area off, or at least delay the US Team's capture of the hill for some time. The easiest way to achieve this is for the support team to take one or two FAVs to the hilltop to use as emplaced weaponry and defend the hill from cover.

Most of the PLA troops should be inside the main courtyard, where there are many nooks and crannies offering a good view of the north or south entrances to the area. **[Screen 03]** Using the building may also be a good defensive strategy. By keeping most of the troops in the courtyard you will help keep the US Team at bay, but be aware that their snipers have multiple views into the area that can be very effective against bunched-up troops.

There are small, temporary sandbag camps around the courtyard that offer good defensive positions, especially the one by the north entrance. **[Screen 04]** However, the US Team coming in from the main road can easily flank this position. There are also defenses at the end of the road to the southwest, around a building. This area also has an emplaced MG, which points out into the fields and behind the buildings. PLA troops here will have to use sheer force to repel the US Team.

If the US Team gets into the courtyard, the PLA should fall back to positions from where the objective itself can be seen, such as inside the main building or between the building next to the south gate and the wall. At this time, the US Fire Team Leaders will be attempting to plant their charges, so players will need to especially aware of them and take them out before they can get near the objective.

05

EXTRA INTEL
CHAPTER 06

In this chapter you'll find Intel to complement your gaming experience. It includes a comprehensive index of military terminology used in the game, an Achievement and Trophy guide to help you unlock them all, and a Fire Team engagement mini-walkthrough. Use this chapter to gain a better understanding of the game, to unlock every Achievement or Trophy and gain a heads-up on the extra FTE missions that are available to download.

MILITARY TERMINOLOGY
CHAPTER 06

The following tables list all the relevant acronyms and terms used in the game. Consider this your 'go to' index for all things military while playing the game, and consult this table to decipher any obscure acronyms or terms. This Intel will make things much clearer as you play the game, and will increase your understanding of every situation.

ALPHABET CALL SIGNS

Lttr	Call Sign	Lttr	Call Sign
A	Alpha	N	November
B	Bravo	O	Oscar
C	Charlie	P	Papa
D	Delta	Q	Quebec
E	Echo	R	Romeo
F	Foxtrot	S	Sierra
G	Golf	T	Tango
H	Hotel	U	Uniform
I	India	V	Victor
J	Juliet	W	Whisky
K	Kilo	X	X-ray
L	Lima	Y	Yankee
M	Mike	Z	Zulu

GENERAL

Term	Meaning
AO	Area of Operation
Arty	Artillery
Copy	Understood or received well
FARP	Forward Arming and Refueling Point
FT	Fire Team
Klick	1,000 meters (1 km)
LZ	Landing Zone
Mikes	M for minutes, as in 2 mikes
On the Hook	On the line or radio
OP	Observation Point
Oscar Mike	OM, On the Move
RTB	Return To Base
SF	Special Forces
Sitrep	Situation Report
SO	Special Operations
Spec Ops	Special Operations

ORDNANCE & EQUIPMENT

Term	Meaning	Term	Meaning
AA	Anti-Aircraft	HMG	Heavy Machine Gun
AAA	Anti-Aircraft Artillery	HMMWV	High Mobility Multi-Purpose Wheeled Vehicle
AAVP	Amphibious Assault Vehicle Personnel (Carrier)	LMG	Light Machine Gun
ACOG	Advanced Combat Optical Gunsight	M	Model (as in M16, M21, etc.)
AGL	Automatic Grenade Launcher	MEU	Marine Expeditionary Unit
AP	Armor Piercing	MG	Machine Gun
AP	Anti-Personnel	MGL	Multiple Grenade Launcher
APDS	Armor Piercing, Discarding Sabot	Mk	Mark (as in Mk16, Mk17, etc.)
APFSDS	Armor Piercing, Fin Stabilized, Discarding Sabot	Mod	Modification (as in Mod 0, Mod 1, etc.)
APHE	Armor Piercing, High Explosive	NVG	Night Vision Goggles
AT	Anti-Tank	RPG	Rocket Propelled Grenade
ATGM	Anti-Tank Guided Missile	SAW	Squad Automatic Weapon
FMJ	Full Metal Jacket	SCAR	Special Forces Combat Assault Rifle
HE	High Explosive	SMG	Sub-Machine Gun
HEAT	High Explosive, Anti-Tank	SOC	Special Operations Capable
HEDP	High Explosive, Dual Purpose	SPR	Special Purpose Rifle
HEF	High Explosive, Fragmentation	UAV	Unmanned Aerial Vehicle

USMC MILITARY RANKS

Abbrv	Rank	Abbrv	Rank
Pvt	Private	CW	Chief Warrant Officer
PFC	Private First Class	2ndLt	Second Lieutenant
LCpl	Lance Corporal	1stLt	First Lieutenant
Cpl	Corporal	Capt	Captain
Sgt	Sergeant	Maj	Major
SSgt	Staff Sergeant	LtCol	Lieutenant Colonel
GySgt	Gunnery Sergeant	Col	Colonel
MSgt	Master Sergeant	BGen	Brigadier General
1stSgt	First Sergeant	MajGen	Major General
MGySgt	Master Gunnery Sergeant	LtGen	Lieutenant General
SgtMaj	Sergeant Major	Gen	General
WO	Warrant Officer		

US FIRE TEAM AND PLA LOADOUTS PER CAMPAIGN MISSION
CHAPTER 06

If you need to know what you and your men will be packing, or if you have to find out how heavily armed the enemy is, this section is for you. Here, we will show you the complete loadouts (weapon and equipment) for every man on your team per mission, including your own personal inventory. You will also find out which PLA types will be present in each mission, and learn what all your PLA enemies are carrying.

US FIRE TEAM LOADOUTS

This section details your Fire Team per mission. Here, you'll discover who is on your team and what weapons and equipment they are carrying. This Intel will come in handy as it will allow you to better understand each man's abilities, and how you can use them most effectively. It is also handy to review your inventory to enable you to plan your attack strategies in each mission more effectively, and to tackle the Achievement and Trophy challenges.

MISSION 1: DRAGON RISING

SABER 2: SO ENGINEERING TEAM

Soldier	Weapons	Equipment
Mulholland (2ndLt): SF Leader	Mk16 Mod 0 (Assault): 9 clips, 9HE, 9 HEDP MEU (SOC): 5 clips Knife	M67 Frag: 2 M18 Smoke: 2 IR Strobe: 3 C4: 4 Night Vision Goggles Binoculars Field Dressing
Knox (Cpl):: SF Machinegunner	M249 SAW: 5 boxes MEU (SOC): 5 clips Knife	M67 Frag: 1 M18 Smoke: 1 Night Vision Goggles Binoculars Field Dressing
Morales (Cpl): SF Medic	Mk17 Mod 0 (Marksman): 9 clips MEU (SOC): 5 clips Knife	M67 Frag: 2 M18 Smoke: 2 Night Vision Goggles Binoculars Medical Kit
Winters (Cpl): SF Engineer	Mk17 Mod 0 (Marksman): 9 clips MEU (SOC): 5 clips SMAW: 3 HEAT Knife	M67 Frag: 4 M18 Smoke: 2 C4: 3 M14 AP Mine: 5 M21 AT Mine: 2 Night Vision Goggles Binoculars Field Dressing

MISSION 2: BLINDING THE DRAGON

SABER 2: SO ENGINEERING SCOUT TEAM

Soldier	Weapons	Equipment
Mulholland (2ndLt): SF Leader	Mk17 Mod 0 (Night Ops): 9 clips MEU (SOC): 5 clips Knife	M67 Frag: 2 M18 Smoke: 2 IR Strobe: 3 C4: 6 Night Vision Goggles Binoculars Field Dressing
Knox (Cpl): SF Machinegunner	Mk48 Mod 0: 5 boxes MEU (SOC): 5 clips Knife	M67 Frag: 1 M18 Smoke: 1 Night Vision Goggles Binoculars Field Dressing
Morales (Cpl): SF Medic	Mk17 Mod 0 (Night Ops): 9 clips MEU (SOC): 5 clips Knife	M67 Frag: 2 M18 Smoke: 2 Night Vision Goggles Binoculars Medical Kit
Winters (Cpl): SF Sniper	MP5A4 Sub-Machine Gun: 5 clips MEU (SOC): 5 clips M21 Sniper Rifle: 12 clips Knife	M67 Frag: 2 M18 Smoke: 2 M18A1 Claymore: 2 Night Vision Goggles Binoculars Field Dressing

MISSION 3: UNITED WE STAND

DAGGER 1 BRAVO: HEAVY ASSAULT TEAM

Soldier	Weapons	Equipment
Hunter (Sgt): Fire Team Leader	M16A4 (CQB): 12 clips MEU (SOC): 5 clips Knife	M67 Frag: 6 M18 Smoke: 2 IR Strobe: 2 M14 AP Mine: 6 Binoculars Field Dressing
Briggs (LCpl): Grenadier	M16A4 (Assault): 12 clips, 9 HE, 3 HEDP MEU (SOC): 3 clips Knife	M67 Frag: 2 M18 Smoke: 2
		M14 AP Mine: 6 Binoculars Field Dressing
Avery (PFC): Medic	M16A4 (Basic): 12 clips MEU (SOC): 3 clips Knife	Binoculars Medical Kit
Jedburgh (PFC): Machinegunner	M249 SAW: 4 boxes MEU (SOC): 3 clips Knife	M67 Frag: 4 Binoculars Field Dressing

MISSION 4: EAGLE OFFENSE

DAGGER 1 BRAVO: ANTI-TANK TEAM

Soldier	Weapons	Equipment
Hunter (Sgt): Fire Team Leader	M4A1 (Marksman): 9 clips MEU (SOC): 3 clips SMAW: 2 HEF, 2 HEAT Knife	M67 Frag: 4 M18 Smoke: 1 IR Strobe: 3 M14 AP Mine: 3 Binoculars Field Dressing
Jedburgh (PFC): Machinegunner	Mk48 Mod 0: 9 boxes MEU (SOC): 3 clips Knife	M67 Frag: 2 Binoculars Field Dressing
Avery (PFC): Medic	M16A4 (Basic): 10 clips MEU (SOC): 3 clips Knife	Binoculars Medical Kit
Briggs (LCpl): Anti-Tank Specialist	M16A4 (Basic): 9 clips MEU (SOC): 3 clips SMAW: 2 HEF, 2 HEAT Knife	M67 Frag: 1 Binoculars Field Dressing

MISSION 5: POWDER TRAIL

DAGGER 1 BRAVO: ASSAULT TEAM

Soldier	Weapons	Equipment
Hunter (Sgt): Fire Team Leader	M4A1 (CQB): 8 clips MEU (SOC): 3 clips SMAW: 2 HEF, 2 HEAT Knife	M67 Frag: 2 M18 Smoke: 1 IR Strobe: 3 Binoculars Field Dressing
Briggs (LCpl): Grenadier	M16A4 (Assault): 7 clips, 9 HE, 3 HEDP MEU (SOC): 3 clips Knife	M67 Frag: 2 M18 Smoke: 1 M14 AP Mine: 3 Binoculars Field Dressing
Avery (PFC): Medic	M16A4 (Basic): 7 clips MEU (SOC): 3 clips Knife	Binoculars Medical Kit
Jedburgh (PFC): Machinegunner	Mk48 Mod 0: 3 clips MEU (SOC): 3 clips Knife	M67 Frag: 1 Binoculars Field Dressing

MISSION 6: HIP SHOT

SABER 2: SO STEALTH OPS TEAM

Soldier	Weapons	Equipment
Mulholland (2ndLt): SF Leader	Mk16 Mod 0 (Stealth): 9 clips MEU (SOC): 5 clips Knife	M67 Frag: 2 M18 Smoke: 2 IR Strobe: 3 C4: 4 Night Vision Goggles Binoculars Field Dressing
Winters (Cpl): SF Rifleman	M16A4 (Stealth): 9 clips MEU (SOC): 5 clips Knife	M67 Frag: 1 M18 Smoke: 1 C4: 3 Night Vision Goggles Binoculars Field Dressing
Knox (Cpl): SF Rifleman	M4A1 (Stealth): 9 clips MEU (SOC): 5 clips Knife	M67 Frag: 1 M18 Smoke: 1 C4: 3 Night Vision Goggles Binoculars Field Dressing
Morales (Cpl): SF Medic	M16A4 (Stealth): 9 clips MEU (SOC): 5 clips Knife	M67 Frag: 2 M18 Smoke: 2 Night Vision Goggles Binoculars Medical Kit

MISSION 7: BLEEDING EDGE

DAGGER 1 BRAVO: ASSAULT TEAM

Soldier	Weapons	Equipment
Hunter (Sgt): Fire Team Leader	M16A4 (Marksman): 7 clips MEU (SOC): 3 clips Knife	M67 Frag: 2 M18 Smoke: 1 IR Strobe: 3 Binoculars Field Dressing
Briggs (LCpl): Grenadier	M16A4 (Assault): 7 clips, 9 HE, 3 HEDP MEU (SOC): 3 clips Knife	M67 Frag: 2 M18 Smoke: 1 M14 AP Mine: 3 Binoculars Field Dressing
Avery (PFC): Medic	M16A4 (Basic): 7 clips MEU (SOC): 3 clips Knife	Binoculars Medical Kit
Jedburgh (PFC): Machinegunner	M249 SAW: 3 clips MEU (SOC): 3 clips Knife	M67 Frag: 1 Binoculars Field Dressing

MISSION 8: LOOKING FOR LOIS

SABER 2: SO RESCUE TEAM

Soldier	Weapons	Equipment
Mulholland (2ndLt): SF Leader	Mk16 Mod 0 (Assault): 9 clips, 3 HE, 9 HEDP MEU (SOC): 5 clips Knife	M67 Frag: 2 M18 Smoke: 2 IR Strobe: 3 M21 AT Mine: 4 Night Vision Goggles Binoculars Field Dressing
Knox (Cpl): SF Machinegunner	Mk48 Mod 0: 5 clips MEU (SOC): 5 clips Knife	M67 Frag: 1 M18 Smoke: 1 Night Vision Goggles Binoculars Field Dressing
Morales (Cpl): SF Medic	Mk17 Mod 0 (Marksman): 9 clips MEU (SOC): 5 clips Knife	M67 Frag: 2 M18 Smoke: 2 Night Vision Goggles Binoculars Medical Kit
Winters (Cpl): SF Sniper	MP5A4 Sub-Machine Gun: 12 clips MEU (SOC): 5 clips M21 Sniper Rifle: 5 Knife	M67 Frag: 2 M18 Smoke: 2 M18A1 Claymore: 2 Night Vision Goggles Binoculars Field Dressing

MISSION 9: TRUMPETS SOUND

DAGGER 1 BRAVO: HEAVY ASSAULT TEAM

Soldier	Weapons	Equipment
Hunter (Sgt): Fire Team Leader	M16A4 (Assault): 7 clips, 7 HE, 2 HEDP MEU (SOC): 3 clips Knife	M67 Frag: 2 M18 Smoke: 1 IR Strobe: 3 M14 AP Mine: 3 Night Vision Goggles Binoculars Field Dressing
Briggs (LCpl): Grenadier	M16A4 (Assault): 7 clips, 9 HE, 3 HEDP MEU (SOC): 3 clips Knife	M67 Frag: 2 M18 Smoke: 1 M14 AP Mine: 3 Night Vision Goggles Binoculars Field Dressing
Avery (PFC): Medic	M16A4 (Basic): 7 clips MEU (SOC): 3 clips Knife	Binoculars Medical Kit
Jedburgh (PFC): Rifleman	M16A4 (Marksman): 7 clips MEU (SOC): 3 clips Knife	M67 Frag: 2 M18 Smoke: 1 Binoculars Field Dressing

MISSION 10: DECAPITATION

SABER 2: SO STEALTH OPS TEAM

Soldier	Weapons	Equipment
Mulholland (2nd Lt): SF Leader	M16A4 (Stealth): 5 clips MEU (SOC): 5 clips Model 82A1 (Night Ops): 9 clips Knife	M67 Frag: 2 M18 Smoke: 2 IR Strobe: 3 C4: 3 Night Vision Goggles Binoculars Field Dressing
Knox (Cpl): SF Rifleman	Mk17 Mod 0 (Marksman): 12 clips MEU (SOC): 5 clips Knife	M67 Frag: 4 M18 Smoke: 2 IR Strobe: 3 Night Vision Goggles Binoculars Field Dressing
Morales (Cpl): SF Medic	M16A4 (Stealth): 9 clips MEU (SOC): 5 clips Knife	M67 Frag: 2 M18 Smoke: 2 Night Vision Goggles Binoculars Medical Kit
Winters (Cpl): SF Sniper	M16A4 (Stealth): 5 clips MEU (SOC): 5 clips Model 82A1 (Night Ops): 9 clips Knife	M67 Frag: 2 M18 Smoke: 2 IR Strobe: 3C4: 3 Night Vision Goggles Binoculars Field Dressing

MISSION 11: DRAGON FURY

DAGGER 1 BRAVO: QCB ASSAULT TEAM

Soldier	Weapons	Equipment
Hunter (Sgt): Fire Team Leader	M16A4 (Night Ops): 7 clips MEU (SOC): 3 clips FGM-148 Javelin: 1 HEAT Knife	M67 Frag: 2 M18 Smoke: 1 IR Strobe: 3 Night Vision Goggles Binoculars Field Dressing
Jedburgh (PFC): Rifleman	M4A1 (CQB): 7 clips MEU (SOC): 3 clips Knife	M67 Frag: 2 M18 Smoke: 1 M18A1 Claymore: 2 Night Vision Goggles Binoculars Field Dressing
Avery (PFC): Medic	M16A4 (Basic): 7 clips MEU (SOC): 3 clips Knife	Night Vision Goggles Binoculars Medical Kit
Briggs (LCpl): Combat Engineer	M16A4 (Basic): 8 clips MEU (SOC): 9 clips Knife	M67 Frag: 2 M18 Smoke: 2 C4: 2 M21 AT Mine: 2 M14 AP Mine: 5 Night Vision Goggles Binoculars Field Dressing

PLA LOADOUT AND CAMPAIGN MISSION ASSIGNMENT

Here you'll find two sets of data, the first of which is a series of charts showing each PLA enemy type you will encounter in each mission, and a master loadout table showing the weapons and equipment carried by each PLA enemy type. Use this information to better understand the threat you are facing and to find out which weapons and equipment to seize from each PLA type. Knowledge of the weapons carried by each PLA will be advantageous when planning your attack strategies and if you decide you need a little extra weaponry to destroy your adversaries.

MISSION 1: DRAGON RISING

Fire Team Leader	Rifleman
Machinegunner	
Mounted Rifleman	
Queen Bee AT Specialist	

MISSION 2: BLINDING THE DRAGON – PLA ENEMIES

Anti-Aircraft Specialist	Helicopter Pilot	Mounted Fire Team Leader	Rifleman
Engineer	Machinegunner	Mounted Medic	Rifleman (Night Ops)
Fire Team Leader	Medic	Mounted Rifleman	Senior Officer
Grenadier	Medium Machine Gunner	Platoon Leader	Vehicle Driver

MISSION 3: UNITED WE STAND – PLA ENEMIES

Anti-Aircraft Specialist	Medic	Rifleman
Fire Team Leader	Medium Machine Gunner	
Grenadier	Queen Bee AT Specialist	
Machinegunner	Recon Rifleman	

MISSION 4: EAGLE OFFENSE – PLA ENEMIES

Anti-Aircraft Specialist	Medic
Engineer	Medium Machine Gunner
Grenadier	Rifleman
Helicopter Pilot	

MISSION 5: POWDER TRAIL – PLA ENEMIES

AFV Commander	Fire Team Leader	Machinegunner	Mounted Rifleman
AFV Crewman	Grenadier	Medic	Queen Bee AT Specialist
AFV Gunner	Helicopter Gunner	Medium Machine Gunner	Rifleman
Engineer	Helicopter Pilot	Mounted Fire Team Leader	

MISSION 6: HIP SHOT – PLA ENEMIES

Airborne SOF Engineer	Fire Team Leader	Mounted Rifleman
Airborne SOF Leader	Helicopter Pilot	Queen Bee AT Specialist
Airborne SOF Light Machinegunner	Machinegunner	Rifleman
Anti-Aircraft Specialist	Mounted Fire Team Leader	

MISSION 7: BLEEDING EDGE

Fire Team Leader	Rifleman
Machinegunner	Sniper
Medium Machine Gunner	
Queen Bee AT Specialist	

MISSION 8: LOOKING FOR LOIS – PLA ENEMIES

Airborne SOF Grenadier	Airborne SOF Medium Machinegunner	Machinegunner	Queen Bee AT Specialist
Airborne SOF Heavy Sniper	Airborne SOF Rifleman (Recon)	Medic	Rifleman
Airborne SOF Leader	Engineer	Medium Machine Gunner	Sniper
Airborne SOF Light Machinegunner	Fire Team Leader	Mounted Fire Team Leader	Vehicle Driver
Airborne SOF Medic	Helicopter Pilot	Mounted Rifleman	

MISSION 9: TRUMPETS SOUND

Fire Team Leader	Recon Rifleman
Grenadier	Rifleman
Machinegunner	
Queen Bee AT Specialist	

MISSION 10: DECAPITATION

Fire Team Leader	Medic
General Han	Rifleman
Helicopter Pilot	Sniper
Machinegunner	

MISSION 11: DRAGON FURY PLA ENEMIES

Airborne SOF AA Specialist	Airborne SOF Leader	Anti-Aircraft Specialist	Machinegunner
Airborne SOF AT Specialist	Airborne SOF Light Machinegunner	Engineer	Medic
Airborne SOF Engineer	Airborne SOF Medic	Fire Team Leader	Medium Machine Gunner
Airborne SOF Grenadier	Airborne SOF Medium Machinegunner	General Zheng	Queen Bee AT Specialist
Airborne SOF Heavy Sniper	Airborne SOF Rifleman	Grenadier	Rifleman

PLA LOADOUT

PLA Enemy Type	Weapons	Equipment
AFV Commander	QBZ95 (Rifle) QSZ92 Pistol	Type 86 Frag Grenade: 1 RDG2 Smoke Grenade: 1
AFV Crewman	QBZ95 (Rifle) QSZ92 Pistol	Type 86 Frag Grenade: 1
AFV Gunner	QBZ95 (Rifle) QSZ92 Pistol	Type 86 Frag Grenade: 1
Airborne SOF AA Specialist	QBZ95 (Rifle) QW-2 Anti-Aircraft Missile QSZ92 Pistol	Type 86 Frag Grenade: 1 RDG2 Smoke Grenade: 1
Airborne SOF AT Specialist	QBZ95 (Rifle) PF89 120mm Rocket (Queen Bee AT) QSZ92 Pistol	Type 86 Frag Grenade: 1 RDG2 Smoke Grenade: 1
Airborne SOF Engineer	QBZ95 (Rifle) PF89 120mm Rocket (Queen Bee AT) QSZ92 Pistol	Type 86 Frag Grenade: 4 RDG2 Smoke Grenade: 2 Type 72 Anti-Personnel Mine: 5 TM62 Anti-Tank Mine: 2
Airborne SOF Grenadier	QBZ95A Assault. 12 HE, 6 HEDP QSZ92 Pistol	Type 86 Frag Grenade: 2 RDG2 Smoke Grenade: 2 Type 72 Anti-Personnel Mine: 5
Airborne SOF Heavy Sniper	QCQ-05 Sub-Machine Gun M99 Anti-Material (Sniper) Rifle QSZ92 Pistol	Type 86 Frag Grenade: 1 RDG2 Smoke Grenade: 1 POMZ2 Claymore (Mine): 2
Airborne SOF Leader	QBZ95A Assault: 6 HE, 6 HEDP QSZ92 Pistol	Type 86 Frag Grenade: 2 RDG2 Smoke Grenade: 2
Airborne SOF Light Machinegunner	QBB95 Light Machine Gun QSZ92 Pistol	Type 86 Frag Grenade: 1 RDG2 Smoke Grenade: 1
Airborne SOF Medic	QBZ95 (Rifle) QSZ92 Pistol	Medic Pack Type 86 Frag Grenade: 2 RDG2 Smoke Grenade: 2
Airborne SOF Medium Machine-gunner	Infantry Type 67-II Medium Machine Gun QSZ92 Pistol	Type 86 Frag Grenade: 1 RDG2 Smoke Grenade: 1
Airborne SOF Rifleman	Type 81-1M Marksman Rifle QSZ92 Pistol	Type 86 Frag Grenade: 4 RDG2 Smoke Grenade: 2 IR Strobe Grenade: 3
Airborne SOF Rifleman (Recon)	Type 81-1M Marksman Rifle QSZ92 Pistol	Type 86 Frag Grenade: 4 RDG2 Smoke Grenade: 2 3x IR Strobe Grenade
Anti-Aircraft Specialist	QBZ95 (Rifle) QW-2 Anti-Aircraft Missile QSZ92 Pistol	
Engineer	QBZ95 (Rifle) QSZ92 Pistol	Type 86 Frag Grenade: 2 RDG2 Smoke Grenade: 2 Demo Charge: 1 Type 72 Anti-Personnel Mine: 3 TM62 Anti-Tank Mine: 2

PLA Enemy Type	Weapons	Equipment
Fire Team Leader	QBZ95A Assault: 7 HE, 2 HEDP QSZ92 Pistol	Type 86 Frag Grenade: 1 RDG2 Smoke Grenade: 1 RDG3 Red Smoke (Grenade): 1 IR Strobe Grenade: 3 Type 72 Anti-Personnel (Mine): 2
General Han	QSZ92 Pistol	
General Zheng	QSZ92 Pistol	
Grenadier	QBZ95A Assault: 9 HE, 3 HEDP QSZ92 Pistol	Type 86 Frag Grenade: 2 POMZ2 Claymore (Mine): 2
Helicopter Gunner	QCQ-05 Sub-Machine Gun QSZ92 Pistol	RDG3 Red Smoke (Grenade): 1
Helicopter Pilot	QCQ-05 Sub-Machine Gun QSZ92 Pistol	RDG3 Red Smoke (Grenade): 2
Machinegunner	QBB95 Light Machine Gun QSZ92 Pistol	Type 86 Frag Grenade: 1
Medic	QBZ95 (Rifle) QSZ92 Pistol	Medic Pack
Medium Machine Gunnerr	Infantry Type 67-II Medium Machine Gun QSZ92 Pistol	Type 86 Frag Grenade: 1
Type 31-1M Marksman Assault Rifle	Type 81-1A Assault: 7 HE, 2 HEDP QSZ92 Pistol	Type 86 Frag Grenade: 1 RDG2 Smoke Grenade: 1 IR Strobe Grenade: 3 Type 72 Anti-Personnel Mine: 2
Mounted Medic	Type 81-1 Rifle QSZ92 Pistol	Medic Pack
Mounted Rifleman	Type 31-1M Marksman Assault Rifle QSZ92 Pistol	Type 86 Frag Grenade: 1
Platoon Leader	QBZ95M Marksman (Rifle) QSZ92 Pistol	RDG2 Smoke Grenade: 2 RDG3 Red Smoke (Grenade): 1 IR Strobe Grenade: 3
Queen Bee AT Specialist	QBZ95 (Rifle) PF89 120mm Rocket (Queen Bee AT) QSZ92 Pistol	
Recon Rifleman	QBZ95M Marksman (Rifle) QSZ92 Pistol	Type 86 Frag Grenade: 2 RDG2 Smoke Grenade: 1
Rifleman	QBZ95M Marksman (Rifle) QSZ92 Pistol	Type 86 Frag Grenade: 1
Rifleman (Night Ops)	QBZ95 Night Ops (Rifle) QSZ92 Pistol	Type 86 Frag Grenade: 1
Senior Officer	QSZ92 Pistol	
Sniper	QBU88 Sniper Rifle QSZ92 Pistol	Type 86 Frag Grenade: 1 RDG2 Smoke Grenade: 1 POMZ2 Claymore Mine: 2
Vehicle Driver	QBZ95 (Rifle) QSZ92 Pistol	Type 86 Frag Grenade: 1

06

INFANTRY CAMPAIGN

You will unlock these Achievements / Trophies when you play as the Fire Team Dagger 1 Bravo and if you complete the mission indicated. As they are all Primary Objectives, you simply have to succeed in the mission and they are yours. Follow the walkthrough described earlier in this guide to get through every mission in the campaign.

Achievement / Trophy	Description
Tide's Out	Successfully hold the beachhead in Mission 3: United We Stand.
Runway Relief	Capture the airfield in Mission 4: Eagle Offense.
Sandman's Saviors	Extract the downed air crew in Mission 5: Powder Trail.
Resource Management	Secure the fuel depot in Mission 7: Bleeding Edge.
Uphill Struggle	Eliminate the PLA Mortar Site in Mission 9: Trumpets Sound.
Ship It	Assault the Naval base in Mission 11: Dragon Fury.

SPEC OPS CAMPAIGN

You will unlock these Achievements / Trophies when you play as the Fire Team Saber 2. Simply completing the mission indicated will unlock them. As these are all Primary Objectives, all you need to do is succeed in the mission, and they are yours. Follow the walkthrough described earlier in this guide to get through each mission in the campaign.

Achievement / Trophy	Description
Without Warning	Destroy Radar emplacement in Mission 1: Dragon Rising.
Saber Beats SAM	Disable the SAM sites in Mission 2: Blinding The Dragon.
Fly Away Peter, Fly Away Paul	Get to the extraction chopper in Mission 6: Hip Shot.
Heroic Rescue	Rescue the hostages in Mission 8: Looking For Lois.
Bug Out	Reach the extraction point in Mission 10: Decapitation.

INFANTRY BONUS OBJECTIVES

These are Bonus Objectives that you can work to achieve when playing as the Fire Team Dagger 1 Bravo. Unlocking these objectives will require some special gameplay to accomplish them.

Achievement / Trophy	Description
Get Creative	Destroy the PLA APC at the top of the beach in Mission 3: United We Stand
Hip Shooter	Destroy the fleeing PLA transport helicopter in Mission 4: Eagle Offense.
Hitchhiker	Destroy the PLA armored units around the ghost village in Mission 5: Powder Trail.
Ruthless Efficiency	Eliminate the remaining troops on the second line with one Mortar Barrage in Mission 7: Bleeding Edge.
Keep 'em Rolling	Ensure all the Abrams reach the supporting fire position in Mission 9: Trumpets Sound.
Vertical Envelopment	Pilot a Seahawk safely to the designated landing zone in Mission 11: Dragon Fury.

Get Creative

This one may prove a tad tricky. Firstly, the AAVPs in the area will quickly advance to the farmhouse and will often take out the PLA APC before you get the chance. Secondly, if you are fast and get to the farmhouse before the AAVPs, the PLA force there will be substantial and aggressive, and will be easily able to cut you down before you can make your shot.

However, it can be done. The best approach is to move fast to the first AA team in the trees to the northeast. Kill them quickly, and then scavenge the Queen Bee from the fallen AT gunner. Now run east and give the farmhouse a wide berth and try not to attract the attention of the PLA there. The PLA APC is further to the east on the road, and you will be able to see the APC if you can make it past the farmhouse to the small field to the east. Once you spot it, use the Queen Bee to take it out to unlock this Achievement / Trophy. **[Screen 01]**

Hip Shooter

Immediately after you destroy the two PLA APCs in Mission 4, you will be tasked with advancing to an emplaced grenade launcher. As you are crossing the field and moving to that new position, look to the south and you'll see a PLA transport chopper taking off and flying off to the west. You will have a SMAW with you but, as it isn't a guided missile, it can often miss. It is best to use your assault rifle and pump the chopper full of lead. A few well-placed rounds is all it takes to knock the chopper out of the air to unlock this Achievement / Trophy.

Hitchhiker

At the end of Mission 5 when you are making your escape to the evacuation point, two PLA APCs will enter the area and take up position to the north and northwest of the village. To take them out, have your men move on to the extraction point while you circle round and attack the APCs. If you saved your Fire Mission that you obtained earlier in the mission, then use it on one of the APCs. Otherwise, you'll need to save the two HEAT rockets for the SMAW you start the mission with; one HEAT rocket for each APC. Since you start the mission with a SMAW, it's simply a matter of saving the two HEAT rockets until the end of the mission to deal with the APCs.

Ruthless Efficiency

When you reach RV7, you'll receive a Fire Mission. There is a PLA Spotter team consisting of four PLA soldiers to the north. They are spread out, but if you use a barrage spread for your Fire Mission and target the middle ground between the PLA, you can take them all out easily with one strike. Use your binoculars to scan the area, locate the PLA and then target the strike to land amongst all four. A PLA will generally be lurking in the woods that will serve as your middle ground for the strike, so find him and launch the strike. **[Screen 02]**..

Keep 'em Rolling

To unlock this Achievement / Trophy, you simply need to quickly push the mission forward. Always ensure that you are well ahead of your Abrams, and quickly eliminate all the AT gunners you encounter. Make sure no AT gunner can attack your Abrams, and ensure that all the Abrams reach RV14 safely and you'll unlock this one.

Vertical Envelopment

In Mission 11, immediately after you secure Skoje village, two choppers will come in (assuming you knocked out the PLA AAA vehicles in time) to give you a ride to the next RV point. You can simply ride as a passenger, but to unlock this Achievement / Trophy, you must pilot the chopper yourself. Enter as the pilot, and then fly the chopper to the southwest where you'll find a purple smoke grenade indicating the landing zone. Land the chopper there to complete this achievement..

SPEC OPS BONUS OBJECTIVES

These are Bonus Objectives that you can attempt to achieve when you are playing as the Fire Team Saber 2. Unlocking these will require some special gameplay.

Achievement / Trophy	Description
Skirinka Island Tour	Find the PLA helicopter and fly it around Skirinka Island in Mission 1: Dragon Rising.
Ghost Ops	Eliminate the PLA Commander in Mission 2: Blinding The Dragon.
Fuel the fire	Destroy all of the PLA fuel trucks in Mission 6: Hip Shot.
Perfect Rescue	All hostages must survive in Mission 8: Looking for Lois.
Two Birds, One Stone	Eliminate Han and the radio station with one JDAM in Mission 10: Decapitation.

Skirinka Island Tour

This Bonus Objective for Mission 1 is fairly straightforward. After you have destroyed the SAM site on the western side of the island, walk down to the beach and you'll find an abandoned PLA chopper. Get in, and pilot the chopper round the coast of the island (either clockwise or counterclockwise). Follow the coastline and fly a complete tour of the island and this Achievement / Trophy is yours. **[Screen 03]**

If you haven't taken out the SAM site and PLA APC to the north, then you'll need to be extra careful in that area, as the PLA and APC will fire on you and could destroy the chopper. It's best to take out the PLA to the north first before trying to unlock this Achievement / Trophy.

Ghost Ops

In Mission 2, near the Sunburn site, there is a village filled with PLA (RV11). You do not have to attack this village unless you want to unlock this Achievement / Trophy. To unlock this one, launch an assault on the village and kill the PLA commander you will find there. Since you're going to the trouble of attacking the village, you'll want to kill every PLA present and, in so doing, kill the commander which will earn you this Achievement / Trophy.

Fuel the fire

During Mission 6 when you are about to the blow the fuel generator, you will find two PLA fuel trucks just south of the generator. Check your map to easily identify them. To unlock this Achievement / Trophy, you need to blow both of those trucks up. The easiest way to do this is to plant C4 on both trucks and on the generator and blow them up all at once. To do so, equip the C4, plant a charge, and then hit the Aim button (left trigger on the 360 or the L2 button on the PS3). Pressing this button will cycle you away from the C4 detonator and place another C4 charge in your hand. This allows you to place all three charges (one on the generator and one on each truck) and then exit the depot to a safe distance to blow them all up.

Perfect Rescue

A straightforward Achievement / Trophy. In Mission 8, simply make sure all four POWs survive. To make this easier, avoid engaging in combat as much as possible on your way to the airport. When you attack the airport, have the POWs hang back and let your men charge in first. Once the majority of the PLA are down, you can then enter the complex, mop up the last few and board the extraction helicopter to finish the mission.

Two Birds, One Stone

In Mission 10, one of your Secondary Objectives is to follow Han for recon to find out what he is doing. If you succeed in this objective (see the walkthrough for more details), you will be awarded a JDAM Fire Mission. Use the Air Strike from RV7 to destroy the radio antenna once Han is there. Using your binoculars, aim for the antenna when you launch the strike. Han should be near the antenna and you will kill him (and destroy the antenna) to earn you this Achievement / Trophy. **[Screen 01]**

MISCELLANEOUS

These Achievements / Trophies will require a particular type of gameplay to win them and, in some cases, a truly concerted effort. While some of them will be unlocked normally by playing through the whole campaign, there are few elusive ones that you'll have to really concentrate on if you want to unlock them.

Achievement / Trophy	Description
Dragon Rising	Complete the campaign on any difficulty.
Dragon Rising – Hardcore	Complete the campaign on Hardcore difficulty.
Shock and Awe	Call in your first air strike.
Hard Rain	Call in your first artillery barrage.
Low Blow	Kill an enemy vehicle with an AT mine.
Scrap Metal	Kill an enemy vehicle with an AT weapon.
Clear Skies	Kill an enemy vehicle with an AA weapon.
The Sky is Falling	Kill an enemy with a helicopter without using its weapons.
Squad Slayer	Kill or incapacitate 25 enemies.
Platoon Pounder	Kill or incapacitate 50 enemies.
Company Killer	Kill or incapacitate 100 enemies.
Unbloodied Hands	Complete a mission without directly killing anyone yourself.
All Patched Up	Apply a field dressing to an injured friend in Co-op mode.
Florence Nightingale Award	Apply the field dressing to other wounded soldiers 20 times.

Dragon Rising

The description says it all for this Achievement / Trophy. Simply complete the whole campaign on any difficulty level.

Dragon Rising – Hardcore

Again, the description says it all here. You'll need to complete the whole campaign in the Hardcore (hardest) difficulty level to unlock this one.

Shock and Awe

The first time you call in an Air Strike, you'll earn this one. The earliest op-

portunity to do this is in Mission 4, when the PLA armored vehicles move in to attack the Control Tower.

Hard Rain

The first time you call in an Artillery Strike, you'll unlock this Achievement / Trophy. The earliest opportunity to do this is in Mission 1, right after you destroy the radar array.

Low Blow

This one is very tricky indeed. You need to plant an AT mine and have an enemy vehicle run over it and destroy it; no easy task. You can get your hands

on an AT mine for the first time in Mission 1 from your teammate, Winters. This of course means that he'll have to be dead for you to take his inventory and, even if you do this, you'll be hard-pressed to find a PLA vehicle that travels a known route on which you can lay the trap. You can also steal AT mines from the PLA Engineer in various missions.

However, the easiest way to accomplish this task is to play Mission 8. That is the only mission in which you'll have AT mines in your personal inventory from the start. You have to clear the airport at the end of the mission, then have your men and the POWs board the evac helicopter. If you don't complete the mission by boarding the chopper yourself, PLA reinforcements will arrive. You have 5 minutes after entering the complex before those reinforcements roll in.

The reinforcements will drive in on the road just north of the complex, which gives you the perfect opportunity. Once you have cleared the complex and everyone but you is on the chopper, go to the road north of the complex and lay two AT mines. Put one in the left lane and one in the right lane. Now all you need do is wait for the convoy to roll in and run over the mines. The vehicles will be PLA APCs and the AT mine will severely damage them. Once a vehicle is hit by the mine, it will smolder and smoke. Wait 1 minute, and the vehicle will explode, thus earning you this Achievement / Trophy. **[Screen 02]**

Scrap Metal

You'll need to use an AT weapon such as the Queen Bee or SMAW to unlock this one. The earliest opportunity to do this is in Mission 1. There are AT gunners in the village to the south. Kill one and take the Queen Bee from him. Now head to the LZ, and you'll soon be assaulted by two PLA vehicles. Blow one of the vehicles away with the Queen Bee, and this Achievement / Trophy is yours.

Clear Skies

The easiest way to unlock this one is to complete the third Secondary Objective of Mission 4. There is a QW-2 AA Missile in a crate on the first floor of the control tower. Use it to take out the PLA attack chopper to unlock this one.

The Sky is Falling

This one may prove a tad difficult, but the easiest way by far to accomplish it is to play Mission 11. After taking Skoje village, you'll be able to board and pilot a chopper. You then fly to the designated landing zone where you can fly through a checkpoint and save your progress. This puts you in a fully functional chopper at a save point. Now from there, head east where

you will see an emplaced gunner on a hill. It will help to switch to the third person view when you try this.

Fly toward the emplaced gunner, and come in low and slow. When you are nearly above him, turn down the engines (thrust) to zero by pulling down on the right stick, causing your chopper to plummet down. Time this accurately, and you'll land right on top of the emplaced gunner and kill him, thus unlocking this Achievement / Trophy. **[Screen 03]**. It may take a few times to get this right, but since you're at a checkpoint in the chopper, all you need do is reload the last checkpoint and try as many times as it takes to do it.

Squad Slayer, Platoon Pounder and Company Killer

These three missions require you to kill 25, 50, and 100 PLA enemies respectively. Just play aggressively through the whole campaign once, and you'll get all three. If you plan to play on Hardcore to unlock the 'Dragon Rising – Hardcore' achievement, and you'll certainly unlock these three as you play.

Unbloodied Hands

For this one, you have to complete a mission without killing anyone yourself. The easiest mission by far in which to attempt this one is Mission 6: Hip Shot; a stealth mission where you spend more time avoiding combat than engaging in it. There is only one necessary kill in that mission; the guard in the small hut at RV4. You can order your men to kill him, and then sneak into the fuel depot to plant the C4 charges. As you move into the depot, try to avoid the PLA guarding the generator, or have your men engage them.

Once you plant the C4 on the generator, run back to the east and backtrack along the RV chain that got you to the depot. Remain in the woods and make your way to the extraction point. Once there, have your men attack the PLA while you hang back. Once the chopper arrives, it will take out any remaining PLA. Board the chopper and you will have accomplished this Achievement / Trophy.

All Patched Up

You'll have to play the game in Co-op mode to unlock this one. As the description indicates, apply a field dressing to a wounded teammate to unlock this Achievement / Trophy.

Florence Nightingale Award

As you play through the game, monitor your men closely and, the moment one is wounded, run over and apply a field dressing. Do this 20 times to unlock this Achievement / Trophy. **[Screen 04]**

FIRE TEAM ENGAGEMENTS
CHAPTER 06

The Fire Team engagements are a series of six short bonus missions. Each of these missions focuses on a single engagement in a critical area, which must be either secured or defended by the player's Fire Team. You may have to download these bonus missions to play them. Once you have them, you can access them from the single mission screen. They can be played either as a single player campaign or as single missions in Co-op mode.

NIGHT RAID
MISSION 01

A short Fire Team engagement, pitting one USMC Fire Team against a number of PLA Fire Teams in and around the pumping station. The player will have to take out the PLA forces stationed inside the complex, and then defend against a co-ordinated counterattack.

	Primary Objectives	Secondary Objectives
01	Eliminate all PLA around the pumping station	N/A
02	N/A	N/A

FORCE SUMMARY

ASSAULT TEAM

All four Fire Team members in this mission are identically equipped, and all use the same Mk17 Mod 0 (Night Ops) Assault Rifle. This means that there's no advantage in preferring one member over the others in a Co-op game.

LANCE CORPORAL TRANH (SF RIFLEMAN)

Initial Loadout	Primary Weapon	Mk17 Mod 0 (Night Ops)
	Primary Weapon Ammunition	12x20 FMJ round magazines
	Secondary Weapon	–
	Secondary Weapon Ammunition	–
	Additional Equipment	4xM67 Grenades, 1xM18 Smoke Grenade, 1xNVG

PRIVATE FIRST CLASS SCHLIENS (SF RIFLEMAN)

Initial Loadout	Primary Weapon	Mk17 Mod 0 (Night Ops)
	Primary Weapon Ammunition	12x20 FMJ round magazines
	Secondary Weapon	–
	Secondary Weapon Ammunition	–
	Additional Equipment	4xM67 Grenades, 1xM18 Smoke Grenade, 1xNVG

PRIVATE FIRST CLASS MORENO (SF RIFLEMAN)

Initial Loadout	Primary Weapon	Mk17 Mod 0 (Night Ops)
	Primary Weapon Ammunition	12x20 FMJ round magazines
	Secondary Weapon	–
	Secondary Weapon Ammunition	–
	Additional Equipment	4xM67 Grenades, 1xM18 Smoke Grenade, 1xNVG

PRIVATE FIRST CLASS LEVESQUE (SF RIFLEMAN)

Initial Loadout	Primary Weapon	Mk17 Mod 0 (Night Ops)
	Primary Weapon Ammunition	12x20 FMJ round magazines
	Secondary Weapon	–
	Secondary Weapon Ammunition	–
	Additional Equipment	4xM67 Grenades, 1xM18 Smoke Grenade, 1xNVG

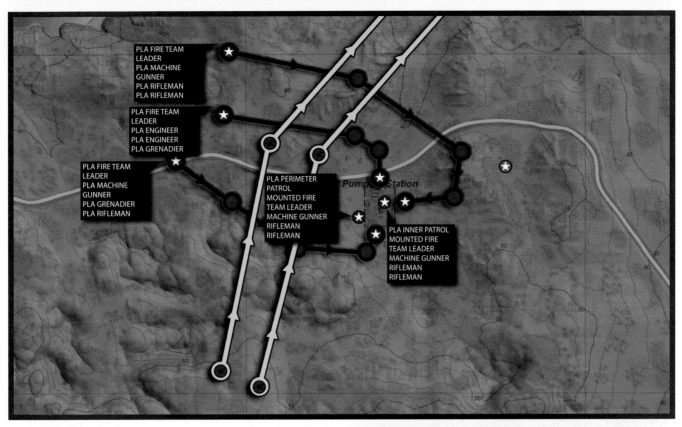

PLA FIRE TEAM
LEADER
PLA MACHINE
GUNNER
PLA RIFLEMAN
PLA RIFLEMAN

PLA FIRE TEAM
LEADER
PLA ENGINEER
PLA ENGINEER
PLA GRENADIER

PLA FIRE TEAM
LEADER
PLA MACHINE
GUNNER
PLA GRENADIER
PLA RIFLEMAN

PLA PERIMETER
PATROL
MOUNTED FIRE
TEAM LEADER
MACHINE GUNNER
RIFLEMAN
RIFLEMAN

Pumping Station

PLA INNER PATROL
MOUNTED FIRE
TEAM LEADER
MACHINE GUNNER
RIFLEMAN
RIFLEMAN

① Starting out

The player's Fire Team starts this mission in the dead of night, only a few hundred meters east of the objective, hidden by the brow of a hill. The team consists of Special Ops soldiers, and their equipment includes night vision goggles and thermal scopes on their weapons. Use these as much as possible; the great advantage over the PLA stationed here is that you can take them out at long range in a surprise attack. **[Screen 01]**

② Scouting the area

Heading toward the complex, use the scopes to note the positions of the PLA; one Fire Team patrols the inner area, while the second patrols outside the perimeter fence. Make sure your team are set to Fire on my Lead so you can choose the best time to strike. Try to wait until the teams are far away from each other and more spread out, and you can take them out individually. **[Screen 02]**

Three PLA teams will advance toward the pumping station from the northwest. Try to move swiftly and precisely to eliminate the opposition, aiming to take them out as early as possible, so that you do not have to fight both sets simultaneously. This will reduce the chance of being easily flanked or overrun. Two PLA attack helicopters are flying overhead on your way to the pumping station. Be sure to stay out of sight, because if they detect you, they will reveal your position to the rest of the PLA forces in the area, and you will lose the element of surprise.

③ Taking the complex

Advance into the complex itself as soon as you can to take advantage of some solid cover. Out in the surrounding hills it will be a lot easier for the PLA to take you down, though it can still be tactically useful to someone who prefers sniping from a distance. If you do head into the station, use the concrete and metal buildings and try to stay away from the pipes, as they can be confusing to navigate during combat. The houses to the southeast, northeast and southwest all give you an advantage as a staging area. Use your thermal scopes to spot the PLA early, and eliminate them as they head toward the complex to finish it with the lowest number of casualties.

01

02

COASTAL STRONGHOLD
MISSION 02

This Fire Team engagement sees one USMC Fire Team taking on a number of similarly equipped PLA Fire Teams in and around the lighthouse to the north of Skirinka Island. The player will have to take out the PLA stationed around the buildings, and then defend as a Troop Transport Truck arrives with reinforcements.

	Primary Objectives	Secondary Objectives
01	Eliminate all the PLA around the lighthouse	N/A
02	N/A	N/A

FORCE SUMMARY

RIFLE TEAM

In Co-op play, the second player may want to select Rios, as the under-slung grenade launcher on his assault rifle can be very useful for shelling the lighthouse area from the nearby hillside. Armistead and Gerrett however, come with demo charges and AT Mines in their inventories, which can be used to take out the PLA vehicles.

CAPTAIN LENTON (SNIPER)

Initial Loadout	Primary Weapon	–
	Primary Weapon Ammunition	–
	Secondary Weapon	M21
	Secondary Weapon Ammunition	7x20 FMJ round magazines
	Additional Equipment	1xM67 Grenade, 1xM18 Smoke Grenade, 2xM18A1 Claymore Mines, 1xNVG

PRIVATE FIRST CLASS RIOS (GRENADIER)

Initial Loadout	Primary Weapon	M16A4 (Assault)
	Primary Weapon Ammunition	7x30 FMJ round magazines, 9xHE projected grenades, 3xHEDP projected grenades
	Secondary Weapon	–
	Secondary Weapon Ammunition	–
	Additional Equipment	2xM67 Grenades, 1xM18 Smoke Grenades, 3xM14 AP Mines, 1xNVG

PRIVATE FIRST CLASS ARMISTEAD (COMBAT ENGINEER)

Initial Loadout	Primary Weapon	M16A4
	Primary Weapon Ammunition	7x30 FMJ round magazines
	Secondary Weapon	–
	Secondary Weapon Ammunition	–
	Additional Equipment	2xM67 Grenades, 2xM18 Smoke Grenades, 2xC4 Demo Charges, 2xM21 AT Mines, 5xM14 AP Mines, 1xNVG

PRIVATE FIRST CLASS GERRETT (COMBAT ENGINEER)

Initial Loadout	Primary Weapon	M16A4
	Primary Weapon Ammunition	7x30 FMJ round magazines
	Secondary Weapon	–
	Secondary Weapon Ammunition	–
	Additional Equipment	2xM67 Grenades, 2xM18 Smoke Grenades, 2xC4 Demo Charges, 2xM21 AT Mines, 5xM14 AP Mines, 1xNVG

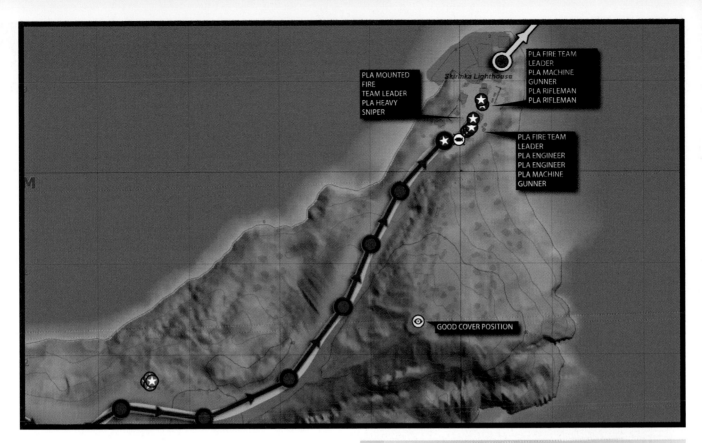

PLA MOUNTED
FIRE
TEAM LEADER
PLA HEAVY
SNIPER

Skirinka Lighthouse

PLA FIRE TEAM
LEADER
PLA MACHINE
GUNNER
PLA RIFLEMAN
PLA RIFLEMAN

PLA FIRE TEAM
LEADER
PLA ENGINEER
PLA ENGINEER
PLA MACHINE
GUNNER

GOOD COVER POSITION

1 Approaching the lighthouse

The player starts this mission not far from the objective concealed under the road close to the cliffs a few hundred meters south of the lighthouse. You are provided with an M21 Sniper Rifle, an excellent weapon to use to pick off the enemy from a great distance. Seek a high flanking vantage point that provides a good view over the objective, and assess the situation as you move closer to your target. There is a large hill to the east of your position that you can use as both an approach and a sniping spot. **[Screen 01]**

2 Using the hillside

Avoid detection by patrolling PLA troops, and keep out of the way of the helicopters. You may find yourself crawling on your belly for quite a significant part of the way to ensure you are not seen. When you move closer to the lighthouse complex, infantry will get out of the helicopter, after which it will fly away to the northeast. This is a good opportunity to get the PLA soldiers before they enter the cover of the buildings. Use your Fire Team to move into buildings, and clean out any PLA soldiers you cannot see, while you snipe from above at any soldier that becomes visible.

3 Defending the lighthouse area

Once the lighthouse complex is clear, the team should move in to check that all the forces there are dead. While you move into the complex, a PLA troop transport truck containing PLA infantry reinforcements will be issued a move command from the south, and starts heading toward the complex. No warning will be given of the PLA truck's arrival, and they can easily catch the player unaware, so keep your eyes on the road. If you have players in control of Armistead or Gerrett, you can make use of their Claymore Mines to set a trap for the incoming PLA truck. This will eliminate the reinforcements in a single blast, but you'll have to act very quickly to set it up in time. **[Screen 02]**

If the truck reaches the defenses just outside the complex, the infantry will get out and start attacking the player and his Fire Team inside the complex. You can get dug in and take the PLA out using your sniper rifle from the complex, while the rest of the team again use the hill to the east as a vantage point. You can also make use of the emplaced grenade launcher located at the entrance to the complex.

AMBUSH
MISSION 03

This is one of the longer Fire Team engagements, with the USMC Fire Team this time having to infiltrate a village from the north. They must secure the consulate building within the village, and take out all the PLA troops. They must then move into the walled house at the far end of the village and repel the PLA counterattack.

Primary Objectives	Secondary Objectives
01 Secure the Consulate Building	N/A
02 Repel the PLA counterattack	N/A
03 Eliminate and remaining PLA forces	

FORCE SUMMARY

ASSAULT TEAM

Traynor is the obvious choice for a second player to control in Co-op play, since his Marksman-type M16A4 Assault Rifle will give the team a much better long range sniping ability. Winslow's M249 can be great for suppressing the PLA in the consulate courtyard however, especially as this is an unavoidably close quarters battle, so choose Winslow as the third player.

CORPORAL VERWAYNE (FIRE TEAM LEADER)

Initial Loadout	Primary Weapon	M16A4 (Assault)
	Primary Weapon Ammunition	12x30 FMJ round magazines, 7xHE projected grenades, 2xHEDP projected grenades
	Secondary Weapon	–
	Secondary Weapon Ammunition	–
	Additional Equipment	2xM67 Grenades, 1xM18 Smoke Grenade, 3xIR Strobes, 3xM14 AP Mines

PRIVATE TRAYNOR (RIFLEMAN)

Initial Loadout	Primary Weapon	M16A4 (Marksman)
	Primary Weapon Ammunition	7x30 FMJ round magazines
	Secondary Weapon	–
	Secondary Weapon Ammunition	–
	Additional Equipment	2xM67 Grenades, 1xM18 Smoke Grenades

PRIVATE ZEVALLOS (MEDIC)

Initial Loadout	Primary Weapon	M16A4
	Primary Weapon Ammunition	7x30 FMJ round magazines
	Secondary Weapon	–
	Secondary Weapon Ammunition	–
	Additional Equipment	1xMedical Kit

PRIVATE FIRST CLASS WINSLOW (MACHINEGUNNER)

Initial Loadout	Primary Weapon	M249 SAW
	Primary Weapon Ammunition	3x200 FMJ round ammo boxes
	Secondary Weapon	–
	Secondary Weapon Ammunition	–
	Additional Equipment	1xM67 Grenades

Madlenka

PLA RIFLEMAN

PLA FIRE TEAM LEADER

PLA FIRE TEAM LEADER

PLA FIRE TEAM LEADER

PLA MOUNTED
RIFLEMAN

PLA MOUNTED
FIRE TEAM LEADER
PLA MOUNTED
RIFLEMAN

PLA MOUNTED
FIRE TEAM
LEADER

PLA FLANK 1

PLA MOUNTED RIFLEMAN

PLA FLANK 2

PLA RE ENFORCEMENTS

① The approach

The player starts this mission on the outskirts of Madlenka village. At the start of the mission, both tanks carrying the two additional USMC Fire Teams are destroyed in an explosion. Once this happens, you must move swiftly to find cover, as the PLA infantry in the area will move in on your position very rapidly. You have a M16A4 with under-slung grenade launcher, some grenades, HE and smoke at your disposal. The grenade launcher will be useful here to repel the PLA from behind their cover. **[Screen 01]**

② Attacking the village

Once you enter the village, be sure to clear the buildings before you enter them, or get close to them as PLA soldiers will try to use them for ambush. Your objective is the consulate building at the far end of the village, and there are a number of ways to approach it. Since taking the open road through the center offers no cover, head to the right of the road and go between the houses and farm buildings, flanking the emplaced MG on the opposite side of the road. Once you are parallel to it, follow the road behind it into the back entrance and to the courtyard of the building.

There are two PLA Fire Teams positioned in the courtyard of the consulate. Use HE grenades as you enter the complex, and get your Fire Team to flank to make sure there is no danger of the PLA flanking you. **[Screen 02]**

③ PLA reinforcements

Move to the front of the consulate and kill the remainder of the PLA guarding its main entrance. While you are engaging the PLA in the consulate complex, a PLA reinforcement force will advance to retake the consulate. This force consists of two trucks and two Fire Teams. Once the trucks stop, the Fire Teams will disembark and immediately move to flank you. Act swiftly using hand grenades to kill as many of the PLA as they disembark, as they will move swiftly on your position.

The PLA reinforcements will split up and attempt to cover both sides of the building. The first Fire Team moves into the main entrance at the front of the consulate, while the other moves around the back to the rear entrance. Eliminate them both swiftly, using your Fire Team to occupy defensive positions. If you have a team member near the mounted MG to the northeast

01

02

of the complex, they can use it to take out some of the reinforcements as they arrive. You could also place some of your AP Mines at one of the two entrances to the consulate courtyard to deal with one of their approach routes, allowing you to focus on the other side.

CLOSE QUARTERS
MISSION 04

This mission is a brief Fire Team engagement which sees the player's Fire Team launching an assault on Taranay village in a bid to stop the PLA forces before they can take control of the area. There are many tactical options in this mission, including an all-out assault, which can lead to a very short engagement indeed.

Primary Objectives		Secondary Objectives
01	Hold Taranay against PLA forces	N/A
02	N/A	N/A

FORCE SUMMARY

ASSAULT TEAM

Gray's Marksman model of the M16A4 Assault Rifle will help a good deal in your approach to the village, and can enable you to take out some PLA as they are still moving into position. Burlingame, on the other hand, does not have a scoped assault rifle, but does come with a very useful SMAW. This can be used to take out enemy vehicles and there are several of these. Either of these two will be a good choice for a second player in Co-op mode.

SERGEANT KELLY (FIRE TEAM LEADER)

Initial Loadout	Primary Weapon	M16A4 (Assault)
	Primary Weapon Ammunition	7x30 FMJ round magazines, 7xHE projected grenades, 2xHEDP projected grenades
	Secondary Weapon	–
	Secondary Weapon Ammunition	–
	Additional Equipment	2xM67 Grenades, 1xM18 Smoke Grenades, 3xIR Strobes, 3xM14 AP Mines

PRIVATE FIRST CLASS GRAY (RIFLEMAN)

Initial Loadout	Primary Weapon	M16A4 (Marksman)
	Primary Weapon Ammunition	–
	Secondary Weapon	–
	Secondary Weapon Ammunition	7x30 FMJ round magazines
	Additional Equipment	2xM67 Grenades, 1xM18 Smoke Grenades

PRIVATE BURLINGAME (ANTI-TANK SPECIALIST)

Initial Loadout	Primary Weapon	M16A4
	Primary Weapon Ammunition	7x30FMJ round magazines
	Secondary Weapon	SMAW
	Secondary Weapon Ammunition	1xHEF Rocket, 2xHEAT Rocket
	Additional Equipment	1xM67 Grenade

PRIVATE FRIEND (MACHINEGUNNER)

Initial Loadout	Primary Weapon	M249 SAW
	Primary Weapon Ammunition	3x200 FMJ round ammo boxes
	Secondary Weapon	–
	Secondary Weapon Ammunition	–
	Additional Equipment	1xM67 Grenade

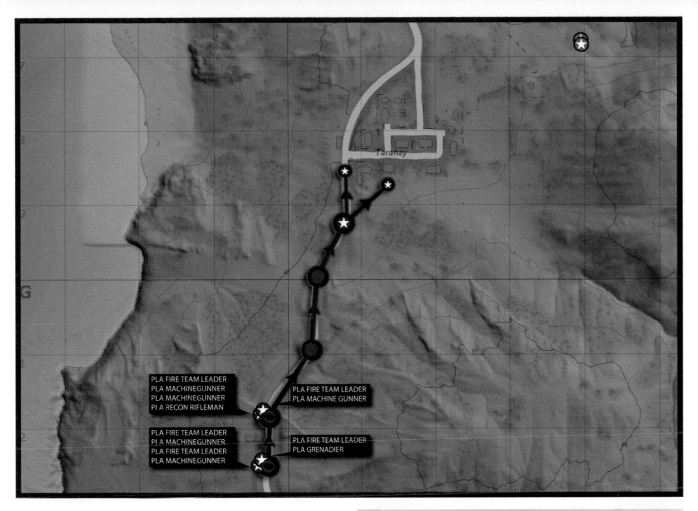

PLA FIRE TEAM LEADER
PLA MACHINEGUNNER
PLA MACHINEGUNNER
PLA RECON RIFLEMAN

PLA FIRE TEAM LEADER
PLA MACHINE GUNNER

PLA FIRE TEAM LEADER
PLA MACHINEGUNNER
PLA FIRE TEAM LEADER
PLA MACHINEGUNNER

PLA FIRE TEAM LEADER
PLA GRENADIER

① Starting out

The player starts not far from Taranay village, just behind the brow of
the hill. From the outset the player can see the USMC helicopter as it takes
off and flies away (presumably the helicopter that brought the player into
this mission). PLA troops will be heading into the village from the opposite
side, and your job is to clear out all the resistance in the area. When the
player's Fire Team begins advancing on Taranay, PLA howitzers will start
dropping around them. You can avoid these by keeping moving directly
toward the village; don't stray from the most direct route, or one of the
howitzer blasts could take out your team.

② Taranay village

Once in the village, the PLA forces will have begun to spread around
and move to different flanking positions, taking advantage of building cover.
There is a lot of good cover in the area for you to use, so don't simply storm
down the streets unprotected. Use your Fire Team to suppress the enemy or
to flank round a known position to attack them from an unprotected side.
Taking your Fire Team on a path roughly from the northeast to the south-
west should lead you to skirmishes with most of the resistance, including
the forces that were the last to emerge from the trucks on the other side of
the village. **[Screen 01]**

③ Clearing the village

Inside the village the player can find and use the HMMVWs distributed
around the village. **[Screen 02]** These vehicles can be used for mobility, as
well as for cover and better firepower. Make sure another member of your
Fire Team operates the turret if you have taken one. You can also have your
team take control of a vehicle and send them to distract the enemy while
you pick them off. Your under-slung grenade launcher can also be an amazing asset in this mission, allowing you to take out the PLA very quickly as
they are getting into position. The mission is completed once the player has
eliminated all the PLA in the village.

ENCAMPMENT
MISSION 05

As the name suggests, this Fire Team engagement has a US Fire Team taking on PLA forces spread out in an encampment in the woods along the west side of the island of Skirinka. The player must eliminate all the enemy forces at the northern and southernmost camps, and pass through any resistance they encounter on the way.

Primary Objectives	Secondary Objectives
01 Secure PLA Camp Alpha	Shoot down enemy helicopter
02 Secure PLA Camp Beta	N/A

FORCE SUMMARY

SPEC OPS TEAM

Suarez is the obvious choice here for a second player to control in Co-op play. He comes with both an MP5 SMG and an M2 Sniper Rifle and Claymore Mines. This kit combo is a great addition to the tactics available to the team, especially at the start of the mission. As heavy combat will be taking place at longer ranges, the Mk17 Mod 0 (Marksman) which Beattie comes equipped with slightly edges out the LMG carried by Bocelli, so you should choose him as a third player.

PRIVATE FIRST CLASS PENDLETON (SF ANTI-AIRCRAFT)

Initial Loadout		
	Primary Weapon	Mk17 Mod 0 (Marksman)
	Primary Weapon Ammunition	9x20 FMJ round magazines
	Secondary Weapon	FIM-92A Stinger
	Secondary Weapon Ammunition	1x3kg HE Frag Surface to Air Missile
	Additional Equipment	1xM67 Grenade, 1xM18 Smoke Grenade, 1xNVG

PRIVATE FIRST CLASS BOCELLI (SF MACHINEGUNNER)

Initial Loadout		
	Primary Weapon	Mk48 Mod 0
	Primary Weapon Ammunition	5x100 FMJ round ammo boxes
	Secondary Weapon	–
	Secondary Weapon Ammunition	–
	Additional Equipment	1xM67 Grenade, 1xM18 Smoke Grenade, 1xNVG

GUNNERY SERGEANT BEATTIE (SF RIFLEMAN)

Initial Loadout		
	Primary Weapon	Mk17 Mod 0 (Marksman)
	Primary Weapon Ammunition	12x2- FMJ round magazines
	Secondary Weapon	–
	Secondary Weapon Ammunition	–
	Additional Equipment	4xM67 Grenades, 2xM18 Smoke Grenades, 3xIR Strobes, 1xNVG

CORPORAL SUAREZ (SF SNIPER)

Initial Loadout		
	Primary Weapon	MP5A4
	Primary Weapon Ammunition	5x30 FMJ round magazines
	Secondary Weapon	M21
	Secondary Weapon Ammunition	12x20 FMJ round magazines
	Additional Equipment	2xM67 Grenades, 2xM18 Smoke Grenades, 2xM18A1 Claymore Mines, 1xNVG

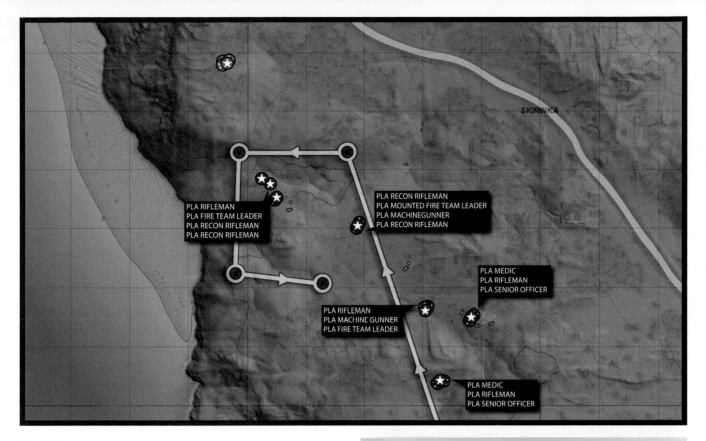

06

① Alpha approach

The player's Fire Team starts this mission just behind the ridge of a hill some distance to the northwest of the first enemy camp. This FTE is about picking your way through dense undergrowth and taking out the PLA defending sandbag emplacements around the camps. The objective marker leads the player south and down a hill toward the first defensive position protected by four PLA soldiers. **[Screen 01]** It is best to take the first two enemies out from long range to start with, and then flank round to one side as you descend to get a better view on the second two, as they are obscured by foliage.

In Co-op mode, a player controlling Suarez can stay back and snipe these enemies while the rest of the team heads southeast down the hill to engage them directly. The natural undulation of the terrain will also largely obscure the advancing players from the other PLA groups to the east while they continue to head south, using the camp for cover before turning east and clearing out any remaining enemies.

② Taking down the chopper

There is also a Secondary Objective that requires you to take down the PLA transport helicopter. The helicopter should begin circling shortly after the start of the mission and, as soon as it is spotted the player in control of Pendleton, should find a place that is safe, but with a clear view of the sky so that they can obtain a solid lock with their FiM-92A. The hill to the south of the first camp **[Screen 02]** is an excellent location from which to do this, and taking it down early will make progress though the mission much easier. Once it is down, head further southeast to the next objective.

③ Clearing camp Beta

The final objective is to progress toward camp Beta and clear the rest of the PLA in the area. You will need to do this quickly, as any PLA forces that spotted the players in their assault on the alpha camp will be closing in. There are up to three Fire Teams out in the open at smaller camps or patrolling across the tree line. You can use small piles of logs and the small camps you have cleared for cover as you advance toward the second camp. Camp Beta sits on top of a small hillock, so be careful on your final advance into the camp and use the tents for cover. Killing all 17 PLA soldiers here will complete the Primary Objectives of clearing both camps.

DEBRIS FIELD
MISSION 06

A short Fire Team engagement of a USMC Fire Team against a number of PLA Fire Teams in a battlefield being shelled by mortar fire. Enemy armor will need to be eliminated to gain control of the area involved.

	Primary Objectives	Secondary Objectives
01	Eliminate all remaining PLA forces	N/A
02	N/A	N/A

FORCE SUMMARY

ANTI-TANK TEAM

All three of the other Fire Team members have useful tools here, and should be considered equally by other players in Co-op mode. Valentine comes with a Mk48, which is as useful as ever for suppressive fire and close quarters combat. Osika and Carter however, are carrying SMAWs as backup weapons, which can make taking out the enemy armored vehicles much quicker. This is especially useful if the team leader runs out of rockets, as they are carrying three extra HEF rockets each.

Combat Support: 1x Howitzer Artillery available from the start.

1ST LIEUTENANT MCDONAGH (ANTI-TANK SPECIALIST)

Initial Loadout	Primary Weapon	M16A4
	Primary Weapon Ammunition	7x30 FMJ round magazines
	Secondary Weapon	SMAW
	Secondary Weapon Ammunition	1x HEF Rocket, 2xHEAT Rockets
	Additional Equipment	1xM67 Grenade, 1xNVG

PRIVATE VALENTINE (MACHINEGUNNER)

Initial Loadout	Primary Weapon	Mk48 Mod 0
	Primary Weapon Ammunition	3x100 FMJ round ammo boxes
	Secondary Weapon	–
	Secondary Weapon Ammunition	–
	Additional Equipment	1xM67 Grenade, 1xNVG

PRIVATE OSIKA (ANTI-TANK SPECIALIST)

Initial Loadout	Primary Weapon	M16A4
	Primary Weapon Ammunition	7x30 FMJ round magazines
	Secondary Weapon	SMAW
	Secondary Weapon Ammunition	3xHEF Rockets, 2xHEAT Rockets
	Additional Equipment	1xM67 Grenades, 1xNVG

PRIVATE CARTER (ANTI-TANK SPECIALIST)

Initial Loadout	Primary Weapon	M16A4
	Primary Weapon Ammunition	7x30 FMJ round magazines
	Secondary Weapon	SMAW
	Secondary Weapon Ammunition	3xHEF Rockets, 2xHEAT Rockets
	Additional Equipment	1xM67 Grenades, 1xNVG

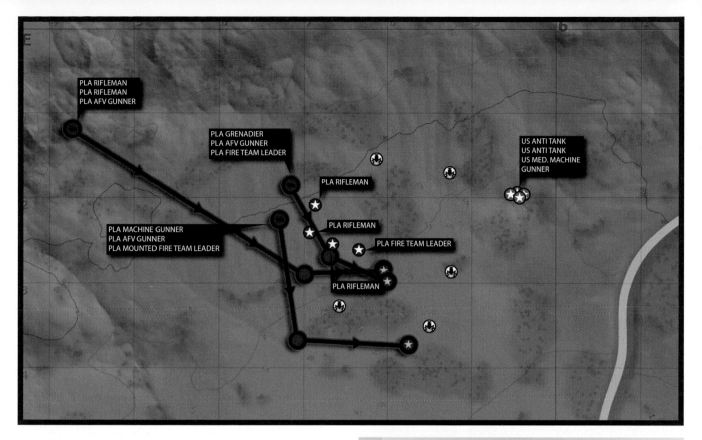

PLA RIFLEMAN
PLA RIFLEMAN
PLA AFV GUNNER

PLA GRENADIER
PLA AFV GUNNER
PLA FIRE TEAM LEADER

US ANTI TANK
US ANTI TANK
US MED. MACHINE
GUNNER

PLA RIFLEMAN

PLA MACHINE GUNNER
PLA AFV GUNNER
PLA MOUNTED FIRE TEAM LEADER

PLA RIFLEMAN

PLA FIRE TEAM LEADER

PLA RIFLEMAN

① Calling in the big guns

The player starts this mission with PLA mortars raining down in front of them. You see a battlefield of wrecked tanks scattered over the open area, and PLA troops are moving up into defensive positions. Heading up the ridge, players will be able to see the troops on the opposite side of the battlefield through the smoke and fire from the group of destroyed tanks. Besides the troops, there are also numerous armored vehicles being deployed by the PLA in the area.

Players are given a single howitzer strike at the start of the mission, which should be reserved until the enemy armored units are in view and have stopped moving. **[Screen 01]** The burnt-out vehicles scattered around the area provide perfect cover as you line up the Artillery Strike. A Barrage Strike will generally work best here, as the armor is spread over quite a large area, so covering as much ground as possible is a good idea.

② Finishing off the armor

While the artillery is raining down on the PLA armor, players should start eliminating the enemy soldiers with their rifles to take advantage of the confusion. Hopefully the Howitzer Barrage would have also taken down some of the enemy troops and, even if it didn't, the added smoke in the area will only aid your cover to make moving around the area a little easier. Once the smoke clears, players should assess the situation and try to spot any PLA armor that survived the barrage and which are still active. Their number one priority should be to identify and destroy these targets with their SMAWs as quickly as possible. **[Screen 02]**

Remain under cover and keep out of the way of the helicopters flying over the area, as these will alert the PLA troops to your position. If a player spots a helicopter coming in, they should alert the other players and the group should move back from the cover of the destroyed vehicles into the trees to mask their visibility from above.

③ Mopping up the remains

Single players should use their Fire Team to suppress or engage enemies to prevent them from being flanked and overrun by the enemy as they press forward. Keep your Fire Team close by and make sure to avoid the Mortar Strikes as you advance. If you use the same approach in Co-op mode,

but with human players in control, things will go much more smoothly, as they will be able to cover more angles. Stalk from cover point to cover point and take out any remaining PLA that have exited the armored vehicles. You will have accomplished the mission when 13 PLA soldiers have been killed and all the armored vehicles are destroyed.

OPERATION FLASHPOINT: DRAGON RISING

Operation Flashpoint: Dragon Rising is developed and published by Codemasters Software Company Limited

PROJECT MANAGEMENT

VP OF CODEMASTERS STUDIOS
Gavin Cheshire

GENERAL MANAGER CODEMASTERS
Trevor Williams

CHIEF TECHNICAL OFFICER
Bryan Marshall

EXECUTIVE IN CHARGE OF PRODUCTION
Julian Widdows

EXECUTIVE PRODUCER
Sion Lenton

SENIOR PRODUCER
Brant Nicholas

PRODUCTION MANAGER
Chris Gray

PRODUCERS
Darren Campion
Martin Klima

ASSOCIATE PRODUCER
Adam Wilkinson

PROJECT PLANNER
Vincent Meulle

LEAD PROGRAMMERS
Steve Bennett
Will Leach

LEAD ARTIST
Michael Smith

CHIEF GAME DESIGNER
Lee Brimmicombe-Wood

CHIEF LEVEL DESIGNER
James Nicholls

DESIGN

GAME DESIGN
SENIOR GAMES DESIGNER
Tim Browne

SENIOR DESIGNERS
Clive Lindop
Philippe O'Connor

EXPERIENCED GAME DESIGNERS
Adam Keyte
Alan Massey

JUNIOR TECHNICAL DESIGNER
Alexander Williams

LEVEL DESIGN
LEAD LEVEL DESIGNER
Gavin Cooper

SENIOR GAMES DESIGNERS
Bob Hands
Darren Kirby

SENIOR LEVEL DESIGNER
Colin Nicholls

EXPERIENCED LEVEL DESIGNERS
Guy Joyner
Steve Prestidge

LEVEL DESIGNERS
Amanda Jeffrey
Christiaan Jones
Daniel Molnar
Graham Sergeant
Jamie Stowe
Jonathan Heckley
Nicholas Hall
Yael Katvan

JUNIOR LEVEL DESIGNER
Joel Beardshaw

ENGINEERING

AI
SENIOR PROGRAMMER
Tomas Nevrtal

PRINCIPAL PROGRAMMER
Dan Kennedy

SENIOR PROGRAMMERS
David Tetlow

Jason Callis

EXPERIENCED PROGRAMMERS
Andrew Fray
Andrew Paul
Carles Ros Martinez

AUDIO
EXPERIENCED PROGRAMMER
Justin Andrews

GAMEPLAY
PRINCIPAL PROGRAMMER
Adrian Smith

SENIOR PROGRAMMERS
James Shaughnessy
Philip Stewart

EXPERIENCED PROGRAMMERS
Andrew Saldanha
David Chalmers
Matt Booth
Phillipa Leighton
Steve Hughes

PROGRAMMERS
Alok Narula
Mark Oxenham

NETWORK
SENIOR PROGRAMMERS
Allan Mulholland
Mathew Gregory

EXPERIENCED PROGRAMMER
Mark McDonagh

PIPELINE
SENIOR PROGRAMMER
Matthew Hildred

RENDERING
SENIOR PROGRAMMERS
Andrew Dennison
David Smethurst
John Longcroft-Neal
Leigh Bradburn

EXPERIENCED PROGRAMMERS
Alessandro Monopoli
Peter Nicholls
Stuart Merry

PROGRAMMERS
Daniel Lawrence
Federico Rebora

SYSTEMS
SENIOR PROGRAMMER
John Pullen

TOOLS
SENIOR PROGRAMMER
Marcin Kalicinski

EXPERIENCED PROGRAMMERS
Pawel Leszkiewicz
Robbie Pallas

UI
EXPERIENCED PROGRAMMERS
Lee Walford

David Gower
Grant Mark
Tomas Jakubauskas

PROGRAMMERS
Adam Parker
David Crook
Rob Lee

ADDITIONAL PROGRAMMING
Tim Austin

TEST ENGINEER
Dan Beasley

CENTRAL TECHNOLOGY

LEAD PROGRAMMER
Chris Brunning

PRINCIPAL PROGRAMMERS
Alex Tyrer
Andrew Wright
Bryan Black
Csaba Berenyi
Graham Watson
John Atkinson
Nick Trout
Simon Goodwin

SENIOR PROGRAMMERS
Daniel Wheeler
David Burke
Pete Akehurst
Tim Owlett

EXPERIENCED PROGRAMMERS
Erika Renlund
Jay Rathod
Laurent Nguyen
Ryan Wallace

PROGRAMMERS
David Buckingham
Samuel Ong
Tadeusz Marianski

EXPERIENCED TECHNICAL AUTHOR
Jason Darby

TEST ENGINEER
Andrew Measures

PROJECT PLANNING OFFICE
PROJECT MANAGER
Steve Eccles

CENTRAL ART

ART DIRECTOR
Rachel Weston

CENTRAL ART MANAGERS
Neil Kaminski

Nicolas Pain

OUTSOURCE MANAGER
Andre Stiegler

ANIMATION
LEAD ARTIST
Jon Maine

SENIOR ARTISTS
Adam King
Rob Strand

EXPERIENCED ARTISTS
Huy Nguyen
Neil Bruder

CHARACTERS
LEAD ARTIST
Toby Hynes

SENIOR ARTIST
Paul Edwards

EXPERIENCED ARTIST
Mark Hancock

CONCEPT AND MARKETING ART
LEAD ARTIST
Max Cant

SENIOR ARTIST
Jim Vickers

ENVIRONMENT
LEAD ARTIST
Erol Kentli

TECHNICAL LEAD ARTIST
Peter Ridgway

GROUP LEAD
Gyanam O'Sullivan

SENIOR ARTISTS
Adam Hill
Joe Bradford
Steven Jackson
Wayne Smith

EXPERIENCED ARTISTS
Karl Davies
Ken Jarvis
Matthew Stott
Peter Kerpcar
Richard Berwick
Richard Priest
Thomas Adams

ARTISTS
James Gerrett
Joseph Stone

TECHNICAL ART
LEAD ARTIST
Martin Wood

PRINCIPAL ARTIST
Andrew Catling

SENIOR ARTIST
Tom Whibley

USER INTERFACE
LEAD ARTIST
Philip Cox

SENIOR ARTIST
Matthew O'Connor

EXPERIENCED ARTISTS
Adrian Waters
Dan Fernando

ARTIST
Elly Marshal

VEHICLES
SENIOR ARTIST
Mitchell Roach

EXPERIENCED ARTIST
Steve Tsang

VISUAL EFFECTS
LEAD ARTIST
Jon Graham

SENIOR ARTIST
Imkan Hayati

EXPERIENCED ARTISTS
James Watt
Marcus Wainwright

WEAPONS
SENIOR ARTIST
Dermot Murphy

CAMPAIGN INTRO SEQUENCE
Surface3D.co.uk

AUDIO

AUDIO DIRECTOR
Stephen Root

AUDIO MANAGER
John Davies

AUDIO DESIGN
SENIOR AUDIO DESIGNER
Oliver Johnson

AUDIO DESIGNER
Jethro Dunn

ADDITIONAL AUDIO
EXPERIENCED AUDIO DESIGNER
Mark Willott

AUDIO DESIGNERS
Claire Woodcock
Ed Walker

MUSIC
COMPOSER
Christian Marcussen

VOCALS, THROAT SINGING
Steve Sklar

VOCALS
Johnna Morrow

IGIL PERFORMANCE
John Pascuzzi

KL STUDIO

DIRECTOR
H.S.Low

GENERAL MANAGER
Maxime Villandre

TECHNICAL ART DIRECTOR
Jason Butterley

PRODUCTION MANAGER
Johan Fariz Lam

PRODUCTION ASSISTANTS
Lau Chee Shyong
Chong Ee Von

HR MANAGER
Kuan Sook Mee

FINANCE MANAGER
Tay Kah Chai

ADMIN ASSISTANT
Farra Nadia Zuhari

TECHNICAL SUPPORT ENGINEER
Chin Cheong Weng

ANIMATION
GROUP LEAD
Adam Harvey Batham

ARTISTS
Chew Tiong Nam
Hong Tuan-Keat (Eugene)
Lee Fook Loy (Roy)
Lee Kean Boon
Shervie Tan
Tan Jing Chun (Shirley)
Teah Wei Han
Teh Jia Shyan
Wong Kew Chee
Wong Mun Poh (Jane)
Zarif Khairuddin

CHARACTERS
GROUP LEAD
Kong Foong Ching

ARTISTS
Kok Chen Yong
Yeap Guan Beng

ENVIRONMENT
GROUP LEADS
Gerome Gan Khoon Deed
Lee Ka Hal
Lor Hang Chuan
Mohd Fazlan bin Abdul Jamil

ARTISTS
Beh Chor Joo
Chee Yim Mei (Jouly)
Chun Zhenhui
Hang Hue Li
Jacob Yuean
Koh Yen Yee
Lew Wai Hong (Joe)
Lim Jenn Yu
Lim Ke Wei
Mohd Munadzam Bin Samsudin
Noor Izmal Mukhriz Bin Ismail
Ong Wei Chuan (Lawrence)
Siah Joon Kiong
Stephanie Yong Jo-Ann
Sung Pei Sun
Syamil bin Abd Latif
Tan Kean Wooi
Tey Hong Yeow
Thum Chee Ket (Jack)

Yap Ann Rose
Yap Wai Mun
Yeo Chuan Tong

VEHICLES
GROUP LEADS
Azmi Bin Mohd Amin
Yoong Wei Siong

ARTISTS
Abdul Khaliq (Alitt)
Cheng Lin Chou (Chris)
Ho Kuan Teck
Liew Seng Tat
Ling Swee Hee
Ma Hanson
Ng Kah Yeow (Kenji)
Ng Say Chong (Raymond)
Ong Hong Tiong (Kelvin)
Tan Jee Hean

WEAPONS
GROUP LEAD
Wong Yee Hsien

ARTISTS
Chong Ri Hui (Saxon)

Gilbert Chong Ming Jin

QUALITY ASSURANCE

QA GENERAL MANAGER
Eddy Di Luccio

FUNCTIONAL QA MANAGER
Danny Beilard

FUNCTIONAL QA TESTING
QA TEAM LEADERS
Simon Wykes

Andrew Stanley

SENIOR QA TECHNICIANS
Adriano Rizzo
Alex Tyc

EXPERIENCED QA TECHNICIANS
Alan Jardine

Edward Copland

QA TECHNICIANS
Akuila Iliesa
Alessandro Naso
Alex Harvey
Angelo Mendola
Ben Russell
Benjamin Earle
Brad Porter
Brett Collins
Chris Armstrong
Daniel Corbett
Daniel Preedy
David Scott
David Wixon
Jack Boad
James Constable
Jens Schneider
Laurence Perkins
Lee Burns
Nelli Ferenczi
Nigel Jordan
Paul Devitt
Richard Ford
Rob Appleyard
Sam Adamson
Shaun Moffat
Simon Pattison
Tim Davies

PLATFORM LEADS
SENIOR QA TECHNICIANS
Robin Passmore
Stephen Terry

EXPERIENCED QA TECHNICIAN
Ricky O'Toole

ONLINE
QA ONLINE MANAGER
Jonathan Treacy

QA TEAM LEADER
Andrew Hargreaves

SENIOR QA TECHNICIANS
Michael Wood
Robert Young
Matt Boland

OPERATION
FLASHPOINT.
DRAGON RISING

Operation Flashpoint: Dragon Rising –
The Official Strategy Guide is produced
and published by Future Press

SPECIAL THANKS...

...to the Operation Flashpoint team for their continuous support. This book
would never have been this good without your overwhelming support.

CREDITS

**FUTURE PRESS
VERLAG UND MARKETING GMBH**
www.future-press.com
feedback@future-press.com

MANAGING DIRECTORS
Jörg Kraut
Frank Glaser

AUTHORS
Chris Andrews
Wil Murray
Bruce Byrne

EDITORS
Carol Aggett
Trevor Howell

CREATIVE DIRECTOR
Jörg Kraut

LAYOUT
Tobias Koch
Sven Kanth
Rico Ketelsen
Frank Bechthold

PRODUCTION ASSISTANTS
Martin Adler
Jean-Reiner Jung

©2009 Future Press Verlag und Marketing GmbH. All rights reserved,
including the right of reproduction in whole or in part in any form.

Operation Flashpoint®: Dragon Rising™ – The Official Strategy Guide is
published in North America by BradyGames Publishing, an Imprint of DK
Publishing Inc.

BRADYGAMES

Publisher
David Waybright

Licensing Director
Mike Degler

Marketing Director
Debby Neubauer

CODEMASTERS SOFTWARE COMPANY LIMITED

Director, Business Development
Peter Chan

STRATEGY GUIDE CONTRIBUTORS
(VERY SPECIAL THANKS, GUYS!)

Adam Keyte, Adam Wilkinson, Alan Massey, Amanda Jeffrey, Bob Hands,
Brant Nicholas, Christiaan Jones, Christopher Gray, Colin Nicholls,
Dan Robinson, Daniel Molnar, Daniel Schaefers, Darren Campion,
Darren Kirby, Gavin Cooper, Graham Sergeant, Guy Joyner, James Nicholls,
Jamie Stowe, Jim Vickers, Joel Beardshaw, Jonathan Heckley, Karl Reader,
Ken Jarvis, Lee Brimmicombe-Wood, Mark Geoghegan, Mark Turosz,
Matthew Stott, Michael Smith, Nicholas Hall, Peter Matthews, Sion Lenton,
Thomas Adams, Tim Browne, Vincent Meulle, Wayne Smith, Wesley Strange,
Will Leach, Yael Katvan

THANKS TO OUR PARTNERS, FRIENDS AND FAMILIES

Antoine Bailly, Autumne Bruce, Beth Guzman, Brian Saliba, David Bugden,
Florent Moreau, Geoffroy Marty, Géraldine Saint-Louis, H. Leigh Davis,
Hiro Yamada, Isabelle Connuel, Jane Best, Jean Bury, Matt Warley,
Patrick Melchior, Priscille Demoly, Richard Deavall, Roman Huber,
Stefan Apelt, Thomas Rickal, Tracy Wehmeyer, Ulrich Mühl

Katja Gerber, Lisa Andrews, Cindy Miner, Patrick and Kathleen Murray,
Lea and Alex Glaser

ISBN-13: 978-074401167-8

ISBN-10: 074401167-1

Unit price: $19.99 USA · $22.99 CAN

OPERATION
FLASHP⊘INT.
DRAGON RISING

GENERAL

ⓟ	Rendezvous Point (RV)
⊘	Checkpoint
ⓘ	Objective Point
🔫	Emplaced MG
🔫	Emplaced AGL
📱	Offboard Support
⊘	Ammo Crate
◯	Staging Point
■	PLA Controlled Area
⌐	Patrol Route Marker
★	PLA Forces
★	USMC Forces

MISSION SPECIFIC

⬆	PLA Counter Attack
⬆	USMC Assault
▢	Defend Sector
◉	Recon Point
●	PLA Mortar Zone
●	Counter Attack Route
●	PLA Vehicle Patrols
◉	Ally Team Route
◉	Explosive
◯	Npc Route

MULTIPLAYER

◎	USMC Start
●	PLA Start

VEHICLES

●	USMC Armor/APC
●	USMC 4x4/DPV
●	USMC Helicopter
◉	USMC Convoy
◉	USMC Helo Route
●	PLA Armor/APC
●	PLA 4x4/FAV
●	PLA Tank
●	PLA Helicopter
●	PLA Truck
◉	PLA Helo Route
◉	PLA Convoy
◉	Fuel Route
⊗	Wrecked Armour
●	Empty 4x4
●	Un-Manned PLA Armor
⊗	Empty Helicopter

1